Just
Vegetating
A Memoir

Just Vegetating

A Memoir

JOY LARKCOM

F

FRANCES LINCOLN LIMITED
PUBLISHERS

TO OUR GRANDCHILDREN WILLIAM AND LUCINDA,
TO MY SISTER ERICA,
AND, ONCE AGAIN, TO DON, FOR BRINGING THAT
BAG OF PIG MUCK FORTY-FIVE YEARS AGO

Frances Lincoln Limited
4 Torriano Mews
Torriano Avenue
London NW5 2RZ
www.franceslincoln.com

Just Vegetating
Copyright © Frances Lincoln Limited 2012
Text copyright © Joy Larkcom 2012
Photographs copyright © Joy Larkcom 2012
except those listed on page336
First Frances Lincoln edition 2012

A catalogue record for this book is available from the
British Library.

ISBN 978-0-7112-2935-8

Printed and bound in China
1 2 3 4 5 6 7 8 9

CONTENTS

PREFACE

I was originally spurred into writing this book by the thought that the articles I wrote earlier in my career were buried in old magazines and unlikely ever again to see the light of day. And I was rather fond of them. So much research had gone into some of them, while others reflected the excitement of learning about gardening, vegetable growing in particular, in the only real school – practical experience. I wanted to bring them back to life.

Another stimulus was looking back on our 'Grand Vegetable Tour' in Europe in the 1970s. I was always saddened by my failure to get those adventures, and Don's resourceful cooking during and after those adventures, into any kind of coherent story. The immediate task of earning a living took precedence on our return. It's too late for a complete account now, but I hope it is still possible to capture its flavour with some of the articles that resulted, woven together with their background and autobiographical bits and pieces.

And once I'd embarked on this, it seemed natural to carry on into more recent times. Writers get as attached to their writings as parents to their children, so it has been an agonizing task deciding what to include and what to leave out. Inevitably there is some repetition, not least because the same themes thread in and out of the four decades covered. Some pieces have been shortened or just extracts used, and some have been updated where necessary. I've sometimes written a short introduction or afterthought, putting them into context or explaining their significance then or from today's perspective. And apologies for what I now realize is excessive use of the word 'obsession'. I'm afraid it's proof, for good or ill, of my obsessiveness.

I hope fellow gardeners will enjoy a window on the world I have inhabited in a lifetime of gardening writing, a world where fun and fact have constantly intermingled.

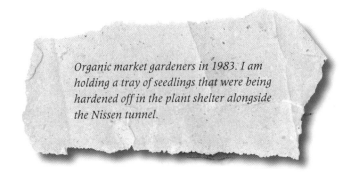

Organic market gardeners in 1983. I am holding a tray of seedlings that were being hardened off in the plant shelter alongside the Nissen tunnel.

I am far right, second row, with fellow horticultural students at Wye College and Dutch exchange students from Wageningen University, in 1956.

1 FIRST FOOT ON THE LADDER

'I believe you may have the basis for a regular weekly feature in *Garden News*,' wrote the *Garden News* editor, Frank Ward, in 25 January 1973. I must have pranced around the house whooping with joy at the news. A chance to write about gardening – at last.

Fifteen years previously I had graduated from Wye College with a degree in horticulture, but it had rusted in the intervening years of globetrotting. I had taught at a school for American missionaries' children in Chiengmai, in northern Thailand, and written plays for them to perform. Then I emigrated to Canada, hoping to become involved in making Shell's natural history films. But neither Shell, nor anybody else it seemed, made natural history films in Canada, so instead I became a library assistant in the science and medical division of Toronto University Library. In my spare time I started writing adaptations of children's books for CBC radio. Then I returned to the UK to qualify as a librarian – well, it did seem silly to be doing the same job as the professionals for half the pay – but mercifully, there were no vacancies in the library school.

So I followed up a lead with the scientific journal *Discovery*, which I had been pestering for years to give me a job. My luck was in. In the hiatus between a take-over and the arrival of the new editorial team the journal needed a temporary assistant. I fitted the bill – on paper. And what a wonderful introduction to the world of publishing and journalism that was! I did everything from picture research to editing. I loved the buzz, soon realized this was what I wanted to do, and asked for a permanent job. My only chance by then was to learn shorthand and become the magazine's secretary – and I had three months in which to do it. The secretarial colleges were scornful. I can still hear those stuffy voices saying, 'You can't learn shorthand in less than year.' So it was teach yourself. I can get very obsessive about learning what needs to be learned, and in those next three months carried a battered second-hand copy of Pitman's *Teach Yourself Shorthand* with me wherever I went, mentally drawing shorthand squiggles in the air at every bus stop. (Fifteen years later I'd be jogging on a disused East Anglian runway tracing Chinese characters in the air before researching oriental vegetables.) I was given the job – in spite of only getting halfway through *Teach Yourself Shorthand*. The editor was sold short: I was a dreadful secretary.

Then a chance came to move to a sister magazine, *Personnel Management and Methods*, as assistant editor. I agonised over it. Writing about industry? In a trade magazine. Me? What could be more alien to my roots, interests and training? Among my mentors at the time, weaning me and my writing from school girl essays into the real world, were a couple of respected Austrian writers. Take it, they said. Nothing but good will come from writing to deadlines for a commercial market. So I did. And they were right.

Five years later I left, having become editor, to write a careers column for *The Observer* newspaper. Far removed though these jobs were from horticulture, I loved them. I loved the challenge of starting with a blank sheet and writing about subjects I knew nothing about. I loved the worlds they took me into – coal mines, steelworks, oil refineries, law courts, holiday camps for disturbed kids, hospitals – I even became intrigued with management; and on 'personnnel management' I had the ideal teacher in the editor, Howard Griffiths – humorous, quietly intelligent, supportive when things went wrong. And being a journalist was exciting: not just interviewing the movers and shakers (sad to think I'm reading their obituaries now), but the sheer pressure and drama, in those days, of getting copy to the press or the printers, dictating to 'copy takers' from phone booths, trips to the all night (was it really?) Post Office off Trafalgar Square, occasionally to Paddington Station to hand copy to the guard for the printers in Bristol. Today you just press 'send'. Where's the fun in that? When I returned to horticulture it was with fresh eyes, questioning much of what I had learned as a student.

Just before starting on *The Observer* I met an American teacher, Don Pollard (on St Valentine's Day in the unlikely setting of a Chelsea party), and a few months later we married and moved to the Cambridgeshire fens. Our first shared gardening experience was a wonderfully fertile allotment. The following year we bought 0.8 hectares/2 acres of land and an old farmhouse, Montrose Farm, in Suffolk, and gardening began in earnest. Especially vegetable growing, for soon there was a young family to feed. It wasn't long before I was getting an itchy pen, and an insatiable yearning to write a 'Kitchen Garden' diary about all I was learning in my vegetable plot.

Several newspapers and magazines rejected my idea before *Garden News* went for it. In the end my brief was for a fortnightly column aimed at the woman gardener, and 'to encourage wives to take more interest in the vegetable side by suggesting recipes, when to pick, how to choose, reducing waste (or waist if you like)'. I was paid £4 for 450 words. It wasn't much – even then. Next year the fee was increased to £5. Later – when we were very hard up – I was bold enough to ask for another rise. I've no record of a reply, but the last letter in the file, from the next editor, was in October 1975, saying that hard economic times meant they had to drop some regular columns – the magazine was 'walking a precarious tightrope between profit and loss' – and after much soul searching mine was one of those to go. (By then the original 'Kitchen Garden' column had been followed by a year's series on gourmet vegetables.) I must have been gutted – I'd never been fired before – but it was time to 'move on', as we say now. I had started to work on my first book, *Vegetables from Small Gardens*, which was published in 1976, and a germ of an idea was forming in my mind, which eventually blossomed into our Grand Vegetable

Tour. This was the year we were to spend travelling around Europe in a van and caravan, collecting old vegetable varieties and studying peasant and modern systems of vegetable growing. But that's running ahead. Back to the 'Kitchen Garden' column.

Re-reading those articles more than thirty years later, between little waves of nostalgia, I'm struck by what has changed and, almost equally, by what hasn't. I can't believe how 'unenvironmental' I was then, endorsing peat as a mulch, artificial fertilizers and chemicals, particularly seeds coated with the fungicide captan. I hadn't yet become the committed organic gardener I have been for many years. And how ephemeral some aspects of gardening can be! Seed companies I wrote about are long gone, or merged into others – a source of sadness. And where are the products I trialled, from cloches to bird scarers? So much for their problem-solving claims. (There's a lesson there: beware the unending tide of gardening gimmicks.) Yet not a mention of modules, the mainstay of my plant raising today. Even vegetable varieties introduced with hyperbole as outperforming all others have mostly gone. Only a few notable ones have stood the test of time.

But the vagaries of the weather sound familiar. I was constantly writing about water shortages, East Anglia being one of the driest parts of the country. Frequent references, too, to rising fuel prices and general shortages . . . What crisis was that, I wonder now? Were there premonitions of our future retirement garden in Ireland's West Cork? Shelter from wind and the value of seaweed both earned columns. And how domesticated I was! Young children, naturally, earned plenty of comment, but so did housework. And recipes. Back then I was a real cook! After our year of travel Don became the chief cook and housework person, a role he has more or less fulfilled ever since, and I'm afraid I have earned a reputation for poor performance in both fields. Spiders sleep peacefully in Donaghmore Farmhouse.

I no longer have copies of the *Garden News* in which these articles were originally published. The only copies I have, now rather yellowed, are those my inordinately proud mother pasted into the large red *Observer* scrapbook for my careers articles. Thank you, Mummy. I appreciate your diligence thirty-five years later.

I've selected just a handful of the 'Kitchen Garden' columns. I've also sneaked in a couple of light-hearted articles I wrote at about the same time for the 'Farmers' Wives' section of *Farmers Weekly*.

WATER FOR THE PEAS, AND 'BLACK JACK' FOR THE CELERY
'Kitchen Garden', *Garden News*, 29 June 1973

It is one of the ironies of this country that even with all the rain we get, most of our vegetable crops respond dramatically to generous watering. So I've been spending a lot of my evenings this freezing June with a hose in my hand. The peas have had high priority, because research has shown that yields can be increased by up to 25 per cent if they are irrigated when they start flowering (not before), or when the pods start swelling.

Ordinary watering apart, there is a lot in the kitchen garden at the moment which would benefit from regular feeding – celery, leeks, lettuces, cucumbers, tomatoes – to name but a few. It's worth making your own liquid manure for this. Alfred Gower, who was a marvellous gardener of the old school, made 'Black Jack', as he called it, by suspending a bag of soot in a barrel filled with farmyard manure and water. This potent brew was diluted before use, 3 parts of water to one of Black Jack, and given to plants once a week. Give a strong solution to young plants rather than a weak solution to mature plants, was a piece of advice Mr Gower passed on to me.

It seems odd in mid-summer to be thinking of winter, but I find this a good time to sow some of the salad crops which will be valuable in a few months' time. I'm thinking of winter radishes ('China Rose', 'Round' and 'Long Black Spanish' and the Japanese 'Mino Early'), chicory, endive, Chinese cabbage and American land cress. I also try and sow an extra row of carrots about now – to give 'spring' carrots in the autumn, as well as turnips, kohl rabi and beetroot.

Beetroot is a sore point with me; my family have almost forgotten what it tastes like. It took me a couple of years of failure before I pinpointed sparrows as the main source of the trouble. Using our hawthorn hedges as base, they make periodic forays into the vegetable patch, and nip off the leaf tips on the young seedlings. The seedlings never seem to recover. I caught them at it the other evening, starting on a row of Thompson and Morgan's 'Snowhite' beet. But a strand of black cotton over the row seems to have done the trick.

The winter crop of parsley should be sown in July, and talking of herbs, if those beautiful flowering chives are cut back, they will throw a second crop of tender leaves.

....

Alfred Gower was the head gardener in the private garden near Reading where I did a year's practical work before going to Wye College. A lovely man renowned for his skill with sweet peas, and a great teacher. He had one of the very first hip operations, and leaned heavily on sticks. As we cut gladioli on my first day as his 'right hand' I heard a squeak. I pretended I hadn't. 'Didn't you 'ear me 'ips?' he asked, turning his bright blue eyes on me. From then on, whenever they squeaked, I'd take my cue with 'Heard your hips this morning, Mr Gower'. Mr Gower infected me with a lifelong love of sweet peas, and to this day, names of the varieties we grew then stir nostalgic memories of that year in the walled garden. I've left out the recipe for asparagus soup, but it ended with 'Don't compromise on the butter and cream'. What trouble I'd be in with that today!

Right: Head gardener Alfred Gower having a tea break on an upturned orange box in the kitchen garden at Calcot Grange. Below: pages from the diary I kept during my year's practical work before going to Wye College.

Pollination — Using a rabbit's tail the apricots and young peach trees were pollinated. The pollen is ~~knocked~~ brushed lightly from the anthers on to the stamen, making sure of pacing flowers. This is repeated twice or even three times, in case the insects do not carry out enough pollination.

Finished planting chrysanthemums, and P.M. planted sweet peas.

(C.S. – Planted sweet pea seedlings – the cuttings)

March 29th.
Stocks— stood some of the stocks in their pots outside, to make them hardier.

Asparagus— The beds are just starting to show shoots, & were raked lightly to get off the weeds. The asparagus grows new crowns during the winter, which throw up shoots in the spring.

Cut about 9 doz. daffodils & polyanthus for market tomorrow.

March 30th.
Watered lettuces, carrots in closed frames, & cauliflowers & May Queen lettuce in boxes in green frames. Carrots etc. need a thorough watering every so often — a sprinkling is useless, as they are wilt beyond recovery when the effect is over.

Finished making over the asparagus beds — did a little hoeing etc.

March 31st.
Did watering, & moved seedlings of zinnias, lobelias etc. to cooler house to make room for tomatoes. Spaced out potted tomatoes to give them more air & light, and potted out some more.

(C.S. – Planted 2 pots of potatoes)

SAVE AUTUMN LEAVES
'Kitchen Garden', *Garden News*, 30 November 1973

This is a relatively unrushed time in the kitchen garden. The only real hurry is to get the ground properly dug over before the bad weather sets in.

With many crops cleared off the ground, it makes sense to work in manure or compost at this time of year. We are lucky here in being able to get spent mushroom compost from the mushroom farm next door. (It's known locally as the 'factory', which tells you something about the way they grow mushrooms these days!) When we moved here in November five years ago digging was almost impossible. 'Slurp' was the only response to plunging the fork into the clayey, waterlogged substance we called soil. But regular applications of mushroom compost each autumn have had a miraculous effect in converting unworkable clay into beautiful loam.

Many gardeners can't get hold of bulky organic manure these days, but there should be a compost heap at the bottom of every garden. It's surprising how much valuable vegetable waste a household and garden can accumulate in a year.

My composting seems to have evolved into a three-heap system: the 'completed' heap, the 'in progress' heap, where most of the weeds, kitchen waste and soft material go, and the 'long term' heap, for tougher material like brassica roots, clumps of grass and trimmings from the herbaceous border. When the 'in progress' heap is completed it is covered with a layer of soil, as insulation, mixed with poultry manure and polythene sheeting is fixed over the top. The 'long-term' heap then forms the base for the next 'in progress' heap. By then the first completed heap is ready for use, so the new 'long-term' heap is built in its place.

While on the subject of waste, it seems to me it should be a criminal offence to burn autumn leaves, not because of what it does to the neighbour's washing, which is bad enough, but because of the destruction of potentially valuable material for the garden. Deciduous leaves collected together into a loose heap (not too thick), turned from time to time so that the air and light can get in, eventually decompose into beautiful leafmould. This is lovely stuff for working into seed and potting composts in place of peat, or for making a layer between the drainage crocks and the soil in flowerpots.

....

I still follow the three-compost-heap system, but now they're spaced at the bottom, the middle and the top of the garden, to minimize the distance for barrowing in old age. The poultry manure has been replaced by seaweed . . . Well, we've no hens and there's seaweed near by. The term 'global warming' was unknown in 1973, but of course burning leaves is taboo now for that reason alone.

TIPS TO TAME TODDLERS
'Kitchen Garden', *Garden News*, 26 April 1974

When I first got married and gave up work (paid work), I thought how marvellous it would be to potter in the garden all day. I hadn't taken children into my calculations. But now I know that gardening with babies and very young children can be an extremely frustrating business.

It's in their nature to empty flowerpots and boxes, crawl over finely raked seedbeds, pour lashings of water over plants 'to help', pull up onion sets, pick the heads of flowers and so on.

For young mothers (or fathers) determined to carry on gardening in spite of children, here are a few tips culled from my personal experience in the last five years.

- Keep spares of everything. Never sow a whole packet of seeds at one time, or chuck out seedlings left over after pricking out. You might need them.
- Labels are like magnets to crawlers and toddlers so . . . mark rows in the middle. If you have a seedbed, keep a record of the order in which you sowed it. All my labels were uprooted one year. I found it impossible to tell the seedling brassicas apart, so was reduced to planting out rows of sprouts or calabrese, etc.
- Use plastic cloches when possible, or at least use plastic for the end pieces. It's safer to fence them off.
- Keep a supply of large seeds (it's worth growing a few sunflowers for this purpose), just for kids to sow. Keep seedlings of forget-me-not and other self-seeding plants for the same purpose. Kids can have lots of fun planting them in a sand pit while you're getting on with something else.
- Don't sow seeds which take more than one season to germinate. They are sure to be 'discovered'. Wait until the children are older.
- Have diversionary 'toys' handy. Suggestions are large round stones for babies and bags full of coffee jar tops when they're a little older.
- Encourage them early in life to take things to the bonfire (provided it's not lit), and the compost heap. It's good training, and you could sow or thin out a whole row while they're gone. (My first introduction to gardening was my father giving me wireworms to take to the hens. It's only now that I'm wondering whether the object was to get rid of the wireworm or me!)
- A pile of mushroom compost is a wonderful diversion. It's sterilized, so won't do them any harm to romp in. Lumps of chalk are an added bonus as they might start drawing with them.
- Dress children in bright clothes in the garden. It's easier to keep an eye on their whereabouts and to track them down when they wander off.
- Pray for earthworms. They are invaluable for the soil, of course, but also a great source of entertainment. I'll never forget the sheer excitement when my daughter saw her first earthworm at the age of about one and a half. She watched it in complete absorption for about five minutes, and five minutes is a long time at that age.

It's surprising how early in life children can join in constructively. An eighteen-month-old child can just about shell broad beans; at two years old they can pick up lawn mowings and help plant potatoes by covering them up – provided you can persuade them not to twiddle off the 'sprouts'. They can also help in sowing broad beans, shallots, onion sets.

By the age of three they are ready for their own garden. Make it in a good open site, and I'd suggest starting off with seeds like calendula (pot marigold), statice, honesty and nasturtium which are nice and large to handle, godetia and nigella which germinate well, radishes, broad beans and cucumbers (started indoors) which grow fast and dramatically. Last year my four-year-old son's garden was trodden hard around his broad bean – he spent so much time watching it grow. People often say kids aren't interested in gardening. I think they are wrong.

....

Nothing much has changed here!

MULCHING MADE SOWING A PLEASURE
'Kitchen Garden', *Garden News*, 24 May 1974

I've had mulching on the mind lately. It started with a couple of conversations with people who believe in the 'No-Digging' approach to gardening.

Once they've got their soil into good condition, the No-Diggers abandon digging and just keep the soil continually mulched – scraping away the mulch for sowing and planting. Cultivation is restricted to light forking or hoeing. It's the sort of theory that becomes progressively more interesting as old age looms.

I don't think my soil is quite good enough for that yet, but the value of mulching was brought home to me a few weeks ago in that dry spell at the beginning of April.

After the soil had been forked over in March, I had lightly mulched part of the vegetable garden with the remains of a very old haystack. When it came to sowing carrots, parsnips and turnips there, I found beautifully crumbly, moist soil under the mulch, and sowing was a real pleasure. But when I tried sowing Brussels sprouts and red cabbage on the strip I'd reserved for this year's seedbed, which hadn't been mulched, the soil was hard and dry, and I had to drench it overnight before sowing.

Mulching benefits the soil in several ways. It keeps it warmer in winter and cooler in summer; it helps preserve moisture; it keeps down weeds; and because the worm population increases in a mulched soil it improves soil structure and fertility.

All sorts of things can be used for a mulch: lawn mowings, dried-up bracken, spent mushroom compost, manure, peat, straw, well-rotted sawdust, leaves, leafmould and so on. With experience you get to know how thick a mulch to use – probably an inch of peat is enough, an inch or two of lawn mowings, but a thicker mulch of less dense material such as old straw.

However, don't mulch when the soil is very dry; don't mulch tiny seedlings; and don't mulch tomato plants before the soil has had a chance to warm up. If your soil is very infertile, it would be best to dress it with dried blood or a high-nitrogen fertilizer before mulching.

At this time of year it is worth checking to see that you have all the seeds you will need for late summer or autumn sowing. They often become hard to find later. I once asked a shop if they had any seeds for autumn sowing and was told they wouldn't be getting them until the spring!

I'm still a firm advocate of mulching, though in my Irish garden I'm aware it can encourage enemy number one, slugs. I'm convinced old rotting straw is one of the best mulches of all: it is amazing how it improves the soil. No way would I recommend peat mulching now, but most of us were unaware, in the 1970s, of the ecological impact of extracting peat. Nor, of course, would I suggest a high-nitrogen fertilizer, encouraging lush, disease-prone growth. Now it would be compost, compost all the way, with seaweed-based feeds to boost growth later on if necessary.

NEW YEAR RESOLUTIONS
'Kitchen Garden', *Garden News*, 27 December 1974

With January a few days away, I've been making New Year Gardening Resolutions in the hope that I will avert some of the mistakes of previous years.

I've also made a list of good resolutions which I wish manufacturers and seed merchants would adopt!

A lot of my resolutions seem to be concerned with pest control.

1. I will set mousetraps under cloches before sowing peas and get the mice before they get the peas.

2. In the belief that a stitch in time saves nine I will keep a sharp lookout for pests. Last year the savoy cabbages were reduced to lace curtains before I realized what the caterpillars were up to. And some aubergines under a cloche were being murdered by aphids before I discovered them. They never really recovered.

3. I will read all labels before using sprays. Last year I used a puffer on ants in the melon frame, then read the warning notice about cucumbers and melons. Luckily no damage was done – but luck was the operative word. Later I did a close-up spray on green peppers, and afterwards read the small print saying don't hold too close. The greenfly died; and the young pepper leaves turned black.

4. I will not waste time sowing autumn peas. I admit defeat in the face of moles, mice and weather.

5. I will not get cross if my husband digs up the tarragon, rosemary or seakale by mistake. It's a small price for all the other digging he does.

6. I will not sow sweetcorn, melons, cucumbers, pumpkins or marrows before at least the third week in April. Last spring my son drew a picture of our house in which the whole of the upstairs window was taken up with a cucumber seedling. That's about how it was. They all grow fast but can't go outside until the danger of frost is over; they just get pale and lanky hanging around indoors.

7. I will not fall for plant clearance offers. If they're being cleared they should be cleared out. Bad plants never make good.

8. When I order seeds in spring I'll include seeds for autumn sowing. It's hopeless chasing around for them in August and September.

9. I will make strenuous efforts to sow brassicas 5cm/2in apart, so that it won't matter if I'm held up transplanting. In fact I'll sow all seeds very thinly; they'll do far better, and besides, seeds are no longer cheap.

Now my resolutions for manufacturers:

1. Please devise labels which won't peel off in damp conditions, leaving one guessing the following year what it is and how to use it.
2. Why not calibrate all watering cans in pints, gallons, or litres?
3. Please make assembly instructions for cloches, frames and other equipment understandable. Some have no instructions at all; others are so vague you hate the thing by the time it's assembled.

And for seedsmen:

1. Please make catalogues strictly alphabetical – peas under P and beans under B and not in front or at the back. One 1975 catalogue has vegetables in near random order and not even an index.
2. Tell the whole truth, not just part of the truth, in catalogues and seed packets. The limitations are often omitted. For example, there's often nothing to say that certain types of lettuce are unsuitable for sowing after July.
3. Cut out extravagant claims. Unfulfilled expectations backfire against the firms concerned. If a moderate claim is exceeded, the gardener is pleased with himself and a satisfied customer to boot.

....

I did seem obsessed with spraying, though mostly with products like derris, which were approved organically. The seed company I had a dig at for not having an index must have read the piece, because I got an apologetic note and a promise to reform. Which it did. I've gone back to sowing autumn peas, but starting them in drainpipes indoors. And we've no moles in Ireland.

I AM A LISTOMANIAC
Farmers Weekly, 6 July 1973

I have listomania. I've had it for a long time, and it's getting worse.

I don't just make the ordinary lists everyone makes – shopping lists and Christmas card lists and thank-you-letter lists – every night I make lists of what to do the next day.

And it doesn't end there. I also have a week list, done on Sunday evening; a month list, made at the beginning of each month; and a 'long-term list' for things I want to do one day but can't possibly do this month.

These lists are clipped neatly together and hung in a prominent place in the kitchen within easy reach. That little pile of paper dominates my existence.

Listomania is a destructive and malignant disease. It destroys the most innocent pleasures by haunting victims with the thought of the thousand other things which they should be doing. It leads to resentment, when one is forced into doing things which are not on the list; disappointment, when you do things you think are on the list, and discover they are not; hypocrisy, when you add things to a list after doing them, merely for the satisfaction of crossing them off.

A listomaniac is exposed to endless temptations. I have gone through agonies trying to decide whether to put 'make pudding' or 'clean kitchen' on the list, knowing that many people make puddings and clean the kitchen every day.

And there is the urge to put down little things that can be done quickly. Instead of simply picking up the watering can and watering the geraniums, how often have I reached for the pencil, found the list, written 'water geraniums', watered the geraniums, reached for the pencil, found the list again, and crossed off 'water geraniums'?

Listomania reveals all human frailties. As the disease progresses, the listomaniac succumbs to even greater absurdities. 'Do next list', written on the bottom of a list, reveals an acute case. The List becomes an insatiable monster, making increasing demands on its weakening victim: clean paper, rather than the back of an envelope; ink or ball-pen, not blunt pencil; legible, not scribbled . . .

In severe phases of listomania – the disease seems to go in cycles – I count each day's items and try to accomplish at least 50 per cent. At other times it suffices to cross out the jobs done by the end of the day. But always the list provides a flimsy framework to my existence. Without it, I flounder; with it, I think I know where I am going.

Lists are giveaways of character. A typical list of mine would reveal a middle-class, middle-aged woman, preoccupied with her garden, rearing a family in the country on an apparently inadequate income.

'De-flea Sam' appeared twice on one old list I found, as well as 'train Sam'. Poor Sam met his end long before he was either trained or de-flea-ed.

'Order seeds', 'potting soil', 'clear vegetable garden paths' – a question mark here, indicating an impossible task – 'clean windows', 'clean silver', 'write Christmas letters', the list continued. There were numerous things to be made or mended. 'Patch Don's trousers' in black felt-tip pen capital letters implied great urgency. How long had Don had holes in his trousers?

So it went on, an embarrassing reminder of yesterday's trivialities. I was relieved to see I hadn't

One of the cartoons that illustrated 'I am a Listomaniac'. At the time I was rather hurt at being depicted as middle-aged; now, of course, I would be flattered!

put 'have baby' on that list, a remarkable feat of self-control as one was due at the time. Crossing it off would have been some compensation for all the effort.

Where did it all start? Could the seeds of listomania have been sown by those hated school uniform lists which plagued my schooldays, with the mysteries of 'liberty bodices' and 'long-sleeved spencers', their optionals, extras, winter-onlys and so on?

Am I today working out the feelings of acute discomfort I suffered twenty years ago, when matron used to try and decipher my mother's complex explanations of why her daughter had only two pairs of green uniform knickers instead of the statutory three?

Or is listomania a hereditary disease? Did I get it from my mother? She still keeps a piece of paper by her bed in case she thinks of something in the night. It certainly looks as if I am passing it on to my son.

At the age of two he grabbed a piece of paper, demanded a pencil, and announced that he was going to write a list.

Is it infectious? Should listomaniacs be isolated? Or certified? It probably is an addiction. Like many drugs, it gets a hold unobtrusively. I cannot blame the friend who, in all innocence, gave me a 'list book' one fateful Christmas. It was a long, thin, lined notebook, and it was irresistible.

When I told my doctor of my complaint he was not much help. Did I have migraines, he asked? I didn't. Well, he said, if I didn't make lists perhaps I would have migraines. I was unconvinced. I wanted a cure.

Perhaps I should form a Listomaniacs Anonymous. Maybe writing this will get it out of my system. But one thing is certain: I've a treat in store tonight.

I'm going to cross 'write Listomania' off today's list, this week's list, this month's list and the long-term list.

....

Although I resisted putting 'have baby' on the list, I did write the due date on the calendar. He came on time – a rare example of punctuality – and I had the immense satisfaction of crossing it out and writing 'baby came'. Writing the article was no cure: I am still an inveterate list maker.

A SERIOUS CASE OF FALL-OUT
Farmers Weekly, 31 May 1974

My first contact lenses were marvellous. I don't look like an owl any more, I thought. No glasses to steam up when I go into a warm room on a cold day; I'll even be able to read in the bath. No more 'erosion' marks, as my friends called them, on the bridge of my nose. No struggling to fit sunglasses or goggles over heavy rims. Everything was fine, except for the hazard I hadn't anticipated – fall-out.

The first time it happened I didn't notice until I prepared to take out my lenses at night. To do this you put your finger on the corner of your lower eyelid, elongate your eye slightly, and the lens drops into your hand. Well, one of them did not drop into my hand this time.

I peered into a mirror. No sign of a lens. It had obviously dropped out during the day.

I remembered my eyes watering in the firm's art department. Next day my suspicions were confirmed. Mysterious pieces of glass had been found on an artist's palette and identified as the remains of a contact lens. They had been carefully preserved in a desk drawer. The insurance company paid up.

The next occasion was in public, during a Friday afternoon rush hour. I was heavily laden with shopping bags and books, in the busy underpass from Waterloo Road into Waterloo station. This time I felt the lens go.

Without moving my feet in case it was underfoot, I stretched out to put my bags beside a pillar and stared at the mottled-grey, dimly lit floor. What could be worse?

I got down on my knees and systematically

moved my hands over the grubby floor, peering at it from all angles in the hope that light would reflect from the lens. On all sides trousered legs rushed by in a relentless homeward stream. One of them, I was sure, would crush my lens. After a few seconds the first offer of help came.

'What you lost, miss?'

'A contact lens. You know, one of those lenses you put in your eye.'

'Oh! What'll it look like?'

Someone else overheard and produced a dilapidated pair of spectacles. 'It'll be like this, will it?' pointing to the heavy glass lens.

'Oh! No. It's much smaller than that. About the size of your little fingernail. It's tiny.'

'What colour is it?'

'It's transparent really.'

'Blimey.'

They stared fixedly at the floor, attracting other helpers. An American woman and her daughter produced a torch and started the hunt several yards from the scene after someone suggested that 'it might have bounced down the steps'. A bowler-hatted gentleman put down his briefcase and joined in.

'Will it flash?' asked the original helper. 'Like a diamond?'

More help came. Hundreds of people now seemed to be walking around, heads down, eyes glued to the floor, looking for something I suppose they imagined was a cross between a flashing diamond and a piece of glass.

I began to feel guilty. They all had trains to catch and people waiting to meet them. I found myself going from person to person, thanking them and imploring them to stop. 'Please don't bother any more . . . Please don't miss your train on my account . . . It's covered by insurance . . .'

But the hard core persisted, including the man with the spectacles. 'It's all right, miss,' he said. 'I got plenty of time. Me lorry broke down. I got nothing to do for the night.'

Several times I moved to pick up my bags, to convince them that I had given up, only to put them down guiltily in the face of continued interest and perseverance. Just as I finally made up my mind to go the lorry driver called: 'Here, miss, what's this?' Carefully sheltered from pedestrian feet, on the far side of the pillar, was my lens.

I licked the tip of my index finger and prised it off the floor. The search party crowded round curiously. I thanked them profusely and escaped into the anonymity of the larger crowd.

The lens was chipped by its fall, but the insurance company paid up.

All sorts of things happen to contact lenses. They are swallowed, dropped into coffee and washed down drains. Mine have been worn the wrong way round, and two in one eye. I have even searched desperately for them when they were still in place.

I have given them up now. As my husband says, I got my man – hoodwinked by false eyes (and a wig). And he can't afford the insurance premiums.

....

After I had written this article dust trapped behind one of the lenses found me one day, eyes streaming, outside a shop in Oxford Street. I felt a hand on my shoulder. 'Don't worry,' said a reassuring male voice. 'Your turn will come.' I was standing in front of a window of wedding dresses!

2 THE GRAND VEGETABLE TOUR

The most memorable year of our lives was August 1976 to August 1977, which we spent travelling in Europe, in a van and caravan, studying vegetable growing and collecting the seed of old varieties. We dubbed it 'The Grand Vegetable Tour'. Whatever the conditions, I kept a detailed diary, which I hoped to make the basis of a travel and cookery book on our return. In my mind I was calling it 'Do you Grow Vegetables and Can I Have a Bath?', which summed it all up for me. (Perhaps unsurprisingly, the title didn't seem to appeal to anyone else.) But it was not to be. Travel books were apparently out of fashion and I was snubbed by the publishers I approached. Our savings had been exhausted by the year travelling and, faced with the need to earn a living, we couldn't afford the luxury of writing on spec. Before we left, Don had been refused a year's sabbatical leave by the education authority for which he was working, so on our return he took a series of poorly paid manual jobs until eventually getting back into supply teaching. We also started a small, experimental market garden, and I put my writing energies into articles for the commercial horticultural and gardening press. It wasn't until 1979, when I wrote an article for *The Observer* newspaper, that publishers showed an interest in a travel book. By then I was writing my book *Salads the Year Round*, which embodied so much of what we had discovered, and the burning urgency to write the travel book had dissipated. I could no longer remember, as I could on our return, what had unfolded every single day.

The *Observer* article 'Random Harvest' in many ways summarizes why we went, what we did and how we felt.

I did draft a few chapters of the never-written book. One of them, 'Blast Off', describes the final few days before departure. It's included here, perhaps as a warning to anyone tempted to do likewise.

The articles that follow are a selection of those written both during our travels and on our return, using material gleaned on the Grand Vegetable Tour. There are also a couple – 'Vendange at Vouvray' and 'Husking Bee in the Lot' – which were never published. I've linked the articles with introductory pieces, which in some cases bring the articles up to date and in others sketch in the background and, I hope, convey the problems, joys and encounters of our nomadic existence.

The weekly *Gardeners' Chronicle and Horticultural Trades Journal,* to give it its full title, was willing to publish something every two weeks and became our financial lifeline during our travels, not least as our other source of income, rent from our house, faltered. A journal for professionals, it was the ideal outlet for the commercial enterprises we visited – with a wonderfully supportive editor in Barry Hutton. I remember in one covering letter saying I didn't really care about the money but I would give anything for a bath. (Not entirely true, I suspect.)

RANDOM HARVEST
The Observer, 20 May 1979

On paper, a plan to study vegetable growing in Europe looked an unromantic reason for throwing up my husband's secure job as co-ordinator in an upper school, leaving the comforts of home, and squashing our forty-year-old selves and two young children into a caravan for a year's travelling on a shoestring.

The idea of 'going somewhere' had been fermenting in our minds for years. We'd tried to teach Eskimos in Canada, and to go to Ethiopia, or to help a missionary uncle in Bihar . . . but nothing had gelled. In the end it was my work as a horticultural journalist which gave us a purpose.

I had written a book on growing vegetables in small gardens and kept coming across references to intensive, old-fashioned systems of growing vegetables which had once been used in Europe. Did they still exist? Then, on a Sunday visit to some Manchester allotments, 'the Italian's' patch was pointed out to me: a mound of earth thrown up on one side for growing potatoes (increasing the surface area); vegetables chopped off to resprout (doubling productivity); unusual vegetables being grown. Something clicked into place.

At the same time a great deal was being said and written about 'saving' rare vegetables, collecting the seed of the old and local varieties which are dying out all over the world under the pressures of conformity, and preserving them in vegetable gene banks. Not only are these old varieties of botanic and culinary interest: they often have unusual characters, such as resistance to disease, which are invaluable to the plant breeder. We had found a reason to travel.

The preparations were a nightmare: a treadmill of financial worries, exhausting decisions about equipment, background reading, paperwork . . .

Lack of money seemed to overshadow everything. It was late 1975 and early '76, that gloomy period when an economic crash, thirties style, seemed highly likely. If the bottom dropped out of sterling the money we had saved and hoped to earn would become worthless overnight. We decided we'd have to be as independent as possible: we'd trust in goods not cash, taking as much as we could with us.

Other decisions then fell into place. A second-hand caravan to live in, a second-hand Mercedes van to tow it: diesel powered to save on fuel, very roomy to give us maximum storage.

We took bikes for short journeys, a tent for emergencies, tins of English humbugs for presents, spares for the van. In every corner of the van and caravan we built cupboards, shelves and hanging pouches for storage. Shelves were lined with cookery books, dictionaries, maps, tourist literature, reference books, biscuit tins with silica gel bags in them for storing seeds. We even took a telescope.

Miraculously, we got a £1,500 grant from the Stanley Smith Horticultural Trust, and on an exquisitely mellow Suffolk day in August we left for the ferry, towing our overladen untidy caravan.

Within no time we had shaken off the old existence and slipped into the new. Don took over the domestic chores – cooking, cleaning, looking after and teaching the children, and driving. I concentrated on 'work' – making contacts, interviewing and visiting, photography, keeping records and writing.

Life became dominated by the basic amenities of water, space, food, a firm level piece of ground on which to park and weather. As our lighting systems were perpetually failing, we geared ourselves more and more to the natural rhythms of day and season, rising at dawn, settling down at sunset. A full moon was a bonus.

The Italians showed us how to use wild plants: how to slice the bitter wild chicory finely, how to strip the outer skin from a thistle stalk to find the tender part beneath, how to suck honey from borage flowers. We were shown the edible leaf rosettes of young poppies, thistles and dandelions and wild asparagus growing in the hedges of the Bologna campsite. We collected buckets of mushrooms in the Belgian Ardennes. In Provence and Italy we learned to cook the Mediterranean vegetables: courgettes, peppers, aubergines and even the marrow flowers; we spoilt ourselves with melons. Don learned to make superb spaghetti sauce.

A French railway worker gave us his recipe for a delicious velouté made from shaggy cap mushrooms.

In a Sardinian camp we were shown the art of cleaning and preparing octopus. We grilled fresh sardines Portuguese style.

We had unforgettable meals with people we met – farmers, peasants, market gardeners, friends and friends of friends. We compensated for the hardships and discomforts of travel with the luxuries of superb olive oil, fresh herbs, good garlic and wine – often gifts from people who had grown it or made it themselves.

The children, five-year-old Kirsten and seven-year-old Brendan, adapted well to our nomadic existence. They plastered the walls above their bunks with stickers, while the floor was perpetually strewn with Lego, toy cars and dolls' clothes. Lessons were fitted in at bizarre times and in bizarre places.

My fears that the trip would prove a failure horticulturally were unjustified. We sent back nearly 150 samples of local varieties of seed, and in every country found something of interest.

In Holland it was the work of plant breeders, seed firms and research stations which proved most interesting. In Belgium I came across new vegetables, such as iceplant, winter purslane or claytonia, and unusual forms of spinach, and found a tremendous interest in the use of herbs and vegetables.

France was the country where we learned most about herbs. We gathered wild herbs from the hills and hedgerows of Provence; saw fields of green and red basil and marjoram; visited a lavender distillery; and, in the Loire, found out about the centuries-old cultivation of herbs for medicine: foxglove, camomile, cat's paw, pot marigold and hundreds more. Unusual crops encountered in France were

truffled oaks, actinidia (kiwi fruit) and chayote. From every gardener one learned something about cooking or growing vegetables.

In Portugal we made one of the most exciting discoveries of the trip – the ancient market gardens or *maceiras*, painfully excavated by hand, deep in the sand dunes along the northern coastline. The steep sides of the gardens are held in place by vines trained horizontally against them, and in the warm microclimate below, created by the sun's rays reflecting off the sandy sides, early crops are cultivated in an extraordinarily intensive fashion. The *maceiras* are kept fertile with seaweed, and we will never forget seeing the skirted peasant women, armed with huge rakes and nets, braving the cold February seas to haul in the seaweed.

Portugal also proved the richest source of old and local varieties of seed: myriad strange beans, a whole new world of cabbages and kales, ranging from the giant 2.5m/8ft tall *couve galega* to types of turnip grown for the flowers, and a host of unusual pumpkins and gourds.

Spain was full of examples of man's ingenuity: in devising irrigation systems, in building tiered plastic greenhouses on the steep, rocky south-facing precipices of the south coast; in using ancient Arab techniques of mulching with stone, sand and gravel to conserve precious moisture and encouraging plants to grow on barren soil. In Italy we found them mulching asparagus and courgettes with mountains of fluffy cotton waste; we found

market gardeners using the 'cut-and-come-again' and intercropping techniques I had read about – but best of all we discovered the marvellous range of green and red chicories, and rugged winter salad plants.

In Yugoslavia we visited a nursery heated with hot springs, and a state fruit farm where trees were dwarfed with a double-rooted system. In Hungary it was the Tápiószele seed bank, breeding of vegetables for mechanical harvesting, ubiquitous small gardens packed with dill and poppies grown for seed and the huge jovial lady who rose at 2.30 a.m. to water her vines and vegetables.

Our memories are rich with the beautiful places we stayed in, famous and unknown, which we would never have visited in a lifetime of holidays. Most vivid of all are the experiences we shared with other people and the generosity of strangers.

Was the most unforgettable evening of all in the Sardinian shepherds' one-roomed farmhouse? We sat in front of their fire with the secretary of the Sardinian Radical Party and her pet sheep Columba, listening to them talking, drinking their home-made wine, sharing their superb but simple supper – home-made salami cut down from the rafters, sheep's milk cheese on damped, wafer-thin cymbal-like pancakes of 'music bread'. Outside owls clucked to each other over the stony ground where, before dusk, we'd been photographing wild cyclamen and peonies.

We're sucked back now into the old routine. We listen to the BBC and take hot running water for granted. We may be using Italian peasant methods to grow unusual vegetables in the garden, but if I hang out the washing at night, I realize with a pang that I no longer know what phase the moon is in.

Back home at Montrose Farm, a rather self-conscious family posing for the local press.

BLAST OFF!

Of course we were never ready to go. Don came out of hospital, kidney stones dispersed, after about a week, but was very weak for some time after. Will you still go, people kept asking? We were determined we would, but I was surprised, and a little hurt, at how many people seemed to wallow in the possibility of a last-minute hitch.

As we entered the last three weeks we seemed to be running from dawn to dusk, going to bed later and later, getting up earlier and earlier. We employed Poppy, who lived in the next village, to help with the work which had to be done. Poppy turned her hand to anything: decorating the house, dismantling my Dexion potting bench for conversion into shelves for the van, scrubbing, ironing, washing.

We started disposing of goods and chattels: grandfather clock and piano to safe-keeping in the village; bunk beds and geese to my sister; Becky the dog, some chickens and sewing machine to other friends; and so on.

There were thousands of last-minute jobs — having a lesson in hair cutting, sorting out social security benefits to which we were entitled, getting the chimney cleaned, arranging for a bulk refuse collection to take away scrap metal which had been left in the yard, collecting a money belt from friends . . . And how friends helped, giving and lending us equipment, cleaning and decorating, helping us pack!

At the back of my mind, during the last few weeks, churned fears of what might go wrong. They were mainly fears for the physical safety of the children. There was a rabies scare in France at the time, which preyed on me. There were constant reports of guerilla outbreaks in Spain, revolutionary uprisings in Portugal, kidnappings in Italy. There was always the vague fear of becoming a political pawn in a Communist country.

The other fear I could never quite shake off was that the whole thing, horticulturally, would be a wild goose chase — that we'd never make any contacts or discover anything interesting, and that I didn't know enough to spot what was of interest. Sometimes I had an awful vision of myself as a rather wet, helpless English woman, wandering tongue-tied from place to place, feebly asking woolly questions.

As inflation continued to soar, the simple fear of the pound collapsing and our being unable to make ends meet was never far from my thoughts. To crown it all, I have a chronic fear of driving and traffic accidents. A whole year on the road. How would we avoid disaster? Beset by these fears I sometimes wondered how or why I'd ever become obsessed with the idea of this Grand Vegetable Tour!

Occasionally friends would start me worrying about Don. It's all right for you, several of them said: you'll have the fun of meeting people and doing your own work. But how's Don going to like doing the cooking and housework and looking after the kids once the novelty has worn off? My instinct told me that Don would love it, but sometimes I'd find myself wondering if they could be right. As it turned out they weren't. Don was marvellous and he loved it, pouring his creative energy into producing meals with whatever was available, under often intolerable conditions, accepting the challenge of keeping the basic systems operating, enjoying the unexpected which every day was to bring.

The last day came. We had to be ready to leave home for the ferry by 6.30 p.m. The house still seemed full to overflowing with our possessions, the caravan unpacked and unsorted, the last-minute lists unbelievably long. We had told the kids, Brendan and Kirsten, they could take only a limited number of toys each, but faced with their eleventh-hour pleadings to take this teddy and that toy, this doll and that digger, we relented.

As the afternoon minutes began to tick away like heartbeats, panic set in. I grabbed three large black plastic sacks, and went from room to room, picking up each object in turn and consigning it to one of the three sacks. Sack one: rubbish to be thrown away. Sack two: to be stored in the spare room upstairs. Sack three: caravan.

It was after six when I jumped into the bath – possibly the last bath for a year. When I got out I realized I'd bequeathed most of my clothes to the rubbish sack. Naked, I streaked across the lawn to retrieve a pair of clean knickers from the caravan.

It was time to leave. We hauled up the caravan jockey wheel, let off the caravan brake and put on the safety chain for the first of thousands of times. The chaos in the van and caravan was indescribable. In the last few hours we had hurled everything in, hoping to find time to sort it later. The main thing was to have things with us. No tidy, chrome-surfaced caravan ours. No surfaces were visible. Through the rear window all one could see was a mountain of bikes and black plastic sacks. From the front and side windows peered an army of dolls, teddies, hand-knitted camels and kangaroos, strategically placed by the children so that they would miss nothing of the excitement. They nodded and jolted like puppets as we set off down our long rough drive.

By the time we had reached Harwich the overhead cupboard doors had burst open and poured the contents of countless bottles of herbs and spices over everything on the floor. Hooking cupboard doors and drawers tight soon became part of our departure drill – but this was Day One. We were novices.

It was an utterly beautiful summer evening. The Suffolk countryside between Montrose Farm and the coast was lush green, the unique jubilant richness of English countryside. I couldn't believe we were on our way, setting out for our adventure. Months of tension dropped away and the tears rolled down my cheeks. 'Mummy's crying,' said Kirsty in disbelief. 'What on earth are you crying for?'

Belgium was the second country we visited on our Grand Vegetable Tour. We had been mollycoddled during our three weeks in Holland, where the kindly Mr Koomen from the Alkmaar Outdoor Vegetable Research Station had organized a ten-day programme of visits to key research stations and institutes, allotments, botanic gardens, auctions, markets . . . Only later, as I struggled with explaining my mission to strangers in languages I scarcely spoke, did I appreciate fully the luxury of an organized programme. And we had been mollycoddled by Peter Beemsterboer, wonderfully eccentric king of the brassica breeders, who became a life-long friend.

But Belgium was a blank sheet: none of the horticultural contacts I had written to had responded. We were on our own, and didn't know what to expect.

Little did we guess how richly that blank page would be filled: how our early visit to Jelena and Robert De Belder's Kalmthout arboretum and their burgeoning kitchen garden would be our first encounter with cut-and-come-again techniques, which were to dominate our salad growing and my books until this day; how the Gonthier seed company would introduce us to several new plants, and how I would spend hours devouring their superb catalogue; how we would return over the years to the fabulous 200-year-old kitchen garden at Hex Castle (see page 291), as guests and speaker at their garden festivals. Nor did I imagine how easy it would be to visit the excellent fruit and vegetable research stations and how much I would learn from them. We met enthusiastic gardeners from all walks of life and learned from all of them. Belgium proved to be a horticultural gold mine.

I put much of this into my article 'Some Belgian Vegetables', for *The Garden*. I am puzzled now as to why I made no reference to finding winter purslane, *Claytonia perfoliata* (formerly *Montia perfoliata*), which became one of my favourite autumn and spring salad plants. We had first seen this pretty little plant in Gonthier's trial ground. In the nineteenth century it was introduced into Europe from North America, where its many

Winter purslane or claytonia, one of the vegetables we 'discovered' in the trial grounds of Gonthier seed company, which has proved so useful in winter salads.

names include miner's lettuce and spring beauty. In Belgium it went under yet another name, Claytone perfolie de Cuba, and since the Cuban revolution, they told me, it had been impossible to get the seed. My ears pricked up. Our mission was to collect seed of vegetable varieties in danger of extinction. Was claytonia to be the first endangered plant we would save for humanity? We bought several packets, sent some to the Wellesbourne Vegetable Gene Bank, and introduced it to gardeners back home. The laugh was on us. After our return to the UK, during the early days of anti-nuclear marches, Don popped into a wood for obvious reasons. He returned with a grin on his face. The wood was carpeted with claytonia. Later we learned of acres of claytonia on a Scottish estate and rampant claytonia in Cornwall. Claytonia has all the characteristics of an invasive weed. It was well able to look after itself.

Belgian horticulture found its way into my notebooks, articles and books, and eventually into what we grew and how we grew it. What stayed indelibly in our minds and memories was our 'campsite' in the Ardennes. After five weeks of constant travel we were tired. We needed to stop in one place for a week or more, so Don could catch up on the domestic chores and give the kids some settled schooling, and I could catch up with my notes – I already had a box of papers to sort and 200 shorthand notebook pages from Holland and Belgium; and it was essential to write a few articles to generate income further down the line. Money was a problem. Belgium was an expensive country, and we were failing to keep to our target budget of £7 a day. Some of the Belgian campsites were £2 a day, and I noted one evening that we had spent £1.40 in one shop buying 'two ginger biscuit things and a loaf of bread . . . so we must start making our own bread!' I added that 'in fact we're eating very well'. No need for tears, just caution! We had decided to look for a cheap but congenial campsite in the Ardennes, before moving on to France.

So at about 5.30 one evening we stopped the van in the village of Maissin, got out the guidebooks and started considering the options. While we were doing so, a character lumbered drunkenly out of a nearby bar, clothes peg stuck jauntily in his felt hat, and tried to climb over Don in the driver's seat, chattering away in German. (The van being a Mercedes, he must have assumed we were German.) He was, it seemed, directing us to his friend's place to stay. 'Let's just go there,' I remember saying, 'shake him off, then we can move on.' So we followed him around a corner to a farmhouse. A short stout man emerged and looked at me severely. 'Are you the advance party of a circus?' he asked me. I assured him we weren't. 'Will you pay me?' I assured him we would. We struck a bargain to stay in his field for a night (far cheaper than any campsite), and drove into a lovely little orchard behind the farm. We stayed ten days in our Walloon-speaking village. It was a haven.

It was beautiful countryside, much of it wooded, the fields white with autumn mushrooms. We biked and walked, enjoying the unspoilt villages with their large farmhouses, typically barn and house in one. We had beautiful views from our orchard, and on clear evenings – it seemed to rain rather a lot – got out our telescope to look at the stars. Our farmer, M. Rossion, soon lost his fierceness and told us to help ourselves to the windfall apples and pears and pick the chanterelles in the orchard. We

Left: Brendan and Kirsten with M. Rossion, the Belgian farmer who let us stay on his farm at Maissin, in the Ardennes. This was taken on our return visit in 1978. Right: Luxury: ten days in one place in the Ardennes. We doubled our living space by putting up the awning.

could buy eggs from the elderly couple across the road, and milk from Marie further down the road. We could use his barn, which smelt sweetly of the recently picked apples stored there. It was also used for scout camps so, greatest treat of all, I could borrow a real chair. (I normally had to make do with folding camping chairs, so rarely enjoyed comfortable typing.)

We loved our taste of village life. Two thin, elderly sisters were our neighbours. Every day they went out with sharp knives and huge baskets, collecting food for their rabbits and mushrooms for themselves. They had two pigs, one cow, lots of black hens and the rabbits. I took photos in their immaculate garden, and several years later we returned to the village and were invited into their equally immaculate kitchen, polished brass implements adorning the huge fireplace. And we met M. Rossion again, by then a widower.

Buying milk always took a while. Marie, who seemed to be the only young mother in the village, was never there, probably busy with the cows or keeping an eye on her three young sons, Jean Paul, Jean Claude and Jean Pierre. We'd knock on her door and sooner or later a neighbour or two would shout out, '*Marie, il'y a quelqu'un . . .*' and eventually Marie would emerge.

Buying eggs was infinitely more complicated and protracted. The old lady, who only spoke Walloon, was the keeper of the eggs. The eggs were kept in an egg tray in the larder. Her husband, a lean, gangly man, was the negotiator and interpreter. I would explain that I would like to buy some eggs. He consulted his wife. She talked mainly in a very low voice, rather like the background clucking of hens, then there would be a couple of cresendoes as if she had laid an egg and then the tone would drop back; all the while she would be knitting furiously. He would then relay the conversation in French. The hens weren't laying very well, they are losing their feathers . . . and he

lifted his shoulders and drooped his long arms in a great imitation of moulting hens. It doesn't matter, I tried to assure him: we can always buy eggs in the shop. But then he disappeared into the larder and emerged with the egg tray. These four, he said, are for the cake my wife makes for the *curé* every Sunday, these two are for . . . and so on. It really doesn't matter, I would repeat; I just thought it would be nice to buy eggs from you. On one occasion the old lady went into the larder and brought out nine eggs. Then she went back and brought out one more, before taking three back. In the end I bought nine eggs that night and arranged to return in a few days' time. And when I did, they had started preserving them for winter in waterglass. The old man was very proud of his eggs. They are so fresh you can hear them being laid, he said, whereas the ones in the shops were so old you could hear them crack open.

Maissin brought history alive to us. It had been run through at the beginning and the end of the First World War, and had its own, sad war cemetery, where the bodies of 3,000 young men, enemies in war, were buried side by side. The German graves were covered with trimmed ivy, the graves of unknown soldiers with juniper. The Scots pines around the cemetery instilled a mournfulness. Our farm had also played its part. We learned that what we had thought was a tumbledown shed had once been a forge, built in 1805 and worked by M. Rossion's father. The lathe had originally been powered by a dog, later with a petrol engine, finally with electricity. There was a workshop below ground, and during the war villagers had taken refuge there, pulling a rock against the door when they were inside. The invading Germans had run through the forge above, but were shot by a Frenchman hiding in the orchard – our orchard. That made a deep impression on us.

Shortly before we left, our other neighbours were picking their plums. Well, they had hung a huge net under the tree and were shaking the tree vigorously. They broke off a branch and gave it to us: a generous gesture but rather a shock to my horticultural soul! Not long before leaving I asked if I could buy the chair I had borrowed; it had transformed my life. M. Rossion was very sorry: it belonged to the commune and wasn't his to sell. There were tap-tapping sounds during the day, but I thought little of them until M. Rossion emerged from his workshop. He had repaired a chair for me, and would accept nothing for it. It still brings tears to my eyes to think of it. And it brought tears to my eyes again, when, months later, in Yugoslavia, I saw it tumble backwards through the caravan door and disintegrate. It had served me well. When it came to the final payment for our stay M. Rossion insisted on far less than he had originally asked. We thanked him with a tin of English humbugs, and I'd like to think we gave him the drawings Brendan and Kirsten had done of his farm. But to be honest, I can't remember!

....

SOME BELGIAN VEGETABLES
The Garden, January 1977

I make no claim to being an 'expert' on the Belgian kitchen garden, but during a three-week stay in the country I couldn't help noticing several striking differences between the average Belgian potager and the typical English kitchen garden – and a few ideas worth stealing.

Two factors, I suppose, contribute to these differences. First, the climate, generally more continental than ours, with a shorter summer growing season and longer, more severe winters, and second, the Belgian's love of his stomach. Ask any ordinary gardener about something growing in his patch, and in no time, he'll talk of béchamels, vinaigrettes, mayonnaise (not from a bottle) and soups.

Several vegetables which we consider oddities, or would only grow in very small quantities, are very common in Belgium – for example, purslane, chervil, corn salad and cress. These all have the advantage of germinating and resprouting quickly in the spring, may give two or three crops from one sowing, and can be used in various ways – in salads, soups, sauces and as garnishes.

HERBS FOR POT AND SALAD

Purslane (*Portulaca oleracea*), related to the ordinary garden portulaca, is seen intercropped, undercropped, and in patches everywhere. It is sown in frames or under cloches in April, then out in the open, and is ready for use two months after sowing. The most commonly grown variety is 'Large Leaved Golden', and according to Gonthier (one of the leading Belgian seed firms) it should be watered in full sun to enhance the golden colour. The leaves are roundish, fleshy in texture, and should be picked off individually, always leaving two or three at the base of each shoot to allow for regrowth. Like garden portulaca, it is a sun lover, and will keep growing until the frost. Mrs de Belder, from the arboretum at Kalmthout, finds a square metre of purslane keeps her family going all through the summer, and that it freezes well. It can be chopped into soup, used in salads or cooked like spinach, and is also recommended as an ingredient of béarnaise sauce.

Chervil (*Anthriscus cerefolium*) is very widely grown for use in soups and sauces and, because of a slightly hairy texture, sparingly in salads. It is often chopped into soups just before the soup is served, and also makes very good green mayonnaise. Normally several sowings a year are made, the first in frames or under cloches, the last very thinly in September, to stand the winter. It germinates best in spring and autumn; summer sowings need to be in a shady position, with the plants being well watered. Germination is sometimes hastened by covering the seeds after sowing with black plastic, or sacks which are kept moist by watering. The covering is, of course, removed as soon as the seed has germinated.

Chervil is cut when a few inches high, between six and eight weeks after sowing. The annual varieties are generally used for kitchen gardens, but there is also an attractive perennial variety, which one of our Belgian hosts found an excellent substitute for parsley during this dry summer, when the ordinary parsley had succumbed to the drought. I now suspect this was in fact sweet cicely (*Myrrhis odorata*), which has a very similar leaf and aniseed flavour.

Corn salad (*Valerianella locusta*, syn. *V. olitoria*) is another salad vegetable which is far more popular in Belgium than England. A quarter of Gonthier's customers order it – and they have eight varieties to choose from, varying in colour and shape of leaf, hardiness and 'heartiness' (a relative term where corn salad is concerned). It can be sown from July onwards, but because it is so hardy, the main sowing is in August for gathering from October until the following April or May. It likes a firm soil, and is a convenient crop for intersowing in the onion patch, shortly before the onions are lifted. A dwarf growing, rosette-shaped plant, like purslane, it is best picked leaf by leaf to encourage more growth. Although hardy, winter protection with cloches or bracken is certainly advisable, as it improves the quality of the leaf.

Used mainly in salads, it is often combined with celery, cooked beetroot and Witloof chicory. Vilmorin's seed catalogue also recommends it for stuffing, and chopped with Roquefort cheese. It is especially worth growing oneself, as it travels badly and is generally of poor quality in shops.

I was very puzzled when I first encountered patches of cress in Belgian gardens, not recognizing ordinary cress (*Lepidium sativum*), beyond the 'blotting paper on a windowsill' stage. But here cress, *cresson alénois* as it is called, is grown a great deal in gardens, mainly for use in salads and soups, chopped off at ground level when 7–10cm/3–4in high. In soups, I gather, it is used very much like chervil, chopped in raw at the last moment just before the soup is served. In Holland I was told they eat cress on toast with a little bit of sugar, which sounds worth trying as an alternative to the traditional cress sandwich.

Several sowings of cress are made each year since it runs to seed quickly. As with chervil, summer sowings need to be in the shade. There are several varieties – fine-leaved, broad-leaved, curled – and I have read about a golden or American variety, which could be an attractive form for salads.

Land or American cress (*Barbarea verna*, syn. *B. praecox*) is also fairly widely grown, and is known as garden cress. This, with its watercress flavour, is much hardier than ordinary cress and can be used in salads or for garnishes during the winter.

Sorrel is another of those vegetables which is far more appreciated and used in Belgium than England, partly because of its culinary value, partly because of its hardiness. Being perennial, it can provide fresh green leaves very early in spring. There are several varieties of sorrel (*Rumex*), but the main variety in catalogues is the common, broad-leaved, French sorrel 'De Belleville'. If sown in spring the first leaves are ready within two months. But most people have a permanent patch, renewed every two or three years by division. In the lovely privately owned kitchen garden at Hex Castle in Liège province, two large patches of sorrel, of different varieties, are a permanent feature in the lee of one of the great brick walls.

Rumex patientia, herb patience, is another form of sorrel which I saw in several formal herb gardens in Belgium. This handsome plant, which sometimes occurs wild in Britain, can grow up to 1.75m/6ft tall. It is said to be very prolific, and to come in ten to fourteen days earlier than common sorrel in the spring.

Sorrel is best known for its use in soup; but it is also cooked like spinach, and John Organ, in his book *Rare Vegetables*, recommends using it in summer salads, or cooking it with turnip tops and spinach, or, when the leaves are very young, using it on thinly sliced bread with cream cheese. Mrs de Belder uses it with Swiss chard in green mayonnaise.

SPINACH AND ITS RELATIVES

In most Belgian gardens there seem to be several rows of leaf beet, apparently preferred to ordinary spinach, which is liable to run to seed in summer. These are forms of *Beta vulgaris*, the garden beet, with the leaf developed rather than the root. I've always thought them preferable to spinach, being tolerant of a wider range of conditions and quite capable of surviving the winter, producing a crop of succulent fresh leaves early in spring.

In the Flemish parts of Belgium and in Holland these leaf beets are known as *snijbiet*, or cutting beet. Two types are grown: the ordinary spinach beet, which is cut off at soil level and treated just like spinach, and Swiss chard, with far more pronounced midribs. The greenery of Swiss chard is stripped off and used like spinach, while the midribs are cooked like asparagus or celery.

One of the substitutes for summer spinach which seems to be fairly common in Belgium and parts of Holland is orach or mountain spinach (*Atriplex hortensis*). I bought a packet of seed in a market in southern Holland, but it was some weeks before I had identified it as orach.

The seeds are sown *in situ* from March onwards, and thinned to about 35cm/15in apart. Early flower heads should be pinched out to encourage the foliage. There are white, green and red forms, but for a striking patch of colour in the vegetable or herb garden, the red form is certainly worth growing. With its brilliant crimson leaves, the upright stance of a large dock, a height of up to 1.5m/5ft, competition between the cook and the flower arranger can be expected. If the flower arranger wins and the plant is allowed to seed, be prepared for many, probably too many, self-sown seedlings in future years.

Orach is boiled like spinach or sorrel, and is often mixed with sorrel to modify the acidity of sorrel. A few leaves look very colourful in a salad, but unfortunately the red colour is lost when the vegetable is cooked.

I saw two other very curious substitutes for summer spinach in the Gonthier trials grounds in Wanze, which, incidentally, are open to the public. The first was the iceplant (*Mesembryanthenum crystallinum*). At a cursory glance the plant is not unlike New Zealand spinach, but on a closer look the stems and

The picturesque iceplant (Mesembryanthemum crystallinum), *with its sparkling, succulent leaves, was another unusual plant we discovered in Belgium and introduced to the UK on our return.*

leaves appear to be covered with tiny lumps of ice or frozen dew. This weird appearance is caused by transparent membraneous bladders. The plant is said to originate in the Cape of Good Hope and is sometimes grown as a house plant. Seed is becoming hard to get.

The other unusual 'spinach' was amaranth 'Fordhook Tampala', which stands summer heat very well and grows with great rapidity. The leaves are eaten like spinach and the stems like asparagus. It is an erect plant, somewhat taller than ordinary spinach. This is the last year Gonthier are selling the seed, as it also has become increasingly hard to find.

WINTER VEGETABLES GALORE

Apart from the green vegetables of summer, Belgian gardens are full of vegetables for winter, most of which are destined to be lifted in autumn and stored in cellars, frames or trenches, covered with leaves or straw, or kept in earth, sand or ashes. Only the hardiest are expected to survive outside. The Gonthier seed catalogue has many illustrations showing the different methods used to store and protect vegetables during the winter.

The only vegetable cellar I actually saw was the 200-year-old cellar at Hex Castle, built alongside the walled-in vegetable garden. It keeps completely frost free all winter. Here cabbages are stored on a semicircular wooden frame, cardoons and celery in pits in the earthen floors, carrots and celeriac in clamps and boxes.

Again with winter vegetables it is a case of what is odd in England being ordinary here: scorzonera, kohl rabi, celeriac and Witloof chicory are seen in almost every garden, along with the expected winter standbys of carrot, beetroot, leeks and onions. Witloof chicory is grown in immense quantities: it must be eaten every day! 'Witloof' is the Dutch (Flemish) for 'white leaf', and Witloof chicory was 'discovered' in Belgium by a farmer who threw his old chicory roots (used for coffee) into a dark shed and found that they sent up tender white shoots. A huge cottage industry developed on the basis of this discovery.

Most Belgians blanch their chicory in pits, or frames outdoors, covering the roots with several inches of earth or ashes, then a layer of straw, and often a final protective covering of, for example, corrugated iron. The trimmed roots are stored in clamps or boxes until required for forcing.

I came across quite an unusual hardy vegetable in Belgium, completely new to me. *Chou côo*, I was told, was 'typically Belgian'. As far as I could make out, it is a kind of sprouting kale, which stands well into winter. The head is picked first, then shoots form in the leaf axils, and these, as well as the leaves, are eaten in winter and early spring.

Curled endive (all sorts of endives and scaroles are grown in Belgium) is another vegetable used in winter, often blanched under mats or pots, or by tying up the leaves. Long and round black-skinned radishes are also grown for winter and stored in cellars. As for celery, our white English blanching celery is unknown, but two types are grown – a bushy green form used only for soup, which is overwintered in the open or under frames, and a green-stemmed blanching type, which is generally overwintered under cover.

No article about Belgian gardens would be complete without mentioning the enormous, vigorous types of climbing French bean (*Phaseolus vulgaris*), which are so widely grown, often on poles up to 4.5m/15ft high. Some types are eaten as green 'haricots', while others are used as dry beans in winter. Many dwarf varieties of French bean are also used. The Belgians are extremely scornful of the inferior flavour of our runner bean, *Phaseolus coccineus* (syn. *P. multiflorus*). But it was, after all, originally introduced solely for its ornamental qualities.

And lastly, herbs. As in England, there is a tremendous revival of interest in herbs. Besides the common quintet of sage, thyme, parsley, mint and chives, one often sees savory, hyssop, tarragon, marjoram, basil and others. Anyone interested in herbs who finds themselves in Belgium should go to the open-air museum at Bokrijk, in Limburg province in the north-east of the country. Here, in the 'domaine' of a castle, there has been an extensive reconstruction of Belgian villages from various parts of the country, spanning the seventeenth, eighteenth and nineteenth centuries. The villages are complete with boundary stones, wayside chapels, mills and so on – all extremely well done. Behind the farmsteads there are many little gardens, often enclosed in clipped hornbeam hedges, which are cultivated by pensioners who act as guides and custodians. In the centre of the park there is a wonderful herb garden (*kruidtuin*), with an excellent collection of old herbs – culinary, medicinal and economic. A fascinating place, and worth a long visit.

One of the pensioners at Bokrijk was very proud to show us around his garden – an immaculate little plot with the dwarf beans grown in ridges (a fairly common practice in parts of Belgium), tomatoes tied neatly and stopped at three trusses, leeks earthed up and in the process of being liberally manured. Around the edge, and between the rows, numerous beer bottles were buried up to their necks. This, he said, was to keep the moles away. The sound of the wind in the bottles frightened them off – more or less. I don't know whether this is an old gardening trick, but it's one idea from Belgium I'll try out in our mole-infested garden on our return.

....

The Bokrijk Museum is still there, but I have to say I've completely changed my mind about the merits of spinach beet versus spinach. I much prefer spinach these days.

When we visited the chateau of Villandry in 1976 its renovation was still underway, and it was far less well known than it is today. Its originality made a deep impression on me, but I little imagined how far reaching that would be, and how it would seep into almost all my gardening subsequently.

About eight years after visiting Villandry I created my first little potager in Suffolk, and now, nearly thirty-five years later, have created a retirement potager, presumably my last, in Ireland. In the years between I have seen colourful vegetable gardens all over the world and encouraged waves of people to 'design' kitchen gardens, or even tiny plots, integrating vegetables, fruit, herbs and flowers to make beautiful but productive places. Villandry was the inspiration which led, twenty years later, to my book *Creative Vegetable Gardening*.

The vivid images of Villandry, garnered on the first visit in 1976, are always with me. Not just the patterns made by the colourful tapestries of vegetables but the features – the arbours, the fences, the benches, the beautifully trained fruit, the fountains. It worried me, on the original visit, that the vegetables were scarcely used, but they are used by the household, and I remember delighting, on a later visit, at seeing a cook out there picking basil.

Today the garden, under the ownership of Henri Carvallo (great-grandson of the garden's creator, Joachim Carvallo, and Ann Colman), has over 340,000 paying visitors a year, there is a staff of ten gardeners for the six different chateau gardens, and the gardens themselves are open all year round.

....

BEHIND THE SCENES
Gardeners' Chronicle, 17 December 1976

Of the many famous chateaux in the Loire Valley, Villandry has pride of place with garden lovers on account of its superbly reconstructed Renaissance garden. The ornately patterned parterres engraved with yew and box, the raised walks of pollarded limes and the use of vegetables and flowers to create a tapestry of remarkable colour and texture make this garden unique.

The garden owes its existence to Joachim Carvallo, who bought Villandry in 1906 and made it his life's work to restore the castle to its sixteenth-century Renaissance splendour and create a garden 'to match'. No plans existed of the original gardens at Villandry, but there were plenty of extremely detailed plans of gardens of the period in the works of Olivier de Serres and the architect and designer Jacques Androuet Du Cerceau. Carvallo used these as the basis of his reconstruction at Villandry.

Villandry is sited on a gentle slope and, making the most of this, the gardens have been created at three levels. At the highest level is the water garden, with a small formal lake, in the shape of a Renaissance mirror, surrounded by four symmetrically placed fountains. Water from nearby springs flows through the lakes and garden, to feed the fountains in the lower gardens, and the moat which partly surrounds the castle.

At an intermediary level are the flower garden parterres, known as the 'salons' as, at drawing-room level, they were considered extensions of the chateau. These elaborate formal gardens, conceived in symbolic designs, consist essentially of wide clipped box hedges interplanted with flowers – generally of a single colour.

The salon nearest the castle is the Love Garden. This is made up of four separate rectangles intersected by gravel paths, centred around a fountain. Tragic love, flighty love, tender love and passionate love are symbolized in the different squares.

Tragic love, for example, is in the shape of daggers and swords, and is planted with blood-red dahlias, as suggested by Du Cerceau to represent blood spilt for women.

Flighty love is depicted by butterflies, fans and 'billets doux' or love letters. Here the dominant colour is yellow, the traditional colour of unfaithfulness.

In 'passionate love' hearts are broken into whirling fragments; in 'tender love' they are intermingled with masks (for whispering sweet nothings at balls!) and separated by red flames of love. Red, pink, yellow and white single dahlias are used for the colour in these gardens.

In a second series of parterres the symbols are historic: the crosses of Malta, Languedoc and the Low Countries respectively. In a third set of 'music' salons, the motif is lyres and candelabras – to light the music. All these gardens are entered at regular gaps in the box hedges. These are marked by upright yews trimmed in dumb waiter shapes, to all appearances springing from the surrounding box hedges. They make a striking break to the monotony of the otherwise dominant horizontal lines.

The best-known feature at Villandry is the potager or kitchen garden. This is at the lowest (perhaps lowlier would be more appropriate) level, i.e. on the level of the servants' quarters. One hectare/2.4 acres in size, 100m/328ft in

each direction, it is divided into nine equal squares, separated by wide gravel paths. Where the squares meet there is a central fountain and, at each of its corners, a trellised arbour covered with climbing roses, honeysuckle, jasmine and vines.

Within each square there is an astonishingly complex symmetrical pattern of beds – no two squares being the same. All, however, radiate from a central fountain surrounded by a low box hedge; all are planted with vegetables and a standard rose and edged again by low box; all are separated from their neighbours by paths of sparkling white sand. The complex of beds in each square is enclosed by a narrow outer ring of beds planted with flowers and spindle-shaped pears with a final outer enclosure of low oak trellis fencing, against which grow espalier apples and pears.

The Renaissance potager evolved as a compromise between the needs of the sixteenth-century aristocracy and the traditional monastic vegetable garden which preceded it. Because so many vegetables were being introduced into Europe in the sixteenth century, the lords and masters wanted their kitchen gardens nearer their mansions to watch the progress of the new arrivals. Therefore, they also had to be beautiful: hence the flower beds around the potager area, the fountains and the arbours.

In the monastery gardens each monk was responsible for cultivating a piece of ground. This idea was retained by dividing the potager into small squares. The monks often planted roses as an ornament, so in the Renaissance garden the standard rose in each plot was the symbol of the working monk. It was the monks who conceived the idea of planting vegetables in groups so that their colours and textures would make beautiful patterns in themselves.

Finally, to symbolize the cloisters surrounding the monastery garden, the raised

The world-famous potager at Villandry in the Loire Valley, where the patterned beds, densely planted with colourful vegetables, herbs and flowers, resonate with medieval symbolism.

walks surrounding the Renaissance potager were planted with trellised vines, open at the sides but covered over the top, as in cloisters.

The raised walks are an essential feature of the Renaissance garden, as only from a height could the effect of the patterns of the parterres, or gardens 'on the ground', be appreciated.

At Villandry the framework of the entire complex of gardens around the chateau is formed by avenues of limes, sometimes arched to form tunnels. On the southern side of the gardens long ramps lead from one level to another. Hedged with trimmed hornbeam, they form dramatic diagonals. Pillars at the head of the ramps are decorated with urns of geraniums.

The most recent chapter in Villandry's history opens in 1971, when, after several years of neglect, it was taken over by Carvallo's grandson and turned into a non-profit-making company. His partner in the enterprise, and the present *régisseur* or working manager, is his brother-in-law Marc d'Estienne d'Orves, who after twenty years in the French merchant and fighting navies has turned his considerable energies to the task of bringing Villandry back to life and making it a commercial proposition.

Running a labour-intensive Renaissance garden on a budget determined solely by the number of visitors is no easy task in these inflationary times. The gardens are open from 15 March to 15 November and, to obtain a high-quality display through the year, two complete plantings have to be made. All the plants (over 300,000 of them) are raised at Villandry. To keep operations on target, Villandry is run with the clockwork precision of a military operation. For example:

1 February – seed sowing starts

15 March – spring planting in potager

15 April – path weeding starts

End April – summer planting in flower gardens

15 to 25 June – uprooting of spring planting in potager

25 to 30 June– summer planting in potager

1 September – start next year's manuring, soil renewal. Seed plans

15 November – start to empty potager beds; start planting bulbs and spring bedding in flower beds and potager for spring display; start pruning limes

Until 15 March – manuring, digging, soil replenishment throughout garden, lime pruning.

The nursery for the Villandry gardens consists of a couple of old greenhouses and a courtyard of frames. All seedlings for the first planting in March are raised in the frames on hotbeds. These are constructed in the traditional way by mixing stable manure with leaves (lime leaves are used for the purpose), which is then made into a layer 1m/39in deep covered with boards and glass lights.

Each winter 3,000 dahlia cuttings are taken to ensure a continual supply of the well-defined colours used in the ornamental gardens. Flowers raised in the nursery include biennials such as wallflowers, forget-me-nots and pansies for the spring display (planted with red, pink, yellow and white tulips), and dahlias, petunias, African and French marigolds, impatiens, carnations and begonias for the summer.

Space is always at a premium. When I visited Villandry in October 50,000 forget-me-nots had been raised for the autumn planting; the problem was where to put them temporarily. Some eventually found homes in the potager where the pumpkins had finished, in the hope that they would be mistaken for corn salad!

Spent manure from the hotbeds is used in the regular replenishment of the soil in the potager, which is carried out on a three-year rotational basis. The basic mixture used is one-third leafmould, one-third turf, one-third ordinary garden soil. In addition the garden receives an annual dressing of cow manure, and every year one-third of the garden is green manured, using grasses such as rye and meadow foxtail, sown as early as frosts permit and eventually dug in. There is little use of artificial fertilizers.

Many of the operations at Villandry, by the very nature of the gardens, have to be carried out by hand. For example, no weedkillers are used on the paths, for fear of damaging the hedges. Regular regravelling controls the weeds to some extent, but most of the weeding is done with an old tool, the *paroir*. This is a fine-bladed broad hoe, which penetrates the gravel and cuts off the weeds at soil level. From 15 April onwards this operation is carried out at fifteen-day intervals.

Trimming of the hedges is another immense task, for there are over 50 kilometres/30 miles of them, ranging in height from 22cm/8½in to 2m/7ft, most being cut twice annually. The trimming of the box has recently been mechanized by using German 'Freund' double-edged cutters. This has reduced cutting time from five men for three months to two men for one month.

Over 1,100 limes have to be pruned, a job which takes four months. For this the traditional hooked knife or *serpe*, used to prune vines, is used. The 300 standard roses, 200 apples and pears and vines also have to be pruned every winter. Some of the vines have died, but replanting is filling in the gaps.

One or two of the yews, a vital feature in the ornamental gardens, are also dying. This is a worrying problem as their root systems are so entwined with the box that removal of the yews for replanting would inevitably damage the box. It takes twenty years to grow and trim a yew into regulation height and shape. The roots of the box and yew naturally tend to grow towards the flower beds, creating an unbalanced effect, but this has been overcome at Villandry by fertilizer injection into the gravel.

Another task which is now being tackled by the staff is the renewal of the picturesque oak fencing around the vegetable garden. The original fencing, now over sixty years old, is sadly rotting away and it is proving difficult to find suitable wood of the same quality.

Because the Loire valley is subjected to dry summers, one of the essential factors in reviving Villandry was to instal an irrigation system. Two years ago a borehole was sunk and a network of underground pipes laid by the staff, a task which took six months. Electric pumps and Wright Rain irrigation were then installed. Watering is done at night, when pumping is cheaper, evaporation lower and there are no visitors.

During the summer months the gardens are irrigated six nights a week, normally from about 10 p.m. until between 4 and 6 a.m. The infinitely varying requirements of the garden mean that the twelve to eighteen sprinklers in use have to be moved every two hours. One of the gardeners is responsible for the job between 10 p.m. and midnight but the régisseur himself takes what can only be called the dawn watch, from midnight until the early hours of morning. Asked when he finds time to sleep, the answer was, in winter, 'Comme les marmots'. (Like the dormice.)

The annual planning of the potager probably ranks as the régisseur's most complicated task as there are so many factors to consider. One major concern is the authenticity and effectiveness of the plants, for as far as possible, the vegetable varieties used must be those that were available in the sixteenth century.

They must also be of a reasonably uniform height, without protruding too much above the box edging in order to maintain the tapestry effect. Adaptability to local conditions is essential so that they will grow well throughout the months of display.

Then there is the question of balancing the colours. For the spring planting the colours are variations of pure green, blue green and yellow green. In the summer plantings the principal colours are blue, red, yellow and green. Finally, there is rotation. When the régisseur starts on the annual plan (worked out, incidentally, to two decimal places) the starting point is the choice of colours for each bed, taking into account that each colour must ensure a rotation from whatever grew there the previous year.

It requires considerable skill to get the massed effects on which the garden depends. For the summer planting most of the vegetables are raised in Jiffy pots and planted out direct. In some cases it is necessary to plant several seedlings in one spot, with beet, for example, to get the density of foliage required. The vegetables, after all, are not there, primarily, to eat!

A tremendous range of vegetables is used in the potager display. Spring planting includes carrots, spring cabbage, radish, spinach, ryegrass, cress, peas, chives, types of 'Salad Bowl' and ordinary lettuce.

In the summer blues are supplied mainly by types of cabbage and leeks, especially the variety 'Bleu de Solaise', which becomes a striking purple towards autumn. Reds are obtained with red cabbage, ruby chard, purple orach, red lettuces and this year a dwarf miniature tomato, brought from the USA. (A slight twisting of facts, d'Estienne d'Orves admits, as although tomatoes were introduced into Europe in the sixteenth century, they did not reach France until later . . . But they could have been seen by travelling Frenchmen of the day.)

Yellow colour is predominantly created by yellow leaf beet or chard (the *poirée blonde* that is so popular in France), sorrel, the pale-leaved leek 'Jaune Gros de Poitou', and celery. New Zealand spinach, chives, chicory, dwarf curly kale and haricot beans are some of the true greens used.

In October the most striking effects were created by 'Rhubarb Chard', a splendid variety with crinkled, deep crimson-bronze leaves and brilliant red stalks; the red-leaved lettuces such as the 'Red Oak Leaf', 'Rouge Grenobloise' and 'Bronze Salad Bowl', and most impressive of all the coloured kales, with an outer fringe of green leaves and a coloured core. The colouring increases with colder weather, making a stunning autumn display that from a distance looks more like a bed of dwarf hydrangeas than a plot of mere brassicas. Whether it was a question of variety or the method of culture, they certainly surpassed any ornamental cabbages or kale I've ever seen in England.

As with any enterprise on the scale of Villandry, the main problems are staff and finance. When the gardens were taken over in 1972 the existing staff were mainly unskilled old men who worked part-time at Villandry and part-time on their own holdings, and so were reluctant to work overtime. To economize on the wages bill no head gardener was taken on and d'Estienne d'Orves doubled as manager and head gardener.

For this reason he is apt to disappear, with a polite apology, in the midst of a guided tour around the gardens. In my case he reappeared on a high stable roof apparently supervising a repair job. (Perhaps the navy is a good apprenticeship for running a Renaissance garden.) Three younger men have recently been recruited, however, who are more willing to take on responsibility and work overtime. The present staff now averages about six.

As already mentioned, visitors' entrance fees are the sole source of income for the garden, currently bringing in about 600,000 francs (£75,000) a year. This income also has to meet the cost of urgent repairs to the castle and buildings, which must be carried out within the next few years (every visitor means four new tiles).

The French government offers some help toward the cost of repairing and maintaining historic buildings, and at present Villandry is applying for a grant towards the cost of re-establishing the herb garden, an expensive enterprise. The bill for the basic plants alone that were ordered this year came to £1,500.

The target for visitors is 200,000 per year, which would, it is estimated, balance the books. When the present team took over in 1971 there were only 50,000 a year. This has been built up steadily; in that first year 20 per cent of the budget went on publicity.

By 1975 the total number of visitors had risen to 30,000, but hopes of reaching 150,000 in 1976 were dashed by the exceptionally hot summer, which lowered attendance. Now 5 per cent of the budget is allocated to publicity. As part of the publicity drive, d'Estienne d'Orves visits one European country and two French provincial regions every year – presumably during the winter hibernation period.

'Vouvray' for us is not just a famous wine from a famous town in the Loire but a campsite that was a haven. We arrived in early October and stayed for ten days – an exceptionally long time for us to be in one place – even staying an extra day after it had officially closed. From my diary entries it is clear we were exhausted from travel when we got there. I was desperate for a quiet spell to write up notes and articles, get photos printed, send seeds back to the UK; the washing pile had reached gigantic proportions during prolonged wet weather (not to mention the mending pile); the van was having problems and needed servicing; and our finances had run low. I waxed ecstatic about the two hours of free hot water every day and hot showers, and that the camp was uncrowded, the management genial. The children were thrilled at having three sand pits to play in and tracks for biking along the river. To crown it all there was 'food for free' on the site – wild garlic and wild mushrooms such as shaggy ink caps and the delicious *bleus* (blewits) I had never seen before. Vouvray was also within easy reach of the many horticultural enterprises in the Loire – Château Villandry, Vilmorin, the famous French seed firm which had recently relocated its headquarters there, and the city of Tours with its network of allotments and gardens to which we had several introductions.

We hadn't intended to pick grapes, but one evening we offered to help two non-French-speaking lads, an American, Dave, and his English friend, Travers, to find a vineyard. Don decided he would join them to earn some extra cash. Then Travers was afflicted with asthma, so I exchanged two days of child minding for two days of grape picking. Travers was great with the kids, I had an experience I wouldn't have missed and Don had a well-deserved break, hard though the work was, from domesticity. His earnings went on servicing the Mercedes van and our camp fees. (We still have his official tax receipt for 297.83 francs.) I split mine with Travers and splurged on a hair-do.

....

VENDANGE AT VOUVRAY, OR A FEW DAYS IN THE LIFE OF A GRAPE PICKER
Unpublished

Whenever I come across a bottle of Vouvray in future, the subdued gold and pale green label will convey much more than a good white French wine. It will bring back an immense vista of vineyards stretching down towards the Loire, the heads and coloured shirts of grape pickers appearing and disappearing between the vines, a sugary stickiness in my fingers and an ache in my legs. For it was at Vouvray that Don and I had our first experience of grape picking.

But first find your grapes. The key word, of which we were previously ignorant, is *vendange*. *La vendange* is the grape harvest: *vendanger* is to pick grapes; the picker is a *vendangeur*. Armed with our new vocabulary and an address in rue Docteur Lebled (which instantly transformed itself in our minds into Street of the Bleeding Doctor) we drove along the Loire on our first day in Vouvray, diving up and down the maze of steep narrow lanes on the hillside above the river in search of the vineyard. It was just after

12.00 when we found it. Lunchtime, of course. The *patron*, they said, would be back at two. We were still not attuned to the fact that the great heart of France stops beating between 12.00 and 2.00 while it tends to its stomach.

When we returned at 2.00, the jovial *patron* regretted that he needed no more pickers, but directed us to a nearby chateau with a scribbled note to say he'd sent us. More driving up and down lanes in the shadow of cliffs, which we later learned housed millions of bottles of wine in caves and passages, some of them miles long. Here and there makeshift chimneys protruded and windows appeared from unconventional cliff-side homes.

We found our vineyard, drove into the courtyard, and had our first glimpse of a tractor-load of grapes and pickers at work. To a man they stopped to stare at us. We felt self-consciously foreign. We would soon realize that staring was not curiosity, just a natural snatching at an excuse to stretch one's back and ease up for a moment.

The supervisor was young, blond and polite. We shook hands all round. Yes, he'd be glad to take us on. Hours were from 8.00 a.m.–12 noon; 1.30– 6.00 p.m. Wages were 8.30 francs per hour for cutting; 9.70 for carrying. If required breakfast was 2.50 francs, lunch 9 francs, supper 7 francs, bed 1.60 francs. The form filling took nearly half an hour: age, date of birth, mother's maiden name, national insurance number, social security number, ability to drive a car, motor bike, etc. English paper work is child's play compared with French.

At 8.00 the next day we started work. As a 'cutter' I was issued with a bucket and secateurs, ritually oiled and sharpened every morning. A kindly old timer made sure each day that I had a decent pair. Don was a 'carrier' or *hotteur*, his equipment being a *hotte*, a fibre-glass triangular-shaped hod carried on the back.

There were between twenty and thirty of us that day. The cutters work in pairs, one on either side of vines, cutting the bunches, putting them into the bucket, then emptying the bucket into the carrier's *hotte*.

It took several hours to get used to the rhythm of standing, stooping or crouching to reach the grapes, cutting, then moving the bucket along the rows to search for more. One soon learned instinctively where to look on the vine for the stem of the bunches. The largest bunches, especially those which were starting to rot, had often become solidified in a congealed sticky mass around the supporting wires, and it could take several minutes to cut into them.

The heavy, putrefying grapes are richest in sugar and the best for wine: steamy clouds of mould spores rose from the buckets when they were dropped in. The grapes were surprisingly weighty, especially when wet. At first I could hardly lift the full bucket high enough to empty it into the *hotte* especially if the *hotteur* was tall, but you quickly acquire the knack.

You also learned to watch out for your fingers. The thick canopy of vine leaves can easily conceal the sharp point of your partner's secateurs, and every day had its crop of bleeding fingers. '*En-core-un*' (another one), the cry would go out, in the rhythm of the 'bee boo bee' of the French ambulance klaxon.

The grapes were collected either in a bulk bin, or in barrels loaded on the trailer, driven off to the caves by an archetypal Frenchmen – red cheeks, checked shirt, moustached, huge brawny arms. Tractor drivers considered themselves considerably higher on the social scale than pickers and, tractor driving apart, rarely did anything more strenuous than rake down the grapes in the bin, pick out a few offending leaves, or press down the grapes in the barrel with a wooden pole. Sometimes they would condescend to pass around the wine.

The *hotteur* has to climb the ladder to the trailer, and balancing on the top step, empty the grapes from the *hotte* with a deft twist of the shoulder; no easy feat with a heavy load of sticky grapes. Each *hotteur* was responsible for four to six cutters. It was a social crime for a cutter to empty a bucket into the wrong *hotte*, unless invited to do so by the *hotteur*, and fierce arguments occasionally broke out if a carrier was considered to be getting away with fewer cutters than the norm. Each *hotteur* had his own system of working: some preferred one long walk with a full load; others made several trips with lighter loads. The day was punctuated by their shouts to the cutters. '*Videz, mon pays*', '*Videz, ma petite dame*', (empty, brother, empty, my good woman) was the cry of the tall humorous character with an endless supply of raucous jokes. '*Seau, s'il vous plaît*', (bucket, please) from the quiet medical student.

Don getting first-hand experience of grape picking as an hotteur, *here emptying his* hotte *into the barrels on the tractor at the end of a long day.*

Sometimes consciencious pickers, held up by a full bucket, would call out '*Hotte, hotte*'.

The end of a row was a welcome respite. We'd stretch backs and legs, aching from the crouching and stooping, have a glass of water or the raw red wine from the plastic drums and two communal glasses which would appear, cleaning the black stickiness off our hands by crushing a bunch of small sour grapes and wiping the juice off with vine leaves. Packets of Gitanes would circulate. We'd chatter and nibble sweet grapes. It was a chance to look at the lovely open landscape, to appreciate the clarity of the light and the cloud formations. While working the immediate task of finding and cutting grapes was so absorbing one was almost oblivious of weather and scenery.

The length of the break depended on the presence or absence of the supervisor. The pickers rarely embarked on a new set of rows unless told to do so. Sometimes the atmosphere was leisurely; at others the pressure was on, notably if either the tall distinguished figure of the patron, or his white Citroën, were in the vicinity.

The pickers were a mixed crowd. There was a very dark-skinned gypsy family. There was funny round Jean François the Breton, nicknamed the Ball, and incomprehensible to us all. Poor Jean François left his suitcase in a bar in Tours one evening, got time off to find it next morning, but got so drunk in the process that he was sacked. We later saw a notice in a shop window in Vouvray, saying if anyone had seen Jean François X, the Breton, please phone this number. We did so, but it seemed to be another Jean François.

Most of the regular employees were elderly men, dressed in traditional blue working overalls, blue jackets and berets. They whipped through the vines at a tremendous rate, doubtless setting the pace for us ignorant casuals. There were several groups of young people, some families and couples who went grape picking every year, and a smattering of foreigners like ourselves.

The camaraderie and friendliness amongst the pickers was unforgettable. Sadly I could only understand a fraction of the banter and chatter. The accents and vocabulary were, I suspect, far removed from everyday French. Jokes would whip backwards and forwards over the vines, and sometimes all heads would 'up' for a communal 'laugh-in'. We paid for the lunch the second day, and thought the soup, green salad, roast beef, tomato salad, cheese and wine excellent value for 9 (old) French francs. Some of the French workers weren't as impressed, and complained to the boss.

Trouble broke out later that day. We were on long rows, 457m/500 yards long, and the pressure was definitely 'on'. It was heavy sloping land, muddy underfoot. The vines were exceptionally heavily laden, so buckets filled rapidly, and because the rows were so long, *hotteurs* had exhausting walks between pickers and tractor. (An empty hod weighs about 7kg/16lb, and a full load could weigh as much as 34kg/75lb – no mean weight to carry a distance.)

The traditional water and wine were missing. One of the carriers asked for it, but the small wiry regular who should have produced it refused. The argument started with words and threatening steps towards and away from each other. It graduated to gestures – shaking of clenched fists, elbows bent menacingly, and a vigorous gesture with thumbs tucked under the teeth which could only be interpreted as 'I'll bash your teeth in'. Then it came to blows. The *hotteur* struck at the older man who fell down, but immediately bounced back and embarked on another round of words and gestures.

The wine eventually appeared; the old man disappeared; the carrier got the sack . . . and the rest of us had an extra break, witnessing as much as we could from a distance, and getting the full details from the other *hotteurs* as they drifted back from the field of action.

The following day was unusually hot for October. There were over eighty pickers scattered over the nearly 40 hectares/100 acres of the vineyard. Power cuts brought the presses to a standstill and chaos reigned. I was no longer working, but had gone back in the late afternoon to take photos. There were the usual warm greetings from one's fellow workers of yesterday, but smiles were tired. The day had been really hard; by the end some of the *hotteurs* were so exhausted they had to be helped up the ladder to empty the *hotte*. It was an undignified and sad spectacle. And when the day ended at 6.00 p.m., there was still a fifteen- or twenty-minute walk back to the courtyard, and another twenty or thirty minutes' washing mud off boots and cleaning out the *hottes*. It would be nearly dark before they started for home. Grape pickers work hard for their money.

After supper one evening we went round the caves. Work was still in full swing with three electrically operated presses crushing the grapes. It takes four hours to extract the grape juice and separate the pips and skins, which are fermented to make alcohol or used as fertilizer. The raw grape juice goes into large glass-lined tanks known as *cuves*, where it starts to ferment. Many stages intervene before it is finally pumped into storage tanks and bottled.

At this vineyard most of the operations were carried out in the vast tufa caves underneath the vineyards, caves that were originally made when the stone was hewn out of the rocks to build the famous chateaux of the Loire valley. The temperature is almost constant year in and year out. The walls are black with fungi. We could smell the yeastiness, and hear the gurgling of fermenting wine in the *cuves*.

As a souvenir the cave manager gave us a bottle of *bernache*, the local word for the young fermenting wine, made from the grapes we had picked earlier in the week. He took the precaution of drilling a hole in the cork to avoid an explosion with the vigorously active young wine. There may not have been a gold and green label on the bottle, but this, at least, was our bottle of Vouvray!

On a cold day in November 1976 we landed on the Pozzer families in the Lot valley where two brothers, their respective families and the Italian grandparents lived together. The five days we spent with these dedicated, pioneering *biologique* (organic) farmers, whose name we had been given by the Henry Doubleday Research Association in the UK, were rich with new experiences and a unique insight into farming in a modern world without using chemicals.

We've probably never worked so hard. Within minutes of arriving Don and I were out in the fields helping the women lift sugar beet by hand: the two husbands, we learned, were at the acupuncturist. The weather had been so wet that autumn that it was impossible to get machinery on the fields. Indeed on the way south we had seen seed being broadcast by hand and had thought it quaint, not realizing that it was of necessity.

We worked until it was dark, innocently assuming the day's work was then done. How wrong we were! The next day was the *biologique* market in nearby Villeneuve-sur-Lot, where the family had a stall. So the wood-fired oven had to be lit, bread, tarts and cakes baked, cheeses prepared, and butter, jams, walnuts, prunes, pig's head *fromage* all collected for the market.

Baking in wood-fired ovens was a tradition the family had helped revive. Commonplace in the past – their farm would once have had four ovens – it had all but died out. Gilbert Pozzer had travelled the country to learn about the old ovens and built his himself. No simple turning on of a switch. It was lit with conifer clippings, kept going with wood, and then, after it had burned for an hour, the ashes were raked out and the vast oven space filled, if I remember rightly with cakes and tarts first, then with bread. The poker was a 1.75m/6ft-long steel bar. We helped Claudette mix dough and make loaves (using her own yeast recipe), the daughter rolled out pastry for a huge number of tarts, while the boys prized little cheeses out of their moulds, trimmed the edges, and set them on maple leaves. It was straight home from school to work for these kids. And when it was all done, we shared a wholesome supper of broth, brown bread, a giant bowl of salad and a tureen of chestnuts. Since the family was unable to lift potatoes from the sodden fields, chestnuts had taken their place as the staple carbohydrate that year.

But still the day hadn't ended. Claudette was involved in planning a summer street fair in nearby Montflanquin, where traditional methods of cooking were to be demonstrated. I went along with her. Food samples had to be tasted, old cooking instruments viewed, options discussed, and fliers to potential customers stuffed into envelopes, under the stern eye of the organizer, who claimed empty envelopes had been sent out the previous year. I had to comb the local phone directory to find suitable people to address them to: lawyers, doctors and so forth. I was more adept at this than might have been expected, having spent hours on our travels mastering the mysteries of French directories to track down contacts. A chaotic but lively evening. I later wrote in my diary: 'Couldn't help noticing how French people enjoy food. They almost smiled as they approached the samples, picked them up, looked at them carefully, smiled as they put them in their mouths, and unashamedly came back for more of those they appreciated most.'

We didn't get home till 1.30 a.m., and Claudette was up at 6.00 a.m. to start getting ready for the market. The market itself was a pioneering venture in France at the time, and much negotiation had taken place to get it established. The potential stall holders had wisely decided they would face the least opposition from the conservative town elders if they opted for a market on the left bank of the river, the traditional market being on the right bank. Eventually they were allowed to do so, but I had a strong sense they were considered pariahs and were treading carefully.

I helped on the stall the next day, and had so much fun, chatting to the other stallholders and arranging to see some of their places later. I loved the way the pumpkin seller asked customers if they wanted seeds when they bought a few slices of pumpkin. No F_1 hybrids here: just the assumption you might want to grow your own next year. This was also the first time I'd seen *chayoté*, an unusual member of the cucurbit family grown in cold frames.

We helped the Pozzers with all sorts of jobs, learning so many things, from how to dry walnut skins to make a furniture stain to making their own Crozefond cheese. These hard round cheeses were stored in the cheese store, the youngest cheeses at the bottom. They had to be turned daily and rubbed with a salted cloth to harden them gradually. Even the shelves had to be turned and wiped. I helped one morning, but didn't realize all the surfaces had to be wiped. So we had to redo mine. (They were nice about it – as they were when seven-year-old Brendan let the bull out of his pen, which could have had far worse consequences.) The clotting agent used in the cheese making was another of their recipes: a mixture of alcohol, salt water and *caillette*, the cow's fourth, or 'rennet', stomach. Empty *caillettes*, which take about four months to dry properly, were hanging up all over the farm.

When we left, besides loading us with their produce, they gave us a packet of heirloom seed, of a large-rooted winter radish which had been in the family for years.

To go back a few days, after returning home after the *biologique* market the family had worked until dark to lift the rest of the sugar beet. They were jubilant when the job was done. It was that same night, Don having turned down the offer, that I went with Claudette and her children to the Maize Husking Bee. Here is the account I wrote later.

....

HUSKING BEE IN THE LOT
Unpublished

Among the most characteristic features of rural France are the *séchoirs*, the slatted structures, raised off the ground to catch the wind, in which the maize for the cattle and poultry is dried and stored during winter.

Today most of the maize is harvested mechanically, but in the old days it was cut, husked and shelled by hand. Husking, stripping off the protective sheath of leaves around the cob, or *épanouillage* as it was called, was traditionally a communal affair, with the whole village participating and relaxing with food, drink and dancing when the work was done.

Last autumn some of the farmers in the Lot valley decided to revive the traditional *épanouillage* for auld lang syne. As it turned out, heavy rainfall in late October created such waterlogged conditions in the fields that some of the maize was of necessity harvested by hand, making the 're-enactment' closer to the real thing than had been visualized.

We were staying with the Pozzers, a French farming family at the time, and I went along with Claudette, the wife, and the three children, hoping to get a glimpse of French country life as it was forty or so years ago.

The gathering was held in a recently converted barn, a lovely stone and timber building. As we arrived two pairs of men, carrying huge baskets of cleaned cobs between them, came out of the building and loaded the maize on to a lorry. For a moment we thought we were late. But we needn't have worried: inside there was still plenty of work to be done.

The room was lined, if that is the word, with a huge semicircular pile of maize cobs, several feet high. Around the cobs people were clustered three to four deep; and in the centre of the semicircle were the large flat baskets in which the maize was being collected.

We took up places at the back of the throng and got going right away, stretching around or through the people in front as best we could to reach the cobs, stripping off the leaves, throwing the cleaned cobs blindly over the heads in front towards the baskets, and dropping the leaves on the floor behind us.

The pace of work was equalled only by the chatter. Everyone grabbed, pulled and chucked feverishly, all the time talking vivaciously to friends, greeting new arrivals, cracking jokes. Children romped on the floor between the baskets, miraculously unharmed by the cobs flying through the air at no mean speed in countless misplaced aims at the baskets. The men who removed the full baskets and returned with the empties seemed heroic to me, braving the unceasing hail of cobs. The floor was thick with maize; one man spent all his time retrieving scattered cobs with a long-handled shovel and putting them back into the baskets where they belonged. Sometimes a giggling boy would be carried back in an empty basket, legs sprawled over the edges.

The pile of maize became smaller and smaller, the semicircle tighter and tighter, with keen competition for the last few cobs. The children and teenagers, who had lost interest in husking, started throwing armfuls of maize leaves around, so soon we were covered in dust and chaff. A determined adult eventually calmed them down.

I've no idea how long we worked, but it was amazing how fast that huge pile of maize was demolished. What a tedious task it would have been if tackled alone!

As the last few cobs were being done the youngsters turned their energies to scooping up the discarded leaves and rubbish from the floor. They trooped outside with armfuls of debris, and made a huge bonfire with it. Within minutes several old ladies had swept the floor clean. The work was done: time for the fun.

All the while we'd been working a group of people, with much laughter and merriment, had been cooking chestnuts over a fire in the room next door. No sooner was the rubbish being burnt and the floor cleaned than the chestnuts began to appear through the door – in everything from ornate silver dishes to plastic crates. The supply seemed endless. They came and they came and they came –

piping hot and delicious. Some people kept supplies, squirrel like, in their pockets while they cooled down; others juggled them from hand to hand until they were cool enough to bite. Several of the men handing round chestnuts were wearing the traditional peasant dress of the area – white flannel shirts, black waistcoats, black corduroy trousers, wooden clogs and berets – and fine they looked. Most of the company, unromantically enough, were wearing jeans and sweaters.

The floor, so clean a few minutes before, was soon littered with the charred shells of chestnuts.

Meanwhile, at the far end of the room two barrels of rough red wine and a limited supply of glasses had appeared. Roast chestnuts, red wine, the dying glow of the bonfire outside, the crisp frosty air coming through the heavy wooden door, the liveliness . . . it was a good combination.

In an atmosphere of increasing mellowness the dance music started up – three accordions and a girl violinist. The dances were all *ancienne* – traditional dances on the verge of dying out. A group who knew them well and went from village to village performing gave us a lead. The dances were easily picked up, the barn dance type, strong rhythms with short crisp steps, broken by jumps and whirls. There were lots of quick waltzes, and a chain dance, in which everyone joined in to form a long dancing snake. The players teased the dancers by slowing down to an agonizingly slow speed, then going faster and faster until one expected to collapse in exhaustion. And all the time we were tripping and stumbling over an ever-deepening layer of chestnut shells.

One old peasant was time and again the first on the floor, with his black beret, button and bar slippers, grubby checked shirt and trousers only just held at a respectable height below his waist by an inadequate belt. Two little girls frequently stole the show — a pony-tailed red-head of about five, who seemed to know all the steps, and her partner, a tiny blonde of two in purple tights and woollen red dungarees. By midnight she was so tired she just sat in the middle of the floor, with everyone dancing around her.

After a couple of hours the players had a rest, and the cry went up for stories. Everyone gathered around M. Simonet, a market gardener from Villeneuve, who jumped up on a table and willingly launched into his repertoire. My French was not good enough to understand them all: I frequently failed on the punch line. But I did understand the one about the priest who careered through a village on his motor scooter, and when stopped by the gendarme, gave as his excuse that God was behind him, guiding him. Whereupon the gendarme gave him two speeding tickets — one for the priest and one for God.

Many of the stories had local roots. 'A tourist came into Villeneuve one day and went into the chemist. It was nine o'clock in the morning . . . they get up so late these tourists . . .' 'You know the old bakery by the square in Montflanquin . . .'

When M. Simonet temporarily ran dry others volunteered their stories. A rosy-cheeked stocky man was a superb mimic and pigs, hens and cows figured large in his stories. In one, centred on the changing sex life of a maturing cock, he picked on members of the audience to illustrate the theme. For the young cockerel, with a raw, undeveloped crow, a young boy; a gangly youth for the cockerel in his prime, crowing magnificently; and amidst much laughter, an old man for the cock with a feeble crow who was evidently 'past it'. Another storyteller launched into the local patois, fascinating to listen to but incomprehensible. It was later translated to me as a classical modern tale of a stoic old lady who refused permission

The classical séchoir, *where maize cobs are dried and stored. I took part in a memorable evening when the traditional communal husking was re-enacted.*

to developers to bulldoze her house to make way for a road. And one more, telling it as it was told. A man craps in the middle of the road. A policeman approaches. Quick as a flash the man whips off his hat to cover the offending item. 'Well, what have we here?' asks the policeman. 'My canary escaped,' the man replies. 'Would you mind it while I go and buy a cage? Just don't move the hat .˙. .'

At times the whole audience, as well as the storytellers themselves, was convulsed with laughter which took minutes to subside. Then M. Simonet launched on a second series – then the musicians picked up their instruments, and the dancing started again.

It was after one in the morning when we tore ourselves away. The dancing was still in progress, though the chestnuts and wine had long been finished. A group of children had climbed on to the lorry of maize outside and were singing. It was a beautiful clear night. As we got into the car to go home, with the petrol gauge needle hovering ominously around zero, Claudette remarked: 'How nice to meet everyone again. We never see our neighbours now, not since television.'

It's easy to be sentimental about the past, but how wise they were! The tedious job of husking had to be done; people need to get together and relax. It made sense to combine the two in a rollicking communal evening.

Perhaps the most unusual crop I wrote about during our travels was truffled oaks – truffles being the edible, tuber-like fungus, so prized by gourmets, which develops underground in association with tree roots.

In Bordeaux we had contacted INRA, the French Institute for Agricultural Research, who had helpfully put us in touch with a range of growers and interesting enterprises. One of these was a pioneering truffle venture working in close partnership with INRA.

So on a Sunday afternoon in November we left our forlorn campsite – the only tap was usually frozen until about ten in the morning and our caravan had been peppered with shot from hunters that morning – to find M. Averseng's fruit and nut nursery. The family gave us a warm welcome, and the youngest son made our visit far easier by taking Brendan and Kirsty under his wing. Not unnaturally for five- and seven-year olds, they hated being dragged around nurseries, botanic gardens and the like. Kirsty once asked: 'Is this the kind of place where you walk and walk and walk then stop and talk and talk and talk and then walk and walk and walk?'

Yes, it probably was. For us it was a most interesting place, and as so often in France, we came away, after tea and popcorn, with a handful of recipes. Don still makes 'Mme Averseng's' chervil soup.

Thanks to the Internet, I have been able to catch up with subsequent developments. Thirty-five years later M. Averseng has retired, but the company, Agri-Truffe, is flourishing. The truffles are still proving reluctant to give up all their secrets. There is no absolute guarantee that truffled trees will in due course yield truffles, so many factors are involved. However, new truffiers have been established with inoculated trees and are in production, some of them within five to six years of planting. In general the hazels and evergreen oaks have proved the earliest to produce. Dogs are now the favoured way of harvesting the underground truffles. As the Agri-Truffe website puts it, they are easier to fit into the car boot than a pig, and have the great advantage of not wanting to eat the truffles when they find them. The current price for a single tree is about €18. About 70 per cent of France's truffles still come from the traditional oak and hazel forests. Research has continued at INRA, and in March 2010 they issued a press release announcing that a French–Italian consortium had cracked the genetic code of the black truffle (*Tuber melonosporum*). It had taken fifty scientists five years.

There is world-wide interest in truffles. A small industry has been established in the USA, reputedly producing about 100kg/220lb a year. In Australia and New Zealand work is being done on the production of truffles which could supply Europe in the summer months, European truffles being harvested only in autumn and winter. So far they can claim only limited success.

And yes, we did taste truffles once during our travels, during a superb Sunday lunch to which we were invited by the Tours Cheminot, the railway workers' organization.

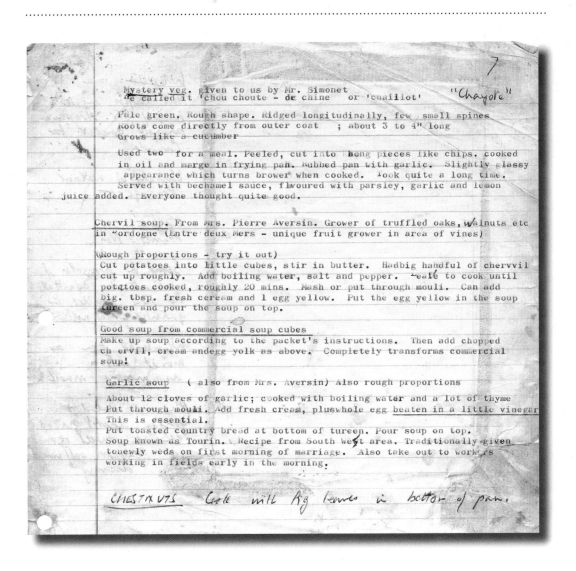

Mystery veg. given to us by Mr. Simonet   "Chayote"
He called it 'chou choute - de chine   or 'chaillot'

Pale green. Rough shape. Ridged longitudinally, few small spines
Roots come directly from outer coat   ; about 3 to 4" long
Grows like a cucumber

Used two for a meal. Peeled, cut into long pieces like chips. Cooked
in oil and marge in frying pan. Rubbed pan with garlic. Slightly glassy
appearance which turns brown when cooked. Took quite a long time.
Served with bechamel sauce, flavoured with parsley, garlic and lemon
juice added. Everyone thought quite good.

Chervil soup. From Mrs. Pierre Aversin. Grower of truffled oaks, walnuts etc
in Dordogne (Entre deux Mers - unique fruit grower in area of vines)

(Rough proportions - try it out)
Cut potatoes into little cubes, stir in butter. Had big handful of chervil
cut up roughly. Add boiling water, salt and pepper. Leave to cook until
potatoes cooked, roughly 20 mins. Mash or put through mouli. Can add
big. tbsp. fresh cream and 1 egg yellow. Put the egg yellow in the soup
tureen and pour the soup on top.

Good soup from commercial soup cubes
Make up soup according to the packet's instructions. Then add chopped
chervil, cream and egg yolk as above. Completely transforms commercial
soup!

Garlic soup   (also from Mrs. Aversin) Also rough proportions

About 12 cloves of garlic; cooked with boiling water and a lot of thyme
Put through mouli. Add fresh cream, plus whole egg beaten in a little vinegar
This is essential.
Put toasted country bread at bottom of tureen. Pour soup on top.
Soup known as Tourin. Recipe from South West area. Traditionally given
to newly weds on first morning of marriage. Also take out to workers
working in fields early in the morning.

CHESTNUTS   Cook with fig leaves in bottom of pan.

PRODUCING TRUFFLED OAKS FOR A SPECULATOR'S MARKET
Gardeners' Chronicle, 25 March 1977

In a nursery in the Garonne valley south of Bordeaux, a fruit grower, Pierre Averseng, has branched out into a unique horticultural product: truffled oaks and truffled hazelnuts.

Truffles – this is the black Périgord truffle – are among the most prized and expensive of France's gastronomic delicacies. Last year (1975) they were fetching the high price of £30 a pound, because of the drought. The annual demand for truffles in France is between 200 and 250 tons a year, but production fluctuates from 40 tons or less when July and August are dry to about 65 tons, the deficit being met with imports from Spain and Italy. In the heyday of French trufficulture, towards the end of the nineteenth century, annual production was reputed to be in the region of 1,800 to 2,000 tons a year.

The truffle is the fruiting body of an underground fungus, *Tuber* sp., which can only exist in a symbiotic relationship with specific trees, most commonly certain varieties of oak, hazelnut, chestnut and some conifers. It will grow and flourish only under specific soil and climatic conditions. Most of the *truffiers*, or truffle grounds, are found in wooded areas on chalky soils, generally south of latitude 47° North. The old *truffiers* were very carefully managed to ensure the continued cropping and spreading of the truffles: much secrecy surrounded the art of truffle culture.

One reason for the rapidly diminishing truffle crop in France is that many of the secrets of trufficulture were lost with the heavy manpower casualties of the two world wars. Without careful pruning of the host trees into an inverted conical shape, which ensures the truffled areas are protected from the midday rays of the sun, correct cultivation, and selective gathering so that the species can multiply naturally, the *truffiers* rapidly fall into decline and cease to produce.

Faced with the prospect that truffles might disappear completely, the French government undertook a research programme to establish the optimum conditions for the growth and fruiting of truffles, and to develop techniques for preparing a truffle 'culture', as the first step towards cultivating truffles or establishing new *truffiers*.

Attempts to 'sow' truffles had always proved unsuccessful in the past, partly because of the problems of breaking the dormancy of the spores produced in the truffle. It was realized that the best hope of establishing new *truffiers* lay in planting trees already impregnated with truffle mycorrhiza. The symbiotic relationship between the truffle mycorrhiza and the tiny rootlets of the host tree is most easily established with very young seedlings. It is very difficult to infect old trees.

The old literature of trufficulture was studied, existing truffiers analysed, and laboratory and field experiments carried out, so that a great deal was relearned about the conditions required for successful growth of truffles. A technique for growing truffle mycorrhiza under laboratory conditions was developed by INRA, the French National Institute for Agricultural Research, and in 1971 the production of truffled plants on an experimental scale was started. M. Averseng collaborated in devising practical methods for inoculating young seedlings with the mycorrhiza produced by INRA. He has the sole licence for production of truffled seedlings, paying 10 per cent of net returns to the government.

The truffled trees have now been on the market for five years. In 1975, 40,000 were sold, two-thirds oaks, one-third hazelnuts. In 1976, 50,000 were sold.

The oaks are grown from acorns selected from 'truffle oaks', oaks which have had truffles associated with them. Whether or not this is essential has not yet been established: it's a question of playing safe. The oaks are subsequently selected for vigour of growth and the quality of their root systems, both important factors in getting truffiers established and in production in a comparatively short time, i.e. about seven years after planting. In March the acorns are germinated in plastic trays, inoculated, then potted into 23cm/5in, tapering pots, with four drainage holes in the base for the take-up of water. They are potted into sterile soil with a reasonably high chalk content.

For the first few months they have to be kept under sterile conditions to avoid contamination with any other fungi, which could be detrimental to the truffle mycorrhiza. The exposed surface of the pots is kept covered with 5cm/2in of stones, again a measure against infection. They are watered from below via a felt material, the water being filtered to prevent bacterial or fungal infection. Once the truffle mycorrhiza are established they are vigorous, and sterile conditions are no longer necessary. There is evidence that certain fungal mycorrhiza could have a beneficial effect on the development of truffles, and it is possible that in future the soil in which truffled plants are grown could be inoculated with these beneficial fungi.

The plants are housed in a plastic tunnel from the time they are inoculated until they are sold, between ten and twelve months. The tunnels are heated during the coldest one or two months.

A similar method is used for the production of truffled hazelnuts.

When the truffled plants are six months old, a 10 per cent sample is taken to INRA and tested to ascertain that they are infected with the truffle mycorrhiza, to a predetermined level, and that no other mycorrhiza are present. The results are compared with those obtained under laboratory conditions, and if not up to the established level, the plants cannot be sold.

Three varieties of oak are at present being used: pedunculate, pubescent and the evergreen oak, *Quercus ilex*. When 'truffled' they remain small, between 1.5 and 4m/5 and 13ft high. The choice of tree depends on the conditions and situation in which they will be planted, the chief criterion being that the tree must grow well. It is essential that the trees establish themselves rapidly, as it seems that the truffles will not form until the soil area is completely covered with the roots, and the roots of neighbouring trees are touching. For this reason planting at a very high density is recommended: for example, 400–600 trees per hectare/2.4 acres (rows 5–6m/16–19½ft apart, trees 3–4m/10–13ft apart in rows). In fact this density can be tripled by interplanting with trees which will be uprooted when the others mature. One practice is to plant oaks in a square, with a hazelnut in the centre which is later removed. The intermediary trees hasten the development of a root network which will be completely colonized by the fungus.

Plants are sold when one, sometimes two, years old for planting in spring, the current price being 12 francs (about £1.50) per plant. To encourage the establishment of *truffiers* the French government is paying 50 per cent of the cost of purchase. Plants have to be looked after carefully in the first couple of years, protected against rabbits for example, and watered carefully so that the mycorrhiza are not destroyed under drought conditions.

At present purchase of the truffled trees is something of a speculation, a wait-and-see game, as it is still too early to have truffles from the trees which have been artificially inoculated.

Many professional people have been buying the trees as an investment for their retirement. With trufficulture becoming a more exact science and less of a gamble, quite a number of farmers with suitable soils are establishing 'truffle orchards'.

Under natural conditions it is often ten years or more before truffles appear. INRA guarantees only that the trees sold have truffle mycorrhiza in association with the roots: they do not guarantee eventual production of truffles, as failure could be due to any number of factors. The first hopeful sign for the purchaser will be when a burnt circle, the *brulé*, appears a few metres around the tree. This is where the truffle mycelium has killed off other forms of plant life, and is a precursor stage to the formation of truffles, indicating that the mycelium is now very thoroughly established.

M. Averseng is carrying out trials with the use of other species for truffles, particularly chestnuts and conifers, which form a particularly close symbiotic relationship with the truffle mycorrhiza.

We never expected to spend two and half months in Portugal on our year-long travels. I think we fell in love with the country from the moment we crossed the border in the north. We had struggled across Spain in hurricane weather, through empty villages with black-shawled figures scurrying into houses, and bleak plains where shepherds were wrapped in woollen blankets against the cold winds, only their faces visible. We were fearful of camping 'wild' (forbidden in what was still de facto Franco's Spain), though few campsites were open in winter and there was sometimes no option. Perhaps reading George Orwell's *Homage to Catalonia* was a bad idea: would one of those paired motorbike Guardia Civil, leaning ominously against granite pillars by the roadside, knock on the door at night? They did once, but let us stay where we were, hearts melted, perhaps, by the sight of two sleeping children.

As we crossed the border into Portugal the sun came out – for the first time in five days. Maybe it was a symbolic transitory moment, for in the next ten weeks we were constantly bemoaning the wind and rain: big black umbrellas feature again and again in the photos I took in Portugal. It was strange how everything seemed to change at the border. The scenery became prettier, with little vineyards and terraced cultivated patches on the hillsides. Previously empty roads were thronged with colourfully dressed, chatting people, almost all carrying something, quite often huge bundles of grass on their heads. There was lively traffic of donkeys and donkey carts, accompanied by a retinue of friendly dogs. Our first, and abiding, impression of Portugal was of a land where everyone was continuously on the move. They all waved at us as we passed.

This was post-revolutionary Portugal. Salazar's regime had only been finally overthrown in 1974, by the left-leaning military coup in the near bloodless Carnation Revolution. The first free election in fifty years was about to take place, and the whole country was ablaze with political slogans, posters and murals – some beautifully executed depictions of everyday village life, rural scenes, fishermen hauling in nets. There were even political graffiti in the campsite's ladies' loo. Political prisoners had been released;

the colonial wars had ended; the campsites were overflowing with the *retornados*, some of the million overseas Portuguese who had returned home, often destitute.

After travelling in rich European countries we felt we had stepped back in time. The roads, frequently close to impassable, were a mass of potholes. 'Revolutionary roads' we dubbed them, after the British vice-consul in Porto had commented, 'Roads are the first thing to go in a revolution.' There were obvious signs of widespread poverty. The cities were full of beggars, maimed soldiers with no means of livelihood. A journalist told us one in five children died before the age of five, and that illiteracy levels were something like 40–45 per cent. Compulsory schooling, as far as we could make out, was from seven to eleven years old. During our three-week stay in the Algarve fishing village of Burgau, living close to the villagers, we saw this poverty first hand, reflected in their poor health and the terrible toll on a family when a member fell ill. They could ill afford expensive medicines or treatment. None of this affected their warmth, the welcome they gave us

On the move northwards after several weeks in a rented house in the Algarve: van and caravan, parked under a cork oak in the Alentejo, Portugal.

strangers and the enormous lengths they would go to help us. Ask directions, and as likely as not, someone would volunteer to take you to your destination. Our Burgau neighbours plied us with samples of whatever they were baking.

The backwardness of the country had one huge advantage for us. Unlike any of the other countries we had visited, it was still the norm for market gardeners and peasant farmers to save their own seed. The international seed companies were only beginning to make inroads with modern varieties – the kiss of death for the seed-saving tradition. On my first venture to a seed company in Porto the owner threw up his hands in mock despair when I explained our seed-collecting mission: 'All our seeds are old,' he said, and there they were, in beautiful striped sacks, being weighed out for customers in whatever quantity they wanted.

During our stay we were able to collect over thirty-five heirloom varieties and send them back to the embryonic Vegetable Gene Bank, being established at the National Vegetable Research Station at Wellesbourne, in the UK. They were mainly brassicas, pumpkins and beans – all cultivated in great diversity in Portugal. Given the ubiquity of vegetables, I was quite surprised to read in my diary in February 1977 'the combined effects of inflation and revolution have led to a revival of interest in vegetable growing and sales of vegetable seeds have risen'. Not so different then, from these twenty-first-century recessionary times – bar, so far, the revolution!

The Portuguese seed companies we contacted willingly gave us samples of local varieties, in quaint little packets. Our early visit to the *maceiras*, the market gardens excavated in the sand dunes (see page 65), saw a boy despatched in horse and cart to get some family cabbage seed from his mother. He was sent by the owner of a shop supplying seed and equipment to the market gardeners – a great find, as he had spent time in France, so we could communicate in French. (It took me a while to pick up enough Portuguese to ask questions and stand any chance of understanding the answers.) On our return visit to his shop after Christmas we bought a small wooden table for a tiny sum, a solid table that transformed my writing existence in the months ahead.

Just before Christmas we had the great excitement of – nearly – finding the seed of purple carrots. Before leaving the UK I had been to see one of my college lecturers, Allan Jackson, for his blessing and guidance. Go to Italy and find the red chicories, he had told me, and look out for the purple carrot. German research into this carrot, and its reputed benefits in night vision, had come to an end with the outbreak of war and it had all but disappeared.

Tired of camp life and the continual rain in northern Portugal, we had arranged to meet up with two sets of fellow Porto campers, motorbiking Alex and Clemency Purvis from Australia and Pat and Bob Barwise from South Africa, in their converted ice-cream van, and rent a place together on the Algarve for Christmas. As arranged, we met up in Lagos on 21 December, but while waiting for the tourist office to open, I hopped on to Alex's motorbike and we went off 'house hunting'. I had, after all, been rehearsing phrases such as 'Do you have a place we could rent?' on the journey south. In Burgau I tried out my phrase on the first person we saw. He turned out to be an Englishman, and within minutes we had rented a roomy flat.

But to return to the purple carrot. Don and I were delegated to buy a chicken for Christmas dinner. We went into a tiny shop, where the owner seemed to be lurking somewhere in the back but evidently not in selling mood. While we waited I noticed a box of carrots by the door – purple carrots. I could hardly contain my excitement. When he eventually appeared we bought our chicken, and a sample of carrots, and I learned their Portuguese name, *cenouras roxo*. I assumed it would be easy to find the seed. It wasn't. The seed came from the USA, and as with so many things, had been unavailable 'since the revolution'. Endless quests failed to find any, and by the time I had thought of sending some carrots home, to be grown for seed, the purple carrots themselves had disappeared. I did fulfil the errand months later, through a Hungarian vegetable professor in Budapest, who put me in touch with a man in Egypt, who had purple carrots from Afghanistan. Today, of course, carrots of all hues are on the market.

The Algarve markets were a rich source of seeds. I bought strange-looking beans from a seed seller in Portimao with great baskets of bean seed laid out on the pavement, blissfully labelled with their local names. Later I was able to contact botanists, agricultural workers and researchers who filled in the detailed information I needed.

Two Frenchmen, André Rabiet and Jacques Romand, became key figures in the hunt for old varieties. Partners in a pioneering agricultural enterprise on reclaimed sand dunes near Alcácer do Sal, they had left Morocco several years previously, travelling around Portugal on horseback until they found a potential site for growing citrus, almonds and other fruit and vegetables. The land had to be levelled and drained, irrigation installed and windbreaks planted before the first crops were grown. We spent several unforgettable days camping there in the woods, a tamed fox and friendly pig near by, Kirsty washing her doll's clothes in the huge washing tubs installed as top priority for the work force. But best of all, the foreman asked the workers – there were over a hundred

Kirsty washing her dolls' clothes in the laundry facilities for workers on a French-owned agricultural plantation, south of Alcácer do Sal, made on reclaimed sand dunes.

of them – to bring us samples of their own saved vegetable seed. And many of them did. We offered to pay, but nobody seemed bothered about money. Nor did there seem to be any of the jealous guarding of family seed we had encountered when trying to collect samples from peasant families in France.

Portugal made a deep impression on us. In the south, it was memories of our weeks in Burgau. On stormy days the plaid-shirted fishermen would gather on the cliff edge, looking out to sea, or sit in the café playing cards. If they could fish, they were out at sea in their colourfully painted boats, and we would sometimes help carry the trays of sloppy octopus and other fish ashore in the morning. In the alley beneath our window we might glimpse the day's catch spread out on a mat, being shared among the crew. Fish dominated life. The smell of sardines being grilled in the open was the hallmark of the village. A pally lick from the roving dog left me covered in fishy scales: guess what he'd scrounged for his last meal.

Our flat overlooked the square, a rough earthen space in the centre of the village. Our caravan, rather perilously, was parked there, among crates of empty bottles, piles of gravel and sand, motorbikes and other vehicles. There was a stream of travelling salesmen. The shelled fish seller came with his donkey cart, announcing his arrival on a conch shell. Some days there would be several stalls selling clothes. The weekly rubbish van would cause a great stir, cries of 'lixo, lixo' (pronounced 'leeshu') summoning the householders with their buckets and bags of rubbish. The square was criss-crossed with washing lines, chickens tethered with strings scratching an existence, children and dogs playing, the fishermen going to and fro in their long waders, wicker basket in one hand, bucket in the other. And then there were the newly dug open drains (a village loo was being built), into which I tumbled one night.

We still remember the coastguard, who fished from his high lookout post, casting his line to the sea below – a hazard for strollers on the beach. One night Don and Alex had the telescope out on the cliff top when the armed policeman approached. They feared they were in trouble. But he handed Don his rifle and asked for a turn at the telescope.

During the festive days of Christmas and New Year the tiny bar beneath us shook with dancing, singing and loud music. We only worried a little when, on New Year's Day, a man turned up with a donkey cart beneath our window, and after much chatter, set off with three mates to fetch wine for the café, taking Brendan with him. Two hours later they returned, along with sacks of potatoes, cabbages and, presumably, the wine. By then Don had biked out to meet them, so Kirsty had a donkey cart ride on the return journey.

The countryside was beautiful too: the almonds were coming into blossom, 6m/20ft-high Agave americana leaned over the cliffs at a 45-degree angle, wild flowers and wild rosemary were in abundance, and the fields were being picturesquely ploughed with oxen and mules. We had better treasure those memories: Burgau today, though in a protected environmental zone, is a tourist centre – with supermarkets, modern bars, restaurants, villas, sports facilities and all.

From the north our most vivid memories were of the maceiras, those unique gardens excavated in the sand dunes to reach the 'magic water' below, the sandy sides held in

Women undertaking the backbreaking work of gathering seaweed to fertilize the maceiras, the highly productive market gardens in the coastal sand dunes in north Portugal.

place with an extraordinary network of vines trained flat against them. They were all but hidden from the outside world by the windbreaks of giant reeds planted around them. An idealistic young couple had taken us there the first time: Jacinto had only returned from France 'since the revolution', having fled the country after being imprisoned twice. It had been a rushed visit in appalling weather, so after our Christmas break we drove north again to try and find them on our own. It was this time that we followed a trail of tractors and carts towards the sea, and saw a large group, mainly women in flaring skirts, hauling in the seaweed in giant nets. We photographed them from afar. It was back-breaking work, and it was clear they didn't want to be treated as a spectacle. Later we climbed up a bank, peered through the windbreak reeds and asked the man working below if we could see his garden. Immediately he welcomed us in, pulling a bottle of wine from under the vines to cement the friendship.

About ten years later we returned to the *maceiras*. As we had feared, many of them had disappeared. The valuable coastal land was being sold to developers, and even as we stood in one of them, negotiations were taking place. A hard, but picturesque and unique, form of cultivation was passing into history.

PORTUGUESE VEGETABLE GROWING
The Garden, July 1977

My first inklings of the nature of Portuguese vegetable growing were gleaned in France, where in the course of visiting French allotments and railway workers' gardens (most of them orderliness personified), one would come across an extraordinary plot, to all appearances an assortment of cabbages and kales of every size, shape and height, planted cheek by jowl. The Frenchman would pause for a moment and say, with just a touch of scorn in his voice: 'That one's Portuguese.'

There is, of course, far more to Portuguese vegetable growing than cabbages, but visiting the country for the first time in winter, as I did, the impression that this is a land where brassicas reign supreme was confirmed. In the north of the country in particular the scenery was, literally, dominated by the tall straggling stalks of couve galega, a type of Jersey kale, often growing 1.8–2m/6–8ft high. Beneath or alongside these were the rugged pencas, varieties of the Portuguese tronchuda cabbage with broad white leaf stalks. In the markets there were headed cabbages of such dimensions they seemed to have been fattened for Christmas, alongside purple cauliflowers, a sturdy form of purple sprouting broccoli and bunches of grelos or turnip tops.

Much of Portugal, with the maritime influence of the long western and southern coastlines, has a moderate climate, enabling a wide range of plants to be grown. Climatically, the country is divided in half by the Sierra da Estrela and the river Tagus, with Lisbon at its mouth. Rainfall north of the Tagus ranges from about 1,270mm/50in a year in the wettest northern regions to about 1,016mm/40in a year in Lisbon itself and dropping to around 508mm/20in annually on the Algarve. Typically of a Mediterranean climate, in much of the country the rainfall occurs almost entirely in the winter months, creating a summer drought without irrigation and making summer vegetable growing quite impossible in most areas.

The need to irrigate in summer predetermines the pattern of much of the vegetable growing, and one marvels at the ingenuity and the physical labour involved in creating the network of channels required to water even a small garden. In some cases the source of water is a distant reservoir or stream, and water is carried long distances on overhead or underground pipes, including the minas, built by the Romans. In other areas wells are sunk, and donkeys are often harnessed to the water wheel to raise water from the well.

Basically there are two ways of irrigating. The first, more suitable for sandy soils, is to make slightly sunken beds with raised edges and to flood them periodically. In the second, the land is worked into ridges and furrows, sometimes rounded, sometimes square, with vegetables planted on the ridges and water channelled into the furrows. This system is more suitable for heavy soils. Frequently the ridges run from north to south, with seedlings planted on the south-facing side, thus giving them maximum sun as well as shelter from the ridge behind.

Characteristic features of Portuguese smallholdings and gardens are intercropping and undercropping. In the wine-growing Minho region of the north, where vines are trained overhead on trellises often supported by immense granite pillars, or even up convenient trees around the edge of a terraced field or along a roadside, the land underneath is cropped with potatoes, cabbage, salad crops or the ubiquitous couve galega, which cheekily peers over the tops

Pruning vines in north Portugal. The vines are trained up trees and telegraph poles as a space-saving measure. The ground beneath is often cropped.

of the trimmed vines in winter. On the Algarve, orchards of citrus, figs, almonds, olives and carob are undercropped in winter and spring with broad beans and peas. Not the most high-yielding practice, perhaps, but one which enables a family to keep themselves supplied with a little of everything all year round. On the poor inland soils in the south it was traditional to undercrop orchards with grains, and both ordinary peas and chickpeas. We saw a great deal of intercropping in small gardens, and this gave the impression that as soon as something was picked, something else was planted or sown in the gap, eventually creating a picturesque patchwork of vegetables.

One consequence of high summer temperatures is that humus is easily lost from the top few inches of the soil and needs to be replaced if good crops are to be obtained. In many areas, green manuring is common practice, lupins often being used for the purpose; one friend was using carob bean waste as an organic mulch in her garden. In the coastal regions seaweed is extensively used for manure and one cold January day we came across a group of between twenty and thirty people collecting seaweed from the sea in a feverish operation. Pairs of short-skirted, aproned women were going out into the waves with triangular nets,

throwing them into the waves and hauling them ashore full of seaweed – a heavy task. Huge wooden-toothed rakes were also being used for the purpose. The seaweed harvest was then loaded on to tractors and donkey carts and made into thatched or plastic-covered stacks, which are left for a year before being used.

Some unique market gardens are found in the coastal belt north of Porto. Known as *maceiras*, they have been excavated out of the sand dunes, some as large as a quarter of an acre in extent, and anything up to 12m/40ft deep. I was told, though was unable to verify it, that the *maceiras* date back to an oceanic cataclysm at the end of the fifteenth century when the sea advanced and then retreated, thereby altering the coastline. Fishermen no longer able to ply their trade became farmers, but first had to dig down through the sand to reach a layer of fresh water and fertile soil. Until relatively recent times sand was still laboriously dug out, basket by basket, to make new gardens in the dunes. The sheer enormity of what has been accomplished is overwhelming when you realize the volume of sand that has been removed from the cultivated areas; the depth of a *maceiras* varies according to the level at which water is found: anything from about 1.5m/5ft further inland, to 9–12m/30–40ft nearer the coast. Fortunately, now that sand is in demand for construction work, dunes are being dug out mechanically and new gardens created the easy way.

A unique feature of the *maceiras* is that in most of them the sandy sides are kept in place by vines trained horizontally against the slopes. The grapes produce the famous *vinho verde* of the Minho region. A second common characteristic is that they are sheltered from the sea gales by tall reeds planted around the edges, effectively hiding them from the outside world. The only give-away sign, in some places, is fresh produce being sold on nearby roadsides.

The soils at the water level in the *maceiras* are very rich, and with the warmth of the sun's rays reflected against the white sand on the sloping sides, an exceptionally warm, sheltered microclimate is created. Three or four crops a year are obtained, and conditions are excellent for the production of early crops, especially potatoes, and seedlings. Prices of this land are three times higher than for other agricultural land in the Porto area. Seaweed is used extensively as a fertilizer here, and the area is dotted with little stacks of seaweed; manure, too, is used when it is available. We also learned, from one of the growers, that his father was a fisherman and used crabs as a fertilizer. The old systems are, however, being replaced with the use of artificial fertilizers.

Cultivation techniques in the *maceiras* vary. Some are divided into narrow strips and squares with the irrigation channels, with patches of one crop grown in each small parcel. Elsewhere, intercropping is practised: for example, cabbage,

General view of a maceiras. The sloping sandy sides, which reflect the sun into the beds below, creating a unique microclimate, are stabilized with a network of vines that produce vinho verde grapes.

+ Also 2 original grape knife trees to be unpacked into
Portugal by her Father a grandfather

<u>Thursday, Dec. 16th, 1976</u> <u>Porto</u>

Raining again. Wrote to Mummy and Daddy and sent Christmas card. Then left to
visit Miss Tait, the old English lady with lovely garden. Had trouble finding
it - old 'quinta' or farm, tucked away up narrow alleys in old daysoverlooking
harbour, but now shielded from harbour by trees. Miss Tait v. lively 90-year
old! Hobbles on a stick, but insisted on taking us all around the garden.
Wonderful collection of camellias, immense tulip trees, immense magnolia,
quite a remarkable place but now scarcely kept up. She's been growing vegetables
"since the revolution!" Then showed us the house - again some beautiful carved
Portuguese furniture and lovely prints of Peninsular war. We had to hurry away
as we were supposed to be meeting Jacinto and Christine at 12.30. But Miss Tait
so chatty we were very late! Luckily they had waited for us, and we drove
north. Stopped for lunch in a restaurant - very nice and quite reasonable tho'
such things make large holes in our budget. (In fact we've nowhad a few v. expensive
days, which have set us back from an economic run!) After we had lunch drove on
to Povoa de Varzim, bought film and had quick coffee, then drove towards sand
dunes to find the 'maceiras' beds in the sand. Eventually parked by sandy road,
climbed up dunes, and saw some. They are far bigger than imagined, but some
about 30' deep - all the sand having been excavated. These beds apparently
extend for a long distance along the coast, and one gathers there is a tremendous
difference in techniques, soil and water conditions. Here there is permanent
underground water (magic water), and only with recent developments and increased
demand on water have they had to start pumping. The cultivated area is divided
into raised portions and channels for irrigation. They can sow and plant all
year round, and grow crops all jumbled together- cabbages, carrots and potatoes,
carrots and onions, lettuces and onions etc. Much is sold at seedling stage.
The sand which surrounds the beds on all sides is kept in place with immense
vines, grained horizontally over the dunes (vinho verde - the wine of the
Minho region). Quite a remarkable sight. The 'maceiras' were kept fertile by
the use of seaweed gathered from nearby coast and some 'imported' horse manure.
They are now starting to use chemicals. There are large haystacks of seaweed,
coverd in plastic, everywhere. Jacinto and Christine talked to one of the growers
which was interesting (they both speak French and some English). He said his
father was a fisherman and used to catch crabs to use as fertiliser.! There is
some planting according to the phase of themoon amongst the older growers. Could
find no confirmation that women sometimes dig about a new maceiras for a young
bride. But the land is three times as expensive as normal land - bec. so fertile
and can get such early crops, with sun reflecting off the sand. Certainly a
unique place, and must visit it again to find out more. We went to a seedsmen in
the village to see about local seeds. Said that most probably imported now, but
sent a boy down road in horse and trap (masses of horses and trps in this area)
to fetch a local cabbage seed from the boy's mother! She didn't charge us anyp
thing for it. The seedsmen was born in France so we ere able to talk to him which
was interesting. Apparently they have a unique way of sowing onions here, but
didn't quite grasp what it was!

Afterwards miserable ride back to Porto - horrible driving for Don. Poor roads,
bikes without lights, pouring rain. However, had been an interesting day for us.
Jacinto and Chrstine very interesting couple - trying out to get things done,
help with illiteracy, housing problems etc. Jacinto twice imprisoned and had to
escape to France - andhad only returned 'since the revolution' .
Wrote to E & R in evening and did some work on Maceiras notes.

<u>Frid. Dec. 17th, Porto.</u>

Kirsty's 6th birthday. Gave her a little china tea set (made in Japan), some
little girls necklaces etc (made in Macao), two tiny dolls (made in Portugal) and
a dolls cothes set (made in Hepworth.) She put on all the jewellery and Brendan
said 'Kirsty looks very pretty. Just like a real girl!' Afterwards Don went to
bank and to Matosinhos for mail, I went to appointment arranged by Consultate.
Tumred out to be main port wine company.' Not really up my street. Very smooth
elegantly dressed English public school type Portuguese who all agreed very odd my
being sent there. But they coughed up an agricultural engineer who was quite helpful. But a bit frustrating as we would like to have left earlier in the day for
southerly rendez vous as roads bad and driving slow. Eventually packed up and left
after 3.30. Soon overtaken by darkness; miles from official camp - Main Porto/
Lisbon road v. slow nightmare. I suggested turning off, and immediately landed
in mountains. Eventually reached flatter land, and after going through endless

Stacks of seaweed, collected from the nearby coast, in readiness for use in the maceiras.

carrots and potatoes are mingled together, or cabbage, lettuce and onions. One practice is to sow onions, and when the onions are lifted, to transplant young cabbages or lettuce in the place vacated by the onions.

This land is very intensively cultivated, with an equally intensive use of labour. For much of the cultivation a *machado* or mattock, a kind of enormous hoe, is used. A garden fork is rarely seen in Portugal, and presumably little deep cultivation is carried out, other than ploughing with donkeys, mules, horses or even cows.

The tall kales, *Brassica oleracea* var. *acephala*, are undoubtedly the backbone of the Portuguese peasant kitchen during the winter months. Various different forms of these kales exist, some smooth leaved, some curled: *couve galega* is the principal cultivated form (*couve* being the Portuguese word for cabbage, kales and leaf turnips). The kales grow to tremendous heights, over 2.4–2.7m/8–9ft tall, and if prevented from flowering can be kept in the ground for two to three years, growing continually and producing new leaves. They are often planted around the edge of a garden, or in fields along the irrigation channel, so that their continued presence will not interfere with other cultivation. They are planted close together, perhaps 30cm/1ft apart, so that neighbouring plants shade each other and keep the leaves tender.

Couve galega is largely used in the Portuguese dish *caldo verde*. This substantial soup is made from potatoes, mashed with olive oil, extremely finely shredded kale or cabbage leaves, and chorizo, the hot sausage which is added just before serving. Pre-shredded *couve* is sold for the purpose in the markets, and I must admit, so finely is it cut that I mistook it for grass being sold as rabbit food until I was enlightened.

The other typically Portuguese brassicas are the Braganza or tronchuda cabbages, *Brassica oleracea* var. *tronchuda*. These large sturdy cabbages have remarkably prominent broad, white, leaf stalks and equally prominent

Two of Portugal's remarkable vegetables.
Left: the giant semi-perennial kale, *couve galega*, which can grow well over 2m/8ft tall.
Right: the stunning hardy northern tronchuda or Chaves cabbage.

leafribs and veins. Most of the varieties come from the mountainous regions of the country and withstand frost well: indeed they are said to need frost to bring out the flavour. The leaf stalks, in spite of their thickness, are very tender to eat and are often boiled first, then fried. I collected seed of a number of different *pencas*, as they are known, including 'Penca de Chaves', 'Penca de Mirandela', 'Gloria de Portugal', 'Penca de Póvoa', amongst others.

Turnips are another member of the brassica family which are widely grown in Portugal, both for the roots and for the tops. For turnips grown for the tops, or *grelos*, later varieties are used, usually sown broadcast in September or October, though they can be sown any time from February onwards. They are picked at a later stage than we would pick turnip tops, with the flowers already showing yellow. In the kitchen they are either cut into inch-long pieces for soups, or into large pieces, 15–18cm/6–7in long for eating with cod and other fish, or they may be cooked and chopped fairly finely into a delicious savoury rice.

Beans probably run a close second to cabbage and kales in the Portuguese kitchen. During winter a tremendous variety of dried haricot beans were being sold in the markets. There were plain-coloured red, black, white and khaki beans, as well as many multicoloured and patterned beans, some of them very striking indeed. Some excellent national dishes are made with beans, but one would have to return in summer to see them actually growing. One of the most popular climbing varieties of French bean is 'Bencanta', with a broad yellowish pod, which is split lengthwise for eating in many of the fish dishes.

There are several Portuguese varieties of broad bean, and on the Algarve coast in January the Algarve broad bean was in full flower. A dwarfish plant, its pods are short and broad and the beans huge with, to my mind, a delicious chestnut-like flavour. In the north a smaller-seeded but longer-podded broad bean, 'Cornichela', is grown. Another, even smaller, variety of broad bean, 'Ratinha', is cultivated for feeding birds and animals.

A pea I would love to have seen growing was the red-flowered Portuguese mangetout 'Colossal Delicia' ('Torta de Flor Roxa'). It grows about 1.8 m/6ft tall and has been selected for its long twisted pods. The knobbly red seeds were on sale in many seed shops. Peas are sown in autumn or early in the year in Portugal, for they succumb to the high summer temperatures.

In February on the Algarve they were already romping away in the citrus and olive groves, with piles of wild cistus twigs, collected from the hillsides, in readiness for use as pea sticks.

All the cucurbits we saw seemed huge, and some had extraordinarily 'warty' skins. Of the main ones listed in seed catalogues, there was first of all 'Porqueira', a large pumpkin with yellow/red flesh, used for feeding animals and in cooking; then there was the long, almost violin-shaped 'Carneira', with earwig-like seed and, like 'Porqueira', also an old Portuguese variety. A third common variety was 'Menina', another huge roundish pumpkin for desserts and also fed to animals. Seeing how extensively pumpkins are used in soups, desserts and as a vegetable in Portugal, I have resolved to make better use of them when eventually I return to England.

One of the oddities I encountered on the Algarve was a deep purple carrot. Having been told to look out for purple carrots on our travels (they were once thought to be unusually rich in vitamins), I was most excited to find them.

Although purple outside, they were the normal carrot orange inside, and seemed very sweet and quickly cooked. Unfortunately all attempts to find the seed failed, though I gather it was originally an American carrot, and was grown mainly for its luscious foliage, which was used to feed animals. It is a warm-weather variety, and is not usually sown until April or May.

Some of our common English vegetables are virtually unknown in Portugal, but a number of, to us, odd things are eaten. Among these are the seed of lupin (*Lupinus luteus*), soaked, cooked, salted and nibbled with beer; the seeds of the stone pine (*Pinus pinea*) are also nibbled; corms of *Oxalis pes-caprae*, introduced from South Africa at the turn of the century and now a pernicious weed, are eaten by the peasants; asparagus is rarely cultivated, but may be collected wild.

Portugal is a country where many herbs grow naturally, and again it was tantalizing to be there in winter, when many are dormant. Even so, wild rosemary, lavender and thyme were prolific on hillsides near the coast, and we found fennel and mint by several picnic spots. In winter the two most important culinary herbs are parsley and coriander. Portuguese parsley is of the broad-leaved type and is considered of superior quality to the French by knowing cooks (the French in its turn, of course, being considered superior to our curled types). Few Portuguese kitchen gardens, large or small, are without a little patch of parsley and coriander, as likely as not surrounded by a few plants of *couve galega*.

The *maceiras* lie along the north-west coast, roughly between Póvoa de Varzim and Viana do Castelo. One group can be found by going north from Porto on the N13, and taking the road to the left signposted Aguçadoura, about 39 kilometres/24 miles from Porto.

Many years after writing this I was put in touch with a lady living in Portugal, who told me that she believed the correct name for what I was calling the *maceiras* was probably *masseira*. This is a piece of furniture commonly found in country kitchens – a small table with sides rising at an oblique angle, which is used for making bread. Seen from above, this would be very much the shape of the sand-dune market gardens – hence their name. In my article I had referred to little stacks of rotting seaweed, but she pointed out that the stacks were not rotting seaweed. After being hauled out of the sea the seaweed was laid out in the sun to dry, possibly increasing its phosphate content, and it only rotted when it was later dug into the ground.

Our steadiest income during our travels was from the horticultural trade journal *Gardeners' Chronicle*. As its readers were mainly professionals engaged in amenity horticulture, part of my brief was investigating what was going on in the flower world. Which delighted me, as all the nooks and crannies of horticulture intrigue me.

The seed trade has probably intrigued me more than any other. In the past much of the seed sold in the UK was grown on the Continent and further afield in Europe, where the more predictable climate allows seed crops to mature well and be harvested at their peak. Besides our insights into flower seed production in Provence in France (see page 74) we had another view in Italy with the Mennella family of Farmen Seeds, camping on a corner of their estate at Torre del Greco in the shadow of Vesuvius. The vast range of microclimates near by, coastal and mountainous, combined with the diversity of soils, some enriched with volcanic ash, make it a unique area for horticulture. I loved the way the ubiquitous lizards were natural predators for the aphids. Four generations of the Mennella family had been involved in growing seed crops. In the early days in the 1870s, when they were growing cauliflower seed for the UK, they had even uncovered new ruins at Pompeii. When we visited in 1977 four of the brothers were engaged in breeding bedding salvias, geraniums and much more beside. We were in touch with Mario Mennella – who switched to his great love, breeding tomatoes of outstanding taste and quality (see page 301) – until his recent death. He will be sadly missed by many.

Time has moved on, and with the high labour costs in Europe, flower seed production and breeding are now far more likely to take place in Asia, South America or Africa.

We also visited a number of plant nurseries, and surely one of the most unusual was the carnation and rose nursery Vrtnarija Čatež, near Brežice, in what was then Yugoslavia. The nursery was heated with water from thermal hot springs, and right next to it was a health spa. When the water had fulfilled its function in the nursery, it was pumped off into a series of swimming pools in the spa. This happened all year round. In winter it was covered, Russian style, creating a huge cloud of steam in the countryside.

The pools made it an idyllic place for camping, and this was where our children finally learned to swim. I have to say I noted in my diary that I had never seen so much human flesh in my life – deck chair after deck chair sagging with what seemed to me exceptionally large people.

There was another flower nursery not far away using waste heat from a power station, and looking back, it is surprising how many examples of recycling and alternative energy we encountered that year. Car manufacturers Fiat, for example, had a research station outside Turin, where they were looking into harnessing solar energy for everything from a pilot rubbish recycling scheme for the small nearby town of Cambiano to seed drying, greenhouse heating and operating insect traps. We did our own bit of recycling too. Gypsies that we had become, we gauged the economic state of the country we were in by what was found on its rubbish heaps. In Holland, with the help of the head of a special school who had honed his make-do skills during the Depression, we found three bicycles, which, with his help, we made into one Dutch bike. It served us well for the rest of the year. In France we found display racks discarded by shops, perfect for keeping our gear off the ground. In post-revolutionary Portugal we found nothing: nothing was thrown away.

But back to Vrtnarija Čatež. It was so hot during the day (this was June) that working hours were from 6.00 a.m. to 2.00 p.m. I missed the manager the first time I tried to see him. It was early afternoon and he was 'at picnic'. So the next morning, by the light of the silvery moon, I biked from the campsite to the nursery to catch him at 6.00 a.m. It seemed very romantic at the time. I was then treated to a right wigging for not having visited a Communist country before! I was forgiven and taken round: it proved a fascinating place. They had produced over 4 million carnation blooms the previous year, and much more besides. The nursery still seems to be operational today, though, as far as I can make out, growing vegetables rather than flowers.

In those Communist countries in the late 1970s life was still fairly drab, wages very low and luxuries few. 'We crave greenery in winter,' my interpreter at the nursery told me, when we were looking at the ferns there. Flowers were like diamonds.

Later, in the picturesque cathedral market in Ljubljana, the capital of Slovenia, we saw the Vrtnarija Čatež flowers being sold. They were going well: Ljubljana had the highest per capita income of any Communist city at the time. Near by were stalls of home-grown flowers – delphiniums, campanulas, nigella, even tiny bunches of the humble garden daisy.

From Yugoslavia we travelled on to Hungary, where flowers played an unexpected role in our lives. Hungary was an important country for us. Long before the West was aware of the need to preserve old varieties of vegetables and edible crops, the Communist countries had established gene banks, and the Agrobotany Institute at Tápiószele was a key destination. Hungary also produced seed crops – peas were one of the specialities – and vegetable crops were grown on a large scale, often for the canning and processing industries. UK seedsmen had been doing business with Hungary for years, and had given me various contacts. It also proved to be a land of keen amateurs. We visited a small, ordinary garden where an elderly couple had a battery of insect traps and recording devices. They were supplying a research station with data that was analysed and used to broadcast information on likely pest attacks, and preventive or control measures.

Every Sunday the couple posted a bulletin on their gate for fellow gardeners in the neighbourhood. It was a small-scale, practical example of integrated pest management, encouraging minimum use of pesticides.

Communicating and making contacts in Hungary was far from easy, though better than Yugoslavia, where I had been reduced to mooing like a cow to get milk and cackle like a hen to find eggs. My Hungarian phrase book was, I think, published in the 1920s – only a hair's breadth away from the 'my postilion has been struck by lightning' era. German would have helped, but my German was minimal. The necessary phoning to the contacts who would then make appointments was a nightmare. Every evening I would go to the camp office and ask to use their phone, and for the first five days the camp boss would affably hand me the phone, waiving any charges, and people near by would help interpret. He was my Father Christmas. Then it stopped. For no reason I could see, one evening he turned on me with fury, implying I had no right to use the phone. Had he been offended by the capitalist activities of our children? They had lined the pavement beside our van with fizzy drinks, unwanted toys and their paintings (they'd been inspired by children's paintings we'd seen in the agricultural museum), which they were selling to the amused Czech and Polish holiday makers at the campsite.

One of my key contacts in Budapest was the horticultural professor at the Agricultural Institute, a gangly, likeable man. His first love had been music but he had failed to qualify for entry to a musical academy; his second love was herbaceous plants, but he had had no choice, and had to become a vegetable specialist. He related a sad tale. Permission to travel overseas was rarely granted, but on a hard-won trip to England he had bought a mass of perennials, which, in true absent-minded professor style, he had left on a railway platform. (On my return I tried to send him 'Esther Read' chrysanthemum cuttings, packed in every kind of disguised package I could invent to circumvent restrictions. I never heard if they reached him.) He showed us around Budapest and arranged several interviews and visits for me, but he being very busy, by the end of our stay in Budapest I still hadn't had a chance to ask him all the things I wanted to about vegetable growing. He apologized, but was busy all day on our last day, and in the evening he'd be picking flowers on his allotment. So I offered to help cut his flowers.

Only relatively recently restrictions had been lifted, allowing people to grow and sell produce from small private plots. It turned out that he and his brother, and several other professors, grew flowers for market, in spite of it not being the 'done thing' to trade. He had orders for chrysanthemums and fifty bunches of gypsophila, so as we cut and bunched, I plied him with questions about everything from Communism to celeriac. Away from the restraints of the workplace, he felt free to talk. It was an evening I won't forget, not least for the salutary experience of seeing first hand the ravages of the Colorado beetle, which had devastated lilies and potatoes on the plot. It was dark by the time we finished, and I went home bearing a beautiful bunch of chrysanthemums and gypsophila.

When we drove out the next morning we stopped at the camp office and I asked to see the camp boss. He came out from the back, still without the welcoming smile from our first days there. I said goodbye, thanked him for his earlier help and presented him with the bouquet. I don't think I have ever seen a man melt so fast: the broadest of smiles lit his face, while the watching office staff collapsed with laughter. Giving men flowers? Perhaps not quite the norm. I like to think Anglo-Hungarian relations were restored as a result.

FLOWER SEED PRODUCTION IN PROVENCE
Gardeners' Chronicle, 12 January 1979

While the main purpose of a visit to Provence was to study the production of herbs and Mediterranean vegetables, it provided an opportunity to see another old-established Midi industry: flower seed production.

For a very long time St-Rémy-de-Provence has been the centre of a flower seed industry due to the unique local geography of the area, with the chalky hills of Les Alpilles to the south heading off coastal storms, and the famous mistral coming down the Rhône valley from the north to chase away the clouds.

These factors combine to give the region, centred on St-Rémy, an exceptionally high number of hours of sunshine. Coupled with a mild climate, high light intensity and soil which is mostly light and well drained, it is particularly suitable for flower seed crops. Land in the area is extremely expensive as a result.

Seed growing everywhere has always been a very traditional, family-based occupation, and flower seed is no exception, with families often specializing in just a few crops, the expertise being passed down from father to son. In France the exodus of the younger generation from the land means it is becoming increasingly difficult to find reliable, skilled growers for these specialist crops.

Most of the flower seed crop in Provence is still grown in very small family-owned plots, rarely much larger than about ½ acre/0.2 hectares. They are protected from the strong prevailing winds with tall windbreaks of cypress, often with secondary windbreaks of the cane *Arundo donax*. Almost all the seed is grown on fixed-price contracts for the major seed houses, who supply growers with seed or plants raised on their own nurseries.

With production for so many firms concentrated in a relatively small area, growers have to get together to ensure that varieties which would cross-pollinate are not being grown close together.

Rooted in tradition though flower seed growing is, production methods are changing, the most notable change being the increasing number of crops which are harvested mechanically instead of being cut, far more picturesquely, by sickle.

Generally speaking, cutting cannot be mechanized unless the plants reach a minimum height of about 15cm/6in and, as purpose-built machinery does not exist, firms have to design their own or adapt existing machinery.

The French seed firm Tézier, for example, has adapted a machine for cutting lavender for harvesting flower seed crops. This is used for many crops, and while other crops could probably be mechanically harvested, the saving in labour costs is often offset by the loss of quality. Where the profit margin allows for hand harvesting, this is still preferable.

After harvesting and drying, the crops are generally taken to a *poste fixée*, such as a

Traditional sickles and a modern thresher, both playing a part in harvesting the seed of Senecio cineraria for the Clause seed company. I think the sickles proved more reliable that day.

concrete ground, for threshing. Threshing also poses a problem, again because the overall demand for machinery is too small to justify the development of purpose-built machinery. It is a case of invention or adapting existing machinery.

Because of the relatively small quantities of flower seed handled at any one time, the thresher has to be designed so that it can be cleaned out easily between crops.

With vegetable seed threshing such large quantities of seed are involved that one can afford to waste the several kilos of seed which may be contaminated when the machine is changed over from threshing one crop to another.

Another sign of the times is the increasing number of crops being grown under plastic, to maintain closer control over growing conditions. Crops I saw under plastic on one of the Clause seed company farms included ageratum, heliotrope, Salvia farinacea, petunias and zinnia. (A lot of zinnia, incidentally, is grown in Egypt, where it is possible to get two seed crops in a year.) Trials have shown that better-quality salvia seed was obtained by growing under plastic than in the open.

Although a wide range of flower seed is grown in Provence, there is specialization in those crops which particularly benefit from the region's high luminosity, notably pinks, portulaca and petunias.

For each of these seed crops, slightly differing harvesting techniques are required.

Petunia is perhaps one of the typical flower seed crops of Provence. Fields of single-colour and mixed petunias are a common, and beautiful, sight. It can be grown in fairly open fields on thinnish soil, requiring very little fertilizer.

In fact, petunia can be grown for several years in the same ground. Many varieties are grown in the area, and there has to be a minimum of 100m/about 330ft between them to prevent contamination.

Petunias are generally sown in March for planting out in May and irrigated, according to the soil, about once a week during the growing period. Irrigation ceases about a month before harvesting because, as it was explained to me, the plant 'needs to suffer' at that point. Indeed, heavy rainfall shortly before harvesting can damage the crop seriously.

During the summer the petunias are rogued several times to eliminate off types, and any that are the wrong colour. In Provence they flower all summer long – even up to Christmas. Harvesting starts when three to four pods on each plant are ripe, generally about the end of September, rather than waiting for the whole plant to be ready.

The field is cut early in the day when the plants are still damp, for the seed starts to fall as soon as the sun reaches it. The cut plants are left in a sheltered place to dry for between fifteen days and three weeks, during which time the remaining seed pods ripen on the plant. They are then crushed by driving a tractor over them before being threshed.

Unlike petunias, portulaca needs a fairly fertile soil to get a good seed crop, and although sometimes grown for two years running on the same ground, it is preferable to rotate. It is often planted after potatoes, the ground having been well fertilized for the potato crop.

Seed is sown at the end of April and, on planting, plants are given fertilizer and irrigated, with a second dressing of fertilizer halfway through the growing season. They are normally irrigated once a week, the plants spreading across the furrows to make a blanket over the field – another wonderfully colourful sight.

Harvesting is generally sixty to seventy days after planting. Plants are pulled up by hand, and those from every four or five rows piled upright in one long row and left for three to four weeks to finish drying.

When there is no more 'life' in the plants, the seed is tapped out on to plastic sheeting laid between the rows. Sometimes drying is carried out in greenhouses. The main problem with portulaca is root rot, which occurs under wet conditions.

Another common flower seed crop is statice, which also needs irrigation while it is growing. Like portulaca, the plants are pulled up, at about the end of August when drying off, and left to dry completely until they are paper-like. They are then beaten so that the flower stalks fall off.

Statice used to be sold with seed heads entire, but now the seed is extracted in a machine which rubs the heads between two discs, so giving a far less bulky product.

Seed of the red variety of statice is far more expensive than that of the blue or yellow, because so much less seed is produced.

Oct 1. Pontoise.
Got up at 7.00 to type diary, becasue must pack up, and be at Clause at Bretigny at 1.30, having found camp site first. Desperately need several quiet days to sort out letters, articles in semi-completed stage, photography etc. But we'll be very sad to leave this friendly place by the canal, even if we can hear the autoroute traffic day and night!

Poured with rain as we started to pack up. Awning got soaked. (very bad for it!) M. Bonhommet very kind and came to help us clear up - gold awning etc. We have piles of unwashed clothes, unironed clothes etc! Decided to go straight to Bretigny as time short, driving slow with caravan. Changed into 'interviewing clothes' just before departure. xxxxixxxxxxxxxxxxxxxxxxxxxxxxxxxxxx- xxx Headed for Versailles, then on south. Still very much in area of heavy traffic south of Parisl. Driving rather a strain. Reached Bretigny around 10.00 Parked by railway tracks, opposite Clause (seed firm.) Had quick lunch. Left Don and kids in caravan. Everything a bit soggy - had to unload bikes to settle in caravan. They did some lessons during afternoon. I went to Clause. Biggest seed firm in Europe for vegetables and flowers. Rather late in year for most of trials, but was taken around plant breeding in greenhouses, remainder of flower trials, and some of vegetables by a multi-lingual Dutchman. (Eventually spoke English to him, as so much easier for understanding technical subjects, which I find hard to understand even in English.) He was very knowledgeable, and had spent 11 years working in Italy. Was shown the autumn lettuce trials (the French hate greenho use lettuce, so commercially grow far more types of outdoor lettuce than Dutch.) Also saw the chicory trials. Quite amazing.Had no idea there were so many different types of chicory. Most of them come from Italy — Catalonia types look like dandelions, used cooked. Other types used raw or cooks. Others forced for chicons. Some typessown very thickly and eaten when leaves only couple of inches high. Some beautiful red colour, reds deepening as season becomes colder; others with red or brown pigment in leaves. All seemed to be hardy, but apparently grow to perfection only in Italian climate. Krommenhoek (my guide) expert on chicory; must learn more about them. Very interesting afternoon. Also learnt incidentally quute a lot about Sicily, Sardinia and Yugoslavia. Apparently in E. bloc countries only allowed to buy seed through official govt. agency   , and foreign varieties only recognised after 3 years trial. So underground chain exists to import good vars. of foreign seed. Clause delivers it from their agent in Trieste, etc. to huge Black Mercedes with red diplomat number plate, or into diplomatic planes - whereit gets slipped into the country with no questions asked!   Didn't finish until nearly 6.0. Mr. K. said he'd guide us to a camp near his village. Unfortunately we misinter- preted his signal. Had terrible trouble finding a camp. When found his it was closed. Had problems reversing on to busy roads - dark by then. Asked several times and eventually found one fo r the night.

One of the more curious harvesting methods is devised for marvel of Peru (*Mirabilis jalapa*), the showy plant whose flowers start opening about four o'clock in the afternoon.

The heavy seeds ripen over a long period and become embedded in the furrows. When the seed is ripe, plants are pulled up and seed beaten out by hand. The fields are then flooded, and the seed caught in grilles at the ends of the irrigation channels.

With some of the flower seed crops birds feasting on the ripening seed are a problem. Scabious and gaillardia are two of the most susceptible, and have to be protected by the Crylde acrylic fibre netting which is put over the crop when in flower, and which disintegrates naturally after about a month. Unseasonal heavy rainfall would cause earlier disintegration.

Dianthus chinensis is one of the crops that are harvested mechanically. Unlike petunias the seed has to be allowed to ripen on the plant, and is generally ready at the end of August. Dianthus is more susceptible to pests and diseases than most flower seed crops, including rust, mildew, a caterpillar which attacks the flowers and root pests. The site for growing the crop is best changed annually.

Finally, *Senecio cineraria* (syn. *Cineraria maritima*) is grown on a fairly large scale in Provence, the crop being left in the ground for three years. It is cut, either by hand or by machine, and left to dry for several days before being threshed. As with most of the seed crop, if rain threatens while it is being dried, it has to be hauled under cover.

Very little hybrid flower seed is grown on the traditional holdings in Provence. The parent lines of F_1 hybrids are generally maintained by the seed houses on their own premises, and much of the hybridization is carried out by them, often under glass.

With the high labour costs involved in the production of F_1 hybrid seed, more and more is now being done in low-labour-cost countries, such as Taiwan, where the women quickly pick up the skills required.

A field of the red variety of statice, ready for harvesting for seed. The red is far more expensive than other colours, as it produces less seed.

Learning more about herbs was always high on my list, and we could hardly have spent eight months in countries like France, Belgium, Portugal and Italy without absorbing endless nuggets of information about cooking, using and growing herbs. Buy strange mushrooms in France and they're bound to tell you what herbs to cook them with. Hungary, too, became associated in our minds with herbs. Every little front garden seemed to be crammed with dill and poppies grown for poppy seed. But it wasn't until the last few weeks of our travels, back in France at the end of July, that we were able to get a real insight into commercial herb growing.

We had headed south for St-Rémy-de-Provence, where two major French seed companies, Clause and Tézier, had research and seed trial grounds. Tézier had said we could stay on their research station when we arrived. I still relish their instruction to 'park by the male-sterile tomatoes', i.e. one of the lines used in breeding F_1 hybrids. Dear Tézier: we stayed there ten days, unashamedly doing our laundry in the nearby stream, hanging it out to dry, feeding on the wild purslane among the tomatoes, and helping ourselves to tomatoes as generously instructed.

After nearly a year on the road our finances were at rock bottom, the van was having mechanical problems, and our gear was beginning to disintegrate. Ten days of free camping was a financial life saver, but with the huge bonus, for us, of being in a working environment. There was the chance to talk to whoever stopped by, researchers, workers, neighbours, getting a real feel for this *coin* and all its horticultural enterprises. Our hosts arranged all sorts of interesting visits, as did Clause down the road, an exceptionally jovial crowd, who later said we'd be welcome to stay there too. I sometimes wondered if an English seed company would have been so eager to tolerate our gypsyish camp on their grounds. (Tézier and Clause later merged, and are today part of a huge international seed conglomerate, but there is still a research station at St-Rémy.)

While we were at Tézier our treasured caravan awning, which doubled our living space, was shredded by a Provence mistral. In fact it rained and rained and rained. An old man I chatted to one night remarked that he had been born in the last century, and had never known a Provence summer as wet as this. Is changeable weather really new? The children didn't seem to mind. Kirsty decided to clean the van one wet day, singing away. On a drier day eight-year-old Brendan helped out on the farm, returning gleefully in the evening with his earnings of biscuits, chocolate and a glowing recommendation.

On our first drive into St-Rémy we discovered L'Herbier de Provence, a treasure trove of a seed shop which had been opened two years earlier as a retail outlet for the products grown and harvested by the Caussade herb company. It was a magnet to us, and we returned day after day, hoping for a chance to talk to 'the boss', Gilles Caussade. The boss was an extremely busy man, probably at that point arranging the major breakthrough into the American market that was imminent. But what better place to wait: so many aromas, so much coming and going! One morning the children helped two old men unpack poppy seed heads. We had several in our medicine cupboard for years. I think it was toothache it would cure. But Gilles Caussade made time for me, showing me around the warehouses and drying operations, taking me out to some of the fields – I'll never forget my first sight of a field of red basil – and sharing his vast knowledge of the herb business. He also arranged for two of his collectors to take us out for a day. Brendan came along with me, and what a great day we had with the two straw-hatted characters, roaming over the hills! We returned home with armfuls of herbs and wild plants, familiar and unknown, and had a very herby supper – herb omelette, tomatoes with herbs, peppers and aubergines with herbs. The mosquitoes were bad that night, but we couldn't remember which of our herbs was a deterrent or remedy. The collectors came by the next morning to make sure we had the right names for all the plants. Altogether it was a wonderful, productive ten days.

After we left, on the homeward stretch, we were able to follow up leads on the lavender industry. We had been longing to do this ever since seeing our first blazing field of lavender, driving down the Rhône valley on the way to Provence.

Our final herb encounters were in the very last days of our travels, in the Loire valley near Angers. In this traditional area for medicinal herbs 25,000 families were once involved in growing or collecting plants from the wild, for the pharmaceutical companies. We drove past colourful fields of pot marigolds, cornflower, hyssop and camomile tucked in among the fields of tobacco and maize. In the past they were dried in the attics of the slate-roofed houses, but it was an unreliable method, so a modern improvement was small-scale drying rooms, or *séchoirs*, with flower heads and herbs on racks dried with hot air. We visited some of them. I loved the neat little rows of pot marigold and camomile heads. One of the more unusual medicinal crops was the wild plant *Antennaria dioica*, cat's paw being one of its popular English names and, guess what, *pied de chat* its French name. (The Chinese name for chickweed translates as gosling weed. How do these things come about?)

We were also excited to find the little town of Chemillé – 'Capital des Plantes Médicinales' emblazoned on its road sign. Part of the public park had been set aside for an artistic and colourful demonstration of medicinal herbs, designed and planted by the growers. I can still remember the huge clumps of inula, which I had never seen before. All the plants were clearly labelled with their names and usage. We returned to Chemillé in 2006 (nearly thirty years later), breaking a long journey, to find that the municipal herb garden had been moved to a much larger site and expanded. Not only was it a beautiful and instructive garden, but it was peppered with huddles of children, some under a tree listening to their teacher, others making collages with leaves and petals, others peering into plants. We could hardly drag ourselves away.

The very last day of our Grand Vegetable Tour, 15 August 1977, started with herbs. It was Assumption Day – one of the many French national holidays. At the crack of dawn I set out to visit a couple of herb growers, but only managed to get to the first, as the accelerator pin on the van was causing trouble, and I fearfully limped back to our camp. Then off on my bike to visit a baker, a chance to fulfil a long-held dream to watch French bread being made. It was fascinating to see the deft handling of the dough and the complex procedure, but I was unable to record it, as my malign Russian camera let me

15 August 1977, France: the family on the last, unexpectedly eventful, day of our Grand Vegetable Tour.

down once again. This time the whole shutter release mechanism had fallen out. Kirsty later found it in the grass at the campsite.

Finally it was time to leave. We had a long journey ahead to catch the ferry at St Malo, and the accelerator pin to be repaired. (We were disobeying the primary law of travel: never break down or be ill on a national holiday.) At the last minute we discovered we had a flat tyre on our caravan, and the caravan, which was exceptionally heavy, had sunk in the mud. Burly fellow campers helped us lift it up to take the wheel off, and in spite of the national holiday, we eventually found a kindly mechanic in Chemillé who fixed the inner tube and the accelerator pin. We were on our way. I could hardly believe we could leave behind the empty fruit boxes and boards that were among our most precious possessions. The upturned boxes enabled us to stand our cardboard boxes of files somewhere dry; the boards were slipped under the wheels – both reminders of the simple priorities dictated by life on the road.

An hour and a half later, on a busy main road heading steadily for St Malo, there was a huge bang. Brendan burst into tears. Our new caravan tyre was torn to shreds. How would we repair it? How would we lift the caravan by ourselves to take off the wheel? Surely our Mercedes car jack wouldn't support its weight? I was trying to lower the wheels when a hand appeared. Odd, I thought. It was, of course, a Frenchman shaking hands before offering to help. He and his family of several kids were returning from mass, he knew no garages near by that were open that day, he was a mechanic, and he thought he had some spare tyres at home or could at least mend one – and off he went, taking Don with him. He sorted us out, surely delaying the sacrosanct festival dinner. He refused any payment, though he did accept a bottle of wine and some biscuits for the children, saying one day we would help a Frenchman in distress. And strangely, one day, a couple of years later, we did. The kindness of strangers: just another of the many kindnesses we had encountered during that year.

Which reminds me of one more. Don and I had slightly dreaded our last month, as it looked as if we would be mainly in campsites, which we found soulless, though the kids loved the facilities and company of other children. About a month previously we had stayed with an old friend's sister, whose husband managed a wine co-operative. They'd promised us a few samples of the wine when we left. One afternoon Don and I returned to find the kids wild with excitement. Our hosts had lined the floor of our caravan with wine bottles: every inch was covered and by chance there was a bottle for every one of our remaining days. Somehow that month didn't seem so bad. These were people who were still addressing us as '*vous*'. How do they treat people who are on '*tu*' terms, I wondered? I suspect we drank the last of our bottles that last night on the ferry, attuning our ears to the English accents around us. They were, to be honest, jarring accents. We had scarcely met native English speakers in our last few months. Our nomadic adventure was over.

HERB REVIVAL IN PROVENCE
Gardeners' Chronicle, 18 November 1977

The soils of Provence have been producing flower seed for European seed companies for many years. But increasing competition in the flower seed business, coupled with increasing world demand for herbs, have led one firm to move away from flower seed into the production of dried herbs and herb seed on a large scale. The firm is Etablissements Caussade, based at St-Rémy-de-Provence, selling under the name of L'Herbier de Provence.

Caussade is a family business, founded by an Englishman, Lawrence Payne, who first went to Provence as a representative for the seed company Hursts and an American seed company. Settling there after the First World War, he started dealing in flower seed and herbs, laying the foundation of the family firm which is today carried on by his son-in-law and his grandsons, Gilles and Gerard.

Gilles Caussade is responsible for production and wholesale marketing. He studied horticulture both in France and at the University of Missouri, USA. He also had a year's practical experience with Hursts (then Cooper and Taber) at Witham, Essex, a year he considers invaluable.

In 1970 he returned from the United States to build up the herb side of the company, armed

Herb grower Gilles Caussade in a field of red basil, grown for leaf and seed. The white chalky soils of St-Rémy-de-Provence make a dramatic foil to the colourful little basil bushes.

with a strong American accent – no mean asset in this international business.

His brother Gerard abandoned a banking careeer to become the commercial director, handling the rapidly expanding retail side from Paris, while their father deals with the accounts and finance.

St-Rémy is in the heart of the traditional flower and flower seed growing area of Provence. While wild herbs have been collected in the area for generations, growing herbs on a commercial scale is a far more recent development.

Until the recent revival of interest in herbs, the herb business had been declining steadily. As Gilles Caussade put it: 'We found ourselves almost alone in a very specialized channel, in the right place, at the right time.'

Caussade are primarily wholesalers, the most important side of their business being aromatic culinary herbs (exported all over the world) followed by medicinal herbs and now, in third place, flower seed production.

Two years ago they branched out into retail sales, opening their first shop in St-Rémy. It was an instant success. Gigantic wicker baskets on the pavement outside, brimming with rose petals, lime flower and lavender, drew in the many tourists in the area.

Inside an enormous collection of herbs and herb by-products are temptingly displayed in jars, bottles and large white hessian sacks.

The shop paved the way for the establishment of others. Two in Paris, one in Lyons, one in Geneva, with others planned in New York and our own Oxford Street.

The list of products sold in the St-Rémy shop is encyclopaedic. Everything from the cook's home-grown herb standbys of marjoram, thyme, basil and mint to exotic imported spices, flowers of hibiscus, heather, calendula, cornflower and camomile, leaves of orange trees, eucalyptus, vines and lemon verbena, dried orange peel, the twisted calyx of the Chinese anise tree, juniper berries, sea wrack and henna.

Concentrated syrups made from fruits and herbs, jams made from almost any European fruit you could name, crystallized fruits, coated almonds or *calissons*, nougat, honey, beeswax, beeswax candles, pollen, teas and tisanes, soaps, bath salts, oil extracts . . . The list of oil extracts starts with angelica and ends with ylang-ylang!

Herbs are grown locally under contract for Caussade, collected locally or imported. Marjoram, basil, parsley, aniseed, fennel, celery, sage and tarragon are some of the more important herbs which are grown in the area.

As far as possible the growers save their own seed. In most cases herbs are planted direct, plants being raised on the company's nursery, and supplied to the growers for planting out in spring.

Finding growers has become a major problem. At present about eighty growers are under contract to Caussade in and around St-Rémy, but as the younger generation of sons leaves the land, the number of potential growers diminishes.

Higher and higher prices have to be paid. More efficient methods of growing herbs commercially must be found if supply is to keep pace with demand.

Marjoram is one of their most important crops, grown both for seed and for drying as a culinary herb. Caussade are France's leading marjoram growers, producing approximately 50 tonnes per annum.

Last year about 40 hectares/98 acres of marjoram was grown under contract, Caussade paying out over 400,000 francs (£44,444) for the marjoram crop alone.

Seed is exported to East Germany, Poland and Czechoslovakia, but now there is competition from Egypt, who produce at lower cost.

The French seed has the edge on hardiness, as the crop is sown outside in February, so subjecting the young plants to cold spring weather. Although germinating rapidly, the 'softer' Egyptian seed is liable to succumb to a cold spell.

The marjoram fields are always full of bees, and very popular with local beekeepers. The crop is cut by hand. If required for the leaf, it is cut when in flower and dried in full sun.

Another important crop is basil, again grown for both seed and leaf. When grown for leaf the crop is cut green. The seed crop is left on the plants to ripen.

Last year 10 tonnes of basil were produced from 15 hectares/37 acres. Much of this is the rampant large green basil, grown supported between strings, more highly flavoured than the lettuce-leaved basil.

Caussade also grow red basil, and claim to be the only people doing so commercially. Several fields can be seen tucked away in odd corners of St-Rémy – and a wonderful sight they are, the neat, beautifully coloured little bushes against the stark white of the chalky soil.

Celery seed has been another Caussade speciality: they grow their own well-known strain. 'Unprovençal' weather, to coin a phrase, earlier this year proved disastrous, so the 1977 crop is almost a write-off.

A surprising proportion of herbs are still collected wild, though the potential area for collecting is continually being eroded. Sometimes land is bought up as a nature reserve and becomes protected. Some landowners, probably because of abuses in the past, have closed their property to collectors. And everywhere, land is continually being 'developed'.

There is still much common land, however, and on privately owned land an annual fee for collecting rights is negotiated between collector and owner. So far Caussade have encountered little difficulty in getting hold of the wild herbs they need.

Much of the collecting is still done by gypsy families, some of whom have supplied herbalists or pharmaceutical companies for several generations. They tackle the difficult work, wandering far and wide in the Alpilles, east and west of the Rhône, and down to the Mediterranean coast.

The peak collecting season is in August and shortly beforehand groups of gypsies come to St-Rémy to see Gilles Caussade, to find out what he requires during the season.

Other collectors work more locally, a family or individual collector often specializing in just four or five different herbs, chosen to give an even spread of work throughout the year.

Rosemary is perhaps the most important of the collected herbs, and is continually in short supply. It has to be grown on dry poor land, and has so far proved difficult, and uneconomic, to cultivate commercially.

Caussade are hoping that 200kg/440lb of wild rosemary will be collected for them this year.

The true wild lavender, *Lavandula angustifolia*, is also collected wild, though there is large-scale cultivation in southern France of lavandin, the hybrid between *L. angustifolia* and *L. latifolia*, for extraction of the essential oils. Flowers of the wild lavender are much smaller but more highly perfumed than those of the hybrid.

Wild thyme, wild savory and wild fennel are other common collected herbs. One gypsy family has undertaken to bring in 3 tonnes of fennel, leaves and stalk, for Caussade this season. Fennel for seed is grown commercially.

At the moment there is a surplus of thyme seed, mainly because 1976 was a bumper year on account of the dry weather during the harvesting period. If it rains during that period the seed capsules burst, spilling the seed,

irretrievably, on the ground.

Caussade find that the medicinal herbs side of the business is growing. They supply all the medicinal plants required to the famous medical faculty at Montpelier, and this has led increasingly to supplying and packaging herbs for pharmacies. They also supply manufacturers of soaps and cosmetics. In July 16,000 bags of herbs were ready for despatch to the Swiss cosmetic firm Biokosma.

Apart from the grown and collected herbs, Caussade import about 200 different kinds of herbs. The policy is to buy only top quality — where vanilla is concerned, for example, only the largest pods.

Imported herbs are normally recleaned. One of the firm's specialities is tea. Large quantities are imported, recleaned, and the best-quality leaf is then mixed with mint, rosemary or other herbs to make up particular blends. Much of this is for markets in Great Britain.

Drying and cleaning the herbs is, of course, a key operation. At least 90 per cent of the herbs are dried naturally in the hot sun, spread out on the concreted area in front of the Caussade warehouse. Among the exceptions are parsley, tarragon and chives, which are dried with hot air in the shade.

Once dried, herbs are crushed, often with a mule drawing a roller over them or, with very hard-leaved herbs such as thyme or rosemary, by running a tractor over them. Collecting the seed or leaf up off the ground often poses a problem. Caussade is considering the use of a giant vacuum cleaner for the purpose.

Virtually all the seed or leaf cleaning is carried out in a very old, electrically powered seed cleaner, using a series of sieves of different dimensions which are vibrated to separate seed and leaves, initially from larger pieces of stalk and unwanted debris, and finally, by altering the sieves, from tiny particles of dust and dirt.

A fan is sometimes perched on the trestle to blow light material into collecting trays. Herbs may be passed through the machine several times before cleaning is completed.

A marvellous herbal aroma escapes from the ventilator in the wall behind the machine to the road alongside – a real Provençal smell. In the same warehouse all the packaging and despatch operations are carried out, from the large sacks of herbs for the wholesale trade to the automated packing of herbs in sealed packets for the retail shops.

....

Caussade's company, L'Herbier de Provence, is now a division of La Vie Claire.

INSIDE THE FRENCH LAVENDER SCENE
Gardeners' Chronicle, 13 January 1978

In the southern provinces of France over 5,000 growers cultivate an estimated total of between 20,000 and 25,000 hectares/50,000 and 61,000 acres of lavender, producing annually about 1,200 tonnes of lavender essences or oils.

An extensive lavender field in full bloom is a beautiful sight. The first one I saw was just north of Montélimar in the Rhône valley, more or less in the centre of the lavender growing area.

A native of Persia and the Canaries, lavender has proved an adaptable plant – England and Bulgaria both grow excellent quality lavender. But the climate and soil conditions of southern France are particularly suitable, and for centuries it has grown wild on the dry hills of the Midi, along with rosemary, wild thyme and wild savory.

Generations of shepherds and peasants, especially the women and children, collected the flower spikes for sale. With the rural exodus at the end of the nineteenth century the lavender spread into abandoned countryside, and collecting began on a more regular basis.

As prices rose, the collectors were encouraged to nurture the wild plants to improve the yields and quality – 'cleaning' the zones where the lavender grew, giving the plants a little fertilizer, weeding them, and encouraging them to grow in rows to make gathering easier. It was a short step to cultivation in fields, which began in earnest in the 1920s.

Production was boosted further in the 1930s, by the establishment of the perfume industry based on Grasse, in the hills above Cannes, and by the development of improved strains of lavender, notably 'Abrialii', which they told me was still the most widely planted cultivar in France.

There are two main types of lavender: the real lavender, *Lavandula angustifolia* (which the French call *lavande*), and the hybrid between *L. angustifolia* and *L. latifolia*, the French lavender, known as *lavandin, L. x intermedia. L. angustifolia* grows best in mountains at a height of over 700–800m/2,300–2,600ft, though, as already mentioned, it has proved very adaptable.

The essential oils from the real lavender are superior to those of lavandin; they contain less camphor and higher quantities of the chemicals responsible for the true lavender scent. They command two or three times the price of lavandin oils.

Yields, however, are much lower. Whereas a hectare/2½ acres of lavandin could be expected to yield between 50 and 100kg/110 and 220lb of oil, it will produce no more than 15–20kg/33–44lb of lavande oil. Lavande is also harder to cut, being a shorter plant, though there is little apparent difference in the flowers. *L. vera* is raised from seed, so there is a variable population in any one field.

The lavandin hybrid, on the other hand, is sterile and raised from cuttings, so populations are far more uniform. A number of good commercial strains have been developed from selected clones, and today about 80 per cent of the commercially cultivated crop is in fact lavandin. It has proved itself even more adaptable than *L. angustifolia*.

The cultivation of lavender is fairly straightforward. Cuttings of lavandin are taken from healthy mother plants in winter, and planted out in nursery beds the following spring, the young plants being planted in the field that autumn or the following spring, according to local conditions. Planting is frequently by machine.

In the first summer in the field the plants are topped, to encourage vegetative growth, and the first real harvest is gathered eighteen months after planting. Yields reach their peak in the third year, and start to decline after the sixth, the life of a plantation being on average about ten years.

The *L. angustifolia*, raised for seed, produces its first harvest a year later, gives best yields in its fourth year, and tends to be productive a year longer.

Much of the cultivation today is mechanized, with herbicides used to control weeds.

A tractor load of lavender en route to the distillery at St Christol-lès-Alès in the Rhône Valley. To me the men's casual chat is a vignette of agricultural life everywhere.

One of the major problems is a decline in vigour, known as *dépérissement*, which lowers the yields and reduces the average life of a plantation to about three or four years. The precise cause of decline is still unknown. It is most serious in the areas where lavender has been grown longest, and is thought to be a combination of soil exhaustion through lack of rotation, parasitic attack, and unsuitable cultural practices.

It is almost entirely confined to the hybrid lavandin, and has doubtless been exacerbated in the past by a practice of taking plants which looked as if they were dying young, and dividing them up or taking cuttings from them to prevent total loss.

The lavender growers' co-operatives are now encouraging selection and propagation from healthy plants to combat decline, as there is no known remedy. New plantations are being made on land which is virgin territory as far as lavender growing is concerned.

Apart from the plant breeding and selection carried out by Professor Abrial in the 1930s, there has until recently been little scientific research into the crop. Cultural techniques tended to be governed by traditional folklore, such as choosing the best phase of the moon for harvesting.

Harvesting at the right moment is the most important factor in determining the amount of essence extracted – variety, age of plantation and the nature of the soil also have an influence. The old adage is that one should harvest when the blue is beginning to fade, i.e. just after the full flowering. Only one cut is made each year, and depending on the region, harvesting takes place between July and September.

In the old days all harvesting was with sickles, the lavender being gathered up initially into cloth sacks carried over the picker's shoulders, sometimes using the women's aprons, then tipped into large cloths knotted at the corners, and taken by mule, or on a man's shoulder, to the distillery. Harvesting by hand at the right moment meant that a great deal of labour was required in the same area at the same time: traditionally Spanish workers came into France for the lavender harvest. Incidentally, because of the disinfectant properties of lavender, it was said that a cut with a sickle never went septic.

Today, except in very remote or inaccessible fields, cutting is almost entirely by machine, either with cutter attachments to tractors, or, in a few cases, with automated cutters. There are now between 250 and 300 machines, and the co-operatives have played a notable role in arranging hire purchase terms with manufacturers, so that small groups of growers could get together and buy a machine over a number of years.

The machines either bundle the lavender or leave it loose, and it is generally left in the field for two or three days after cutting, either on the ground or laid over the bushes, to make it easier to handle and distil. A lady I spoke to working in a field alongside a main highway admitted that they have been forced to cut down on this, as so much lavender was being stolen by passing motorists.

Most of the distilleries are run by the co-operatives, with only a few of the larger growers having their own stills. In the distillery the lavender is piled on to a grill which has been lowered into the bottom of a tank, and as much lavender as possible compressed into the tank before the lid is made fast. In the distillery I visited a large rubber tyre, suspended overhead, was used to compress the lavender into the tank.

Steam is passed into the tank, and the lavender essences are extracted in the steam, the mixture of steam and vapourized essences being passed through a serpentine condenser, cooled by a stream of cold water. The liquid end products are separated simply by gravity, the lighter oils forming a floating layer over the water which is easily tapped off.

Growers are paid according to the weight of oil obtained from each load, and they wait while their load is being processed. The boilers are fired entirely by the waste lavender straw, the spent lavender after distillation, perhaps every other load being used as fuel. This makes it a satisfying self-sufficient process.

The essential oils are mainly in the flowers, although some are also extracted from the stems of the plant. The tanks generally have a capacity of 1 tonne of lavender straw, as the raw material is called, and the steam is passed through for about 30 minutes. Between 5 and 10kg/11 and 22lb of lavande essence, and 15 and 20kg/33 and 44lb of lavandin essence, would be extracted from each load.

For the top-quality essences, those used in perfumes and cosmetics, a more refined process is used. The lavender is soaked in solvents such as hexane or benzene, which dissolve the principal essences and certain waxes. The solvent is then evaporated, and a paste, known as the *concrète*, is obtained. This is treated with alcohol, which dissolves the essences but not the waxes; the essences are then obtained in a pure form by evaporation from the alcohol and filtration.

In the 1880s, in the early days of commercial lavender production, distillation brokers toured the countryside with portable stills, carrying out the distillation for the peasants, and buying the end product from them.

This system was in part responsible for the tremendous fluctuations in prices which have plagued lavender growers. The brokers, having the facilities for storing the essences, were unscrupulous about hoarding and playing the market. The small growers, unable to afford storage, were bound to sell at harvest time when supply was greatest and prices lowest.

Even between 1955 and 1965 prices of lavender fluctuated by as much as 5 to 50 francs per kilogram/2.2lb. As a result many small growers could no longer afford to grow lavender, and between 1964 and 1967 overall production fell by 70 per cent.

In an attempt to remedy this deteriorating situation, the first lavender growers' co-operative was formed in 1968, followed by a number of others. These have now been grouped together under the umbrella of Sicalav (Société d'Intérêt Collectif Agricole).

With their stronger position the co-operatives have been of considerable help in steadying the market and guaranteeing a fair reward to growers, although there are still fluctuations in the market prices. I was told that this year (1977) growers were getting approximately £7 per kg/2.2lb for the agricultural essence, which was being sold to the American buyers for somewhat less than £9 per kg/2.2lb.

Lavender is best known for its use in perfumes, but is also used in the pharmaceutical industry and is in great demand for use in the manufacture of detergents and soaps. About 70 per cent of the oils are bought by the USA soap companies such as Procter and Gamble, Unilever and Unigate. There is also considerable export to Great Britain, Germany and Japan.

The lavender industry is facing growing competition from Asia and Spain, and from the increasing substitution of the real thing by synthetic products.

Apart from the lavender essences extracted from the plants, there is a world market for the dried flowers. These are gathered fresh, dried carefully, cleaned off the stalks, riddled to remove the dust, and packed in 10–15g/⅓–½oz sachets. Over 50 tonnes of dried lavender flowers are sold annually.

Snatches of nomadic life. Above: a page from the list of collected seeds I sent back to the Wellesbourne gene bank. Below: typing outdoors at Capo Caccia in Sardinia while Don makes a start on soda bread.

Cuneo   Seeds 'Zucca' long
.... narrow waisted pumpkin in shops.

61/77 a b	Apr. 22/77 SASSARI, SARDINIA. [8°30'E; 40°40'N]
	Cultivated rocket; Eruca
	(Rucola coltivata) Algherese. (from AGHERO)
	Sown here Apr Cut - re-grows. Green also in wilds

62/77 a b.	Apr 22/77. SASSARI, SARDINIA [8°30'E; 40°40'N]
	RADISH
	Ravanello Sassarese (from SASSARI)
	Long with white roots(?) Lungo a punta bianca
	Sown in Apr For winter use
	90 days from sowing to harvest

.... SASSARI, SARDINIA [8°30'E; 40°40'N]
.... Oval shape; Green skin,
.... early var a late var. for
.... Pinna Nossai: Giacomo, SASSARI,
.... contacted via Dr. Milia, Agronomy
.... Institute, Sassari

L'escalier : 226 marches.
De Trap : 226 treden.

Dear Granny:
I Went to
Waterloo. I climb
ed 226 steps
and counted
them. I saw
the cows
being milked.
It is raining
in Belgium. xxx
Love, Kirsten xxx♥

Mrs. L.
The
12
TRL 5'BA
L

Etat-major
de Napoléon

To Grandpa

We went to water-
loo where the Battle
was fought We went
on a bike ride
and the rain
came and I got
home first. Dad is
our teacher and
gives us lessons. Brandon
love
xxx X
xxxx

Rob. E.H.
The Wh
12

*Wherever we stopped or stayed, the kids
started playing. Lego earned its keep here in
Brežice in Yugoslavia. Schooling was erratic,
so writing postcards to grandparents was
probably part of a lesson.*

Early experiments at Montrose Farm on our return, using peasant systems such as narrow beds separated by permanent paths, close equidistant spacing, intercropping, and cut-and-come-again patches of salad crops like red lettuce, rocket and alfalfa.

3 EXPERIMENTING, CONSOLIDATING

The immediate years following our return from the Grand Vegetable Tour in 1977 were busy ones. While I was working on my book *Salads the Year Round*, we were starting our small-scale organic market garden, mainly supplying bags of mixed salads to wholefood outlets in London. And our Suffolk garden became a small-scale trial ground, in which we experimented with new and old techniques and varieties, including those we had discovered on our travels.

I spent a lot of time tapping into research into vegetable growing, attending open days at research stations, conferences and demonstrations, and visiting seed trial grounds. The publication in 1979 of the classic work *Know and Grow Vegetables*, spearheaded by the National Vegetable Research Institute in Wellesbourne, was a landmark, distilling so much of this research into a readable form for amateur gardeners.

At about this time the Royal Horticultural Society offered me a contract to write a certain number of articles each year for their monthly magazine *The Garden*, with few restrictions on subject or length – a dream for me. The RHS articles selected here were still heavily influenced by our travels, our subsequent experiments and research findings. In those pre-sound-bite days, it was a luxury to have the scope to write at length about the aspects of vegetables and vegetable growing we had uncovered that would interest amateur gardeners.

I did a lot of soul searching before including this article. Perhaps it should be labelled 'dedicated vegetable growers only', with 'licence to skip' for everyone else. I gave in as I feel, more than thirty years since it was written, that it is still very relevant to today's gardeners. Gardens have got even smaller, and the need for the best possible use of them has increased. Moreover, the research on which I drew at the time, detailing the effects of close spacing on yield, size of crop, early ripening and other factors, has all but disappeared from the public domain. I hate to think of it being wasted!

The cut-and-come-again technique, innovatory back in the 1970s, has become popularized for growing 'baby leaves', with seed companies now selling a huge choice of mixtures for gardeners. It has certainly become our main method of growing salad crops and Asian winter greens. I should add that I have now discovered a way to 'two time' potatoes, by sowing rocket or cress on top of them when they are first planted. The seedlings can be harvested before the potato leaves peep through: that's a very satisfying use of space.

....

PRODUCTIVITY IN THE VEGETABLE GARDEN
The Garden, April 1978

The average vegetable garden today is considerably smaller than the vegetable garden of ten or twenty years ago, so there is a lot of interest in ways of making the most of all available space – increasing productivity, as the industrialists would put it. The key way to do this is to use various intensive techniques, such as growing vegetables closer together in patches or blocks, intercropping and the highly productive 'cut-and-come-again' systems.

There is no doubt that vegetables can be grown much closer than is generally recommended and a number of experiments in recent years have demonstrated this. On a commercial scale, it has been shown that with many vegetables, for example, carrots, onions and runner beans, total yields increase with increasing density up to a certain point, and that beyond that point total yields remain constant, in spite of increasing the density of planting. So if one is aiming for quantity there is, within reason, nothing to lose by over-planting.

Other vegetables, however, the prime example being beet, demonstrate the law of diminishing returns. While giving increasing yields with increasing density up to an optimum point, beyond that point the total yields fall off gradually. On an amateur level, experiments carried out in 1977 by members of the Henry Doubleday Research Association on Dutch brown beans grown for drying suggested that highest total yields were obtained by planting beans 5cm/2in apart, compared with planting at distances of 10 and 15cm/4 and 6in – distances which most of us would have considered far more appropriate.

CLOSER PLANTING

It is certainly beginning to look as if amateurs could plant more closely and obtain higher yields. But of course the size of vegetables is largely determined by spacing, and individual vegetables are liable to be smaller if very close planting is adopted. Again research has shown that the size of some vegetables can be very accurately controlled, simply by choosing the appropriate spacing. For example, if commercial carrot growers want to produce small carrots, the recommendation is to aim for 320 carrots per sq. m/30 carrots per sq. ft. (Rows could be as close as 9cm/3½in apart. But if they want a large carrot, they are advised to aim for 106 per sq. m/10 per sq. ft. If some varieties of cauliflowers are planted as close as 23 by 10 cm/9 by 4in apart, they produce a high yield of 'mini-cauliflowers', small curds of between 4 and 9cm/1½ and 3½in in diameter – a practical size for cooking. These mature far more evenly than conventional full-sized cauliflowers, which is useful where one wants to strip a crop for freezing or to clear the ground for a follow-on crop.

Closer spacing also appears to lead to earlier ripening in onions (because of the increased competition between plants) and to more uniform ripening of peas and beans, giving a substantial pick at one time.

The key question for every crop is how close? To do really well, vegetables must be grown in fertile soil, with plenty of moisture, shelter from strong winds and draughts and enough space for their leaves to be fully exposed to the sun to absorb the energy on which the plant's growth depends. With most ordinary vegetables, grown in normal conditions, it is apparent that the roots absorb the nutrients and moisture required from the soil immediately beneath the plant's foliage: one rarely finds strong roots radiating horizontally away from the plant, such as those found with soft fruit bushes. From the plant's point of view, the space between rows, with which we are traditionally extravagant, is out of reach and in effect wasted.

Taking this to its logical conclusion, the most economical way of growing vegetables is to grow them equidistant from each other, with the leaves of neighbouring plants, when mature, just touching. This can be achieved either by thinning out as they grow so that seedlings are always just touching, or by planting so that on reaching maturity all the ground between plants will be covered. Plant or thin using the normal distances recommended between plants, for both between plants and between rows.

Growing vegetables in this way, virtually replacing rows with intensive blocks, patches, strips, or in what is known commercially as the 'bed system', has a number of beneficial side effects. Because the soil surface is in effect covered by a canopy of leaves weed growth is suppressed, soil moisture is preserved and the activity of worms and microorganisms in the soil is encouraged. The soil structure, a key factor in soil fertility, benefits from the fact that there is less treading over most of the ground. It also seems possible that the higher yields obtained at close spacing may be due to the mutual sheltering effect which closely grown plants bestow on each other.

The main disadvantage is the problem of access. Getting at plants in the early stages for weeding and thinning and in the later stages for picking and harvesting is more awkward and time consuming than when they are grown in traditional rows.

To minimize this disadvantage, blocks or strips of closely grown vegetables should probably never be more than about 1m/1 yard in width, so that plants in the middle can be reached without too much difficulty. This is also a convenient size for covering with low plastic tunnels, a cheap and effective method of increasing productivity further, especially at the beginning and end of the growing season.

In my own 'patches' I mulch between plants in the early stages, with rotted lawn clippings, bracken, compost, etc., to eliminate weeding altogether and to conserve moisture. This has proved an invaluable practice in the dry East Anglian summers encountered in many recent years. I also mulch around the perimeter of the block or the edges of the strip. This is partly to keep weeds down and preserve moisture, but primarily to prevent the perimeter soil (a fairly heavy clay) from becoming muddy and compacted. Due to the elimination of rows, the edges of a patch take an abnormal amount of 'traffic'.

Some vegetables seem to lend themselves to patch cultivation. Self-blanching celery, for example, does far better in blocks than rows: the reduced light in the centre of the block encourages blanching. It can be planted about 20cm/8in apart, with a little straw loosely piled on the outside of the block or strip to assist the blanching of the exposed outer plants. Sweetcorn should always be planted in blocks to aid pollination, the plants being between 30 and 45cm/1 and 1½ft apart, depending on variety. Dwarf varieties of broad beans, dwarf French beans and dwarf runner beans are also very suitable for patch culture, as are all the salad crops, as well as carrots, onions, beet, spinach, leeks and celeriac. Probably the only really unsuitable vegetables are tall varieties of peas, beans and tomatoes which need staking or support, making access to the centre of a block almost impossible, and very sprawly vegetables such as marrows or pumpkins, unless they can be trained to sprawl down the length of a strip.

CUT-AND-COME-AGAIN

The fact that many leafy vegetables will resprout when cut off just above the lowest leaves, close to ground level, makes for some very good returns from closely grown vegetables in what has been called the cut-and-come-again technique. The best candidates here are lettuces (cos lettuce and the 'Salad Bowl' type are most suitable), leaf beet types of spinach such as Swiss chard and perpetual spinach, chicories such as 'Sugar Loaf', 'Grumolo Verde' and 'Spadona', turnips grown for their tops, parsley and some of the less common vegetables such as Chinese mustard, chrysanthemum greens (shungiku) and sorrel. The simplest method is to broadcast the seed by scattering it on the surface, and then raking it over, once in one direction and a second time at right angles, to ensure that the seed is covered with soil. Alternatively seed can be carefully station sown by hand, sowing a couple of seeds at each station, 2.5–5cm/1–2in apart. Pelleted seed is ideal for this, provided the ground can be kept moist enough to ensure good germination. However, it is surprisingly easy to pick up individual seeds, such as lettuce, with a small piece of broken glass, moistening the tip, and then to sow them accurately where required.

In Italy lettuce and chicory are frequently broadcast in long beds, with only the minimum, if any, thinning. Leaves are cut off for use in salad when a few inches high, and three or four cuts are made from the same plants. The first cut is naturally the best, and after the 'crisis' of cutting, as it was explained to me in typical Italian terms, plants are left for three or four days to recover, then fed with a liquid or foliar feed. The National Vegetable Research Station in England has carried out research into the cultivation of what they have called leaf lettuce, spacing seeds 2.5cm/1in apart in rows 10cm/4in apart. Cos lettuce varieties were used, leaves were cut initially at about 10cm/4in high, and total yields were roughly double those obtained by growing lettuce at conventional spacing, although of course what was produced was a mass of crispy individual leaves rather than a hearted lettuce. Doubtless amateurs could get similar results by broadcasting, or sowing seeds at equidistant spacing of about 6.5cm/2½in between plants.

An Italian market grower I talked to near Venice was growing perpetual spinach and parsley this way. He sowed the spinach beet in mid-February, and cut it four or five times in the season, usually uprooting it finally in mid-October. With parsley he claimed to get anything from four to eight cuts in a season, manuring the soil very heavily before sowing, and giving supplementary feed periodically.

For any of these intensive techniques to succeed it is essential that the soil is extremely fertile, and that growth is never checked by lack of water. In my own small-scale trials, the failures have all been due to inadequate watering.

Turnips (as turnip tops) and cabbages both lend themselves to productive forms of patch cropping. For early spring greens I normally broadcast a patch of turnips in the autumn – the latest I have done so being 19 October, using 'Golden Ball'. Even though in this case the turnips were only small seedlings throughout the winter, with the first hint of warmer days they grew rapidly and were an invaluable source of spring greens in early April, when fresh vegetables are so often scarce. They are best eaten when about 10–12.5cm/4–5in high, before the leaves become coarse. Growth is so rapid that a cut can be made every few days. Dwarf kale can also be grown very densely in a patch, and the young leaves chopped several times for fresh spring greens.

Cabbage greens can be grown very rapidly by station sowing groups of two or three seeds, 7.5–10cm/3–4in apart each way, in spring or early summer, using any variety of spring cabbage. Thin to one seedling per station, and within six to eight weeks, when the small young leaves are about 7.5–12.5cm/3–5in high, they can be chopped off and eaten as 'greens'; the stalks will resprout. Or alternate plants can be pulled up, leaving the intervening ones to make solid hearts. The old gardener's trick of not uprooting mature cabbages, but cutting a cross about 6mm/¼in deep in the stalk, and leaving it to resprout, is well worth doing. When the sprouted growths have reached 2.5cm/1in or so in height a top dressing of a general or seaweed-based fertilizer stimulates growth. As many as five cabbages can grow from an old stalk.

INTERCROPPING

Intersowing, intercropping and undercropping are all forms of double cropping which enable garden space to be used very productively. In intersowing, two or more vegetables are grown in the same row, the principal crop being a slow-growing vegetable – brassicas, leeks, fennel, or one of the root crops such as parsnips, Hamburg parsley, salsify or scorzonera – intersown with a fast-growing crop such as lettuce (small varieties such as 'Little Gem' and 'Tom Thumb' are ideal), spring onions, radish or short carrots. The quick-growing crop is ready and cleared within a few months, leaving the main crop space to mature fully.

To take an example of parsnips being intersown with lettuce. The parsnips are eventually thinned so as to be spaced about 20cm/8in apart, so that when the drill is drawn out, groups of three or four parsnip seeds are station sown at 20cm/8in intervals. In the same drill small groups of three to four lettuce seeds are sown between each group of parsnip seeds. Although somewhat laborious initially, this parsimonious sowing minimizes thinning later, and is very economical with seed, besides ensuring maximum use of the row. Incidentally, if sowing in poor light conditions, it is advisable to sow the most 'visible' seeds first, or it may be hard to spot where one has already sown. White-seeded lettuce shows up very well.

Radish and spring onion can even be mixed with other seed – carrots, turnips, beetroot, parsnip or parsley for example, and simply sown together. The radish and onions grow very rapidly, and can be pulled carefully when required without disturbing the main crop in the row. Some people sow leeks and spring onions together, pulling the onions in summer and leaving the leeks to develop.

In intercropping the general principle is the same. A quick-growing crop is sown or planted very close to, or between the rows of, a slower-maturing crop. The quick one is cleared before the space between the rows is required for the final stages of development of the slower crop. The possibilities for intercropping are endless, but care must be taken to avoid overcrowding and so growing two inferior-quality crops. Both must have enough space, light and moisture to

Sweet corn, here interplanted with lettuce, is one of my favourites for intercropping and undercropping. Its leaves allow light through to a crop below, and space for an adjacent crop to develop to maturity.

develop fully, and there must be enough space between crops for any essential cultivation or picking. So it is advisable to space the rows of the main crop just a little further apart than normal. As with patch cropping, the soil surface eventually becomes completely covered and weeds cease to grow. Again, mulching between rows is very beneficial. The following are a few examples of intercropping which I have found successful, but there are many others:

- between rows of shallots: carrots, lettuce, radish, turnips to be pulled young, spring onions;
- between winter brassicas planted out in mid-summer: carrots, summer cabbage, turnips, kohl rabi, Chinese mustard, salad crops such as lettuce, land cress, lamb's lettuce, rocket;
- between rows or blocks of peas (preferably dwarf or of medium height): winter brassicas, turnips, carrots, lettuce, summer spinach, green peppers, tomatoes;
- alongside broad beans, dwarf French and dwarf runner beans: winter brassicas, small turnips, summer spinach, salad crops.

The one case of intercropping which I have never found successful, though it is sometimes advocated and is always tempting, is between rows of potatoes. In my experience the second crop is always swamped by the potatoes, whether it is brassicas planted out between the rows, or marrows trained to romp along the furrows. Intercropping with potatoes can probably only succeed when the potatoes are planted considerably further apart than normal.

There is considerable scope for intercropping tall and climbing vegetables with those of a dwarfer or trailing habit. Sweetcorn is a good example, partly because its somewhat scanty foliage allows plenty of light to reach the ground-level crop. Dwarf beans, bush marrows and lettuce do well under sweetcorn, as do trailing marrows, pumpkins and cucumbers.

Climbing vegetables such as runner beans, the lovely purple-podded climbing French bean, the round climbing squash 'Little Gem (Rolet)' and climbing outdoor cucumbers can be grown up 'tepees' of bamboo poles or any similar kind of support, with a quick catch crop of lettuces or radishes taken from the ground between the plants in the early stages of growth.

I was very pleased one year with a tepee of 'Little Gem' squash, grown in a patch .84 sq. m/1 yard square. About sixteen lettuce seedlings were planted in the square early in spring, then a bamboo pole was erected at each corner, and a couple of squash seeds sown under a jar at the foot of each pole. The lettuces matured as the squashes made their way up the poles, and by mid-summer, when the lettuces were finished, the squash plants had completely covered the tepee. It made a very striking feature in the kitchen garden, with the combination of the large prettily shaped silver-edged leaves, bright yellow flowers and finally an abundant crop of little round squashes. We not only ate the lettuces and the squashes but also the flowers once the fruit had set (they are delicious fried or used as the basis of a light soup) – so we really did get our money's worth from that particular square yard.

Where double rows of climbing beans are planted about 76cm/2½ft apart and trained to grow up poles or strings, the space beneath can be utilized by crops which tolerate shade. Autumn-maturing vegetables such as Witloof, 'Sugar Loaf' and red chicory, endive and spinach have proved suitable, being sown at the same time as the beans. They grow almost to their full size before the beans cover the supports completely and block out the light, and are ready for use in late autumn when the beans are taken down. They must, however, be well watered or the competition from the beans will prove damaging.

One further undercropping idea. After a year's absence from my garden, the only parsley I could find had sown itself in the asparagus bed, and was flourishing in the shady protection of the asparagus fern. It might seem sacrilegious, but in future I will sow a little parsley between asparagus crowns, to make full use of that idle, expensive space in an asparagus bed.

Mulching is a subject that continues to fascinate me, although I have had to do some rethinking since moving to Ireland and a garden where slugs, multiplying in the neighbouring grass fields, are a major problem. Is mulching with old straw, a long-time favourite, the equivalent of providing a duvet for the slugs? Yet the way the wind dries out the soil surface and, believe it or not, the shortage of rain are compelling arguments for mulching, slugs notwithstanding. Our favourite material now is seaweed, gathered fresh from nearby Ballinglanna beach with its convenient slipway, though we have to wait for a south-westerly wind to bring it in. Bare soil in a vegetable garden will always disturb me. To me, mulch is the lid on a cooking pot, ensuring that all those vital interactions in the soil are ticking away steadily. Incidentally, the experimental plastic mulching techniques mentioned at the end of the article have all been shown to have useful applications.

MISCELLANEOUS MULCHES
The Garden, October 1978

Mulching the soil is a very ancient horticultural technique, highly developed by many of the world's most skilled gardeners such as the Arabs and Chinese. Closer to home, a friend recently told me about an entry he had found in a thirteenth-century account book for Norwich Cathedral priory: paying labourers four pence for three days' work 'thatching' fields with straw! Probably as sound a practice then as it would be in East Anglia today, where three-quarters of the year's (normal) scanty rainfall is lost through evaporation and transpiration. The purpose of this article is to describe some of the unusual mulching techniques which we encountered in European market gardens on our recent vegetable tour.

Undoubtedly one of the most striking and extensive examples is the sand mulching which I first saw on the intensively cultivated coastal regions of Spain between Málaga and Motril, and which is common practice in Almeria, Granada and Málaga. Known as *enarenados* or sanded cultivation, this technique may have its origins in ancient Arab stone mulching. Modern use in Spain, however, is said to date from about 1880, when growers noticed that tomatoes growing beside ant hills, where sand dug up by ants had been deposited, cropped earlier and were far more productive than other tomatoes. *Enarenados*, which consists essentially of covering the land with a layer of manure and then a layer of sand, was developed as a means of cultivation in adverse conditions – for example, in sub-desert areas where soil and irrigation water were very salty, or simply in areas where irrigation water was extremely scarce. In these hitherto unproductive areas it has been used for the production of family vegetables,

high-value market garden crops in the open, and today, for intensive commercial cropping under low and high plastic tunnels mainly for dwarf beans, tomatoes, peppers, aubergines, cucumbers, melons and marrows. It has also been used in orchards and vineyards, growing table grapes, citrus, and pears, where it has resulted in earlier, heavier cropping than would otherwise have been the case.

The sanding process involves a great deal of labour. The first stage is to make the land as level as possible. It is then divided into sections surrounded by low concrete walls, which help prevent the loss of both water and sand. For irrigation purposes short concrete channels are then built, generally running down the length of the beds. As Spain is subject to strong winds some kind of windbreak is essential, both to prevent the sand being blown away, and to give normal windbreak protection to the crops. Either permanent windbreaks of thuja, cypress or oleander are planted, or windbreaks made with reed canes, 2–3m/6–10ft high, placed at right angles to the prevailing winds at intervals of 8–10m/8–11 yards apart. These have to be renovated every winter.

The next stage takes place in winter when the ground is watered very thoroughly with the aim of washing the salts down from the surface layers of the soil. The land is then drained, and the beds are covered with a 1–2cm/½–1in thick layer of well-matured, weed-free manure, preferably horse manure without too much straw. Care has to be taken not to overmanure or the growth, particularly of tomatoes, aubergines and peppers, can be too lush. On top of this layer of manure the sand mulch is laid, anything from 7–12cm/3–5in in depth, 12cm/5in being considered the optimum depth).

Either sea or river sand is used for mulching, after being washed and sifted. The ideal size of sand particles is about the size of rice grains, large enough not to be easily moved by wind or water. If particles are too small they may be blown away or crumble, or if they become mixed with soil or clay they will become too damp and absorb salts. If they are too large irrigation is more difficult, and as the large particles are liable to get hotter, plants can be scorched as a result.

When the sanding is completed the ground is then ready to be divided, with ridges and further irrigation channels, into plots of a suitable size and shape for the cultivation of the different crops.

When cultivating and planting in the *enarenados* great care has to be taken not to mix the earth layer with the sand, and, as far as possible, to prevent invasion from weeds. If looked after well the initial sand mulch can last for as long as eight to twelve years, especially if it was laid in a 12cm/5in-thick layer. However, every three years an operation known as *retranqueo* is undertaken, when the sand is pulled back carefully to the edge of the beds, a new layer of manure spread, and then the sand replaced again over the manure. This ensures renewal of the organic matter, and if sand has been lost by mixing with the earth, or by being washed or blown away, more can be added to the surface to make up the loss.

There are a number of reasons for the success and usefulness of the sanded cultivation in the hostile soils on which it is used. One of the most important is the reduction of the salt levels in the soil. Normally, in salty land, water containing dissolved salts rises to the surface by capillary action and evaporates from the surface, either depositing salts in the upper layers of the soil in the root zone of the plant, or forming a crust on the soil surface.

However, a surface mulch of sand breaks the capillary channel in the soil, and so instead of being evaporated, the salts are washed down by the irrigation water (particularly in winter) and tend to accumulate in a layer at a depth of approximately 0.75–1m/2½–3ft deep, well out of the way of plant roots. In fact it is said that by using the *enarenados* technique, horticultural crops can even be grown on old salt pans.

One of the main effects of the sand mulch, of course, is to prevent evaporation of water from the soil, thus greatly reducing the amount of water required for irrigation. Moreover, because the sand heats faster than the soil during the day, and cools faster at night, moisture is condensed on the soil surface, keeping it moist, encouraging growth, and preventing the dangerous and sudden falls in temperature which occur in hot regions. The combination of the heat given off by the manure and radiation from the sand leads to soil temperature rises of up to 10°C/50°F, so giving the market gardeners one of their greatest benefits: crops which come in ten to fifteen days earlier than normal. Moreover, high yields are obtained in the warm humid microclimate which is created. Another important factor is that the physical properties of sand enable irrigation to be carried out with water which is high in chlorides and would normally be considered unsuitable for irrigation.

Naturally there are problems. The initial expenses incurred in preparing the ground are extremely high; weeds are difficult to control and the use of herbicides tricky; and fungus diseases can spread very quickly in the warm humid conditions. However, in skilled hands very profitable crops can be grown, especially in the winter months. To get maximum returns from the sanded areas they are generally intensively intercropped. A common practice is to sow dwarf beans at the beginning of January, then to interplant them with tomatoes, peppers and cucumbers, all of which are harvested in spring.

The *enarenados* technique is widely used today in both low plastic tunnels and high plastic tunnels and greenhouses. The sand mulch prevents the high rate of evaporation from the soil which occurs under plastic and glass, and so cuts down on irrigation, which in winter leads to lowering of soil temperatures. In addition the sand throws out heat at night, so raising the air temperature and benefiting the plants accordingly.

In some of the coastal areas of Spain the mulching is with small stones or gravel instead of sand. At first sight the acres of vigorous-looking plants, growing in gleaming grey soil, are completely mystifying. Close examination reveals that the grey 'soil' is stone. When, after scraping away the top few centimetres of dry warm stone, one comes to the surprisingly moist and warm layer on the surface of the soil, the reason for this laborious method of cultivation is abundantly clear.

One can find interesting accounts of stone mulching in other parts of the world. In South Africa farmers make trenches about 30cm/12in deep and the same width, which are lined with compost and then filled with water. Trees are planted in these, and the trenches are then filled with stones, packed right up against the bark of the tree trunk. Similarly in China there are accounts of fruit trees being mulched with coke and stones. In this case buckets of compost are occasionally thrown on to the coke or stones, and flower seeds sown on the compost. Alternatively holes were made through the stone mulch with a dibber, and flowers planted in the holes.

Moving on into Italy, there are some very interesting examples of mulching to be found in the market gardening areas of the Ligurian coast, where the good light levels, the mild

Ingenious cropping on the Spanish coast near Málaga. Sheltered by windbreaks, the low polythene tunnels were mulched with gravel, which helped retain moisture during the day and then gave out heat at night.

Examples of unusual mulching materials in Italy: asparagus is mulched with sand in Liguria, and courgettes with cotton waste in Albenga.

maritime climate and the rich light soils favour the production of early crops. Here asparagus is one of the crops most frequently mulched. In some cases a fairly thin layer of river or sea sand is used, spread over the asparagus beds in February or March to bring the crop forward by about fifteen days. Another material used is a type of cotton waste, *scarto di cotone*, and I must admit my first sight of this was another mulching mystery. The cotton waste has the appearance of cotton wool, light, white and fluffy, and it is put on the beds in layers up to 30cm/12in thick, literally blanketing the soil. Being organic in nature, it eventually rots into the soil.

The cotton waste is also used to mulch other crops, both outdoors and under glass. I saw it used on outdoor spring-planted zucchini or courgettes, and on an early cucumber crop under glass. I was told it was also used in other parts of Italy. (Incidentally, experiments carried out at the research station at Salerno comparing the effect of mulching asparagus with straw, earth and sand showed that the best results are obtained by mulching with sand. The growers in Liguria, however, found the cotton waste even more effective than sand.

On an organic farm in Piedmont sand was being used as a mulch on a small carrot crop. The sand was spread on the ground after sowing, partly to help warm up the soil, partly to keep the weeds down. The sand was dug in eventually to lighten the soil, which was a heavy clay.

A market garden in Sardinia provided another bizarre example of mulching. It had been created in very poor soil alongside a municipal rubbish tip, and the market gardener had taken the unrefined rubbish and spread it several inches thick over his soil. The collection of broken bottles, plastic containers, tin cans, rags, shattered glass and miscellaneous domestic rubbish was a far from pretty sight, and undoubtedly hazardous to work on. But the owner had purposely left an area in the centre of his land unmulched, and the difference in the quality of the crops was remarkable: the area mulched with rubbish was far more productive.

The eastern Adriatic coast of Italy, south of Bari, is another of those areas where horticulture is favoured by high temperatures, but growers have to contend with the adverse factors of strong winds and severe shortage of water. To make irrigation possible, fields are laboriously worked into small beds, with miles of low earth banks and a network of irrigation channels, often hand dug. Here again mulching has been developed to a fine art. One notable use is the mulching of seedbeds to protect the seeds from the heat and wind before they germinate. In this case the seedbed is covered with a thin layer of very fine straw and manure, the seeds being watered through the straw. Throughout the area large fields of aubergines, tomatoes, peppers and other crops are mulched with straw – a twentieth-century Italian example of the thirteenth-century East Anglian 'thatching'!

Finally, no article on mulching would be complete without mentioning the widespread use in Europe of plastic mulches. In Spain water melons are sown in ridges over which a tight sheet of transparent plastic is stretched to warm the soil before the young plants are eased through. In France black plastic mulches are used to keep crops such as tomatoes weed free, while white plastic is used to hasten the growth of melons. Black and white plastic mulches are widely used in greenhouses in northern Europe to conserve moisture, warm the soil, and prevent the growth of weeds. And for the future, experiments are in progress with the use of chequered plastic mulches to ward off aphids, with perforated film mulches which 'grow' with seedling crops, and even with mulches of brown and violet-coloured plastic. It certainly looks as if an ancient technique is adapting itself to modern materials.

Economic pressures have changed the face of the seed trade since this article was written, with seed production now concentrated in the hands of a few, very powerful, international companies. Happily, when it comes to the retail companies supplying gardeners, the number of small seed companies seems to be increasing, although some long-standing names have inevitably disappeared. Nothing changes the fact that seed is where it all starts, and for me, insights into how seed is grown and harvested, the people involved in the trade and the problems they face have provided some of my happiest horticultural adventures.

One sour note: the 50p packet I thought exorbitant would be a cheap special offer today. Seed prices have risen outrageously.

BACKGROUND TO VEGETABLE SEED PRODUCTION
The Garden, February 1979

The twentieth-century vegetable grower takes seeds completely for granted. We order them through catalogues or buy them over the counter, assured, in 99 cases out of a 100, of getting a packet of clean, reliable seeds which will germinate well. In the plethora of vegetable books on the market today, I doubt if there is so much as a paragraph of practical information on how to save your own seed: it is no longer necessary and has become a lost art.

But for previous generations of gardeners knowledge of how to save seed was of fundamental importance, and was much emphasized in the old gardening books. The earliest known manuscript on gardening in this country – Jon Gardener's poem, written in c.1440 – devotes many lines to seed saving. With onions, for example, you're told to sow them in April or March, to support the tall heads with forks made of ash, and to harvest the seed when it is showing black:

They wul be rype at the full
At lammasse of Peter Apostull.

John Parkinson, in his famous *Paradisi in Sole Paradisus Terrestris*, written in 1629, states firmly that the best gardeners save their own seed. He devotes a whole chapter to the subject of growing vegetable seed, and it is full of sensible advice, for example not selecting the carrots which have bolted in their first season. He also comments on how some seed is best imported (as was the fashion at the time) but how in other cases English seed was the best, and he cites radish, lettuce, carrots, turnips, cabbage and leeks. How surprised he would be if he knew the extent to which our seed now comes from all quarters of the globe!

For the business of growing seeds today could well be described as the world's most international cottage industry. Our seed catalogues this spring will list bean seed from the mountains of Africa; peas from the plains of Hungary; herbs from tiny cypress-sheltered fields in Provence; carrots from the Loire valley; onion, lettuce, cauliflower and tomato from peasant plots in eastern Italy or the San Joaquim Valley of California; cabbage from Denmark; melons from the Imperial Valley of California or the Puglia region of Italy or even the Rhône valley in France; and F_1 hybrid seed from sites as diverse as greenhouses in Holland and Japan, Indonesia or Taiwan; and perhaps only brassicas such as kale and cabbage, or cress seed, will have come from our own East Anglia.

The very steep increases in the price of seed in recent years – one can easily pay between 20 and 50p for a small packet of vegetable seed – have made us far more aware of the value of seed. In the 'old days', three or four years ago, the value for money represented by a small seed packet was indisputable; at today's prices it is less self-evident. Yet when one looks at the problems the seed growers face, the stringent measures taken to obtain seed of the high quality we now expect, the cost of the long-term breeding programmes behind the new varieties, and the expensive techniques needed to produce, for example, F_1 hybrid seed, one is less inclined to grudge the outlay.

Growing seed is what the French would call a 'delicate' business – subject to many variables. In any one year seed can vary enormously in quality, from total failure (those depressing crop failure entries in the catalogues) to the production of a bumper crop of plump, sound, disease-free seed with high germination. Weather, harvesting and

A flourishing seed crop of the famous 'De Barletta' pickling onion being grown for the De Corato seed company in Andria, Italy.

storage are the three factors which determine the quality of seed and of these, weather is probably the most important. In a poor year there are 4,000 onion seeds in an ounce: in a good year a mere 3,000.

With a few exceptions, the main requirements for the majority of seed crops are a moist warm spring in which the plant will make healthy growth, and for assured dry and warm weather for the period in which the seed is maturing, drying and being harvested – with high enough temperatures to kill off the fungus diseases which can blight a seed crop, or infect the seed and cause seed-borne disease. For many species, the ideal environment for producing seed would be an irrigated desert: the Mediterranean climate, with its rainless summers, is also very suitable. There's no corner on earth where weather conditions can be guaranteed, but in general seed production is concentrated in those areas where the basic climatic requirements are met and the weather is normally reliable.

One reason for the high price of seed is the labour-intensive nature of seed production. While seed of brassicas, peas, beans and various other crops is now usually cut and harvested mechanically, so lowering costs, there are still crops which, to obtain quality seed, have to be cut and harvested by hand: onions, leeks and cauliflower among them.

Another time-consuming and labour-intensive aspect of seed production is 'roguing', walking through a seed crop at various stages and pulling out any plants which are poor, diseased or not true to type, so that they won't set seed and lower the standard of the harvest. A cauliflower seed crop, to be sure of a good end product, should be rogued three times while it is growing.

Seed growing is a highly skilled business in many ways, but probably one of the most testing aspects is judging the right moment to harvest. If harvested too soon the seed may be immature, lightweight and germination poor;

leave it too long and it starts to spill on to the ground leading to wastage. Growers judge the readiness of their crop by plucking off seed pods and rubbing the seed in their hands, by the colour of the crop, even by the presence of birds such as linnets feeding on the seed. Often the actual harvesting is done early in the morning, when the seed is less likely to burst out of the seed capsule and be lost.

Because of the skills involved, seed growing has traditionally been a family business, with one family specializing in perhaps two or three crops, the expertise being passed on from one generation to another. The problem facing seedsmen today, as labour costs rocket in the traditional seed-growing areas in France, Holland, other parts of Europe and the United States, is to find the rare combination of the right climate for seed growing, coupled with the necessary skills, in areas where labour costs are still low. The search for alternative areas continues, but the fact remains that today, as for the last twenty years, three-quarters of the seed used by the Western world is grown in the United States, Italy and France. Great Britain, interestingly, is the largest importer of that seed.

Left to its own devices any stock of seed will deteriorate and provide progressively poorer crops. The onus for ensuring that the quality of modern seed is maintained lies with the major seed houses, the most important being in Holland, France and the United States. The seed houses maintain a nucleus of basic or mother stock seed for each of their varieties, and it is this seed which they send out to their contract growers all over the world, to multiply up for bulk sale.

The basic stock itself is frequently grown on the seed company's premises, or near at hand, quite often in greenhouses or plastic tunnels where the conditions can be carefully controlled. It is frequently inspected, and any plants below standard rigorously eliminated. It is then carefully harvested by hand. After harvesting, as the storage life of seed is affected by its moisture level, the stock seed is immediately dried to the optimum moisture level for the species, before being stored in moisture-proof containers, at low temperatures, to prevent deterioration.

With biennials such as onions and carrots, the seed is sown in the normal way in spring, on 'home territory', then in late summer or autumn the onions and carrots are lifted, the best selected, and these roots and bulbs shipped to the contract growers for growing on for seed the following year.

Growers of seed crops face several problems which are unique. One of these is the need to grow seed in relative isolation. If two different varieties of seed of the same species, two varieties of cabbage for example, are grown close together, there is always a risk of cross-pollination and therefore contamination. Similarly closely related species, such as kale and cabbage, can cross-pollinate. In areas where seed growing is concentrated this constitutes a problem and neighbouring growers have to get together to avoid clashing. In East Anglia the Essex Seed Zoning Committee co-ordinates the siting of brassica seed crops to prevent possible disasters.

Seed growers also have to be very careful about rotating their crops. When a seed crop is harvested, seed inevitably falls to the ground, and could well remain in the soil for a number of years, maybe germinating five or six years later and contaminating a future seed crop. Such things explain the occasional appearance say, of a few red round radishes in a packet of long white radishes!

East Anglia provides another example of the kind of hazards which can face seed growers, in this case due to the increasing acreages down to the relatively new crop of oil seed rape. Oilseed rape is very susceptible to the seed-borne disease known as blackleg, which spreads to brassica seed crops in the area, affecting seedlings, and also affecting the seed itself – so creating a double problem. Moreover, a lot of rape seed spills out of the lorries when it is transported to the presses (as bright yellow patches of flowering rape at roundabouts testify) and the volunteer plants which result are not only disease carriers but are liable to cross-pollinate with brassica seed crops in the vicinity, so contaminating the seed crops.

So high is the intrinsic value of any one field of a seed crop, and so vulnerable is it to disaster – anything from a freak hail storm just before harvest to contamination from another crop – that individual growers and seed firms hedge their bets; growers by having a small plot of a variety here and another there, while the seedsmen, whenever possible, grow some in one country and some in another.

A 'special case' in the seed world is F_1 hybrid seed, always the most expensive in the catalogue, but nevertheless accounting for a higher proportion of seed sales every year. F_1 hybrids are produced by plant breeders selecting two promising lines of a species, inbreeding (i.e. self-pollinating) each line for several generations until a pure inbred line is produced, and then crossing the resulting pure lines with each other to produce the F_1 hybrid. Such hybrids are exceptionally vigorous and useful plants, but to obtain the seed, the cross between the inbred parents has to be re-made every time. Seed saved from an F_1 hybrid would, generally speaking, produce a motley collection of valueless plants.

The first stage in producing F_1 hybrid seed is therefore to maintain the parent lines, and very frequently, partly as a result of their being inbred, they are most reluctant to set seed. To overcome this problem they are sometimes propagated vegetatively by cuttings; or

techniques such as bud pollination may be used, the flower being more fertile while still in bud. This has to be done by hand.

Once one has the parent lines, further problems may arise in making the actual crosses to get the hybrid seed. In some cases the two parent lines can be allowed to cross freely in the open field; in others, to get the required hybrid, one line has to act as father and the other as mother, so the mother line has to be castrated by removing the anthers – again by hand. (In some species naturally occurring 'male sterile' lines, i.e. forms without the male parts in the flowers, have been found; this simplifies the process enormously.) Even when the F_1 seed is obtained, yields tend to be much lower than with open-pollinated varieties. All of which goes to explain the very high cost of F_1 hybrid seed.

After harvesting and drying, the seed has to be cleaned – a vital process if good seed is to be obtained. Much seed cleaning today is done with highly automated, electrically and electronically operated equipment. The underlying techniques are much the same as have been used for centuries, based on a series of sieves of different dimensions, shaken by hand in the old days, vibrated mechanically today. With these sieves the seed is separated initially from the relatively large material such as leaves, bits of broken stalk, stones and earth – and then from progressively smaller material, using smaller sieves, until finally it is separated from tiny particles of dust and dirt which are blown away. For centuries a centrifugal device, a spiral with a toboggan-like surface, has been used to separate round seed from misshapen seed. Some seed requires special treatment: barbs have to be removed from carrot seed, the hard outer seed coat from beet, and the fuzz from tomatoes. Spinach seed is cleaned in three different machines, the last of which separates round seed from prickly seed.

The major seed companies are continually carrying out tests on the samples of seed which they have obtained from their contracted growers, to see how they perform both in the field and in the laboratory. In most cases samples are sown in the trial grounds the spring after they are received (the bulk of seed crops being harvested in summer); but in some cases, to get quicker results, seeds are tried out in greenhouses in winter with artificial heating and light.

The laboratory tests on seed samples assess their germination, their cleanliness, their purity (i.e. freedom from weed seed and trueness to type) and, where necessary, their freedom from seed-borne disease. Tomato seed, for example, is tested for tomato mosaic virus by inoculating the leaves of a tobacco plant with an inoculum from the seed: symptoms of disease show up relatively fast on tobacco. Similarly seed-borne virus diseases in lettuces are tested for by using chenopodiaceous weeds as the indicator plants. Tests for anthracnose are carried out on peas and haricot beans.

To ensure that seed remains top quality for as long as possible, it is stored in air-conditioned warehouses, with carefully controlled humidity and temperature. The warehouse floor may even be plastic coated to prevent condensation. Many firms today pack their seed in special air-sealed foil packs, which are an additional insurance against deterioration until the pack is opened.

These are some of the steps taken to maintain the high quality of seed we take for granted. And because seed is now so expensive, perhaps a final word on how to keep it, once purchased, would not come amiss. As already mentioned, seed keeps best in cool dry conditions – the cooler and drier the better. A simple way of storing seed at home is to keep it in something like an airtight biscuit tin, with a bag of silica gel in the bottom, stored in a cool dry room. Unopened packets of seed can even be stored successfully in a refrigerator or deep freeze. Countless germination failures, I am sure, can be traced to seed being kept, at one extreme, in a 'handy place' such as the kitchen or the mantelpiece above the sitting-room fire, or at the other, in a damp garden shed. Even a short exposure to dampness can substantially lower the viability of seed.

Sacks of seakale seed heads and stalks drying in the polytunnel at Kings Seeds in Essex, prior to being cleaned. Kings was probably the only UK company growing seakale for seed at the time.

Fabulous flavour, beautiful looks: no wonder globe artichokes have stolen a place in my horticultural heart. They command strategic points in the fan potager we have established in Ireland, appearing to love the maritime climate and be oblivious to the salt-laden wind, although I've had to modify that view: several succumbed completely in the more recent, severe winters, with the survivors only making slow recoveries. It's the same with their giant relative, cardoons, that most architectural of vegetables. I'm still convinced cardoons are considerably hardier than globe artichokes, but twice now, in the UK and Ireland, we have lost magnificent mature specimens to exceptionally high winds in storms.

It was globe artichokes, specifically the Bari University Cynar Research Station – probably the largest collection of globe artichokes in the world – which enticed us to Bari on the Italian Adriatic coast during our Vegetable Tour. They called Bari 'the city of thieves' (there were quite a few 'cities of thieves' in Italy at the time), but our stay was memorable for an exceptional taste of Italian hospitality, gorgeous food and an insight into the cultural and horticultural diversity of the area. In a city that was constantly invaded over the centuries, the Viking legacy is seen in the many fair-haired, even red-haired people, while in the mountains behind the coastal plain there were village enclaves where Spanish, Greek and Turkish – often in ancient forms – were still the predominant languages.

We parked on university property, in the shadow of a beautiful house where Mussolini had once stayed, then being restored for university seminars. Only with the most dedicated persistence on the part of caretaker Rosario did we squeeze our van and caravan through the curved paths between the low-walled flower beds. His jovial family took us under their wing – insisting we share barbecues and fabulous salads, bringing real coffee to the caravan for breakfast, hot showers, the loan of a steam iron, spoiling the children as only Italians can . . . And I had a wonderful evening, sitting on one of those flower-bed walls, while Grandpa demonstrated the full range of Italian gestures – pulling down the corner of one eye, boring an imaginary hole in the cheek with a forefinger, clenching one wrist with the other . . . I even took photos. I'll write a book on facial gestures one day, I thought, but of course I never did. It's in the pending file, along with a book on street food.

Professor Bianco of Bari University, one of Italy's three 'vegetable' professors at the time, was a mine of information on all the edible wild and cultivated plants in this exceptionally dry area. (They hadn't had any rain for nearly five months.) That was where I first came across *carosello*, a local cucumber-like melon adapted to dry climates. We sent seeds to the Vegetable Gene Bank, and maybe it will come into its own with global warming. It has appeared recently in UK seed catalogues, and you can even Google it. It seems to be known, appropriately enough, as 'Carosello Barese'.

The Bari Research Station was indeed unique: I had no idea artichokes had such potential for food, drink, medicine and fodder. But we also remember it for an exceptional lunch of local specialities cooked by the station caretaker's wife. Afterwards I was writing down some of her recipes with help in translation from the young horticulturist accompanying us, when her husband burst in, hysterically grabbed a gun from the bedroom, and tore out again. The large snake he was after got away!

··

GLOBE ARTICHOKES - AND CARDOONS
The Garden, March 1979

The globe artichoke (*Cynara cardunculus* Scolymus Group) is indisputably one of the aristocrats of the kitchen garden: handsome, of ancient lineage and a delicacy to eat. It originated in Ethiopia, and was extensively cultivated by the Arabs, the Greeks and the Romans, who were probably the first to introduce it into Britain. But like various other of the good things of life, it seems to have disappeared from our shores during the Dark Ages, and was probably only re-introduced to England from Italy in Tudor times. The gastronomically minded Henry VIII did much to establish its popularity with his renowned 'hartichoake' garden. It was then, and always has been, a rich man's vegetable.

The artichoke is almost unique amongst vegetables in that, in the main, it is the flower buds that are eaten, specifically the small fleshy pad lurking at the base of the flower bracts, and most delectable of all, the succulent receptacle, known in culinary circles as the heart, the *fond* or more prosaically, the bottom. It is less generally known that the root and peeled stems are also edible, and that the leaves can be blanched and eaten as chards. Moreover, for centuries an infusion made from the dried and fresh leaves has been used in medicine (for liver complaints), while in more recent times the dry leaves have been the source of the popular Italian aperitif Cynar. The leaves are also used for fodder, particularly for feeding hens. Today, at the Cynar Research Station in Bari in southern Italy where over 100 varieties of artichokes are being grown, research is carried out into the

Globe artichokes have stolen a place in my horticultural heart.

medicinal, alcoholic and culinary properties of the plant.

The Italians can still claim the closest association with globe artichokes, two-thirds of the world's artichokes being grown in Italy, mainly in Campania. It was originally introduced into Sicily by the Arabs, and now countless different varieties bear the names of Italian towns. The French have also long appreciated the delights of artichokes, generally growing the larger-headed, summer-maturing varieties, while the warmer Italian climate is more suited to spring- and winter-producing varieties.

Artichokes display a tremendous variation: in colour, from rose violet to green to near white: in form, from pointed to round; and in height, from fairly broad squat forms to very branched forms well over 1.2m/4ft high. The shape and prickliness of the scaly bracts also vary enormously. Today it is thought that the cardoon is the same species, merely a form in which the leaf stalks and leaf midribs have developed rather than the bracts and receptacle. Cardoons are more vigorous than artichokes, often attaining heights of over 1.8m/5–6ft or more, making stately architectural plants with their striking greyish green foliage.

Artichokes can be propagated in a number of ways: seed, suckers or offsets, division of old plants and root cuttings. For English conditions the most satisfactory method is by offsets. The drawback with seeds is that seedlings are very variable, and it is impossible to spot the good plants until they are flowering. But seed is the cheapest way of obtaining artichoke plants, so where it is used it is best sown in heat in February (or in the open in March), pricked off singly into pots, hardened off (if necessary) in May, and then planted out *in situ*. A few artichokes should be produced in the first season. Some of the plants will be good, the rest poor: propagate from the best,

to build up a good stock. It is probably best to start by buying plants of good stock. 'Gros Vert de Lâon', a fairly hardy, pointed-headed variety, is frequently recommended for the quality of the artichokes.

For artichokes to flourish, rather than merely exist in an unproductive state, as is so often the case, they must have fertile, well-drained soil which will not dry out. The roots must be kept moist during the summer. The site selected should be open, but if possible protected from strong winds. Artichokes will repay the effort taken to prepare the ground by digging in well-rotted farmyard manure.

Plants or offsets should be planted out in spring, any time from February to April depending on the area, ideally about 1m/3ft apart to give them plenty of room. Remember they will occupy the ground for at least three years. In the early months the space between the plants can be used for intercropping lettuce, radish, onions, dwarf French beans, etc. After planting, mulch with well-rotted compost or similar material as a means of preserving the moisture. A few artichokes should be produced by late summer, although the main crop will be borne in the following and third year. Artichokes require very little cultivation other than weeding and watering well in dry weather. They will benefit from occasional feeding with liquid manure, and if many suckers are thrown up around the base of the plant, they should be thinned out to a maximum of five.

Artichokes are not totally hardy, though they are probably hardier than is imagined provided they are in well-drained soil. However, before the onset of winter, I usually cut off any remaining immature flower stalks and cover the plants with a protective layer of bracken. William Robinson, at the turn of the century, suggested that in the south of the British Isles earthing up was sufficient protection, while in the north and midlands, plants should be protected with litter or leaves. It is important to uncover the plants on warm days, or when warm weather returns, or the protective covering is liable to cause the crowns to rot.

If well looked after, with careful removal of excess suckers and good feeding and watering, artichoke plants can continue cropping usefully for up to five years. However, it is generally felt best to discard plants after their third year, enthusiasts renewing one-third of their plantation annually, planting offsets selected from the best plants. This is generally done in February or May, choosing offsets from around the base of the plant that are between 15 and 23cm/6 and 9in high. Scrape away the earth from the base of the plant and, with a sharp-bladed trowel or knife, slice down between the offset and parent plant, bruising the parent as little as possible, and being sure to get some root on the offset. Trim off the jagged edges, and plant the offsets shallowly but firmly in their permanent position, watering them well, mulching, and protecting from cold winds and extreme sunshine until established. If a second crop of offsets is taken in May, a succession can be established.

With care, the artichoke season can be made to last six months. The established overwintered plants come in first, generally in May and June. They will be followed, in July and August, by strong March-planted suckers. A May planting of suckers gives a crop in late summer and autumn. In addition a few suckers can be taken in November, potted up and overwintered in frames or a greenhouse for extra early plants. Another old trick to obtain a late flush is to cut back some of the old plants in early spring, and occasionally during the year. This will encourage them to make a thicket of shoots, but if these are thinned out, they will give a succession of nice young heads.

The problem with a long-established planting of mature artichokes is that they all tend to come into flowering at the same time.

Judging the precise moment to harvest artichokes is an art that is learned by experience. The heads are ready when plump, when the scales are still soft, just before they start to open. The main heads, which are the largest and best, are cut first, leaving the secondary heads on the laterals to mature later. (If only very large heads are wanted, the lateral 'buds' can be removed when no more than 2.5cm/1in in diameter.) Cut the artichokes with a knife or secateurs with a generous piece of stem, which can be very tender. Cut off the rest of the flower stalk at ground level if there are no laterals on it. Rather than leaving surplus heads on a plant too long, they can be cut off with long stalks and kept in water in a cool place for a few weeks until required. Old gardening books also recommend preserving the heads and stalks in sand.

When the commercial crop of artichokes is harvested in Italy the heads are cut with a piece of leaf, because they 'look prettier that way'. They are then loaded on to a special horse-drawn cart, with a sledge-like base rather than wheels, to make it easier to pass through the narrow rows between the spiky plants. The man leading the horse wisely wears thigh-high boots to protect his legs.

On average one can expect about five heads a year from one plant, although they get smaller and smaller as the season advances. Very productive plants in Italy yield up to fifteen heads a year. The Italians waste nothing where artichokes are concerned, and have recipes for all sizes and stages of artichoke, from tiny babies to the largest grandads of all. The spiky Sardinian artichokes are eaten raw dipped in oil and butter; artichokes are also baked, stuffed, boiled, made into pies, omelettes, casseroles, salads and soups, while the hearts are pickled or preserved in oil.

Growing artichoke chards is a practice which has fallen into disuse, but seems a useful way of getting a final crop from old plants before discarding them. Some time after flowering (recommendations vary from between July and October) cut down the old plants to within 30cm/1ft of the ground. Keep them well watered and mulched, and when the crop of new shoots has grown to about 60cm/2ft in height, tie them together and blanch them like celery, either by earthing them up, or by wrapping them with black polythene, brown paper, straw, etc. The blanching takes between five and six weeks. The shoots should be cut off before severe weather, and can be kept packed in sand in a dry cellar for use during winter, cooking them like cardoons.

And now for a few words about the cardoon (*Cynara cardunculus*), a vegetable which has never caught on here, but is very highly rated by the French for the delicacy of its flavour. As long ago as the early seventeenth century John Tradescant was telling John Parkinson how he had seen 3 acres of cardoons growing around Brussels, which were 'whiteth like endive' for selling in winter. But Parkinson added, 'We cannot yet find the true manner of dressing them that our country may take delight therein' – and I feel the same holds true today.

Raising cardoons is no problem. They come true from seed, the easiest method being to sow small groups of three seeds about 1m/3ft apart, in very well-prepared soil, eventually thinning to one per station. Like artichokes, they need very rich, well-drained soil, with plenty of moisture, so that they can be grown without any check. The French used to make special trenches for cardoons, partly filled with well-rotted manure. As with artichokes, the plants can be intercropped when young.

In autumn the thick stems and midribs are blanched, and it is most important to blanch them thoroughly or the delicacy of the flavour is lost. There are numerous methods. It is best done on a fine day when the plants and soil are dry. The usual method is to draw the leaves into an upright position, and tie them up. The base of the plant is then earthed up, and the main stalks tied with black polythene, matting, newspaper or brown paper leaving only the tips of the leaves exposed. They should be ready after three weeks, and if left much longer, are liable to start rotting.

A French hotelier told me how he lifts his cardoons in October – the plants often put on a late summer spurt and are then of enormous dimensions – and plants them in his cellar, along with the endive, chicory and coal, to blanch naturally in the darkness.

Another method was related to me at great length by an old man in Provence, leaning on his lissade as the moon rose over Les Alpilles. Having sown his seed in June, four to five weeks before Christmas he would make a trench in the soil alongside the plant, and very carefully, bend down the stems, covering them with wheat or oat straw and then soil. These specially prepared cardoons (he did some others in the traditional way) would be eaten raw, at midnight, on Christmas Eve – in anchovy sauce made with pepper, mustard and anchovies. His brother-in-law, he said, lifted his plants whole and buried them in sand, so getting cardoons that were 'as white as snow', and without a trace of rotting, a hazard when blanched in soil. Apart from eating their cardoons raw on Christmas Eve, the family ate them blanched with vinaigrette or a bechamel sauce, or made into fritters, or cooked in the oven with a cheese sauce.

When preparing cardoons for cooking it is important to discard all the tough outer leaves, and to remove any stringy threads from the midribs. They are cut into pieces about 8cm/3in

The magnificent spectacle of cardoons grown for seed, at Ansaloni's nursery in Italy. On the Continent they are prized for their culinary and medicinal uses, as well as their decorative qualities.

long, and cooked either in a court-bouillon, or in a *blanc* made by mixing flour with water, to prevent discoloration. The water is brought to the boil, salt added, and the cardoon cooked in it until tender and then served with a sauce such as bechamel.

Cardoon heads are much smaller and spikier than artichokes, but can be used in soups. Textbooks say that cardoon is not hardy and needs winter protection. In my experience this is not true. The plant I preserved from my only attempt to grow cardoons ten years ago (it was so beautiful I couldn't bear to discard it) has come through ten East Anglian winters, several fairly severe, with no protection and no hardship.

Both cardoons and artichokes are sought after by flower arrangers, for the beauty of the young thistle heads and for the flowers. Perhaps I may be forgiven for quoting from Parkinson again, whose description of an artichoke flower could hardly be bettered: '. . . and after the head had stood a while, if it bee suffered, and the Summer prove hot and kindly, in some there will breake forth at the toppe thereof, a tuft of blewish purple thrume or threds, under which grow the seede, wrapped in a great deal of downie substance . . .'

For ornamental purposes, the heads are best picked when the flower is just forming and hung up to dry; otherwise the colour is lost. They will continue to open up, a fascinating sight, when off the plant.

I have to include something about pumpkins. They give me more pure, visual, pleasure than almost any other vegetable. I can't wait, each year, to see their large expansive leaves, damp with dew in the morning; then the huge flowers being busily worked by bees; and by the end of the summer, the plants taking over the arches which link my new raised beds. So there will be pumpkins dangling overhead, pumpkins clinging to the wire halfway up and pumpkins drooping over the sides of the beds. Every year I devote a precious raised bed to them, interplanting them with sweetcorn. It's a fabulous combination, with the corn silks shimmering above the pumpkin plants in mid-summer. Having less space than in the past I grow only one variety, the smallish, grey-skinned F_1 'Crown Prince'. These are exceptionally dense pumpkins, with deep orange, dry flesh and an excellent flavour. They keep until June. Our culinary repertoire has increased in leaps and bounds since moving to Ireland, thanks to Denis Cotter's renowned vegetarian restaurant Cafe Paradiso, in Cork city, and the inspiring recipes in his books.

I'm happy to say that pumpkins are no longer a neglected vegetable. Everybody loves them now.

A NEGLECTED VEGETABLE
The Garden, May 1979

For me, 1978 was the Year of the Pumpkin — the year I learned to love and appreciate this mocked and misused vegetable. Not only did my pumpkins grow vigorously and decoratively in the summer months when much else failed, but they provided many of the bright spots of our cuisine during the bleak winter which followed. With the garden still suffering from the setback of a year's absence and neglect, our normal supply of winter greens and roots had fallen short. But what compensations there have been in tasty and filling pumpkin soup, in spiced pumpkin pie, in roasted pumpkin seeds by the fireside of an evening and in pumpkin pickle as a substitute for mango chutney. The surplus pumpkins were in great demand for Hallowe'en — though how I begrudge the desecration and waste of those beautiful mature gourds in the name of festivity.

Unlike most of my vegetable obsessions, I can date the precise moment at which I fell in love with pumpkins, and vowed I would grow more pumpkins, different kinds of pumpkins, and learn to use them. It was in the Potager du Roi at Versailles, the huge kitchen garden adjoining the Palace of Versailles which De La Quintinie created for Louis XIV in 1678, today both a French national monument and a horticultural college. It was a fresh day in October and time to harvest the pumpkins. Waggonloads of huge, ribbed, deep orange-red pumpkins were being cut, carted, and stacked outside the cellars before being stored for winter. It was a magnificent sight. I discovered they were 'Rouge Vif d'Etampes', one of the leading varieties on the Paris markets a century ago.

As a result of this encounter, the two main varieties I grew last year were French — 'Rouge Vif d'Etampes', and 'Galeuse d'Eysines', paler, rounder, but equally picturesque, with its grey, barnacle-like encrustations on the skin — aptly known also as the warted marrow squash.

Recently harvested 'Rouge Vif d'Etampes' pumpkins in the Potager du Roi in Versailles, the place where my love affair with pumpkins began.

Pumpkins are varieties of *Cucurbita maxima*, members of the large cucurbit family, and generally believed to have originated on the American continent. In central and south America they have been cultivated for many thousands of years. In China they've been grown for nearly 1,000 years, though, with characteristic Chinese wisdom, primarily for the seeds, which are rich in protein and oil. (Although a marvellous base for dishes, the flesh of pumpkin is of little value nutritionally, especially in older varieties, being 95 per cent water.) Pumpkins were apparently unknown in England until the sixteenth century, when they were introduced from North America. Winter squashes, as they are known in the United States, have always been an important vegetable there, particularly for storage in harsh winter conditions.

The name pumpkin has been modified over the years – pompions, pumpions, pompons and, as late as 1871 in a Carter's seed catalogue, pompkin. In England the most widely grown variety has always been 'Mammoth' (syn. 'Hundredweight'), though there are many more which could be cultivated. Over fifteen varieties were listed in Vilmorin-Andrieux's *Vegetable Garden* of 1885. These ranged from the curious double-decker turk's cap or turban gourd (still grown in France), the well-known American 'Hubbard' squash (one of the best for storage), white, grey and green pumpkins and the flattened 'Chestnut' squash to the lemon-shaped 'Valparaiso'. The 'Blue Hubbard' pumpkin, a traditional favourite around Boston and now much grown in Australia, with bluish green outer skin and yellow flesh, has matured successfully in this country and is said to be excellent. Excellent too are what are becoming known as Japanese pumpkins or *kabocha*. These are very variable, but tend to be smallish, sometimes onion-shaped, with firm flesh and good storage qualities.

Opposite ends of the pumpkin spectrum. Left: our first crop of 'Rouge Vif', drying off at Montrose Farm. Right: the miniature, 'one helping' 'Munchkin', which I found in the USA several years later.

Pumpkins are no harder to grow than ordinary marrows, and require much the same treatment. Their principal requirements are sun, as long a growing season as possible, fertile soil and plenty of water – especially if you are aiming for prize-winning giants.

Most pumpkins are trailing in habit, though a few are bush types. So they require a fair amount of space, unless one is prepared to go to the trouble of training the growths in a circle around the plant. They will also clamber over a framework, provided it is strong enough to bear the weight of the plant.

The ground should be well prepared by digging a hole about 45cm/1½ft deep and wide, filling it to within a few inches of the surface with rich compost or well-rotted manure, and covering with about 15cm/6in of soil. If this is done, relatively little extra feeding will be required unless, again, one is aiming to produce a giant. Like any moisture-loving crop, mulching is worthwhile once the plants are well established.

Last year I sowed the seed in peat blocks on 4 May in gentle heat, hardened them off, and planted them out under plastic bell cloches on 29 May, between rows of early potatoes. The first pumpkin, a 35-pounder (15.8kg), was harvested on 20 September, and apart from having been mulched, the plants had little attention paid to them.

Sometimes problems are encountered in getting the fruit to set. If this is the case they can be hand pollinated by taking the male flower and dabbing the pollen on the stigma of the female flower, easily differentiated by the embryonic pumpkin seen at the base of the flower. In normal years, however, insects carry out the pollination quite satisfactorily.

In spring the flowers are sometimes attacked by grey mould (*Botrytis cinerea*), which may spread to the young fruits. In my experience plants usually grow out of this, but any infected flowers and fruits should be removed, as well as any surplus foliage, to ensure good air circulation around the plant.

In general one only needs two or three fruits per plant, so in late summer any remaining flowers or small developing fruits can be removed. Once the fruits are swelling, the main shoots can be trimmed back to a couple of leaves beyond the fruits; surplus laterals can also be removed to concentrate the plant's energies on feeding the fruit it is carrying. Pumpkin stems are liable to root and where this occurs, they can be covered with a little soil to encourage rooting.

As the fruits mature, they can be turned gently from side to side, to 'tan' more easily. They can be left on the plants to mature until the skins feel hard, or the first frosts are imminent – though mature fruits will stand light frost. Cut them off with a piece of stalk attached, as this makes a useful handle. The fruit can be ripened off finally in a sunny spot against a wall for a week or so. For the winter they should be kept in a cool, dry, frost-free shed. If there is any risk of frost, give them extra protection with a layer of straw or matting. I say this with feeling, having lost my last and most beautiful 'Rouge Vif' to Jack Frost this last winter – in a huge airy barn.

Incidentally, never scorn those small pumpkins which fail to mature to full size. They are quite edible, and in some ways, being small, are more practical than large pumpkins. For one of the snags with pumpkins is that while a whole gourd will keep well – up to a year in some cases – once cut the exposed flesh goes mouldy rapidly. I usually solve the problem of disposing of a large pumpkin by deep freezing the raw or cooked pulp. The simplest means of cooking it is to bake sections of pumpkin in a moderate oven, shell side upwards, until it is soft. Then scrape the pulp away from the shell.

As already mentioned, the seeds are the most nutritious part of pumpkin, and it is a shame to throw them away. I once watched a lady selling slices of pumpkin in a French market: she carefully offered a few seeds to each customer – and most of them accepted. Seeds can be dried by spreading them out on newspaper, or if the pulp is adhering determinedly to the seed, put them in a tightly closed plastic bag in a warm place for a few days. This causes the pulp to ferment, and it is then easily washed away from the seed.

Select some of the healthiest, plumpest seeds for sowing another year. (Don't, of course, save seed from F_1 hybrids, which won't breed true.) Kept in cool dry conditions they should retain their viability for up to six years. The rest can be deep fried and salted (the pepitos of South America and pépites of France) or roasted or baked in a little oil, in a fairly hot oven, for about fifteen minutes. Pumpkin seeds can also be sprouted, but for this the varieties with hullless green seeds are best, such as 'Lady Godiva' and 'Triple Treat'.

Now for a few words on what can be done with pumpkins. Certainly one of the most original treatments is to stuff them. In the Argentine the stew *carbonada* is partly cooked and served inside a scooped-out pumpkin. John Parkinson, writing in the seventeenth century when pumpkins still had something of a novelty value, suggests filling them with pippins. As he put it: 'They use likewise to take out the inner substance with the seedes, and fill up the place with pippins, and having laid on the cover which they cut off from the top to take out the pulpe, they bake them together, and the poor of the city as well as the Country people doe eate thereof as of a dainty dish.' He also suggests fairly plain treatment: boiling in salted water, beef stock, or even milk, and then eating 'as it comes' or buttered.

Still on simple methods, pieces of pumpkin can be baked or roasted in the oven and eaten much like baked potatoes, perhaps with a little extra seasoning of nutmeg or pepper. The French make the pulp into fritters. A surprisingly good dessert is made by mixing semolina, previously cooked in milk, with boiled or steamed pumpkin. The two can be heated together for a short while in the oven before serving.

There are numerous recipes for pumpkin soup, and finally, there is pumpkin pie.

To most English minds pumpkin pie conjures up a rather soggy unappetizing substance, but a good American pumpkin pie is surely one of the best desserts, flavoured with cinnamon, ginger, cloves and a touch of brandy or rum, enriched by black treacle, brown sugar, and evaporated milk or cream.

It seems apt to end the chapter with this article, which gave a fair picture of how our nomadic year moulded our gardening in the next three decades. Some things, inevitably, have changed. For a start derris is no longer considered a 'safe' spray, but others – such as slug collecting at night – remain the same.

....

GROWING VEGETABLES THE EUROPEAN WAY
The Garden, December 1979

It is now two years since we returned from our nomadic year in Europe looking for old and new ideas on vegetable growing – an appropriate time, perhaps, to take stock of subsequent progress in our own kitchen garden. How quickly does a garden recover from a year's neglect? What peasant market gardening techniques have proved to be worth adopting? Which unusual vegetable species and varieties have crossed the Channel happily?

I'll start with the result of a year's neglect. The obvious effect, of course, is the growth of weeds: 1.8m/6ft high in the fruit cage; thistles, nettles, bindweed, docks, all previously under control, again in command; prolific crops of fat hen and other arable weeds, along with masses of self-sown brassica seedlings. In the satisfaction of clearing them away and starting to sow useful crops, we overlooked the seven years' seed they had bequeathed to the garden. I could hardly believe it that first spring as my carrots, onions and spring-sown crops were engulfed in a blanket of weeds which seemed to rise before my eyes. It would have been far better to have waited, allowed at least the first spring flush to germinate, and then to have started sowing – albeit rather later in the year than one would have wished.

The second effect of neglect was less immediately obvious: the loss of humus from the top few inches of soil. A heavy soil by nature, that first year it seemed to turn from winter mud to hard-baked clay in record time. One needs to be working in organic matter continuously to keep such soils workable.

We made two big changes on our return. First, we reorientated the kitchen garden, laying it out entirely in narrow beds. Second, we went organic.

The use of narrow beds, generally 1.2–1.5m/4–5ft wide or 'a man's reach', is one of the oldest systems of vegetable growing. It is still used all over the world in market gardens, and was universal in both market gardens and large private gardens in this country until the introduction of the horse-drawn hoe led to the practice of spacing rows farther apart. But seeing how intensively the modern Italian market gardeners work their narrow beds – broadcasting some crops, planting others close together – it seemed to me to offer many advantages to the amateur trying to get high yields from relatively small areas.

We made the beds here about 90cm/36in wide, separated by paths 30cm/12in wide. The yard bed width was chosen partly because it is an easy 'stretch', partly as a convenient width for covering with low polythene tunnels in winter, though for this purpose 75cm/2½ft would probably have been better. The paths are kept weed-free and dry by mulching with whatever material is available – currently sawdust, sadly plentiful as a result of Dutch elm disease. Experience has shown us that in a fairly large kitchen garden it is advisable to make every fourth or fifth path somewhat wider, to allow for the passage of wide wheelbarrows with bulky loads. The traditional narrow beds were frequently raised, partly to improve drainage. The drawback is that they dry out more rapidly in summer. Ours are flat, though in the course of time, through working organic matter into them, they will doubtless become slightly raised.

Generally speaking, they have worked extremely well. The following are the main advantages as I see them:

- *Accessibility.* In spring it is possible to work the beds from the paths, when the state of the soil is such that I would otherwise delay sowing or planting, or be forced to put boards on the soil to avoid treading it directly.
- *Preservation of soil structure.* The permanent paths make it unnecessary to tread on the cultivated ground for any operation. This avoids the compaction of the soil, which inevitably destroys its structure and so reduces yields.
- *Weed control.* By adopting equidistant spacing for virtually all crops (onions are one of the exceptions) the natural canopy formed by the crops is an effective means of keeping down weeds. Where necessary in the early stages of growth it is relatively easy to weed rapidly, though I try to mulch as soon as seedlings are through – both to preserve moisture and to prevent germination of weed seed.
- *Productivity.* I have no figures to compare the yields from the previous widely spaced rows with the spacing in the narrow beds, but certainly the impression is that we are getting far more from the equivalent area.
- *Rotation.* It is far easier to work out a rotation system for a small garden if it is divided into about a dozen narrow strips rather than three or four large beds.
- *Broadcasting crops.* Narrow beds lend themselves to broadcasting, which can be a most productive way of raising certain salad crops, kale and turnip tops for early spring greens.
- *Covering with low plastic tunnels.* This is the cheapest way of protecting winter and spring crops and narrow beds are easy to cover with low tunnels or cloches.

So, the narrow beds are here to stay.

The impetus for 'going organic' at this point was unashamedly commercial. We needed some income from the garden and, operating on a very small scale, it was essential to aim for a specialized market. The wholefood market was a suitable outlet. It tied in well with our 'philosophy' of gardening, as we had always tried to minimize the use of chemicals.

On the fertilizer front there was no problem. Having ample handy supplies of farmyard manure, spent mushroom compost and our own compost, I had rarely used 'artificials' other than for tomato feed in summer. This was easily replaced with a seaweed-based fertilizer.

As for pests, our principal problems, being a rural garden, have always been two- and four-legged rather than six-legged. And there are few chemical remedies for rabbits and birds. That first winter the rabbits stripped the garden of every vestige of green and we had no option but to go to the expense of wiring in the entire kitchen garden with low fencing.

Next down the scale of destruction were birds – not the large birds we had expected, but sparrows – devouring young beet, chard and chicory seedlings, destroying luscious young lettuce and making mature plants unsaleable. We had hoped the high windbreak netting we erected around much of the garden would deter them: not a bit. We hoped they would ease off in summer when surrounding fields offered more choice: but that was wishful thinking. So the garden is strung with plastic sacks with the edges cut into flapping fringes, single lines of strong black cotton are put over newly sown rows, glass bottles, which reflect light and seem to have a deterrent effect, are stuck into the ground, and young plants are covered wherever possible with netting laid over hoops.

Our other major pest is slugs, appearing in droves from nowhere when a particularly appealing crop such as celery, lettuce, Chinese cabbage or young brassicas is planted. Orthodox pellets were taboo, approved 'organic' slug killers prohibitively expensive to use on any scale, so we resorted to old-fashioned baits and traps – saucers of beer, jars of salt water with bran on top sunk into the earth . . . But the catch of beneficial beetles seemed to be as high as that of slugs (quite contrary to the spirit of the thing, we felt), so we have concluded that the only effective way of reducing the slug population is to go out with a torch at night, hunt around the vulnerable crop, and to collect and kill them. If done over the course of several nights, this simple method reduces damage appreciably.

For other pests we pick off caterpillars by hand, try to catch and squash aphid attacks at an early stage, and use the permitted sprays such as derris and pyrethrum, though admittedly less effective than modern insecticides. Losses have been lower than expected. It does seem that where no sprays are used, the natural predators play a larger part in pest control than would otherwise be possible.

For weed control one misses the use of chemical weedkillers in rough corners and on paths; but mulching, though taking time, energy and materials has provided the answer.

We have taken to very extensive mulching within the vegetable garden, becoming the scavenger beetles of the neighbourhood with our insatiable appetite for the straw farmers would burn, old rotten hay bales, unwanted sawdust and carpets for paths. Pots and window boxes are being mulched with stones, but I have still to experiment with stone mulching in greenhouses as we saw so widely practised in Spain. It seems such a promising method of preserving moisture during the day and giving out some heat during the night.

Besides adopting narrow beds, the main idea we brought back with us from Europe was that of broadcasting crops in small patches. On the Continent these are often cut young and used as seedlings and/or cut-and-come-again crops (cut several times in a season), or used to provide continuous supplies of herbs for the kitchen, e.g. parsley and chervil.

They have proved particularly successful here for early spring crops, both indoors in the polytunnel, when still too cold to sow outside, and later outdoors. Small patches of rocket (used both in salads and as cooked spring greens), and kale and broccoletti (an Italian brassica) were sown in an unheated plastic tunnel very early in March. They made rapid growth and went a long way towards filling the 'hungry gap', often providing several substantial cuts. Both indoors and outdoors, a spring-sown patch of cress gave remarkably good value, providing up to five cuts. Outdoors the 'Salad Bowl' types of lettuce have proved suitable for broadcasting to give a quick supply, as have various types of chicory.

One of the most interesting seedling crops has been the mixed salads, known as *mesclun* in France and *misticanza* in Italy. I made the first trial sowing of mixed seed in a plastic tunnel in March, when temperatures were still low. In this case rather too high a proportion of rocket germinated. The second sowing was made outdoors in May, and all through summer one small patch has provided continuous salading: broad and curled endive, corn salad, red, green and Catalogna chicories, cos and cutting lettuce, and rocket. There always seemed to be something coming on, while during the same period the majority of salad crops in the garden had gone to seed. Cuttings were made repeatedly from July to September, and look likely to continue into October.

Our travels made us aware of the value of intercropping – peasant gardens in Portugal and Italy being intercropped so intensively. Now I feel a twinge of guilt if there is too much unused space around, for example, brassicas when first

Utopia for the family: finding a field of red chicory right next to a campsite (seen in the background). While the kids enjoyed swings, slides and sand pits, we got our first insight into the intriguing world of chicory growing from this father and son.

planted. I try to use such space for small quick crops of radish. Sweetcorn has proved the ideal 'mother crop' for intercropping. It forms only light shade, and even when planted in blocks, can be undercropped with dwarf beans, salad crops and so on.

Among some of the unusual species and unfamiliar varieties which I have been trying out, one of the most successful 'novelties' has been claytonia, or winter purslane, which I first saw in Belgium. It has proved gratifyingly hardy and been most useful in winter and spring salads (see also page 30).

In spite of the climatic differences, many Italian vegetables seem to take to our conditions. I have been experimenting with the various chicories and now, in the light of further experience, recommend sowing the red chicories in late June or early July, and covering them with straw at the onset of cold weather. The leaves turn from green to red in winter, and the loose heads close to form tight hearts, not unlike a dwarf red cabbage. Although more bitter than lettuce, they can be shredded into a mixed salad or cooked – braising being a suitable method.

The squat green 'Grumolo Verde' chicory has become a great favourite, especially after seeing it struggle through the 1978/79 winter in a poor, weed-infested, waterlogged piece of ground, still to produce its fresh green rose-bud rosettes early in spring. I let them run to seed in early summer, partly as a precaution against failing to get more seed, partly as their tall blue flowering spikes are so spectacular. And in the meantime I learned that chicory flowers (also succory, the wild chicory) used to be pickled for winter. I can now vouchsafe that they do make a pleasant and unusual pickle, layered with sugar and covered with cider vinegar seasoned with mace.

Several Italian lettuces have proved superb: especially the frilled *riccio* (curly) 'Lollo', and the deep red 'gathering' lettuces, which need to be sown early in the year if they are not to run to seed. The leaves are a little coarse, but for me, the colour compensates.

The silver- and red-stemmed Italian chards have also been a success, robust, handsome, and especially useful as a protected winter crop, planted late in autumn, again to help fill the 'hungry gap' in spring.

'Grumolo Verde' chicory: a hardy little chicory from northern Italy. It makes its presence known early in spring whatever the weather, and has become a firm favourite in the lean months of winter to early spring.

Thoroughly deserving the title 'heritage vegetable', the picturesque 'Chioggia' beet earns its place in our kitchen gardens for its looks, flavour and ease of cultivation.

Also of interest has been the 'Chioggia' beetroot, from the region just south of Venice, said to be the only native European variety of beet. It is very variable, some beets being almost white, some pink, but all with very marked white rings. To my surprise the small samples we grew last year stored extremely well, while this year's module-raised plants have produced huge, superb beet.

From France there were also many successes: old varieties of pumpkins; the purple leek 'Bleu de Solaise' with its excellent flavour; the large knobbly 'Marmande' tomatoes; and the broad-leaved endives 'Cornet de Bordeaux' and 'Cornet d'Anjou', so useful for summer sowing for autumn and spring harvesting. Last year I planted 'Cornet de Bordeaux' in a plastic tunnel alongside several varieties of winter lettuce: while a great many of the lettuces succumbed during the winter, the endives boasted almost 100 per cent survival.

From further afield we tried Hungarian peppers, and liked best of all the picturesque bonnet or tomato-shaped, which ripened well even under English conditions. Less popular were the bush tomatoes bred for mechanical harvesting. They were certainly dwarf, prolific and uniform in fruiting . . . but where had the flavour gone?

The only real success story from Portugal was the broad-leaved parsley, which withstood a very different climate with great fortitude, producing very well-flavoured, deep green leaves. But there were many germination failures amongst the Portuguese samples; and so far I have failed to sow many of the exciting beans, the unusual pumpkins, the red peas and the many unusual cabbages which I brought back.

There are, sadly, many other seed samples I have still not found time to try: the Bari melon 'Carosello Barese', adapted to exceptionally dry conditions; the yellow, red and white orachs; Yugoslavian beans; black and brown radishes, edible lupins and types of lupin for green manure; the curious Belgian kale . . . and I have yet to try blanching cardoons. There is still time to try some of these things, but with others, the seed is losing its viability.

In the meantime the kitchen garden is a living autograph book. In every corner there is a plant to trigger a memory of people who helped us, a place we enjoyed, a happy occasion. And what a bonus from a kitchen garden!

Less than a year after returning from our European trip I was invited to help with the Victoria and Albert Museum's exhibition *The Garden: A Celebration of One Thousand Years of British Gardening*, on the Vegetable and Kitchen Garden section. Little did I guess where this would lead, and how the rich heritage of garden history would come alive to me as it never had before. It was Rosemary Verey, superb gardener and meticulous historian, who opened the door to the past, inviting me to her house to research in her unique collection of historic gardening books. She taught me so much (see also page 295).

I went on to spend countless hours closer to home, in the Cambridge University Botanic Garden library, with its treasure trove of historic garden books. How they spoilt me as I scribbled and typed away in the Reginald Cory Room, plying me with advice, tea, coffee, biscuits, sherry – though the sherry had to be forgone the day the police were checking the decanter for fingerprints after a Christmas break-in! I still remember the excitement of the rare books room at the British Museum, looking at the precious copy of a fifteenth-century cookery book with its list of salad herbs: carefully written five centuries ago, yet giving us ideas for the 'saladini' salad packs we were then growing and delivering to London. Historic research revealed so much that was relevant to our work, above all the detailed advice in John Evelyn's classic *Acetaria* (1699), and Batty Langley's *New Principles of Gardening* (1728) with its lists of plants for year-round salads, describing how he mixed the 'mild and insipid' with the 'hot and biting' – the lists and the mixing so resembling our salads and mustering methods.

Again and again I was bowled over by the beauty of these old books and, so often, their practicality. I can't resist a few quotations from master gardeners of the past which ring so true today:

'Above all be careful not to suffer weedes (especially Nettles, Dendelion, Groundsill and all downy plants) to run up to seeds; for they will in a moment infect the whole ground . . .'
John Evelyn, *Directions for the Gardiner at Says Court*

'As for quantity of Plot of ground to make a Suitable Garden . . . let me caution all, not to undertake more than can be well looked after . . . for a small Plot of ground well ordered, turns to greater advantage than a large one neglected . . .'
Leonard Meager, *The New Art of Gardening*, 1697

On 'the delightful prospect of a kitchen garden in the spring': 'here we see artichokes rising as it were from the dead; and there asparagus piercing the ground in a thousand places . . .'
Stephen Switzer, *The Practical Kitchen Gardiner*, 1727

'It is most miserable taste, to seek to poke away the kitchen garden, in order to get it out of sight. If well managed, nothing is more beautiful than the kitchen garden.'
William Cobbett, *The English Gardener*, 1845

'From first to last gardening in this country is a continuous conflict with difficulties.'
Shirley Hibberd *The Amateur's Kitchen Garden*, 1877

What insights, too, into the extraordinary lengths gardeners went to, over the centuries, to extend the seasons! In more recent times, what energy plantsmen and seedsmen put into acquiring new and improved varieties, illustrated in stunningly beautiful catalogues!

Working on the exhibition forged friendships. There was a great spirit of co-operation among those working on related topics, many eminent in their fields. It really was a privilege to rub shoulders with them and learn from them. At times we shared a sense of frustration. The pressure was almost unbearable and, we felt, the much needed direction was minimal. Most heartbreaking was the fact that, with late cuts made in the size of exhibits, much of the material we had assembled was never used. There were even murmurs of putting together a follow-up exhibition utilizing this discarded material, but it never happened.

And there was the little question of money. Yes, we were paid a modest fee, but this was a job you did for love, not money, and in the aftermath of our wanderings, the latter was in short supply in our household. When I tried to work out my hourly rate it came to pence per hour – not much even in 1979! Never good at negotiating money, I once tried to hint that the payment was inadequate. The reply was that the lovely lunches and dinners we were being invited to compensated. They *were* lovely dinners – I still have some intriguing addresses scribbled down on the backs of menus – but lovely dinners don't pay bills. Which is why I took my milk bill up to London for the final night before opening, intending to give it to Roy Strong, then Director of the V&A, as a little hint. It ended in 1s. 2d., which made a poignant point, I hoped! But he was in *such* a tizzy, desperately searching in a drawer for mislaid captions, that I hadn't the heart . . .

The experience made it all worthwhile. The article here was part of the catalogue which accompanied the exhibition. I hope it captures something of the vitality of our gardening forbears.

It only occurs to me now, re-reading it years later, to wonder if any of my Huguenot ancestors were responsible for introducing digging!

··

KITCHEN AND VEGETABLE GARDENS
From *The Garden: A Celebration of One Thousand Years of British Gardening*,
the book of the exhibition at the Victoria and Albert Museum, 23 May–26 August 1979

When Henry VIII's first wife, Catherine of Aragon, fancied a salad she had to despatch a messenger to Holland or Flanders to procure it, and that, I'm afraid, gives an accurate insight into the history of vegetable growing in this country. (Over 400 years later, in 1932, we find the government slapping a tax on lettuce to slow down imports from Holland!) In spite of an amenable climate and a deep-seated national interest in gardening we have almost always, apart from in a few exceptional periods, lagged behind our continental neighbours in the range of vegetables we grew and appreciated, and in knowing how to grow and, alas, cook them. Time and again the contemporary classics on vegetable growing have been translations – or cribs – of foreign works: Greek, Latin and Italian in the early days; Dutch and French in more recent times.

The Romans, during their invasion of these islands nearly 2,000 years ago, were the first beneficial foreign influence on our vegetable growing. Before their arrival the native Britons were probably eating mainly wild fruit, nuts and plants gathered from the countryside: their vegetables would have included pignuts, wild parsnips, seakale and celery, the leaves of chenopodium (good King Henry), docks and sorrel, and many other herbs. (The Druids were reputed to have been good botanists.)

The Romans were highly skilled gardeners, however, and no doubt introduced the art of cultivating the many vegetables they knew: cabbage, leeks, onions, garlic, globe artichokes, radish, broad beans, asparagus; lettuce and endive, to name but a few.

Horticultural records from these early centuries are extremely sparse. During the centuries of turmoil which followed the Roman withdrawal, successive invasions by Angles, Saxons, Jutes and Danes probably meant only a few of the Roman introductions remained in cultivation, or were sufficiently naturalized and acclimatized to survive on their own. Cabbage, leeks, beet, onions, parsley, radish and peas and beans for eating dried were likely survivors. The others were reintroduced centuries later.

During the Middle Ages it was the monasteries who kept alive the arts of gardening. Their main interest in plants was medicinal, though they grew a few vegetables for food. Records from monasteries at Ely and Norwich indicate that onions, garlic, peas for pottage or soup, leeks, beans and herbs such as parsley, mustard seed, hyssop and savory were all grown for the kitchen.

By the latter half of the fourteenth century England had become a more peaceful country and most small manors and farms had gardens and orchards. The poor were still eating wild plants, along with peascods (peapods), beans, chibols (spring onions) and chervil, but the rich fed mainly on meat and game. Vegetables (synonymous with herbs) were grown primarily for seasoning, stuffing, soups and salads.

We get a clear indication of this from a list of 'herbs' in a fifteenth-century cookbook. Many of them were wild plants, evidently brought into the almost fortified gardens for cultivation: borage, violets, dandelion, spinach, coleworts and alexanders for pottage; sorrel, pellitory, violets and mint for sauces; costmary and rosemary for 'cups'; tansy, endive and hyssop for distilling; violet flowers again, cresses, purslane, chickweed, primrose buds and borage flowers for salads; while roots used were parsnip, turnip, radish, carrots, galingale and the saffron crocus, which was widely cultivated for the spice obtained from the stigmas. Vegetables and flowers were grown together indiscriminately in these functional medieval gardens. Even the flowers were grown for practical purposes: medicinal, culinary or for distilling.

The earliest original English treatise on gardening dates from c.1440, the poem *The Feate of Gardening* by Jon Gardener. It gives practical advice on, for example, sowing 'worts' (cabbages or kales) to have a year-round succession, on growing onions for usage and for seed, and on preparing saffron beds. Of the ninety-seven 'herbs' he mentions, garlic, leek, lettuce, orach, turnip, radish, spinach and 'worts' are those we would consider vegetables today.

Thus we come to the sixteenth century, a century of progress, learning and travel – the Renaissance expressed itself in a revival of interest in vegetable growing throughout Europe. In the early days of Henry VIII's reign vegetables were still surprisingly little used and grown in England. Salads, carrots, turnips and even cabbages were imported when required. The King was responsible for the reintroduction into England, from Flanders and elsewhere on the Continent, of many of the 'Roman' vegetables: asparagus, melons, globe artichokes, tarragon, horseradish. The Tudors are also credited with reviving the culture of many vegetables which had fallen out of use, such as radishes, skirrets, parsnips, carrots, turnips and various salad 'herbs'.

The explorations during Elizabeth's reign, in the second half of the century, brought exciting introductions from the American continent, among which were French or kidney beans, sweet potato, 'our' potato, Jerusalem artichoke (known as the Canadian potato and destined to become very popular until people 'grew sick of it'), maize, American marrows and gourds and the tomato, which for many years was grown only for ornament and, like so many other plants, as an aphrodisiac.

From the 1540s onwards, new ideas and skills were brought into this country by the persecuted Huguenot refugees, many of whom were highly skilled market gardeners. They may even have introduced the practice of digging: William Lawson, writing in 1617, reported that gentlemen who had leased their land to refugees feared 'they would spoil the ground because they did use to dig it'. 'So ignorant were they of gardening in those days', he added scornfully.

Gradually the increased sophistication of Tudor gardens, with their arbours, galleries, knots, mounts, raised and railed beds, led to the banishment of 'herbs' from the main garden. As John Parkinson was to put it in 1629 in his famous *Paradisi in Sole Paradisus Terrestris*, 'your herbe garden should be on the one or other side of the house . . . for the different scents that arise from the herbs, as cabbages, onions etc. are scarce well pleasing to perfume the lodging of any house.'

Responsibility for this garden of 'herbs' rested with the housewife. Apart from growing basic vegetables, salads, herbs for soups and flavouring, she would also grow strewing and medicinal herbs, and have a stillroom in which to make medicinal potions and fancy 'waters'. Advice on these tasks is given in another gardening poem, Thomas Tusser's *A Hundreth Good Pointes of Husbandrie*, written in 1557. One stanza is on gathering beans:

Not rent off, but cut off ripe beane with
    a knife
For hindering stalke of hir vegetive life
So gather the lowest and leauing the top
Shall teach thee a trick for to double
    they crop.

Kitchen gardens have always been the slowest feature of the garden to change, which was probably just as well in the dizzy fashion-conscious seventeenth and eighteenth centuries. While the gardens of the great worked their way through the formal, then exaggerated French and Dutch styles of the 1600s, into the informal, then exaggerated landscape styles of the 1700s, slow but steady progress was maintained behind the kitchen garden walls – walls mercifully spared when Humphry Repton and 'Capability' Brown swept away other offending barriers.

The horticultural pace setters of the seventeenth and eighteenth centuries devoted their time and wealth to the cultivation of oranges, imported exotic 'greens', tulips and foreign fruit, but a steady stream of new vegetables was also being brought into cultivation: savoys and cauliflowers, runner beans and swedes, celeriac and seakale.

The layout and design of the kitchen garden never threw off the yoke of formality. Within the protecting outer walls, fences or hedges, beds were generally laid out symmetrically. In early Stuart times they were designed in imitations of complex knots and parterres; later the layout became simpler although some extraordinarily elaborate designs were conceived. However, it is safe to assume that the majority of kitchen gardens, in practice, were square or rectangular, with beds arranged in an orderly fashion within the overall design.

One's social status determined the size of one's kitchen garden; but by today's standards these seventeenth- and eighteenth-century gardens were magnificent. A nobleman's garden probably boasted a beautiful pavilion set in the south-facing wall, flanked by vinehouses and orangery.

Fruit of all kinds was grown against the kitchen garden walls. (By Georgian times many north walls were heated with flues.) The wide borders running inside the walls were used for growing perennials such as asparagus and globe artichokes, for seedbeds, for early crops of peas and beans or for salads – early salads under the south wall, summer salads under the north.

Individual beds were usually narrow, no more than 1.2m/4ft wide, so they could be worked easily. Unlike the raised and boarded beds of Tudor and Elizabethan times, when ground was less well drained, they were at ground level and divided by narrow paths. Wider gravel paths dissected the whole garden, bordered perhaps with espalier fruit growing against painted rails or dwarfer gooseberry bushes, and edged with flowers, strawberries or herbs. Melonries and cucumber grounds figured prominently, often sited in the 'slips' outside the walls, where the immense loads of manure for the hotbeds, and the piles of soil (known as 'mould'), peat and sand used in the garden, could be screened off out of sight.

Modern scientific ideas on gardening spread slowly. Rotation was practised, ground was heavily manured to maintain its fertility, the value of drainage and shelter was stressed by the leading gardening authorities. The agricultural writer Samuel Hartlib, son of a Polish immigrant and patronized by Cromwell in his efforts to improve agriculture, expounded the Flemish practice of green manuring. Ridging ground to expose it to winter frost was another recommended practice, as was intercropping; salad herbs were grown among young globe artichokes, skirrets among onions. In his plans for kitchen gardens the famous designer Batty Langley shows savoys planted between kidney beans, and carrots or parsnips mixed with lettuce, radish and spinach.

Much attention was paid to the now neglected art of saving seed. Parkinson devoted a whole chapter of *Paradisus* to the subject. Interested amateur gardeners today would find it worth consulting. Another almost lost technique was blanching. Artichoke chards, endive, chicory, succory (wild chicory), alexanders, celery and cardoons were all blanched to make them more tender and crisp. Methods included putting them in dark cellars or under blanching pots, burying them in sand, or wrapping them around with straw.

From all accounts salads were an important part of the diet, and what imaginative salads they were! In 1699 John Evelyn wrote his *Acetaria: A Discourse of Sallets*, in which he lists thirty-five

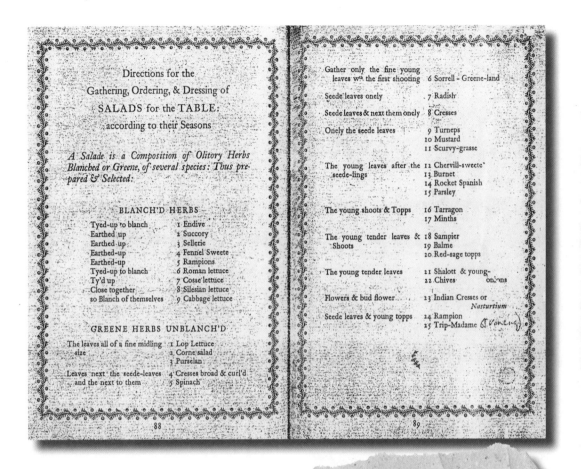

Directions for the
Gathering, Ordering, & Dressing of
SALADS for the TABLE:
according to their Seasons

*A Salade is a Composition of Olitory Herbs
Blanched or Greene, of several species: Thus prepared & Selected:*

BLANCH'D HERBS

Tyed-up to blanch	1 Endive
Earthed up	2 Succory
Earthed up	3 Sellerie
Earthed-up	4 Fennel Sweete
Earthed-up	5 Rampions
Tyed-up to blanch	6 Roman lettuce
Ty'd up	7 Cosse lettuce
Close together	8 Silesian lettuce
so Blanch of themselves	9 Cabbage lettuce

GREENE HERBS UNBLANCH'D

The leaves all of a fine midling size	1 Lop Lettuce
	2 Corne salad
	3 Purselan
Leaves next the seede-leaves and the next to them	4 Cresses broad & curl'd
	5 Spinach

88

Gather only the fine young leaves wth the first shooting	6 Sorrell - Greene-land
Seede leaves only	7 Radish
Seede leaves & next them onely	8 Cresses
Onely the seede leaves	9 Turneps
	10 Mustard
	11 Scurvy-grasse
The young leaves after the seede-lings	12 Chervill-sweete
	13 Burnet
	14 Rocket Spanish
	15 Parsley
The young shoots & Topps	16 Tarragon
	17 Minths
The young tender leaves & Shoots	18 Sampier
	19 Balme
	20 Red-sage topps
The young tender leaves	21 Shalott & young-onions
	22 Chives
Flowers & bud flower	23 Indian Cresses or *Nasturtium*
Seede leaves & young topps	24 Rampion
	25 Trip-Madame (Voreng)

89

species for use in salads. While many of these were blanched, the majority were eaten green and unblanched: the young leaves and first shoots of sorrel, the tender shoots and tops of tarragon and mint, the flowers and flower buds of nasturtium, the tender young leaves of shallots, chives and onions. Many seedlings were grown for use in salads: - cresses, mustard, rape, turnips, radish, spinach and lettuce. By using hotbeds and bell jar cloches, a supply was maintained all year round. Many types of lettuce were known – cos and cabbage, green and brown, hardy and tender. Wild plants were gathered for salads: dandelion, violet flowers, cowslips, blossoms of borage, all 'as part of the

John Evelyn's Directions for the Gardiner at Says Court is still a charming and informative guide to producing salads the year round.

Sallet Furniture'. Radish seed pods, nasturtium flowers, broom buds, cucumbers, purslane, onions and 'hartichoaks' were some of the plants pickled for adding to salads.

The most notable feature of English kitchen gardening, from about the mid-seventeenth century into Victorian times, was the extensive and sophisticated use of forcing techniques, for which the main tools were hotbeds of fermenting dung and large glass bell jars or 'cloches', forerunners of the twentieth-century tent-shaped cloches.

In 1727 the much travelled gardener Stephen Switzer wrote with immense enthusiasm of 'the great improvements in modern times, particularly in hotbeds and glasses'. He gives examples of some of the many vegetables being successfully forced (and retarded): peas and beans available for seven or eight months instead of two; asparagus ready in time for Christmas; and cauliflower 'which previously only threw its beautiful head three or four months but now six or seven, and by good management mocks the severity of our unfriendly climate'. He had learned the arts of forcing in the Neat House Gardens of Pimlico, where, based on the availability of manure from the nearby 'neat' or cattle stalls, there had been famous market gardens since the fourteenth century. Foreign visitors to London were continually astonished by the intensive production of this area, with its fields of bell jars housing three or four cauliflower seedlings apiece, endive grown on slopes, and the closely timed intercropping in the frames to get a succession of unseasonal produce.

Similar practices were adopted in the kitchen gardens of the gentry, especially for the culture of melons. Hotbeds were made in pits, in raised brick or wooden enclosures, or sometimes just temporarily, between bales of straw. They would be covered with heavy lights of the greenish glass of the time, made from numerous small panes, and protected, in severe weather, with extra layers of straw, canvas and matting. Later frames were heated with hot air flues, then with circulating hot water. The labour and skill involved in the making and management of these hotbeds was staggering – but this was an age of cheap labour.

During the nineteenth century the most significant changes in the kitchen garden took place in greenhouse development. The ancestor of the modern greenhouse was the stone-built, glass-fronted, opaque-roofed orangery of restoration times, designed primarily to house orange trees and other exotic fruits in winter. Very early in the eighteenth century the idea of glass-framed lean-tos was imported from Holland. They were soon to be found erected against south-facing kitchen garden walls. But it wasn't until the 1780s that the first freestanding, glass-roofed greenhouse was recorded.

With the development of the new glass manufacturing processes in the 1830s large sheets of good-quality sheet glass at last became available, and this, coupled with the removal in 1845 of the long-standing tax on glass, gave the stimulus to glasshouse construction and design which culminated in the magnificent Victorian conservatories: the Palm House at Kew; Sir Joseph Paxton's conservatory at Chatsworth; and the Crystal Palace at the Great Exhibition of 1851. Everybody who was anybody had a conservatory.

There was immense interest in improving heating systems and in boiler design. Until about 1780 the two commonest methods of heating greenhouses had been hotbeds inside the greenhouses and flues built in the walls to carry away the smoke from stoves and 'subterranean ovens'. Steam heating was first used experimentally in 1788, but was not in general use for another thirty years. It was in turn superseded by hot-water heating, first introduced from France in 1818.

These greenhouses were primarily built for growing fruit and ornamental plants, but they were also used for out-of-season crops of cucumbers, melons, French beans and salads.

With the growth of the middle classes in the nineteenth century gardening became a popular pastime. There was a mushrooming of gardening societies, with their competitions for the biggest and best. The first popular gardening magazines were launched. The retail seed firms which were to dominate the market until present times –Suttons, Carters, Thompson & Morgan – were established.

But what of the twentieth century? The labour-intensive techniques of the past had a final flurry in the 'French gardening' craze, which, starting in 1908, took the country by storm until brought to an end by the First World War. It was an imitation of the techniques of the Parisian market gardeners: hotbeds of manure, frames, bell jars, highly skilled intercropping – all very similar to the techniques of the Neat House market gardeners two centuries earlier. The war and the gradual demise of huge country house gardens were the death knell to these skills, along with the other old skills of forcing, blanching and seed saving. Consequently the number of species cultivated in kitchen gardens has been declining ever since.

On the credit side plant breeders have given us greatly improved vegetable varieties: higher yielding, hardier, dwarfer (and so more suitable for small modern gardens) and often with pest and disease resistance. Seedsmen now supply better and more reliable seed than they did in the past.

There have been enormous developments in the gadgetry of gardening. In 1912 Mr L.H. Chase designed the first continuous glass cloche, which was to become the gardener's most important aid for half a century. (Only recently have plastics begun to replace glass in the kitchen garden.) Standardized John Innes composts were introduced in the 1930s, chemical weedkillers and many modern insecticides in the 1940s, systemic fungicides in the late 1960s. Foliar feeds, hydroponic kits, peat-based composts and 'grow bags' are now commonplace, while garden frames are heated electrically, and domestic greenhouses can be completely automated.

Interest in vegetable growing has waxed and waned, at its peak in times of war and economic stress. Recent years have seen an increase in the number of 'organic' vegetable growers, reacting against the modern reliance on chemicals by using only organic manures and natural remedies against pests and diseases: a return to the tools which have served the previous ten centuries of British kitchen gardeners.

There is always something to observe or check in the garden. This photograph was taken by John Walker, who contacted us when he was a student at the Royal Botanic Gardens at Kew and helped us out over the years with hard labour, farm watching and collaborating on writing projects.

4 HOME PATCH TO FOREIGN FIELDS

The 1980s was a busy decade of book writing, research, reporting, experimenting, plotting potagers and getting a small income from our little market garden by bagging up 'saladini' for Wholefood in London and supplying local shops and chefs with salads, herbs and oddities.

Salads the Year Round, the first fruit of our year's travels, was published as a Hamlyn paperback in 1980. The following year I revised the RHS classic *Vegetable Garden Displayed* for the first time; the revised edition was published in 1982. Then along came a chance to do an illustrated book on salads for the publisher Frances Lincoln. This became *The Salad Garden*, and was published in 1984. What fun it was working with photographer Roger Phillips and his assistant Jacqui Hurst, what a roller coaster growing all the plants to be photographed in our barn, and what gorgeous salad dishes we sampled at the end of the photoshoot days, created by chefs Ethel Minogue and Paul Laurenson!

It was a great decade for garden writers with an interest in science, with a lot of research taking place in mainly government-financed institutes. Much, though carried out primarily for commercial growers, was relevant to amateur gardeners. It just needed an interpreter, and the RHS journal *The Garden* continued to let me carry out that role, as did *Popular Gardening*, in a more light-hearted way. It is a tragedy, in my eyes, that so many of these research centres were subsequently closed down or effectively lost their identity.

I was writing for other magazines too – *Practical Gardening*, *Gardeners' Chronicle*, *Greenhouse Magazine* among them – and in 1983 worked on an *Observer* magazine series, *Dream Gardens*, with Christopher Lloyd. That was a wonderful opportunity to visit unique gardens and to meet and learn from exceptionally creative gardeners. Christopher Lloyd, who died a few years ago, and Beth Chatto both became lifelong friends. My garden is full of plants they recommended, and fragments of their perceptive comments constantly float into my mind when I'm gardening.

Hot on the heels of *Dream Gardens* came *The Observer Good Gardening Guide*. As the youngest of the team I was persuaded to undertake the publicity – mainly through radio stations around the country. My children were impressed with some of the disc

Clockwise from top: head gardener Fergus Garrett and Christopher Lloyd at Great Dixter, Sussex, counting morning glory flowers; Alice Waters outside her San Francisco restaurant Chez Panisse; Mark Musick, founding member of Seattle Tilth.

jockeys I encountered. I was less impressed with the interviewer for an overseas forces programme who picked up the tome, looked at it seriously, and pronounced, 'This book's got chapters.' The others at least had a stab at reading it.

In 1984 I went to East Lansing, USA, as a guest speaker at Michigan State University's Farmer's Week, where I 'ran myself ragged' as my American hosts put it, doing radio and TV interviews to publicize *The Salad Garden*. For boosting morale there is nothing to equal American hospitality and enthusiasm. Back at home I was involved in the first 'organic' TV gardening series, *All Muck and Magic*, and wrote the booklet which went with the series. Ground breaking, it seemed at the time. Growing without chemicals: whatever next?

Oriental vegetables, and the determination to write about them, dominated the decade and led to two research trips, to China and Japan in 1985 and to the USA and Canada in 1987. Then followed several years of experimenting, researching and writing for my book *Oriental Vegetables*; these and my travels in the Far East are covered in Chapter 6. *Practical Gardening* magazine commissioned articles from my trip to China and Japan, helped pay my film costs, and continued their support during my American travels.

I tried to finance the five weeks I spent in Canada and the USA by giving talks along the way. It was a case of having a hunch about where there were Asian communities growing vegetables, then finding groups or gardening clubs near by who would pay for a talk. I narrowly escaped being deported on arrival, as I didn't have the right kind of immigration permit to earn proper fees. Devious ways of circumventing the problem included participants putting donations into a model of a compost bin at Seattle Tilth!

The trip proved a great way to meet gardeners. The United States may not have the European tradition of 'pretty pretty' gardens, but what so impressed me was the hotbed of ideas I encountered. So much energy – youthful energy above all – was being poured into community gardens, school gardens, energy-saving projects, organic gardening and seed-saving projects. An awakening awareness of environmental issues was paralleled by a huge surge of interest in growing and cooking.

What is so gratifying – well over twenty years on – is to see how many of those embryonic enterprises have taken root and flourished. So many of the people who helped me then – Mark Musick of Seattle Tilth (winning a major sustainability award in 2008), Jane Pepper of the Pennsylvania Horticultural Society (only recently retiring as much lauded President in 2010 after thirty years at the helm), inspirational Alice Waters of Chez Panisse restaurant in San Francisco, who has spearheaded countless educational and culinary enterprises, the pioneering seed companies, growers like Chino Farms in California – have had a far-reaching influence that continues to this day.

I hope the articles here reflect some of the goings-on in the 1980s. They are grouped roughly according to subject matter.

THE 'PETIT POTAGER'
The Garden, January 1987

I've always been conscious of the fact that the entrance to our kitchen garden is – well – a bit of a mess. The gate is a typical farm inheritance, made of 7.5cm/3in-square iron mesh (the stuff used to reinforce concrete) and fastened with baler twine. The anti-rabbit fencing and windbreak netting both need to be repaired, the plastic-covered greenhouse and ersatz polythene tunnels are a motley collection, and try as we might, bits of wire, corrugated iron, bamboo canes and ageing wheelbarrows gravitate towards what should be a neat row of workmanlike compost heaps near the gate.

Between the gate, the compost heaps and the first greenhouse is a smallish area, 4 × 5m/4 × 5 yards. It occurred to me one day that I should make a herb garden there: it would make a pretty entrance to the garden, would be useful, and making it would be valuable experience. A friend drew me a lovely plan. But that's when it struck me that a plot that size is all the garden some people have . . . and into my mind sprang the idea of the 'petit potager' (*potager* is simply the French term for a vegetable garden.) Could I make a pretty miniature vegetable patch there, something decorative enough to liven the entrance to our garden, but suitable also for any urban or suburban front garden, where the longing to grow vegetables conflicts with the desire for 'something pretty in front'?

At the back of my mind, of course, was the lovely formal Renaissance garden at Villandry in the Loire Valley, where vegetables are used decoratively, and Rosemary Verey's wonderful, more practical potager at Barnsley House in Gloucestershire. Mine would be the 'poor man's Villandry', a 'mini-Verey'. Subconsciously I set myself three objectives: it had to be pretty; as far as possible everything in it had to be edible or have some practical use; and I wanted it to be attractive all year round, not just in the summer months.

To say the petit potager was designed would be to exaggerate. It 'evolved' during the two rather wet and dreary seasons since its conception in the reluctant spring of 1985. It's essentially a rectangular area, the main axis lying in an east–westerly direction. While the western ends are more or less squared off, the eastern ends are gently rounded, giving it an almost oval shape overall. It is divided into four matching but unequal sections with two paths, the longer running east–west, the shorter north–south. A simple arch straddles the main path at the centre.

Within these bare bones each section is subdivided into four – the dividing lines drawn with plants. There's a circle of approximately 3m/10ft diameter radiating from the centre, intended to be a unifying element linking the four segments. Diagonals are planted across each segment, starting in the outer corner and extending sometimes just to the edge of the inner circle, sometimes through the circle to the central arch. My intention was to grow neat, low-growing plants and cut-and-come-again seedling patches in the eight smaller segments or triangles as I called them, pivoting around the centre, and to use the larger outer segments for bolder, taller, more spacious vegetables.

Within this moderately formal framework I wanted the potager to look natural and informal. So the dimensions of the beds were never measured precisely, nor was the potager ever planned in detail. I decided on the whole to play it by ear, sowing and planting according to how things were growing and what was available.

Left: the central squares of the winter potager, its design based on one in the potager at Villandry. In autumn (right) it was colourful with red and curly kales, red-leaved beet and flowering Chinese chives.

I did, however, draw up a summer and winter list of plants suitable for different purposes in the potager, i.e. for edges, for the diagonals and circle, for 'dot' plants, for the central triangles and for the larger areas. All plants on the list had to be both decorative and productive, but productive was interpreted very widely. Not only did it include herbs but a number of edible flowers such as *Bellis perennis*, calendula, pansies, borage and nasturtium, as we grow these for the restaurants we supply with unusual salads.

I had wanted each segment to develop a character of its own, but what I hadn't anticipated was the character that would be stamped on the garden by the plants that just 'appeared'. These were self-sown seedlings from previous years – borage, 'Pink Chiffon' poppies (quite legitimate as we use the poppy seed on buns and bread), calendulas, the old salad plant

buck's horn plantain, and in the second season dill and nasturtium 'Alaska'.

This surprise element often created dramatic effects that could never have been planned. But on the other hand, effects I visualized never materialized. In 1985, for example, the unifying circle was giant chives, and so successful had a patch of 'Hammond's Dwarf Scarlet' runner beans been the previous year, I decided to encircle the chives with red- and white-flowered dwarf runners. The idea was to create a lovely broad, even, band of red and white flowers, contrasting with the lush upright foliage of the chives. (The white-flowered beans were a new Hurst's variety I was trying out.) It never happened. By mid-summer both the chives and the beans had been engulfed by sprawling borage, calendula, dill, dun peas and ornamental kale – just a few bean flowers poking through bravely from time to time. I was learning lesson number one: desired effects can only be achieved by ruthless rooting out of all competition.

As with any gardening, ideas came as one worked. When weeding the dill patch one day

I found an asparagus seedling, and thought how pretty a permanent clump of asparagus would be, or maybe just one plant. It would be pretty over a long period – one of the main criteria for a good potager plant.

Did I succeed in my three objectives? First, was it pretty? I think so, but then I was a little in love with it and perhaps blind to its faults. I loved the way its moods and character changed with the seasons and with the morning and evening light. Its colour cheered me every time I went into the kitchen garden.

But aware of my bias, I was interested in the more detached reactions of visitors. Some were obviously delighted – 'What a lovely idea', 'Fancy vegetables being so colourful' . . . They instantly saw how the idea could be transformed to a small front garden. But others, I have to say, walked right by. I'd feel obliged to say casually, 'Oh, by the way, this is my experimental "pretty bit" – what do you think of it?' And I'd start to explain the underlying pattern. The inescapable truth is that its high points were interspersed with messy phases (the word messy appeared all too frequently in my notes); and to the casual observer the messy phases were, at best, colourful chaos. Now I'm a sucker for colourful chaos, but it's not everybody's taste.

Let me share some of the high points. In the first year the north-westerly section looked dramatic, in an orderly way, throughout August and September. In the background sweet peas clambered colourfully up the arch (there wasn't time, that first year, to grow an edible crop of climbing beans). The central triangle was ablaze with the variegated leaves and brightly coloured flowers of nasturtium 'Alaska', mixed with a few plants of sparkling iceplant (*Mesembryanthemum crystallinum*), which we use in salads. The semicircle of mixed broad- and curly-leaved parsley made a strong contrasting green band behind them, and behind that were

first dwarf runner beans, later chard. Further out was a semicircle of the ornamental kale 'Cherry Sundae', 30–38cm/12–15in in height, the frilled and puckered green, white and purple leaves looking stunning, the colours becoming stronger as the season progressed. The section was rounded off neatly with an edge of the frilly green 'Lollo' lettuce.

By September the adjoining south-westerly segment was striking, largely because of the diagonal band of the calendula 'Neon' – its wonderful vibrant gold and bronze petals almost iridescent in sunlight. Soft, blue-green downy buds of borage threaded their way through the calendula. At the same time the dill was starting to run to seed, and it too looked brilliant when the sun caught it, contrasting with the red spires of seeding 'Red Salad Bowl' lettuce, which I couldn't bear to pull up.

In spring the following year I found much satisfaction in the dense neat triangles of seedling crops – cress, glossy pak choi seedlings, salad rocket, 'Red Salad Bowl' lettuce, mizuna mustard, clearly circled then with freshly planted giant chives, some already flowering, and enlivened too by the early pansy flowers at the foot of the arch.

By July the relatively prim orderliness of the early months had given way to a rampant blaze of colour, and I was writing enthusiastically: 'I love it now, the intermingling of orange calendula, the soft blue haze of borage, the odd poppy still pink though most of them forming seed heads and the very tall spikes of seeding dill – delicate, glistening greeny gold seed heads.' I did admit that 'you have to look for the vegetables. There has been lettuce around the edges all summer, and the 'Lollo' in a central triangle are developing. Also developing quietly is a triangle of fennel, the recently planted curly parsley, the 'Painted Lady' runner beans on the arch. Asparagus peas and dwarf runners are ready for harvesting.' A border of alternating 'Salad Bowl' and 'Red Salad Bowl' was at its peak then: 'Marvellous rounded bushes, almost a foot high and two feet across, the frilly indented leaves merging with each other: a superb edge.'

The miserable summer probably accelerated the onset of the messy autumnal phase, but even so, in September the combination of the red and white 'Peacock' kales and the 'Lucullus' chard in the north-east section took some beating. The kales were planted in groups of four making very strong patches of colour with their stiff serrated leaves, the red with a light purple centre, the other leaves a contrasting blue green, and the whites creamy and green. As for the chard its huge, glossy, emerald green crinkly leaves radiated vegetable well-being. Again, the section with seeding dill, borage, fennel and kale, all contrasting foliage textures and different heights, had its glorious moments.

What I must do, to improve the overall impact of the potager, is to grow some unobtrusive backgrounds. Visually the greenhouse, fencing, compost heaps and water tanks constantly intrude. Perhaps this year I will plant screens of sunflowers, Jerusalem artichokes, climbing gourds or beans. Or should I make a second potager in the uncluttered setting of the front lawn?

Did I succeed in growing only edible and useful plants? Not entirely. There were the sweet peas up the arch in the first year (and how lovely they were), and both years I sowed a mixture of annual flowers and carrots, my favourite way of disguising a carrot patch and warding off carrot fly. That's how the flax worked its way into the '85 potager, and again, it was so pretty I never grudged it its place.

What did the potager supply? There were always plenty of herbs. There was also quite a choice of cooking vegetables, even if in some cases the quantities were fairly small. We picked asparagus peas, French beans, dwarf and climbing runner beans (I was amazed at the number of dwarf runners I found, even though the plants appeared to have been swamped); peas for drying, beetroot, carrots, Chinese artichokes, various types of chard, mizuna mustard, the pretty Chinese rosette pak choi. Then there were the salad plants – lettuce galore, iceplant, endive, red chicory, purslane; the spring patches of cress, salad rape, salad rocket, pak choi; buck's horn plantain, salad burnet, land cress and claytonia, all of which appeared spontaneously, and lastly the edible flowers and ornamental kales. I felt the potager did fulfil its functional as well as decorative purpose.

So far I have failed in my third aim, to make the potager attractive in winter and spring as well as in summer.

It's not that there aren't vegetables which can look decorative in the winter months. How about the curly kales, savoys, blue-leaved leeks, red Brussels sprouts, red Italian chicories, the hardy Chinese mustards with their purple-veined foliage and the fern-like mizuna, endives, chards, leaf celery, ordinary and Hamburg parsley, as well as buck's horn plantain, chervil, salad burnet and claytonia and again, the ornamental kales which survive at least a few degrees of frost?

Unless protected by cloches, these vegetables inevitably become tattered and torn during the winter months, but even so, it should be possible to create a small potager that is more pleasing to the eye than the average winter vegetable patch.

The problem lies in the fact that if these vegetables are to grow and develop well, most of them need to be planted by July or August. But in July and August the potager is in full swing, crammed with colour, and it is hard to

Clockwise from top: the original little potager in June; me weeding it; aerial view of Montrose Farm; basket maker Martin Nunn weaving the willow seat for the later little potager; the completed arch and seat; the garden plan drawn up for an open day.

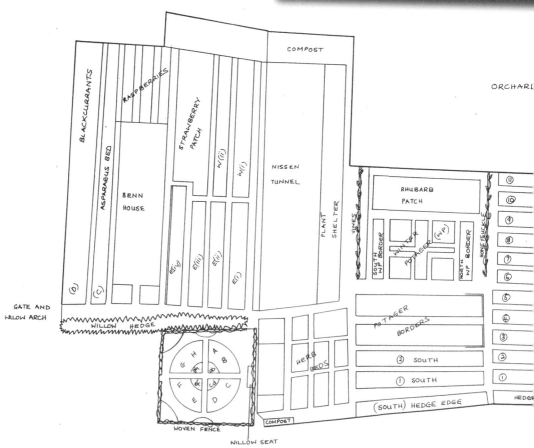

COMPOST

ORCHARD

BLACKCURRANTS

RASPBERRIES

ASPARAGUS BED

STRAWBERRY PATCH

BENN HOUSE

W(ii)

W(i)

NISSEN TUNNEL

PLANT SHELTER

VINES

RHUBARB PATCH

SOUTH WP BORDER

WINTER POTAGER (WP)

NORTH WP BORDER

HONEYSUCKLE

⑪
⑩
⑨
⑧
⑦
⑥

E(iv) E(iii) E(ii) E(i)

(Q) (C)

POTAGER BORDERS

⑤
④
③
②
①

GATE AND WILLOW ARCH

WILLOW HEDGE

HERB BEDS

③ SOUTH

① SOUTH

G H A
F   B
E D C

POTAGER

WOVEN FENCE

COMPOST

WILLOW SEAT

(SOUTH) HEDGE EDGE

HEDGE

FRUIT
CAGE

steel oneself to sacrifice productive plants to make way for the winter fledglings. And if these young plants are tucked into small spaces, they get overshadowed by the mature plants around them and their development is hampered.

Perhaps the solution is to earmark a couple of potager sections in late spring, refrain from growing summer plants in them – or grow only catch crops such as seedling cress, rocket, or radishes – so they can be planted in July and August with winter- and spring-maturing vegetables. Or one could raise winter vegetables in large pots for transplanting at a fairly mature stage in September, when it is easier to make room. I'm sure a solution can be found, but it demands the detailed planning and discipline that my summer/autumn potager has been denied, and doesn't seem to need. Another option would be to create a separate winter potager. That could be fun!

And that's exactly what I did!

SLUGDUGGERY
Practical Gardening, March 1988

Wonderful warm wet evenings again . . . can't wait to go out for an evening graze. Mouth's watering at the thought of those spring seedlings – so tender, so sweet compared to the tough old stuff we have to exist on in winter.

Can't help wondering what this year will be like. Never get another like '87, I suppose. That was Utopia in our patch in East Anglia. Spring was dry, as it often is, but from May until late autumn rain, rain, rain. Far more than usual. Day after day. Did marvels for the birth rate. As my sister said, it's worth bringing young into a kindly world like this. Mind you, the younger generation were completely spoilt: they've never had it so good. Completely self-assured and quite foolhardy. You'd get them brazenly striding across open ground in broad daylight! Rule Number One of the Slug Survival Code: never go out without cover of darkness! What with the birds, that woman, and one thing and another there's a permanent state of war. But you can't tell the young anything.

We're very lucky here; we've an excellent patch. That woman's garden is organic, and you know what that means. None of those nasty pellets – so tempting but so fatal. (And she won't use the organic ones: she says they're too expensive. Thank God for her mean streak!) Then there's always rotting organic matter around: piles of straw and so on – marvellous safe places for the kids to play. She doesn't weedkill the paths either, so there's always some nice weedy grass to hide in within easy reach of the veg.

Another thing, she's mad about plastic mulches. Now that's a modern invention I can go along with. A whole bed of bush tomatoes were mulched with half black, half white reflecting plastic last year. Heavenly. We kept cool and hidden under it during the day, but as soon as it was dark just a minute's creep up through the planting holes to those lovely juicy tomatoes – all within easy reach – then slip back down to sleep it off. Sheltered housing, we called it!

Only snag with these organic gardens is there are a lot of frogs and toads about. Never seen as many as last year . . . and they're rather partial to us!

But the grub here's good. That woman is experimenting with Chinese vegetables. Take Chinese cabbage. I'd go yards for that . . . it's easy to find; you can smell it a long way off. Even the outer leaves are soft – we make lace curtains out of them! The hearts are even better.

Pak choi is good too, especially when it's young. But I got nowhere with that Chinese kale, *kai-lan*. Horrible waxy leaves. And that mizuna with its shaggy leaves is a bit tough – emergency rations only, I'd say. Mind you, some things are an acquired taste. Take red chicory or radicchio – quite a fashionable thing now. I couldn't stand it once, and still don't bother with it in summer. But it seems quite palatable in the autumn when you want a break from cabbage, cabbage and more cabbage.

You asked about last year's delicacies. The French beans were a walkover in June. Put up no resistance whatsoever. (Here's hoping for another cold summer!) We polished off a lot of lettuces too, especially the ones that woman planted for winter. Silly thing, you'd think she'd know better by now. The only one I didn't care for was that new 'Parella Rossa' from Italy. Funny taste. We left them alone. The fennel and celery were delicious, and the basil – and the potatoes. We got through an awful lot, just leaving the skins. They even had my favourites – 'Golden Wonder'. (I love 'Maris Piper' too.) You *can* spot the difference. The large winter radishes are a case in point. I much prefer the long ones – you can get a grip on them and 'hole in'. Personally I keep slipping off the round ones!

The thing we all dread is that woman and her husband coming out at night to look for us.

They come with torches. Luckily their batteries are dim half the time, and if you lie quietly on the underside of a leaf they're quite likely to miss you. That woman's eyesight isn't what it used to be, but she's now got the sneaky idea of running her hands up the undersides of the leaves. She's got quite a few of us that way. The other bad news is they've started collecting us in Coke and beer cans. It was open cottage-cheese pots in the old days, and with the co-operation of a snail or two, you could tip them over and escape in the dark. Soil is wonderful camouflage: they never pick you up again. But those beer cans have such steep sides and only a sharp narrow hole at the top. (There was one survivor, who got to their kitchen. Poked his head out the following morning and gave a visitor a hell of a fright!)

But I digress. That woman doesn't half nag her husband about hunting us at night. 'I'll do a quarter of an hour then I'm going to watch *Spitting Image*,' he says . . . 'I'll have the good torch when you go,' she replies in a martyrish tone. We dread that point. Eleven at night, pitch dark, and you wouldn't believe how obsessive she gets. Against blood sports and boxing, but it's the killer instinct against us. I'll never forget the night she remembered the late summer cabbages which we'd been working our way through steadily for weeks. Sheer slaughter. I only escaped because her fingers got so cold and slippery she dropped me. Trouble is we've put on so much weight this year we're big targets. When you're small – or young – you can curl up into almost nothing and they can't grab you.

There's a lot of prejudice against slugs. Snails eat twice as much as us, but no one hates snails. I heard of an organic extremist who couldn't bear to kill snails. He put them on the compost heap instead so they could feed on the compost. Never entered his head to retire us to the compost heap.

Even the media is biased against us. After the Great October Storm ADAS (the Ministry people) warned farmers to guard against us. Said we would be taking advantage of the wet conditions to attack those fallen Brussels sprouts.

Oh well, we'll survive. We'll go on skirting around their beer traps and slug pubs, laughing at the beetles who've been caught. We'll ignore the unpleasant things they put around their precious plants – soot, lime, wood ash, coils of human hair and sheep's hair. And have you heard the latest? They're making sprays from slug bodies, caught when the moon is in Cancer. Makes you sick! They must be desperate to come up with something like that. We'll slug it out!

PARKINSON'S LAW ON THE HOME PATCH
From '1980 Retrospective', *The Garden*, February 1981

A thought which swam consistently into my mind last year was an attempt to formulate a sort of Parkinson's law of gardening, to describe that unintended chain of events which seems to arise when one sets foot in the vegetable garden. The scenario goes something like this.

A voice from the kitchen says, 'Could you bring in a few onions?' You pop out willingly. On the way to the onion bed you notice how weedy the parsley has become. As it will only take a minute to put right you tackle the job. Ten minutes later you remember the onions . . . Tripping over a cane on the way to the onion bed you realize that was just what you were looking for yesterday to stake that Brussels sprout which is toppling over. The sprouts have been invaded by a new batch of caterpillars since you last looked at them. Better deal with them on the spot or it will be too late. Takes quite a while. Then you remember you'll need string to tie the cane – and it's in the shed. On the way to the shed, just as you had spotted an isolated cloche which would be better used covering some basil plants, there's a voice from the kitchen, 'Have you got those onions?' . . .

Will I be more single-track minded and efficient in 1981? I doubt it, and secretly hope not. For surely part of the enjoyment and recuperative nature of gardening lies in its surprise elements and spontaneity.

. . . .

This was probably a misappropriation of Parkinson's law, which is that work expands to fill the time available for its completion. But I think it struck a chord. The editor of a gardening newsletter reprinted it in his publication.

PESTILENTIAL THOUGHTS
From 'Review of '82', *The Garden*, January 1983

It's becoming something of a tradition, at the turn of the year, to look back in anger, joy or sorrow at what befell my garden in the previous twelve months. So here we are again, and this time I'm starting with my war memoirs . . . thoughts, that is, on the permanent war between me and certain pests.

The first thought that struck me, in turn with rabbits, birds, slugs and leather-jackets, is how systematically the enemy works. Night after night, or dawn after dawn, depending on the nature of the beast, they return to raid the same patch, row or plant. A young rabbit, presumed to have slipped in through an open gate, concealed itself for days in an overgrown mint bed before we flushed it out, but every night gorged itself on Hamburg parsley, working steadily down the rows from east to west. Pigeons seem to do the same. They discover a patch of brassicas, peas or chard, drop some kind of marker flare, and inevitably return to finish off the dirty work they have begun. Last year they took all my perpetual kale, carefully raised from cuttings. I thought I'd read that pigeons don't touch kale . . . Ah well, never believe what you read in print!

As for other birds, gardeners are bound to develop a schizophrenic attitude towards them. What is lovelier than a quiet evening, digging, sowing or planting, serenaded by blackbird or wren, or watched in flattering trust by a perky robin? Yet in our garden 75 per cent of our crops have to be protected from birds – and any aesthetic pattern there might be is lost under a sea of wire and Correx hoops covered by netting. The temptation to protect the whole garden with a giant, fruit-cage-style net is enormous. But judging from the scores of birds which sometimes fly off the garden, obviously having feasted on insect pests and weed seeds, the garden would be the poorer for their total exclusion.

We rely on three measures. When sowing or planting seedlings birds like – beetroot and spinach seem to be among the most tempting – I run a thread of strong black cotton (button thread) a couple of inches above the row. This is just as effective as a complex network of threads. We also, mainly in spring, put unturned bottles in the ground here and there. Perhaps it's the sun glinting on them, but they seem effective for short periods though, as with all bird scarers, they must be moved about. Birds quickly become accustomed to anything permanent or semi-permanent – glinting or not. Our principal protective device, as already mentioned, is netting, and I usually seem to be putting the netting over the hoops in the gathering dusk, cursing as it catches on twigs, wires, even my buttons! But if it's not done then 'you know who' will be gathering before dawn.

There was a new pest last year; asparagus beetle. As far as I was concerned, asparagus beetle had hitherto been a textbook pest. I'd never encountered it and didn't quite believe in its existence. Then in June I suddenly noticed a lot of small black grubs on the asparagus foliage, which was prematurely losing its soft green bloom and becoming brown and brittle. Ever reluctant to spray (though derris eventually proved to be very effective) I diligently squashed grubs every time I passed the bed, which fortunately lay on a main thoroughfare. Five or ten minutes 'squashing' and all foliage within comfortable arm's reach (I have a very lazy streak) was cleared. Pass again two or three hours later, and the upper echelons of asparagus fern would be repopulated! I pictured bands of heroic larvae, lurking in the depths, ready to march forward and replace their fallen comrades. The adult beetles emerge from hibernation in May and June – so I'll be on the lookout next year. I would hate to lose my asparagus bed.

I was pleased with the way both whitefly and red spider were kept under control in the greenhouse. For the former, I am completely converted to interplanting with French marigolds. It's one of the few 'organic' preventative measures I believe works, and it's simply a question of planting a marigold between every pepper, aubergine and tomato plant. In spite of the very warm spells, the whitefly never built up seriously, and the marigolds, of course, look very colourful. I assume it's their powerful scent which deters the insects. I sowed them in April, which seems to be soon enough for their role as bodyguards.

As for red spider, the important thing is to maintain a damp atmosphere, with maximum ventilation and regular sprinkling with water once a day, or twice a day in hot weather. It's important to sprinkle thoroughly, on both paths and foliage, as evaporation is rapid when temperatures are high.

ALTERNATIVE PEAS
The Garden, April 1980

A dismal sign of the times is that it is almost impossible to buy fresh garden peas on the Continent; green peas only come in tins and frozen. And the way things are going the situation will soon be the same here.

So was there ever a stronger case for growing one's own? Is there anything to equal the exquisite taste of fresh garden peas, plucked in their prime from the garden? Probably not. But what happens? In my experience there is no crop as hit and miss as the capricious pea. There is no crop where painstaking effort in preparing the ground, in sowing, in protecting seed and seedlings from rodents and birds, in erecting supports and so on can bring so little reward.

Last year was a case in point. My ordinary garden peas were a total failure. I'm still not quite sure why. But fortunately I had decided in February that 1979 was going to be my year for trying 'alternative' peas – namely mangetout peas and peas for drying. Probably an atavistic urge: centuries ago the common folk of this country gathered their peascoddes – mangetout types of peas with edible pods – in summer; while pease pottage, the thick nourishing soup from dried peas, sustained them during their long, protein-starved winters.

First to look at the mangetout or sugar peas, *Pisum sativum* var. *saccharatum*, described as long ago as 1677 by J. Worlidge as 'the sweetest of them all'. In many varieties of peas the pod is lined with a thin tough membrane which gives it its solidity. As the pea ripens and dries this membrane contracts, eventually causing the pod to split into two sections and so ejecting the peas. Edible-podded peas, however, are virtually free of a parchment-like membrane. They remain soft and tender even when ripe; so the entire pod is edible – though occasionally strings have to be removed from the outside, as with French or runner beans.

In the 'old days' there were many different types of sugar peas. In some the peas were tiny, glued tightly between the two sides of the pod; in others they swelled into a substantial size. In some pods were straight; in others they were flattened, and curved or crooked in a distinct scimitar shape. In the butter pea the pods were very swollen, thickened and succulent, containing large fat peas.

There was also tremendous variation in height – from climbing forms up to 1.5m/5ft high to dwarf forms like the 'Dwarf Dutch' or 'Dwarf Crooked Sugar' pea, no more than 20–25cm/8–10in high. A curious semi-dwarf was the 'Early Dwarf Brittany' sugar pea, with erect stiff intertwining stems which supported each other, so eliminating the need for stakes. To complete the picture there were black-eyed, yellow-podded and dwarf grey sugar peas, while flower colour was white, yellowish green, purple or red.

To return to modern varieties, the three I grew last year were 'Tézieravenir', a French-bred, scimitar-podded variety; 'Sugar Snap', dubbed the snap pea by its American breeders and from all accounts very similar to the old butter pea; and snow pea 'Melting Sugar', one of the medium-height Chinese sugar peas.

One is always told to grow mangetout peas just like ordinary peas, but the way I sowed those peas broke every rule in the book. Ordinary peas, of course, need rich well-drained soil, they should never be sown in cold wet conditions, never on freshly manured ground. In suitable conditions mangetouts can be sown as early as February, but it was 10 May before I sowed them. 10 May 1979. I remember my fingers becoming progressively numbed with cold as I sowed the three plots!

The bed was 90cm/1 yard wide, and using a dibber, I dibbled in the seeds across the bed, 4–5cm/1½–2in deep, approximately 7–10cm/3–4in apart. The ground oozed with wetness; it was soggy with heavy manure which had been dug in too recently and subsequently drenched with rain. I was ashamed to be sowing peas, but was torn between the overpowering urge to sow something, given the lateness of the season, and the realization that it was dire stupidity and a waste of effort to sow pea seeds in such appalling conditions. The failure rate was bound to be high – if not total. Nevertheless, I covered them optimistically with wire netting to protect them from birds – mangetouts being just as appealing to birds as ordinary peas. By 15 May, to my astonishment, all three sets were through.

As they grew taller, we edged the plots with 1m/3ft high wire netting as a means of support, hoping that by growing them in closely sown blocks they would to some extent support themselves. For again, as with ordinary peas, support is vital if yields are to be substantial. In fact support was unnecessary for the snow peas, which were only 75cm/2½ft high, whereas the snap peas, which grew over 1.5m/5ft tall, would have benefited from taller, more substantial support. The only other treatment the mangetouts received was a very heavy watering in the second week of July when the pods were forming. This was in line with modern recommendations for ordinary peas: to water well at the start of flowering and/or as the pods begin to swell. They would probably also have benefited from mulching, as peas, a cool weather crop, hate to be dried out at their roots.

The plots looked pretty as they were growing, especially the white-flowered snow peas, which had delicate neat foliage, and 'Tézieravenir', with its striking purple flowers.

Claims that the peas would be ready within seventy days proved justified, as picking started on 15 July. With most mangetout peas picking should start when the peas are just visible inside the pods; and regular picking is advisable, as they are undoubtedly at their best when young. The great advantage of the 'Sugar Snap' type is that it is virtually two vegetables: a classical edible-podded pea when young, and when mature, a pod that can be shelled – though in this case, providing pod strings are removed – both peas and pods can be cooked separately.

We thought the flavour in all cases excellent: sweet, tender and distinct. All the pods could be eaten raw or cooked. The secret of cooking mangetout peas is to minimize the cooking and so retain their delicate flavour. Preparation involves no more than simply snapping off the stalks and, if wanted, cutting the pods into 2.5cm/1in pieces.

Chinese recipes suggest either stir-frying, i.e. frying in hot oil for about a minute, or 'flash cooking'. This means dipping the peas into boiling salted water, ideally a few at a time, for no more than a minute. Chopsticks are the best tool for this manoeuvre, but failing chopsticks a strainer can be used. The pods can then be chilled and used in salad, dressed either with oil and vinegar, or a more Chinese mixture of soya sauce and sesame oil.

Dry peas are a different kettle of fish altogether. They have never been widely grown in gardens. Even in their heyday in the Middle Ages and later they were considered a field crop, often sown along with rye or strong-stemmed oats, on which they would climb. When overwintered they were sown with hardy varieties of oats. 'Carlin' was probably the most famous of the old peas grown for drying.

Today there is a revival of interest in dry peas as an alternative source of protein, especially in the EEC (EU) countries where 93 per cent of the vegetable protein now used for animal feed is imported. On a domestic level the high price of meat in recent years has encouraged more gardeners to consider growing their own leguminous crops for use dried – and given our climate, peas are the most likely to succeed.

Last year I grew two varieties of drying peas: one ancient, one modern. The ancient was a Dutch so-called 'grey' pea, a rough-looking, rugged brown-coloured pea from western Holland, once widely grown and now an increasing rarity, much sought after by those who appreciate its culinary qualities.

The modern pea is 'Filby', a neat round pea, pale green when fresh, a creamy colour dry. It was bred at the John Innes Institute for the processing industry. 'Filby' has been hitting the headlines since it first appeared (it was even mentioned on The Archers), because it is a leafless pea. Anything more akin to a barbed-wire fence in the natural world would be hard to imagine! 'Filby' is not, as yet, on the amateur market, but if it ever becomes available, it will prove a certain conversation stopper in the kitchen garden. In its prime, before it starts to fade, I find it an extraordinarily pretty plant. The stems and tendrils are a very delicate shade of green, the flowers white and dainty, and the plants twine together into a neat attractive lacy hedge, no more than 45cm/18in high.

In peas a plant in which the leaves are converted into tendrils turns up from time to time, and just such a plant was one of the 'Filby' parents. Interestingly, in spite of the lack of leaves, photosynthesis is as high per unit area as with ordinary peas. Moreover, because there are no leaves, light penetrates through to the entire plant, whereas in normal peas many of the lower leaves are obscured.

'Filby' arose during the plant breeder's search for improved vining peas – peas harvested on the vine for freezing, canning and dehydrating. Vining peas are wrinkle-seeded peas, which have a high sugar content; but they are only at their optimum point for harvesting for a very brief period – perhaps at the most twenty-four hours – before they start to deteriorate.

The semi-leafless pea 'Markana' makes an almost self-supporting feature in a potager, with masses of intertwining tendrils. These taste like pea tips if picked young.

Before this point is reached they often start to lodge (the technical term for falling over) and the foliage is liable to rot, resulting in stained and spoilt peas. Leafless peas, however, stand very much better because they support each other – and so looked like solving some of the pea growers' problems. As it turns out, leafless peas will probably prove most suitable for the dry pea industry, and semi-leafless peas, another variant on the theme, for the vining industry.

I grew them in exactly the same way as the mangetout peas. Yields per plant are relatively low, but they are of course meant to be grown at high density on a field scale. In the field the lighter-weight crop has some advantage in that the vines are better able to stand until harvested. From my small patch I eventually gathered a sizeable jar of healthy-looking peas.

Peas intended for use as dry peas should be left as long as possible on the vines. When the foliage begins to yellow and the pods to wrinkle, pull them up, tie them in loose bundles, and hang them in a shed or well-ventilated building so that air can get through them. When the pods are crackly and snap open easily shell them and store the peas in jars. Traditionally peas were dried on wooden supports in the field, with a ventilation draught skilfully engineered up the middle of the stack.

The Dutch grey pea first caught my eye at the drying stage. It was on a late summer trip to Holland, and all the allotments seen from the road seemed to be splattered with light structures on which what turned out to be grey peas, were being dried. Like the old field peas, most of which had purple flowers, it has a very attractive flower with cream and purple standards. Again, yields are not high, but the individual peas are large and as with all peas, higher yields per plant would be obtained if they were grown against some kind of support.

As for cooking dried peas, they must be soaked first, the general rule being the older the pea, the longer the soaking. I've been told to boil the Dutch peas until soft, then to put bacon in a pan, heat it until the fat runs, and to stir in the peas mixed with raw or pickled onion, pickled gherkin or cucumber and French mustard.* For the 'Filby' peas I may be tempted to try an old-fashioned recipe for pottage, spiced with herbs such as thyme, mint and savory. Or to treat them like the 'Carlin' peas traditionally served on Sundays, sprinkled with rum and sugar after being cooked. (I have just learned that tinned pease pudding is produced in the UK from a conventional pea called 'Birte' – a pea which looks just like 'Filby'.)

One way and another, I hope to make good use of my alternative peas – hoping meanwhile that the plant breeders will come up with a tall, wrinkled seeded but leafless and therefore free-standing pea, so that even in this pea-stickless society, we can once again reap the benefits of a high yielding, tall variety of garden pea.

*STOP PRESS: Since tried and approved! And now many excellent varieties of semi-leafless peas are widely available.

SALAD DAYS
World Gastronomy, 1988

'We have said how necessary it is, that in the Composure of a Sallet, every plant should come in to bear its part, without being over-power'd by some Herb of a stronger Taste, so as to endanger the native Sapor and Vertue of the rest; but fall into their Place, like the Notes in Music, in which there should be nothing harsh or grating: Altho' admitting some Discords (to distinguish and illustrate the rest) striking in the more sprightly, and sometimes gentler Notes, reconcile all Dissonancies, and melt them into an agreeable Composition.'

So, in 1699, wrote John Evelyn, celebrated diarist, horticulturist and salad guru, in his masterpiece on the art of making salads, *Acetaria*. What wonderful mixtures those salads must have been – mixtures of sweet and sharp flavours, of coarse and tender textures, of fresh young seedlings forced out of season, herbs and plants gathered from the wild, the whole enlivened with the 'discords' of pickled roots and buds, and the 'gentler notes' of colourful flowers and petals!

A cool and gentle climate of the English kind is perfect for growing a host of salad plants. Judging from the detailed accounts of how to grow them and how to mix salads in sixteenth-, seventeenth- and eighteenth-century gardening books, this was not lost on our ancestors. Did the Industrial Revolution dull the English palate? Somewhere along the line the love of a lively salad disappeared, and the art of making 'an agreeable composition' vanished.

Fortunately the art didn't die out all over Europe. Take Italy, where in spring cars are parked on the edge of motorways while their occupants scour the fields for the first young leaves of wild dandelions and chicory, salad rocket, lamb's lettuce, edible thistles and wild poppy leaves, and where baskets of salad seedlings and colourful red chicories and lettuce are sold on market stalls, destined to play their part in the making of a mixed salad.

Is it stretching the imagination too far to suggest that the flame that was kept alive on the European Continent, fanned by the contemporary search for lighter, healthier and vegetarian food, has sparked the revival of the traditional mixed salad in modern guise? Pre-packed 'designer' salads can be found in upmarket chain stores and greengrocers; the word Saladini (which my husband and I claim to have invented, since it stems from our mishearing the Italian word *insalatine*, used to describe small seedling leaves used in salads) is nosing its way into the culinary vocabulary. Long-neglected salad plants are reappearing in kitchen gardens. In the United States salad bars have swept the country, where the subtle flavours of an imaginative range of salad materials risk – at times – being drowned in Thousand Island dressings and other complex concoctions.

This gives us a wonderful opportunity to rediscover forgotten salad plants, to investigate new plants and new varieties to see which could be used in salads, and even to revive some of the old methods of salad growing, such as 'seedling salads'.

In the past many salad plants were sown fairly thickly, often in heated frames, and cut when an inch or a couple of inches high. This of course gives quick and good returns (several successive cuttings can be made), but more important, young seedlings are far more nutritious than tired middle-aged leaves, look wonderfully bright and fresh, and taste superb.

Traditional English seedling salads were cresses, turnips, mustard, radish – all grown for their tiny leaves; spinach, spicy salad rocket, chervil, used when a little larger. Even orange tree seedlings were briefly in fashion.

The French cultivated several varieties of lettuce for seedling salads, now sold as cutting lettuce, but most varieties of cos or romaine lettuce, and the 'Salad Bowl' and oak-leaved type, can be grown as seedlings, 'Red Salad Bowl' producing lovely red leaves. In Italy 'Sugar Loaf' chicory seedlings were, and still are, a prized spring treat.

As for new ideas, there is salad rape, a fast-growing milder alternative to mustard; the recently developed, highly nutritious Texsel greens with a snappy spinach flavour; and the numerous varieties of Chinese cabbage, especially the crunchy-stemmed pak chois, superb seedling salads when cut 10cm/4in high, as are the milder oriental spinach mustards like komatsuna. In Japan pots of seedling radishes are sold like cress, and another type of radish has been developed solely for its pleasantly flavoured leaf, cut when 5–10cm/2–4in high.

What can be used to get interesting textures into a salad? Summer purslane was a popular salad plant in the past, its refreshing succulent leaves either green or a shiny golden yellow. Less well known is winter purslane or miner's lettuce (*Claytonia perfoliata*, formerly *Montia perfoliata*), an American plant that escaped to Europe in the nineteenth century and became naturalized. The pretty, heart-shaped juicy leaves make a perfect spring salad. The flowers and stem are also edible. Children love it. It deserves to be far more widely grown. So does the fascinating *Mesembryanthemum crystallinum* or iceplant. The glands on its very thick, sink-your-teeth-into-me leaves sparkle like dewdrops. It has a slightly salty taste and stays fresh for days when picked.

For delicious sweet crunchiness nothing can beat the pods of sugar or mangetout peas and the new 'Sugar Snap'; narrow matchsticks of fennel have an aniseed crispness; the pak chois, mentioned above, and Chinese cabbage have a cool white crispness, as have well-grown mung bean sprouts.

Interesting curiosities are the seed pods of radishes, popular today in the East, and in the past in the West, both fresh and pickled. If they

are picked young and green, while still crisp, many people prefer them to radishes. As for radishes themselves, the large white Japanese radishes (*daikon* or mooli) are deservedly becoming popular, the many varieties varying from mild to spicy in flavour. A radish that should be known and grown in the west is the Chinese Beauty Heart ('Xin Li Mei', syns. 'Shinrimei', 'Rose Heart') – a huge radish, green outside, red, pink and white inside, beautiful to look at and sweetly flavoured. It needs a long warm summer and autumn to grow to maturity without bolting. Also sweetly flavoured and little known in the West are the green-fleshed Chinese radishes.

Let's move to the more powerful flavours that can add those carefully placed discordant notes. Evelyn disapproved of garlic, unless used very moderately, but recommended instead rocambole, a milder, chive-like wild form rarely found today, although it is easily grown. An answer

This photograph of overwintered salads was taken for the Observer *in the early days of our market garden. We were so proud to find over thirty salad plants and edible flowers.*

could be Chinese or garlic chives, sometimes called Chinese leek (*Allium tuberosum*), a flat-bladed, emerald green leaf with a delicate half-garlic, half-chives flavour. It's a lovely plant with star-like white flowers: the flowers and buds can be used in salads. Country dwellers can try the wild hedgerow plant garlic mustard or Jack-by-the-hedge (*Alliaria petiolata*). Just a few young leaves in an early spring salad will do the trick.

For a lemon flavour there's a marvellous choice of herbs that can be mixed into or sprinkled on to a salad: lemon basil, lemon thyme, lemon balm, lemon verbena, or the

bolder, acidic, but superb taste of sorrel. Basil, of course, has a unique clove-like taste – just a hint in a salad would be enough. Easily cultivated chervil is another source of an aniseed taste, while the distinctive flavour of angelica is found not just in the beautiful angelica leaves and stem but in the young leaves of ground elder (*Aegopodium podagraria*), dreadful weed though it is. Lovage – just a leaf rubbed around a bowl – adds the strongest of all celery flavours; chopped coriander contributes its own haunting mustiness, and for pepperiness the flowers and leaves of nasturtiums are unequalled.

Lastly, the decorative element – and here there is still a wonderful choice. The crinkly moss-like leaves of curly endive, the jagged spiky yellow and cream leaves of blanched dandelion, and the dark green, fern-like leaves of Japanese mizuna mustard (also known as kyōna) all look marvellous in salads. As for lettuce, the plant breeders are at last waking up to the decorative and red forms and starting to develop beautiful improved varieties. Two outstanding decorative lettuces are the deeply crinkled Italian pair 'Lollo Rossa' and green 'Lollo' (syn. 'Lollo Bionda'), named after film star Gina Lollobrigida.

The red Italian chicories too are benefiting from the attentions of the plant breeder. Success in enticing the plants to produce the tight nuggets of crisp, rose-white leaves in autumn used to be a gamble, seed was so variable and unreliable. The new varieties produce far larger hearts, far more reliably, over a much longer season. They are even improving the thin, blade-leaved variety 'Rossa di Treviso', the hardiest of them all – a deep red leaf when grown outside in winter, but if blanched like Witloof chicory, transformed into an exquisite pinky white, rose-tipped blade – perfect for a winter and spring salad.

And after a salad has been dressed with a simple French dressing, the final touch is the addition of flowers. Some suggestions: sweet-tasting, brilliant blue borage; pale blue chicory flowers (where they can be picked straight from the garden); tiny heartsease, violas and pansies; the deep orange and yellow petals of pot marigold (calendula); petals of the common double daisy *Bellis perennis*; nasturtiums, rose petals, geranium petals, sage flowers, elder flowers and, perhaps the subtlest way of adding onion fragrance to a salad, chive flowers. Gently break the globular chive heads into hundreds of tiny flowers and filter them into a salad — purple polka dots, perfect among lush and varied greens.

UNUSUAL TOMATOES - IN SEARCH OF FLAVOUR
The Garden, May 1982

When sketching out my garden plans last spring I made a firm decision to grow fewer tomatoes in 1981, and to concentrate on just a couple of what I consider really well-flavoured varieties, probably 'Marmande' and 'Gardener's Delight'. How easily gardeners are tempted from a path of single-mindedness into the wilderness of diversity! In the end I grew nineteen varieties, including some of the more ornamental ones, with unusual hues and shapes.

First to broach the subject of flavour — minefield though it is – for one of the attractions of unusual tomatoes is the hope of finding some in which a colourful, enticing appearance is matched by exceptional flavour. Of course it is impossible to agree on flavour: for some people sweetness and flavour are synonymous; others equate flavour with tangy tartness; for others texture is the most important feature. Perhaps all that can be said with certainty is that flavour is a positive character as opposed to bland tastelessness.

I sent myself on several tasting trips around my nineteen guinea pigs (I had tried to grow each variety both inside and out), noting my reactions. I was horrified to find that I had made contradictory statements at different times. But then why shouldn't flavour vary during the course of a season, even from one year, or one site, to the next? For many factors are involved in the complex balance between sugars and acids which determines flavour — variety, sunshine, feeding, watering, the amount of leaf on the plant . . .

For example, plenty of sunshine, and also I suspect direct sunshine, as opposed to sunshine filtered through glass or polythene, seems to bring out the best flavour in the 'Marmande' and 'Roma' types, and perhaps in the yellows too. The intensive watering and feeding regimes to which commercial tomatoes are subjected probably accounts for their acknowledged lack of flavour rather than the fact that they are modern hybrid varieties. In amateur conditions there is some evidence that heavy watering increases the size of the fruit at the expense of flavour, while some organic growers on the Continent feel that good flavour is encouraged by soaking the ground and allowing it to dry out completely before watering again. They never water more frequently than once a week even at the height of the season, and would water only every two or three weeks earlier in the season. Potash influences acidity and 'tanginess' — one reason for the high-potash feeds given to tomatoes.

It is in the leaves that the carbohydrates are manufactured, which are converted into sugars and create the sweetness. Bush varieties, which often have only one leaf between trusses, have a lower ratio of leaves per fruit than cordon tomatoes, which tend to have about three leaves between trusses. This, tomato expert Brian Tree* believes, is why bush varieties generally have a poorer flavour than an equivalent cordon variety. In the interests of flavour he advocates removing leaves only when really necessary, rather than excessive deleafing. So much for flavour.

The most spectacular of the unusual tomatoes are the giant American 'Beefsteak's – huge, fleshy, succulent, well-flavoured tomatoes, marvellous for slicing. The world weight record is held by a 2.9kg/6lb 8oz sample of the variety 'Delicious Red'. Several varieties are now listed in English catalogues. These tomatoes are multilocular: i.e. there are several compartments to each fruit, so increasing the flesh-to-cavity ratio. They are grown like traditional cordon tomatoes, sideshooting and stopping, and bear large fruit even on the third and fourth trusses. They tend to be later ripening than other tomatoes, though 'Better Boy', not as far as I know available here, ripens almost as early as standard round tomatoes.

The other drawback is getting the fruit to set. Most tomatoes self-pollinate, the stigmas being enclosed within the anthers. With the giant varieties the stigma protrudes well clear of the flower, so they tend to be cross-pollinated. If the atmosphere is dry, pollen falling on the stigma may shrivel. Brian Tree thinks there is a case for hand pollinating – going around the greenhouse with a paintbrush or rabbit's tail and picking up pollen (if possible from any smaller-fruited varieties in the house, which always have loads of pollen to shed) and brushing it on to the stigma of the 'Beefsteak' flower. It

should be done on a bright sunny day. Even jogging the flower heads is a help, as it shakes the pollen from overhead anthers on to stigmas below. Commercially an 'electric bee' is used to jog the flower stalks: Brian Tree suggests an electric toothbrush with the bristles removed. The Dutch variety 'Dombo', incidentally, sets quite well unaided.

The 'Marmande's are the ugly ducklings of the tomato world. The large, multilocular, misshapen fruits are a (glorious) feature of the Mediterranean. Their growth habit is generally semi-determinate: in other words they stop growing after five trusses. If you want further growth, take up a sideshoot. (A truly determinate tomato stops growing after about three trusses and then usually sends out sideshoots. Many bush varieties are in this category. A truly indeterminate variety continues growing on a main stem until the growing point is stopped artificially.)

'Marmande's tend to have their heaviest, and ugliest, fruits on the lower trusses, sometimes running out of steam afterwards. However, if kept growing steadily they will continue to bear, producing more respectable-looking, rounded fruits in middle age. Train them up canes or strings, and sideshoot them as with standard varieties.

It is often stated in seed catalogues that 'Marmande's can't be grown indoors. In my experience (and Brian Tree's), this isn't true; though sometimes they are reluctant to set indoors early in the season. If so, help them along, as suggested for the giants.

As mentioned earlier, bright sunshine does seem to be an important factor in getting that superb flavour. My first fruits of 'Marmande' last year, which ripened during a period when the sun was notable for its absence, were poor in flavour compared to later fruits, which had the benefit of prolonged sunshine.

Where flavour is concerned, I've realized recently, there are 'Marmande's and 'Marmande's. In breeding disease resistance into some F_1 varieties flavour has been sacrificed. (This is even acknowledged in one plant breeder's catalogue, where the claim for excellent flavour has been omitted for their newer hybrids.) Perhaps, once they have got the disease resistance sorted out, they'll start putting the flavour back. Certainly a sample of a new Italian F_1 Marmande type I was sent to try out last year had superb flavour – and the plants were very healthy too. But if you find yourself disappointed with any particular Marmande variety, that may be the reason.

The golden and yellow tomatoes have tremendous visual appeal, and many people rate them very highly for flavour. Round, so-called plum-shaped, pear-shaped, and tiny 'currant' forms can be found. About five round varieties are listed in this country, the largest and most orange being 'Golden Jubilee', a beautiful-looking, smooth, very fleshy variety. Its only drawback is that it sometimes tends to be shy of setting, again on account of the large flowers with protruding stigmas, so hand pollinate them if necessary.

In poor light there can also be a setting problem with 'Golden Sunrise', a globe-shaped deep yellow variety. Mine cropped reasonably well last year under cover, but I thought the flavour on the watery side compared with 'Golden Jubilee'. Brian Tree rates 'Tangella' highly, an orange-fruited variety bred by the Glasshouse Crops Research Institute. It is a good setter, and has orange-yellow fruit and a pleasant mild flavour. For outdoors Unwins recommend 'Yellow Perfection', claiming it is the earliest and most prolific tall yellow in existence.

The pear-shaped yellows are attractive and well flavoured, but interestingly, the true pear shape doesn't develop under short days, only later in the season. All these yellow varieties are indeterminate, and should be grown in the normal way.

A different kettle of fish altogether is the far more primitive yellow currant tomato, which, although indeterminate, throws out an abundance of sideshoots in every direction and has a naturally bushy, sprawly habit. Left to its own devices it would fruit on every lateral, covering a square yard of ground outdoors. Under cover the seed company Robinsons* suggest limiting it to three or four branches and pinching out the laterals. It's advice I should have taken! Mine were grown in a way that can only be described as 'free range', both indoors and out, smothering everything within reach indoors, but producing masses of tiny, literally currant-sized, golden-yellow fruits, which had to be hunted out from beneath piles of foliage.

Outdoor crops were mulched with Reflecta mulch plastic (black on the lower side to suppress weed growth; white on top to reflect light up on to the plants). It was a great help in keeping the fruit clean. The tiny tomatoes went on ripening late into the season, and were only killed off by frost. They look delightful in salads, and would be equally effective in soups, in casseroles, or for purely ornamental purposes.

Robinsons comment that both 'Yellow Currant' and 'Red Cherry' tomatoes are easily propagated and grown, possibly because they are descended from the wild varieties, and seem to be resistant to mildew. They are also relatively hardy, and when grown outdoors in Lancashire, where outdoor tomatoes are a difficult crop, have compared favourably with 'Tiny Tim' and 'Pixie'.

The cherry tomatoes are one size up from the 'currants', being about 2.5cm/1in in diameter. Although Robinsons bracket them with the 'Yellow Currant's as regards habit and culture, I found them less invasive and more controllable, and grew them with no difficulty as cordons. My children insisted on cherry tomatoes for the school packed lunches: living proof of their genuinely sweet flavour.

This doesn't apply to all small-fruited varieties. Someone will no doubt disagree, but I've been disappointed with the flavour of the small, recently introduced 'windowsill' tomatoes such as 'Minibel', and with the flavour, or lack of, of the undoubtedly early, small-fruited Sub Arctic varieties. On the other hand 'Gardener's Delight' (or 'Sugarbush', as it used to be known), which is only a little larger than a cherry tomato, has an excellent flavour, and the very similar but newer 'Sweet 100' is not far behind.

The Italian plum tomatoes, of which the variety 'Roma' is probably the best known here, are long and almost square sided. They are widely grown for making paste and canning, and with their firm flesh and oblong shape, are ideal for bottling. The flavour does seem to vary. I was very disappointed the first time I grew them several years ago; they seemed insipid, and were late to ripen. Yet last year they seemed no later than any other variety, were pleasantly flavoured, and cropped well. I suspect, as with 'Marmande's, that there are 'Roma's and 'Roma's, some selections being better than others, and that climatic factors also play an important role.

'Britain's Breakfast', one of the varieties from Robinsons which I tried last year, proved to be very much like 'Roma' in appearance, a plump, longish tomato. It bore prolifically both indoors and out, had a good flavour, and freezes well.

Various pink varieties thread themselves in and out of gardening literature and catalogues, usually with favourable comments about their flavour and merits. Unfortunately none seem to be available in current English catalogues. The Japanese are busy breeding them: 'Pink Panther' is one of theirs. 'Ponderosa' and 'Oxheart' are available in the USA. Brian Tree, who has grown both, favours 'Ponderosa' but was unimpressed by 'Oxheart', yet John Organ, in his excellent book *Rare Vegetables* (now out of print, but worth every penny if you come across it second-hand), waxes ecstatic about it, saying individual fruits have remarkably good flavour and can weigh up to 0.45kg/1lb. I tend to agree.

The white tomato originated in modern times in the United States, and is also highly recommended by Organ, not just as a novelty but for its 'massive, freely borne fruits which possess a superb smooth flavour'. Tomatoes taste best, of course, picked fully ripe with no further to travel than kitchen garden to kitchen. Occasionally, when mine are especially tempting, they fail to make the journey!

*When writing this article I had a great deal of help from Brian Tree, who had been responsible for the outstanding exhibit of unusual tomatoes, peppers, aubergines and melons which Fisons had mounted at the Chelsea Flower Show over the previous six years. Sadly, Brian died not very long afterwards. I also had help from W. Robinson & Sons, the remarkable Lancashire family seed firm, now run by the fourth and fifth generation, one of whose specialities is unusual tomatoes. Thirty years later, I would add to my favourites the yellow cherry 'Sungold', and two with deep purple flesh, 'Dallas' and 'Capri Rose', bred by our Neapolitan friend Mario Mennella.

THE AVANT GARDENER
Daily Telegraph, 25 May 1988

Is there such a thing as *l'avant garde* in vegetable growing? I think there is, and that the kitchen garden or vegetable plot of the avant gardener reflects the drift of current culinary, scientific and social ideas, converting them into something down to earth – and edible.

So this is what I would expect to find in the avant gardener's kitchen garden today.

First, there would be lots of salad plants, for salads epitomize modern notions of healthy eating. There would be crisp and crunchy lettuces like 'Little Gem', along with pretty red-leaved lettuces like the old French variety 'Merveille des Quatre Saisons' and the exquisite curled and frilled 'Lollo Rossa', a new Italian variety – perhaps coupled with its equally lovely stablemate green 'Lollo'.

Maybe there'd be a border of 'Salad Bowl' and 'Red Salad Bowl' lettuces. Forming loose heads of oak-shaped leaves, these don't run to seed, so provide pickings over a long season – a valuable quality for the time-pressed gardener of the twentieth century.

Coloured lettuce and the stunning Italian red chicory are now almost commonplace in chic restaurants and good supermarkets, but the avant gardener would have several salad plants still unknown to the general public. I'm thinking of the succulent-leaved summer purslane and the spicy salad rocket – both popular in the Mediterranean. In winter and spring, there's the dainty round-leaved, mild-flavoured winter purslane or claytonia, known as miner's lettuce or spring beauty in the United States, where it originated, as it was such a health-giving standby for the miners in spring.

Some salad plants in this progressive garden would undoubtedly be growing in attractive little broadcast patches for cut-and-come-again treatment. Possibilities include salad cress, salad rape, perhaps Chinese pak choi, curly endive, spinach and old-fashioned varieties of 'cutting' lettuce, as well as the purslane, claytonia and rocket already mentioned.

These closely grown crops would be cut when the young leaves were no more than 5–7cm/2–3in high, at their most nutritious, and tastiest, stage. Moreover, as the seedlings normally resprout after cutting, each patch would be cut two or three times, giving wonderful returns in small places.

This old gardening technique was employed in the past to force 'spring saladings' in hotbeds and frames for the tables of the gentry. It has found a new niche in the space-starved modern garden.

Avant gardeners scour seed catalogues in search of varieties of vegetables with real flavour. So they would have discovered the super-sweet varieties of sweetcorn, such as 'Candle' and 'Extra Early Sweet', which, unlike the traditional varieties, retain their sweetness after picking. But they must be grown apart from the traditional types, or the sweet characteristic will be lost by cross-pollination.

The dwarf French beans should all be varieties with exceptional flavour – purple podded varieties, the gold waxpods, or the fine, sometimes speckled 'filet' varieties such as 'Aramis'.

There would be several interesting varieties in the pea patch and these would certainly include some mangetout or sugar peas. These are the flat, edible-podded peas – expensive to buy but easy to grow and with a lovely flavour. A new type of mangetout is the American-bred 'Sugar Snap': it combines sweetness with a crunchy texture and, like all the mangetouts, is delicious sliced into salads or lightly cooked.

Another intriguing novelty is the semi-leafless pea, in which most of the leaves have become 'modified' into tendrils. Developed commercially to facilitate the combine harvesting of dry peas, they are a boon to gardeners as they are almost self-supporting. There could even be purple-podded peas in this adventurous garden. They are a tall old variety with striking purple pods though, sadly, the peas are green.

The brassica bed would be interesting, too. Incidentally, you would be unlikely to find a row of anything in the avant gardener's kitchen garden. The owners would have switched to the (old-fashioned) bed system, laying out the garden in 1–1.25m/3–4ft-wide beds, with plants grown at equidistant spacing in the beds. But I digress. Back to the brassicas.

If space was at a premium, as it tends to be, the avant gardener would spurn slow-growing cabbages and cauliflower and grow instead fast-maturing, space-saving brassicas such as sprouting calabrese (grown about 25cm/10in apart and ready in less than four months). Pride of place should go to the lime-green, superbly flavoured variety 'Romanesco'. Another worth trying is the recently introduced Texsel greens, developed from an Ethiopian oil-seed plant. Highly nutritious, it has an excellent, slightly spinachy flavour, and can be grown as a seedling salad crop or like spring greens. Also rated for its nutritional qualities, and also quick growing, is kohl rabi.

I would hope, too, as this is one of my obsessions, that there would be some exciting oriental greens in the garden – perhaps the serrated-leaved Japanese mustard mizuna or the very hardy, mild-flavoured komatsuna mustard 'Tendergreen', both providing generous pickings over a long season, including autumn, much of winter, and spring.

Adventurous vegetable growing and adventurous cooking go hand in hand and the vogue for ethnic cooking – Chinese, Indian and Middle Eastern – would be reflected in the chilli peppers growing in a warm spot or in the greenhouse. In the well-stocked herb garden a few exotics would be found, such as coriander, dill and perhaps the pretty Chinese or garlic chives. Their flat grass-like leaves have a refreshing, subtle, part-onion, part-garlic flavour, and in summer they produce beautiful, white, starry flowers, which can be used for flavouring. Which brings me to the revival of another lost art: the use of flowers in cookery. Surely this garden would be colourful with nasturtiums, old-fashioned pot marigolds, borage – its sweet, clear blue flowers can be sprinkled on salad or entombed dramatically in ice cubes – and more beside.

Common chives would be left to flower; the purple flowerets look beautiful in salads or in omelettes.

Culinary flowers could give our avant gardener an excuse for embracing another old gardening concept which is returning to fashion: growing flowers and vegetables together, sweeping away the demarcation lines. I should not be in the least surprised to find climbing runner beans, probably the lovely old variety 'Painted Lady', with flowers of apple blossom colours, romping over the garden pergola. And the recently revived dwarf varieties of runner bean – 'Hammond's Dwarf Scarlet', 'Pickwick' and 'Gulliver' – would be there too, glowing in the midst of flower beds, far prettier than a patch of salvias and quietly nurturing a welcome crop of beans.

THE KELSAE ONION FESTIVAL
The Garden, February 1982

If nothing else of note happens in my lifetime, at least I'll be able to tell my grandchildren that I was present at the 7th National Kelsae Onion Festival, held at the Harlow Car Gardens, Harrogate on 26 September 1981, when the World Record for the heaviest Kelsae onion was broken by Mr Bob Rodger of Crail, Fife, with an onion weighing 2.93kg/6lb 7oz, so breaking the record he had established the previous year. I might add that the century's record for cold and wet September Saturdays was probably set the same afternoon; mercifully such unspeakably foul weather is as rare as 6lb onions, but it must have deterred some of the 300 entrants who had been nurturing onions all summer. Absolutely nothing, however, would deter the enthusiastic hard core, who were there in force – albeit in wellington boots.

I should make it clear at the outset that I'm very ignorant of the showman's world, and have never so much as displayed a pea pod in a village show. But knowing only too well the numerous hazards which beset the production of ordinary vegetables grown for the kitchen, I have nothing but admiration for the patience and skill required to produce perfect show specimens – those unblemished sticks of celery, beetroot 60cm/2ft long with a full 30cm/12in of what can only be called 'rat's tail', smooth-skinned shiny onions neatly bound at the necks, parsnips and carrots which could have been moulded in a potter's studio rather than exposed to nature in garden soil, and in this case, these enormous, heavyweight, Kelsae onions.

Weight competitions, I learned, are a relatively new development. Indeed the rules are not yet fully established. There is controversy over the trimming of the neck: a political hot potato which must be grasped by the heavyweight establishment.

What is so special about the Kelsae onion? Apart from its remarkable capacity to grow to an enormous size, it is a handsome, good-quality onion with very high neck and shoulders, giving it a flask-like appearance. It is very popular as an exhibition onion.

It originated over forty years ago in an old Scottish country estate, and was introduced to the public by the Kelso nurserymen Laing and Mather, who maintained it for many years. A few years ago their business was taken over by the seedsmen Sinclair McGill, who are now guardians of the Kelsae, the sole producers of the seed and the sponsors of the annual Kelsae Onion Festival.

But back to the festival itself. Just before 2.30 p.m. the assembled throng were allowed to walk the plank (almost literally), between the general marquee and the exhibition marquee, to witness the public weigh-in. On the benches down the side and centre of the marquee were the mannequin-like vegetables in the show classes, while on a long table across the far end, lined up beside the scales, were the hopeful Kelsae heavies. Notable for 'their high shoulders and distinctive shape' (I quote from one of the organizers), some rough skinned, some smooth, most about 23cm/9in high with a girth of 10–15cm/4–6in, each was mounted on a little plastic stand and bore a label round its neck – a label with all but the most vital of its various statistics. They had been well protected overnight – or did I imagine the notice outside saying 'Beware: Alsatians on Guard'? As I was told later, 'It can get a bit cut-throat when there's big money at stake!'

At the appointed hour the solemn weigh-in began. Each onion in turn was picked up, gently

A spectator holding one of the giant onions at the 1981 Kelsae Onion Festival.

turned over, and checked for the last time, presumably for any signs of cracking or rot. They must 'be sound and true to type'. Surplus dirt was rubbed off the trimmed roots. Were they also, I wondered, looking for secret slugs which might tip the scales? Inspection completed, they were passed smoothly to a second man, who put them on the scales. The weight lit up on the illuminated register; the judge behind the scales wrote the weight on the label and hung it back around the onion's neck; the name of the grower, his area, and the weight were announced over the microphone; and the onion journeyed further down the human conveyor belt, either to be placed on the stand in the first, second or third position – or to join the dejected group of 'also-rans' at the far end of the table.

It took time; interest flagged and conversation mounted towards the middle of the procedure, but when only a few remained tension mounted until, on a nod from Radio Leeds, master of ceremonies Philip Swindells, Superintendent of Harlow Car Gardens, cracked the inescapable joke 'It looks as if someone here knows their onions', and the winner topped the scales.

In no time a Miss World scene had broken out – cameras flashing, reporters jostling around the ebullient, £500-the-richer Scottish farm worker, Bob Rodger, who with infinite patience and good humour answered the first of countless questions on how he'd done it.

Some vegetable champions are very unwilling to discuss their methods. They'd 'rather not say' – a polite equivalent of 'No comment'. But Bob Rodger and his clan of relations and friends, who between them walked off with most of the festival prizes, were not at all secretive. Bob Rodger himself is a relative newcomer to showing, only starting six years ago. He was taught the basics by his brother. Then perhaps, as often happens, he applied a fresh outsider's view to the received wisdom of generations and started beating the old hands at their own game. But very friendly rivalry it seemed to be.

For example, the traditional method of preparing the beds in autumn is to build up sandwich-like layers of soil and manure, adding fresh manure each year. But Bob decided this created too rich a mixture, so this year omitted the manure – and got healthier onions and far better results.

It's the early stages that matter in producing the champs, along with attention to detail and a good strain of seed. (Many of the best growers save their own seed.) The seed is sown at Christmas in a greenhouse or frame in 7.5cm/3in pots, and the seedlings moved in stages into 12.5cm/5in and finally 23cm/9in pots, the greenhouse being kept at a temperature of 13–15.5°C/55°–60°F. They are planted out in the open ground in April or early May with polythene protection, and during the summer measures are taken to keep them free of pests and disease. But it's all a question of good husbandry, the winners I talked to agreed, helped along in the north, which seems to produce all the winners, by the long hours of daylight in summer.

Bob Rodger goes to about nine shows a year, and selects his winners from about 135 onions planted out in his garden. He'd grow more if he had the space, but it's only a small council house garden and as he says, you've got to have them on your doorstep. You can't keep your eye on them if they're on an allotment a couple of miles away.

Producing the seed for the Kelsae onion is an interesting story in itself (and here I'm indebted to an article Philip Swindells wrote for the *Northern Gardener*). On their site at Kelso Sinclair McGill have 743 sq. m/8,000 sq. ft of glasshouses where the seed onions are grown. Everything is done by hand, so exactly the same procedure could be used by anyone saving their own onions for seed.

Seed for the 'mother' bulbs – those which eventually produce the seed sold to the public – is sown under glass in January. They are grown in frost-free conditions until the middle of April, when they are gradually hardened off before planting outdoors in May. During the summer they are left in the ground and grown normally, until lifted in the autumn. The key to maintaining the quality of the seed lies in roguing out any substandard onions when harvesting. Only the very largest onions, absolutely true 'Kelsae' in shape, completely free from any sign of disease, are selected for growing on for seed. All others are rejected.

These prime onions are planted in January and February in the greenhouses in slightly acid, sterilized soil, treated with John Innes base fertilizer and limestone. They need as long a growing season as possible. In June or early July they are given a top dressing of nitrate of soda to encourage growth, and in mid-August a dressing of sulphate of potash to encourage the tissues to harden. Although they are treated with the necessary pesticides while growing, these are withheld when the onions start to flower for fear of harming the pollinating insects. In dull weather pollinating has to be done by hand to ensure a good crop.

The seed heads ripen unevenly over a period of time, so as soon as any head looks black it is cut, and laid on newspaper on plastic trays in a dry and airy seed store. When the seed is thoroughly dry, it is threshed and cleaned.

So that's what goes on behind the scenes. Sinclair McGill are pleased with the way the festival, which is held in a different place each year, is progressing. The quality is improving, there's a lot of keen competition and the weights are getting heavier. But then, 1981 was a good year for onions and everyone assures me that the Kelsae onion is very good to eat.

....

Sadly, the Kelsae Onion Festival came to an end about twenty years ago, when the sponsors faced financial problems.

GOOSTREY GOOSEBERRY SHOW
The Garden, December 1982

Surely the prize for the best living horticultural tradition should go to the giant gooseberry competitions of mid-Cheshire? Having just returned from the annual Goostrey Gooseberry Show (Goostrey is a stone's throw from Jodrell Bank), I find it hard to decide whether I've been to a rather unusual but exceptionally friendly twentieth-century village produce show, or stepped back into history – so steeped in ritual and tradition is the whole procedure.

Records show that the giant gooseberry shows were in their heyday in the mid-nineteenth century, but started much earlier. The first edition of the *Gooseberry Growers' Register*, the main chronicler of the shows, was published in 1786, and recorded weights from shows which had already been held in previous years. The origins of the Goostrey show are shrouded in lost records. It was, however, mentioned in the 1875 *Gooseberry Growers' Register*, but evidently subsequently became moribund, for in 1897 the minute book records how growers were called to a meeting at the Red Lion inn with a view to reviving the show: which they did.

The old shows were held mainly in Lancashire, Cheshire and the Midlands. Today, as far as I know, the survivors are restricted to mid-Cheshire – eight shows in the Mid-Cheshire Gooseberry Shows Association, one other Cheshire show outside the association and a show at Egton Bridge, near Whitby in Yorkshire.

The Goostrey show is restricted to a maximum of thirty-two exhibiting members,

known as 'gatherers', who must be house-holders in Goostrey or one of four neighbouring parishes. The show really starts the night before when each gatherer collects his berries in the presence of another, paired with him as a witness. This is to prevent any cheating: for it's one of the fundamental rules of the show that you exhibit your own berries, grown in your garden.

We were sent along to John Egerton's garden on Friday evening to see the gathering. We'd be sure to see some good berries there, we were told, both John and his 21-year-old son Kevin being prizewinning growers. We arrived at 6.45 p.m., to find an average-sized council house garden, with a strip of vegetables along the back wall, some flowers at the front, but every other square inch taken up with gooseberry 'pens', specially wired off areas in which the 'trees' are grown. And how well those trees were protected – first with a layer of large mesh net to keep off blackbirds, then a layer of finer windbreak net to keep off wasps, and on top several portable polythene and wooden frames which could be put over them quickly at night to protect them from heavy rain or bad weather.

Mrs Egerton stood ready for the berries, with a tea tray covered with cotton wool. The polythene covers and nets were removed from the pens, and in front of the watchful eye (and witty tongue) of witness Bill Lynch, John Egerton moved carefully from one bush to the next, selecting the berries he wanted. You had the feeling he knew every berry along every branch, but with another show the following week, it was a fine art judging which could be left to swell, or whether, in the ensuing days, they would be overcome by the fate of bursting.

There are a whole range of classes: triplets – the heaviest three berries on one stalk; twins – a pair on one stalk; the steward's premium prize for the heaviest berry in the show; colour classes for the heaviest red, yellow, green and white respectively; and the 'plates' – the champion showplate of the heaviest twelve berries of any one variety, followed by lesser plates with berries of one colour, or mixed.

The picked berries were examined carefully, and handled as delicately as if they were new-born babies, were laid in groups on the tray, no doubt with their destined classes in mind. The pens were re-covered and we went indoors to check the weights.

Most growers have their own sets of apothecary's scales, the berries being weighed, as they always have been, in troy pennyweights (dwts) and grains. All over Goostrey and the surrounding villages at that hour men were poring over their scales, their hopes alternately being dashed and raised by their monstrous berries. (Some of the 'also-rans' I brought home were 5cm/2in long and 4cm/1½in wide.)

After weighing the berries are arranged in home-made wooden boxes designed for the purpose. Compartment by compartment, drawer by drawer are filled with triplets, twins, premium berries, coloureds and those which will end up on the plates. Finally the box is closed, tied with tape, and sealed with wax by the witness. Small buttons, halfpennies and penny pieces are preferred for the seal. The box is put somewhere cool for the night – for the berries can sweat and lose weight, maybe – unspeakable horror – even burst overnight. The holes drilled neatly in the sides of the box, like

John Egerton weighing his gooseberries at home on apothecary's scales, in troy pennyweights, the night before the contest. One became the champion berry.

pigeonholes in a dovecot, serve to keep their precious cargo well ventilated in the critical hours ahead.

And so to the show the following afternoon. By 1.45 p.m. all the exhibitors are assembled behind tables drawn up in a square around the edges of the room, sealed boxes in front of them, brimming beer mugs beside them. The boxes are a lovely sight: some recently made, most mellowed with years of use, some no doubt passed from father to son. Accumulated blobs of broken red wax on the lids testify to their owner's show pedigree. There were even a couple of mavericks such as a shoe box – the chairman's, I think – while the most recently joined member, still by his own admission very much a novice, had his two berries in a cottage cheese pot, duly taped and sealed. And inside the boxes, rows of plump fat berries, some hairy, some smooth, nestling on a bed of cotton wool or Kleenex.

Facing the main body of competitors are the officials – the chairman, the secretary, his assistant and the weigher, with small scales for the single berries, twins and triplets, and larger scales for the plates. On one side is the still empty show case into which the winning fruits will be placed during the course of the afternoon, each with a handwritten record of its weight, colour, variety, grower, ranking and so on. Two of the members have been elected scrutineers. They have to settle any disputes: verify, if there's doubt, that a 'green' berry is not a 'white' (the two colours are almost indistinguishable to the layman's eye), vouchsafe that all berries said to be one variety are indeed the same variety and so on. In the centre of the room, journeying constantly between the gatherers and the weigher are the two carriers, whose job it is to take offered berries to the scales where they are weighed against any challengers, and to return the losing berry to its owner – to fight another round if necessary. It's another of the basic rules that you must always send up your heaviest berry.

Each witness checks that the seals on his partner's box are intact, the seals are broken, lids opened, and business begins.

They start with triplets. Not much competition there. Then twins. 'Twins, gentlemen please. Anyone got any twins?' The carriers wander to the tables, waiting for candidates. Someone lifts the lid of his box and volunteers a pair. They're put on the scales. 'Any more against these?' asks the carrier. Someone brings out another pair. 'Good pair, that'll shift them,' says an admiring voice. They're put on the other side of the scales. The scales hover uncertainly, necks crane to see which side will dip … but the first pair has it. The second is taken back to its owner. When there are no more successful challengers the winner is weighed and put in the showcase. Then challenging for the second and third place starts. It's all very leisurely, accompanied by muttered chatter. 'Where's them twins you had Alfie? . . . 'Mine bursted on Tuesday' . . . 'Lost mine two nights ago' . . . and so on.

From the twins to the prize for the heaviest berry. And here all the exhibitors are ranked in order, from one to twenty-seven this year – and each gets a prize. First berry on the scales, by tradition, is sent up by last year's winner, in this case the much-respected raiser of seedlings, Frank Carter. 'That's a fair berry and all,' someone says as he hands it over, but it was challenged and beaten by John Egerton with a 'Firbob' weighing 33 dwts 5 grains. So we'd seen the champion being picked. Then weighing begins for all the other places, simply balancing berry against berry.

They work on through the classes. The show plate was won, for the second year in succession, by Terry Price, with the variety

'Woodpecker'. There's a break in the middle of the afternoon, and the day ends with tea and prize giving in an adjacent room.

How are these giant gooseberries grown? There must be many, probably untold variations, but as far as I could gather, this is broadly how it's done. The starting point is a cutting taken in the back end – from your own bushes if you're a real enthusiast. All but the top four buds are rubbed off to get a leg of 23–30cm/9–12in. Two autumns later these are planted in the pens.

The pens have been well prepared. Good medium loam is the ideal soil, enriched with farmyard manure. As most of the trees are grown in small gardens there is little chance of moving to fresh ground: so when it comes to replanting, the top foot or so is replaced with a barrowload of fresh soil. Soil from stacked turves was, and still is, used. One old grower's formula, passed on shortly before he died, was to plant 'with a clod of turf below and a clod above'.

A grower with one show might have up to 20 or 25 bushes; if he belonged to two clubs, it could be up to 50 bushes.

Pruning and training is generally done in the autumn. Old wood is cut out, and five to eight shoots of new growth selected (the lower number for shy growers), from as near the centre of the tree as possible. These are trained outwards so that they radiate like spokes from a wheel – stretched out horizontally like signposts, as Frank Carter put it. The branches are then shortened to about 18cm/7in, and encouraged to remain horizontal by pinning them in position with large pegs. The berries hang free along the branches. In summer very little pruning is done, as it would tend to let in sunlight, which would ripen the berries.

There's a lot in knowing your varieties and treating them accordingly. Hazards include finches and tits attacking the buds in winter, spring frosts, summer wasps and blackbirds, but most of all 'bursting' towards ripening – generally from heavy rain, but also in very dry conditions. Some growers keep their trees covered, and water and sprinkle to create a moist atmosphere; others believe in exposing their bushes to the elements. According to old accounts, chickweed was grown beneath bushes to encourage a moist atmosphere, and as Gavin Brown relates in the 1949 Fruit Year Book there was 'suckling' – 'saucers of water under the pendant fruits so that the calyx just dips into the water'!

Thinning is another key operation, generally done in two or three stages in May and June. Nineteenth-century growers thinned to four or five berries per tree, but far more berries are kept on today. It's a gamble with the weather. In an early year more may be left on as an insurance against berries being lost by bursting.

Generally the best berries are borne on young wood on three- to four-year-old trees. John Egerton leaves his for about three years, and if they're not shaping up, it's straight on to the rubbish heap. Some trees may be kept for up to ten years, but once a tree has produced a really good berry, it is felt, it should be ripped out, cuttings taken, and another planted.

The Goostrey growers concentrate on about twenty varieties. In the reds there's 'Lord Derby', 'Lloyd George', 'Red London' and the modern varieties 'Jodrell Bank', 'Blackden Gem' and 'Just Betty', raised by Frank Carter. Green varieties are 'Admiral Beatty', 'Surprise', and 'Village Green', a new variety raised by Tom Blackshaw. White varieties include 'Transparent', 'Lord Kitchener', 'Fascination' and the new variety 'Kathryn Hartley', and the yellows, which tend to be the heaviest, are 'Edith Cavell', 'Woodpecker' and 'Firbob'.

Growers have always improved their stock by selection and raising new seedlings. Special fairs used to be held after the show season ended when new varieties were 'let out', i.e. sold, for the first time. In the Goostrey area Frank Carter has raised fourteen successful varieties, two of them, 'Blackden Gem' and 'Firbob', a red and a yellow, coming from the same berry. He starts simply by squeezing the pips from a ripe berry into a pot, covering with sand, and allowing them to winter outdoors before planting the seedlings out in spring. Within three years one gets the first berries.

Gooseberry show enthusiasts will find more information in the *1949 Fruit Year Book*, in back numbers of the *Gooseberry Growers' Register* housed in the RHS Lindley Library, and in R.A. Redfern's *Gooseberry Shows of Old*, enlarged and reissued by Mr Allan Hill. This lists all the prizewinning berries between 1809 and 1895. The most remarkable variety of all was 'London', a consistent winner over a span of sixty-five years. It set a record weight of 37 dwts 7 grains in 1852, which stood until 1978, when it was beaten by a Cheshire grower, Mr A. Dingle, with a 'Woodpecker' of 37 dwts 15 grains.

Manchester University houses the national collection of over 200 gooseberry varieties – a fine collection, all grown as upright cordons. Frank Carter was responsible for them until his recent retirement. There are still uncertainties and anomalies in their naming, not least because in the past seedlings raised by different growers were sometimes given the same name.

One can't leave gooseberries without mentioning flavour, but I have to report that I didn't meet a single grower who ate his berries; I'd been led to believe that, as they are selected and grown solely for size, they would not be worth eating. But if the samples I had after the show are anything to go by, the gatherers and their families are missing out. They were delicious! (So incidentally, were some of the old varieties from the Manchester collection.) However, as this is a competitive not a culinary world, I'll end by echoing Mr Hill's closing sentiments in *Gooseberry Shows of Old*: 'Here's wishing you bigger and bigger unbursted berries for the future.'

'FRUIT & VEG': A PHOTOGRAPHIC EXHIBITION
The Garden, March 1981

The history of gardening is a subject which has commanded steadily increasing interest in recent years; but as anyone who has tried to carry out research has discovered, the pictorial record of fruit and vegetable growing, both in the distant and the immediate past, is sparse compared to that of the ornamental aspects of horticulture.

A photographic exhibition touring East Anglia goes some way towards filling the gap. Entitled simply *Fruit & Veg*, and sponsored jointly by the brewers Tolly Cobbold and the Eastern Arts Association, it is a collection of modern and historic photos on the theme of fruit and vegetables in East Anglia. The contemporary photos are taken by Charles Hall, who was awarded the commission on the basis of an open national competition. He also did the research for the historic photos.

The two sections complement each other beautifully, giving the whole a compelling, and appropriate, historic perspective. For in trying to capture the essence of what Charles Hall calls 'the richness of horticultural experience in the area' one cannot escape the feeling of standing at a watershed. The East Anglian region has always been better known

Our Nissen tunnel, made from a wartime Nissen hut, took on a romantic air in Charles Hall's exhibition of East Anglian horticultural enterprises.

for its commercial rather than its amateur horticulture, but in both immense changes are taking place. *Fruit & Veg* hints at many of these, in particular those where tradition is being forced to adjust to the streamlined demands of the space age – or disappear.

It can be seen disappearing in the great houses of the area: in the orangeries, paint sadly peeling from the walls, no longer harbouring exotic fruits in winter; in walled kitchen gardens only partially exploited, in the best sense of the word – a shadow of their former productive selves.

Signs of modernizing change are evident in the pumping stations, which regulate the water table in much of the area, still an essential feature of East Anglian commercial horticulture. The wind- and steam-powered pumps have all but gone; and the diesel and manually operated electric pumps which followed, machines with a human face lovingly cared for by their staff, are being replaced by automated electric pumps, sealed in a soulless stove enamel box, tended by an itinerant technician.

Many of the most memorable pictures in the exhibition are of commercial horticulture. One example is a remarkably detailed panoramic view of the Chivers jam factory at Histon in 1910 (a tall platform was built to enable the photo to be taken). It shows the extensive, intensively cultivated grounds around the factory, in which all the produce needed was grown, including even the willows to make the baskets. Detailed also is a late nineteenth-century photo of Deal Cullen's seed warehouse – still functional, still in use today, as recorded in one of Charles Hall's photographs, proof of the continuing vitality of the seed industry in the area.

The clean efficiency of modern fruit production is captured in a beautiful rust-toned print of a well-pruned apple tree; while photos taken in the glasshouses of the modernized Buntings Nurseries at Great Horkesley highlight an unusual aspect of modern horticulture, whitefly being maintained on tobacco plants as part of a biological control programme.

Two photos stand out as epitomizing a timeless element in commercial horticulture. The first is of two brothers cutting 'January King' cabbage in a large field. Only the improvised plastic sack apron, held in place with baler twine, ties the picture to the 1980s. The other is of the nightly fruit and vegetable auction in Wisbech – one of two held in buildings on either side of the road. Taken today, it could as easily have been yesterday. During the fifteen-second exposure the figures, unaware that they were being photographed, scarcely moved enough to blur the photo.

Although much of modern horticulture is bypassed in this exhibition (often, evidently, because it failed to strike a chord of sympathy with the photographer), the homely end of the spectrum obviously appeals to him. There are several photographs of allotments, lingering, perhaps too much, on their Heath Robinson, corrugated iron elements, leaving one wondering if East Anglian allotments are perhaps less immaculate and loved than their counterparts in more populous parts of the country. Notwithstanding, one of the most appealing photographs in the exhibition is of Mr and Mrs Webster, an elderly couple who keep a fine allotment in Welwyn Garden City.

Research and education is another strand of the fruit and veg tradition in the region, represented in this case by the John Innes Institute at Norwich, pushing back the frontiers of science, the Henry Doubleday Research Association, trying to stem the tide, and the Cambridge University Botanic Garden. What greater contrast can be imagined than escaping from a muddy allotment to wander through the jungle of foreign foliage, fruiting dates and bananas in the tropical greenhouse at Cambridge?

This quiet, unpretentious exhibition provoked as many thoughts on the unchanging, as on the changing elements of English horticulture – the simple charm of cottage gardens, half-timbered houses shielded from the world by shrubbery, the backache of strawberry picking. I found it also left many, sometimes contradictory images, lingering in my mind. For example, Emerson's photo 'A Spring Idyll': a demure, innocent young girl peeling potatoes in a sun-drenched orchard, contrasted starkly with the wizened, weatherbeaten face of the old woman in the Cambridge market, her bunch of home-grown onions on the pavement – an English counterpart of the *vieilles femmes* which have not yet quite disappeared from the French market. Did the one become the other with the passage of years?

COLOURFUL MEMORIES OF '84
The Garden, January 1985

NORFOLK LAVENDER

When twenty years from now the youngsters of today are telling the youngsters of tomorrow how much better summers were in their youth, it could well be summer '84 colouring their memories. For it was, for most of us, an exceptionally sunny and colourful summer. Certainly for me some wonderful horticultural memories were culled, hopefully to be 'recollected in tranquillity' in those cold wintry days when gardening is best enjoyed as a cerebral activity.

Perhaps most unforgettable of all was a visit to Norfolk Lavender, by chance on the first day of the lavender harvest in the third week in July. It was a brilliant day, but the blue of the sky was pallid in comparison with the brilliant purple of the 4-hectare/10-acre field of lavender being harvested, vivid beyond anything one could have imagined. The humped, rounded bands of lavender hedges seemed to stretch to the horizon, the soft green of the cut rows, splashed with blobs of blue where a few sprigs had escaped the cutter, contrasted dramatically with the solid purple of the unharvested rows. And within the field itself there were distinct shades of purple: in this case the darker rows were 'No 9' and 'No 6', cultivars grown for distilling, and the lighter rows 'Fring A', a cultivar grown for dried lavender. To complete the assault on one's senses the air of course was laden – no other word will do – with the scent of lavender and the inevitable buzz of contented insects.

It was intoxicating just to stand there, watching the cutter move steadily across the fields astride the rows, virtually shaving the bushes, as the cutting and pruning are done in one operation. The stems jog up the conveyor belt – creating another band of purple colour – and are stuffed into hessian sacks. Most are destined for the distillery, as 70 per cent of the crop is grown for the extraction of the oils, used as the basis of perfumes. The rest is used in various forms as dried lavender, and is initially piled on a specially ducted floor in the drying shed, where warm air is blown through it.

Norfolk Lavender Ltd is at Caley Mill, in the north Norfolk village of Heacham, 2.5 kilometres/1½ miles from the sea. It's an area of low rainfall and high sunshine, with well-drained, slightly alkaline sandy soils, ideally suited to lavender growing. With 40.5 hectares/100 acres of lavender under cultivation, they are today the largest growers and distillers of lavender in the country. The products they make with their lavender – soap, talcum powder, sachets, toilet water – are virtually the only genuine 'English' lavender products on the market today.

The company originated in the 1930s when nurseryman Linn Chilvers and landowner 'Ginger' Dusgate joined forces to plant up the first 2.4 hectares/6 acres, hoping to revive the English lavender industry which had once flourished around Mitcham in Surrey but had been devastated by modern development and disease. (At the time farmers were reluctant to have lavender grown on their land, as it was believed to rob the soil of its fertility.) The company has now passed into the ownership of the Head family, who have been involved with it since 1953, and is run today by Henry Head and his mother, Ann.

Besides growing lavender for oil and drying, plants are also raised for garden use and sold to the public. Almost all the cultivars grown for all purposes are hybrids of true lavender, *Lavandula angustifolia*, and they have been raised by Norfolk Lavender over the years. Originally the wild or spike lavender, *L. latifolia*, was used commercially, but it had to be abandoned as it proved so susceptible to the disease shab, the scourge of lavender production both here and in France. The company is continually experimenting and raising improved lines with improved oils and extended harvest. But it is a slow, painstaking business. Once a cross has been made, the necessary testing, trials and bulking up from cuttings can mean it is ten years before a promising new hybrid is in commercial use. The six oil-bearing cultivars now used have been selected from nearly a hundred hybrids.

New planting is done as the need arises, but the bushes have a long life of usefulness: some in fact have been in production for twenty years. Herbicides are now used to control weeds, and though it used to be thought that fertilizers were unnecessary or harmful to lavender, a high-potash fertilizer is now used to encourage flower development. The bushes don't come into full production until five years after planting.

Visitors are welcome at Caley Mill, and can see the stills, the drying room, a film about the industry, the fields and the attractive lavenders and herbs planted in the grounds. Anyone interested in learning more about the romantic history of English lavender should read Sally Festing's *The Story of Lavender*, recently reprinted.

WELEDA HERBAL MEDICINES

In Ilkeston, not far from Nottingham, in a somewhat unlikely built-up area, is what can only be described as a modern physic garden. Weleda (UK) Ltd is a company making homoeopathic medicines, natural and herbal medicines, and more recently toiletries – all from natural products. Most of the raw material for its 1,500 or so products comes from a small garden, no more than 1/10 of a hectare/1/3 of an acre in size, situated beside its laboratories and factory.

I visited the garden in June, in beautiful early summer weather – and in the quiet way of more or less unfettered herb gardens it was enchanting, not least because of its air of purposefulness.

The diversity of plants used in making medicines is astonishing. At least eighty different species are grown in the garden: trees such as hazel, willow, birch, blackthorn; raspberries and wild strawberries; vegetables like garlic, horseradish, broad and French beans; ordinary weeds such as chickweed, annual nettle and dandelion; very many common wild flowers – bluebells, cowslips, foxglove, for example; and of course 'ordinary' herbs – borage, marjoram,

Harvest time at Norfolk Lavender in July, the deep purples of the uncut bushes contrasting with the soft greens of those already harvested by the gentle action of the mechanized cutter.

angelica, thyme, camomile and so on.

They are grown in rectangular beds with grassed paths between them, though unkempt corners are allowed to develop to provide a range of environments. Some of the wild plants it seems, don't take too kindly to being 'cultivated'. Indeed one large patch of stinging nettles is purposely left undisturbed, as their presence is said to intensify the essential oils in the herbs.

Many of the 'herbs', to use the word in its old-fashioned sense, are colourful and decorative. Beds of greater celandine (*Chelidonium majus*) were flowering when I was there (used medicinally); there were straggly clumps of yellow woad and blue comfrey along the hedge, dainty patches of Jacob's ladder, St John's wort and heartsease, and, stealing the limelight, huge dashing plants of variegated milk thistle and the Scotch thistle (*Onopordum acanthium*).

In homoeopathic medicine the mother tincture extracted from the plant is diluted to such an extent that a handful of plants is sufficient for the manufacture of a great deal of medicine. With natural and herbal medicine larger quantities of plant material are needed, and Weleda grows some of these on a nearby field. Oats (*Avena sativa*) are grown there, cut in flower to make a stress relieving drug for which there is increasing demand; and so is pot marigold (*Calendula officinalis*), used to make calendula ointment, a traditional medicine now being supplied to the NHS.

All medicinal plants have to be grown in very pure conditions, without the use of artificial fertilizers or chemical sprays: they must also be disease free. The Weleda garden is operated on the biodynamic principles advocated by Rudolf Steiner. This has many facets, one of the most important being the use of special preparations which are applied to compost when it is made, to the soil or to plants when they are growing.

Organic methods of pest, disease and weed control are also used. Teas made from camomile and marsh horsetail (*Equisetum palustre*) are used against fungal diseases; lemon balm is interplanted with wormwood to counteract the rust to which balm is prone. Perennial weeds such as thistles are controlled by collecting them, burning them, and making a weedkiller spray from their ashes.

Apart from the plants it grows, Weleda also collects from the wild – very carefully, I should add. And from all that everyone said about it, it sounds the greatest fun, a most unusual works outing! A wide range of plants is collected: common wild plants like eyebright, plantain, bittersweet, daisies, violets, dandelion, yarrow, cleavers and poppies; several types of fern; the berries, flowers and leaves of sloe; green horse chestnut conkers, even the bark of some trees. The biggest job of all is collecting ripe haws, as several hundred kilos are needed each year to make a tincture for treating heart conditions.

All the collecting has to be done with great care – at the right place, the right way and at the right time. The chemical composition of the plants changes – not just with the season, but with the time of day, which can make all the difference to their quality for medicinal purposes.

It's reassuring to know that this ancient knowledge is still being put to practical use – easing the ailments of the modern world. But after summer '84, gardeners, at least, should have no need of stress-relieving drugs – or am I writing from the smug vantage point of one of the few who didn't suffer from a water shortage?

....

I'm happy to say that Norfolk Lavender and Weleda are still both flourishing in the twenty-first century.

I can't expect everyone to share my fascination with earthworms, which goes back to my childhood, when my favourite record was Arthur Askey and his song about worms. 'Hello, Playmates, I'm going to sing you a song about worms.' 'You jolly well can't,' says his inner voice. 'I jolly well can,' he replies, and so it went on until he burst into:

I'm such a dear little wriggling worm
Covered in mud from head to stern
Passing the time from night til morn
Making little casts in the middle of the lawn
Just an or-din-ary little worm
Squiggle squiggle squiggle . . . [and finally, an ever-ascending]
Squirm, squirm, squirm!

I asked for it when – surely the pinnacle of my achievements as a garden writer – I was on a sort of *Desert Island Discs* on Ipswich local radio. Sadly they couldn't find it. Assuming there are some gardeners out there as fascinated with earthworms as I am, I'm tempted to echo Arthur Askey and say I jolly well *can* reprint these articles – at least in part. Some time after they were written I went to an international conference on earthworms in Cambridge. The participants, myself included, had a great deal of trouble finding the venue, the 'To the Worm Conference' signs having proved irresistible to students. A fellow delegate was the indomitable Mary Appelhof, one of the pioneers of worm composting.

....

EARTHWORMS - PART I
The Garden, April 1983

At a horticultural press gathering several months ago I overheard a remark which in no uncertain terms discredited earthworms. Surely worms aren't 'out'? I thought; don't gardeners still believe in worms? The chain of thought set in motion made me decide to burrow in the literature, or cast about should I say, to catch up with contemporary thinking on the habits and value of the earthworm. Let's start with some facts about worms and their habits.

There are over twenty species of earthworms in the UK, but only about five are of practical significance. Among the most important are the burrowing and casting worms

Lumbricus terrestris and *Allolobophora longa*, and the manure worm or brandling *Eisenia fetida*. The number of worms in cultivated soils varies tremendously; an average number in good, cultivated soil would be about 100 per 10 sq. ft/sq. m, in grassland about 150 per 10 sq. ft/sq. m, and in non-acid woodland as many as 300 per 10 sq. ft/sq. m. The amount of organic matter present has a spectacular effect on the numbers of worms: a plentiful supply can lead to a tenfold increase in the worm population in three years.

They are by no means distributed at random in the soil. They tend to congregate where there is a food supply. Clusters of young worms can often be found on rotting roots, such as parsnips. This might explain why it used to be thought that earthworms cause disease. When Darwin published his controversial observations about the beneficial activities of earthworms (his classic work *Formation of Vegetable Mold through the Action of Worms* was first published in 1881) contemporary garden books were full of remedies for killing earthworms, so harmful were they considered to be to plants.

Worms also congregate where there is moisture. They are much more active in moist than in dry weather, and overall tolerate cold and wet conditions better than hot and dry. It may take two years for the worm population to recover from the damaging effects of a prolonged drought.

The depth at which they operate varies with the species and the season. The deep vertical burrows of *L. terrestris* can go as deep as 2.5m/7ft, and on the whole worms go deeper, i.e. below the top 7cm/2½in of soil when it is very dry or very cold. Many of them, in fact, go into a quiescent state of comparative inactivity in mid-summer, and sometimes in mid-winter, because of the extremes of temperature. The surface feeders, incidentally, tend to be a darker colour than the deeper species.

They reproduce by producing cocoons containing eggs, which are slipped off their bodies and deposited near the surface in wet weather, but deeper in dry conditions. The cocoons can survive adverse conditions which would destroy adult worms. They are also one means by which worms are spread, for they are easily picked up on the soles of feet or on tools.

The eggs in the cocoons hatch into tiny worms. The rate of breeding depends upon circumstances, but one of the fastest breeders is *Eisenia fetida*. Its pale, lemon-shaped cocoons, each a couple of millimetres long, are easily spotted in decaying compost. Each adult worm can produce two to five cocoons a week, each with up to five eggs in it, resulting in ten to fifteen hatchlings per week. These will be mature in seven or eight weeks. *Lumbricus terrestris*, on the other hand, takes at least four months to reach maturity.

Although most worms probably only live a matter of months, some live for several years. The longest recorded life span is twelve years.

An interesting characteristic of earthworms is their ability to regenerate parts of their bodies which have been damaged. *L. terrestris* is poor in this respect, but *Eisenia fetida* can replace almost any damaged organ. On the whole segments 'aft' are replaced more readily than those 'for'ard'. Moles, which catch and store worms in caches, capitalize on the fact by taking the precaution of biting off the first three to five segments so that their prey can't escape before required.

Like all living creatures, worms require oxygen. They normally utilize the oxygen in the air in the soil, but rather surprisingly perhaps, they can also utilize the oxygen in water. Provided the water is aerated, most earthworms can survive in flooded conditions for several months, the limiting factor on their survival probably being lack of food rather than oxygen. Worms which have suffered in very dry conditions recover if put into water.

As for food, the worm feeds on organic matter, which is generally extracted from the soil which passes through its gut. *Lumbricus terrestris* is exceptional in feeding directly on the leaves which it drags into its burrow to plug the burrow. (An interesting observation, first made by Darwin, is that worms almost always drag leaves into the burrow by their tip, effectively leaving the far less digestible stalk out in the open.)

Given a choice, all worms prefer to feed on dung, or really succulent green material, rather than drier material such as tree leaves. The more nitrogen in their diet, the faster they grow. More cocoons are produced when they feed on decaying animal matter than on decaying vegetable matter. Bacteria, fungi and nematodes all form part of their diet, extracted, along with other animal and plant material, from the soil passing through their gut.

Worms are extremely sensitive creatures. First of all they are sensitive to soil pH, though tolerance of very acid or very alkaline conditions varies with the different species. Very few worms are found in acid soils with a pH below 4.5. For most worms the optimum pH seems to be 5 to 6, i.e. slightly acid. *Lumbricus terrestris* is known to flourish in increasingly alkaline conditions – at least up to a pH of 7.5. In practice, extreme acidity is sometimes a limiting factor on the worm population; in such cases liming should be the first step towards encouraging their increase.

The earthworm is also very sensitive to touch. A good example of this is *L. terrestris*, which scavenges for food on the surface, but likes to keep its tail at home base, in its burrow. Touch the tip and it withdraws sharply. Grab hold of the top half of its body, and it will prove almost impossible to pull it out of the ground. The worm's posterior segments swell to fill the hole and its setae – bristles which project from the body – grip the burrow wall. The result is that it is more likely to break in half than to be drawn out of the burrow. And while on the subject of burrows, another of the characteristics of *L. terrestris* is that it never leaves its burrow unplugged. Any plug that is removed is immediately replaced, and if there's no organic material available, even stones will be used – hence the worm 'cairns' on gravel paths.

Thirdly, worms are sensitive to many chemicals. Fortunately most commercial fertilizers, applied at normal rates, do not harm worms; indeed nitrogen fertilizers help to build up the worm population. But an important exception is the commonly used fertilizer sulphate of ammonia, which is antagonistic to worms, driving them away from the surface layers of the soil.

Few herbicides (weedkillers) are directly damaging to worms but they may change the population of worms by altering the availability of organic matter.

However, many pesticides, both insecticides and fungicides, are toxic to worms, in particular several used in orchards such as copper fungicides and benomyl. It is one of the ironies of orchard spraying that benomyl, used to control apple scab, also destroys the worm population. For left to their own devices worms can remove most of the scab-infected leaves in the autumn, preventing reinfection in the following year.

Some top fruit growers who have eliminated worms by the use of benomyl are running into drainage problems, worms playing an important role in the creation of a free-draining soil. It must also be said that cases have been noted where blackcurrant yields in plantations with no worms were no lower than those in plantations with worms. Similarly there was no loss of yield in an orchard where, as a result of fifteen years of spraying with copper fungicides, the soil was virtually without worms, where an unrotted vegetation mat had accumulated on the surface as a result, and where there was deterioration of the soil crumb structure. However, where worms were inoculated into orchards of young trees on Dutch polders, yields increased noticeably. It looks as if the extensive rooting system of established fruit trees can compensate for the loss of fertility in the upper layers of the soil. But as a scientist recently pointed out, a great deal of work in the last ninety years has demonstrated that worms are beneficial, but not that they are essential!

Be that as it may, work is now being done at Rothamsted Experimental Station on the long-term effect of pesticides on worms. (In future all new pesticides must be tested for their toxicity on worms before they are approved for use.) Another aspect is that even when the worms themselves are not killed by pesticides, toxic ingredients are absorbed into their bodies, which in due course may be eaten by predators such as birds and moles. This also happens with metals such as lead and zinc, which are concentrated in the worm's tissues, so increasing their toxicity.

When worms burrow they are literally eating their way through the soil, turning over and churning enormous amounts of soil. Much of this is subsoil brought up from the lower levels and eventually deposited on the surface as casts. Anything from 2 to 250 tonnes per hectare/2.4 acres per annum can be deposited on the surface, equivalent to a layer up to 5cm/2in thick. This is in addition to the huge amounts turned over in the soil. The long-term effect is to produce a stone-free layer on the surface: in old pastures it can be as much as 15cm/6in deep.

In the course of these immense earth-moving operations earthworms are playing a key role in the breakdown of organic matter.

They consume huge quantities of organic matter and litter and start the cycle of its breakdown. Enzymes in the worm's stomach break it down further and combine it intimately with particles of soil; other bacteria in their stomachs probably help to break it down even further into the ultimate particles of humus from which plant foods are released.

Casts, the end product of the process, are extraordinarily rich: they contain more microorganisms, more inorganic minerals and more organic matter than the soil from which they were derived – all in forms available to plants. They also contain enzymes which continue to break down organic matter when the casts are on the soil surface. Casts also play a key part in the formation of soil aggregates, the basis of good soil crumb structure.

Not only do the activities of worms make nutrients available to plants, but their own excreta, and the decay of their protein-rich bodies when they die, add large quantities of nitrate to the soil. A single dead worm can yield up to 10mg of nitrate, the average life span of a worm is probably about a year, there are several million worms in 1 hectare/2.4 acres of average soil, their bodies decay very rapidly . . . All in all it is estimated that the average population of worms in the soil could produce as much as 100kg/220lb of nitrate per hectare/2.4 acres per annum. That's twice the amount of nitrogen required by the average horticultural crop.

EARTHWORMS - PART 2
The Garden, May 1983

Good soil structure is the key to soil fertility. In an ideal, well-structured soil, the mineral particles are bound together with humus to form permanent granules or aggregates, separated from one another by large pores. These pores join to make a network of channels through the soil, and it is this network which allows surplus water to drain away, roots to penetrate deeply so they utilize water and mineral reserves in the lower levels of the soil, and air to permeate the soil so that all the biological processes flourish.

That's the ideal soil. In practice, in the typical British loamy soil, the granules are not stable: they break down under heavy rain, or with cultivation, or by treading on the soil. As a result the pores between them, and hence the vertical channels, get clogged up with tiny particles of clay and silt, and the whole system operates at far less than optimum efficiency until such time as the structure recovers.

Earthworms can do a great deal to improve the soil structure, particularly our burrowing and casting worms such as *Lumbricus terrestris*, *Allolobophora longa* and *A. nocturna*. The burrows themselves, some of which are permanent with 'cemented' sides, open up the soil and create aeration and drainage channels. This has been recognized for a long time. What has been less widely appreciated is the role of casts in forming the soil aggregates, most notably the casts deposited within the soil, rather than on its surface.

In the course of their burrowing activities worms take in soil and fresh organic residues, which are intimately mixed with gums and lime in their passage through their intestines. Finally the mixture is formed into long cylindrical ribbons which are deposited in the soil as casts, in what has been picturesquely described as a 'walnut-like' coil. These casts (always provided there *was* organic matter in the soil) are very stable and do not disintegrate easily after heavy rainfall. They are, moreover, rapidly invaded by soil microorganisms, and probably by plant roots, which reinforce them mechanically, making them even more stable. This is the beginning of the 'nutty' structure which typifies a really good soil.

Truly stable casts are only made if there is plenty of organic matter in the soil. In other words, to make the most effective use of your earthworms, they must be well fed. It's the old story of working in as much organic matter as you possibly can.

Worms casts are exceptionally rich in nutrients in forms available to the plants. It has been proved that soil structure and fertility can be greatly improved by adding worm casts to the soil: not an easy thing to emulate in practice! It is probably easier to add the earthworms – or the organic matter which encourages them.

Another rather bizarre quality of worm casts, noted in a report from Rothamsted Experimental Station, is that they have a deodorizing effect. It may be possible to filter the gases from piggeries through earthworm casts to remove the smell.

Many experiments have been done in which earthworms were added to poor soils to improve them. This has been successful in a wide range of situations, from poor pastures in New Zealand to Russian prairies, in the reclamation of Dutch polders and land flooded by sea water, in peat bogs where peat has been removed, and on land denuded by industrial enterprises such as strip mining. A National Coal Board farm in South Wales is being gradually restored to agricultural use after coal mining by a combination of drainage and cultivation techniques and the large-scale introduction of earthworms.

In many cases the first step in improvement or reclamation is liming, to bring the acidity down to levels at which worms will flourish. The next step could be the addition of plenty of organic matter as food for the worms – and then the worms are introduced. Some dramatic examples of reclamation and yield increases have been obtained by these means. For example, grass yields were doubled in New Zealand by introducing worms to poor pastures. In this case the method used was to

Mary Appelhof making me a worm bin after we had met at the Cambridge Worm Conference. Her sweatshirts were emblazoned with 'Worms Eat My Garbage', the title of her influential manual.

dig up turf and establish it on the wormless pastures. This is far more effective than trying to introduce individual 'loose' worms, whether they have been gathered or bred for the purpose. Generally speaking, earthworms do not adapt well if moved to a new environment: they are likely to die, or will only build up their numbers extremely slowly.

On a smaller scale, i.e. in flowerpots, it is beginning to look as if earthworms are beneficial. In my student youth I was taught to remove all earthworms when potting up, because, I was told, they had a disturbing influence. But a series of experiments at Aberystwyth, designed primarily to investigate the earthworm's role in soil granulation, also showed quite clearly that plant growth (in this case grass) was best in pots with, rather than without earthworms, though sometimes it took as long as a year for the difference to show up. Since learning this I've been scooping up stray worms and adding them to potted up house plants, herbs and so on, optimistically hoping that they will prove adaptable enough to survive the change to a new environment and will, in due course, 'do good'.

Worm compost can be made on a small scale, to utilize household and garden refuse, and a means of doing so has been worked out by Jack Temple, a nurseryman who now concentrates on organic methods. This system is ideal for people with small gardens, or even city dwellers who find it hard to produce enough waste to make an effective compost heap.

In essence, the worms are bred in converted rubbish bins and fed with the wastes. It can also be done on a larger scale in specially constructed pits in the garden.

The compost is ready within about six months, and with the addition of a little lime and wood ash, can either be used as a concentrated plant feed, or as the basis of a potting compost. Since switching entirely to worm compost for plant raising, Jack Temple claims to have had far better results, with exceptionally healthy plants. An unexpected benefit is that he no longer finds it necessary to take routine hygiene measures such as cleaning out seed boxes.

A sign of the times perhaps, he was recently asked to supply millions of earthworms to an Arab country to help make deserts fertile. He had to decline: his worms wouldn't have liked the move from Surrey – being the species *Eisenia fetida*, they would have died because of the lack of organic matter in the desert soils.

Last word to Darwin and his classic *The Formation of Vegetable Mold through the Action of Earthworms*, published in 1881. It's a thoroughly good read – clear, concise and full of interesting observations. One of these particularly caught my eye, for I had noticed and puzzled over it myself. He writes: 'The mere compression of the soil seems to be in some degree favourable to them [earthworms], for they often abound in old gravel walks, and in footpaths across fields.'

Since converting our garden into narrow beds with well-trodden paths between them I have found huge numbers of worms in the paths, just below the surface, far more than are evident in the beds. I had always imagined when digging over the garden that I was creating soil conditions the worms would enjoy. Yet here they were, obviously attracted to the solid, compacted paths. I wonder why? Is this an argument in favour of 'no-digging'?

A paragraph from Darwin's concluding chapter summarizes the worm story as accurately today as it did then. 'Worms have played a more important part in the history of the world than most persons would at first suppose.' Darwin would be very comforted to learn that the students at Aberystwyth wear T-shirts saying 'Lumbricus Rules'.

PHILADELPHIA GREEN
From *Practical Gardening*, June 1988

My excuse for going to the USA last autumn was to look at oriental vegetables being grown by the various Asian communities who have settled there. It was also an excuse to meet American gardeners and to get some first-hand experience of the widely differing climatic conditions and attendant problems they have to cope with in that vast continent.

I landed in Philadelphia, which I'd fondly imagined to be a balmy sort of place. The first shock was that it felt like the tropics: hot, humid, with a very tropical background chorus of croaking frogs and chirping insects.

My guide was Jane Pepper, the energetic Scottish-by-birth President of the Pennsylvania Horticultural Society. A project very dear to her heart is Philadelphia Green – a remarkable community gardening programme. Philly, I discovered, may be the home of Liberty Bell and boast some of the finest old buildings in the USA, but it is also a huge, sprawling industrial city with more than its quota of inner-city problems, rubbish-strewn lots and desolate slums, occupied by low-income families, mainly black, Hispanics and immigrants. Perhaps I should say it *was* like that, for Philadelphia Green is, literally, transforming the city.

Originating in a window box programme started by a small gardening association, it is now run by the Pennsylvania Horticultural Society with funds from the city, commercial benefactors and proceeds from their Flower Show. Employing twenty-five full-time workers, Philadelphia Green last year worked with more than 600 inner-city groups on over 1100 gardening projects.

These range from street schemes for window boxes, plant tubs – one district planted eighty-five wine barrels with flowers – and tree planting, to the creation of flower and vegetable gardens, orchards, miniature parks or 'sitting gardens' and even a wild garden – all on disused lots.

Once started, very few projects fall by the wayside, perhaps because the initiative comes

The colourful Glenwood Community Garden in Philadelphia, profuse with vegetables and flowers, and exemplifying the success of the Philadelphia Green programme to encourage gardening.

from the grass roots. Tree planting and garden creation projects must start with a petition signed by 80 per cent of the neighbourhood, with a guaranteed core of active gardeners and a once-off fee of 25 dollars per block. At that point Philadelphia Green steps in with help in preparing the site, supplies of construction materials such as fencing, soil (sod to Americans), mulching material, plants, seeds – often delivered in the project's own green and white 'Gardenmobile' van. Supporting activities include a training programme for 'garden interns', who dispense gardening advice and a 'tree corps' of residents trained in the care of street trees.

As we drove away, we peeped into a tiny 'sitting garden', an oasis squeezed between two buildings, and visited another community garden started by the Korean Senior Citizens Association. True to oriental tradition not an inch was wasted. Beautiful crops of Chinese cabbage, peppers, oriental onions, radishes and a few medicinal plants were grown in immaculate raised beds. Several elderly Korean ladies were harvesting beans, and we interrupted a man sowing spinach. These gardens not only enable immigrants to grow their own food but allow them to pass on their rural skills to an urban generation.

WAY OUT IN THE WEST
Practical Gardening, August 1988

Flying over the skyscrapers and traffic filled highways of Seattle I chuckled to think my stay in the metropolis had been spent visiting P-patches and the Back Yard Compost demo, and learning about Zoo Doo. Zoo Doo, to quote from the Seattle Engineering Department's elegant leaflet

printed on 100 per cent recycled paper, is 'a sweet smelling composted mixture of elephant, pony, bison and llama manure, straw bedding, grass and leaves from the grounds of Woodland Park Zoo'. And it's a very popular substance among Seattle's 2,500 P-patchers, residents lucky enough to have one of the 1,000 or so plots scattered over twenty sites where they can grow their own fruit, flowers and vegetables – organically.

A lively young Laotian refugee took a group of us to the Danny Woo P-patch gardens, built and maintained by the Asian community and perched on a hillside in the heart of the built-up international district of the city. To qualify for a plot you had to be Asian, over sixty-two, and live in the district.

It was a microcosm of Asian ingenuity, cunningly terraced, with the use of old railway sleepers and telegraph poles, to create as much land as possible. I saw a wider range of crops on that little hillside than in the rest of the USA put together: tiny trellises of bitter gourd, 'bean poles' supporting bottle gourds, taro, sweet potato, yard-long beans, peppers – all marginal crops for Seattle's coolish maritime climate, but helped by an unusually warm summer. Mustard leaves were pinned on a line to salt and dry for winter pickles, and dandelion, mint, Chinese chives, amaranth, wolfberry, black nightshade (not to be confused with the poisonous deadly nightshade) and lemon grass were some of the herbs being tended in the main by elderly ladies, for use in their traditional dishes.

An imaginative education programme is run by the Seattle Tilth Association – an enthusiastic group of organic gardeners. In their attractive demonstration garden there's an excellent demonstration of the theory and practice of different composting methods, from simple rubbish-filled trenches to a wide range of home-made and commercial composting bins. My favourite was the worm composting bin innocently disguised as a somewhat coffin-like garden bench, but harbouring an army of red manure worms energetically converting household wastes into a wonderful rich compost.

I can't leave Seattle without mentioning the wonderful salads I had there, in large measure due to the activities of Mark Musick, one of the founders of Tilth. He had been instrumental in growing and introducing unusual herbs, vegetables and salads (some included fennel and shepherd's purse blossoms) to restaurants and supermarkets. Many of these ideas had been pioneered at Pragtree Farm, set in a beautiful valley north of Seattle, so a visit there was a must.

In a garden full of interesting plants what caught my eye was the Garden Giant mushroom (*Stropharia rugosoannulata*). It's a large edible mushroom up to 454g/1lb in weight. In a moist climate it can be cultivated along the edge of vegetable beds, provided it is fed with a diet of wood chips, sawdust or even wheat straw. European in origin, the spawn is now available in the US.

From Seattle I travelled on to the horticultural mecca of northern California. By chance two of my contacts were fairly recently established seed companies, Le Marché Seeds and Shepherd's Garden Seeds, both founded by women, dedicated to making the best European and American varieties available to home gardeners (as 'amateurs' are called). Where vegetables and herbs are concerned, they concentrate on varieties with flavour and good culinary qualities. It has to be said that while many American vegetables look fabulous, they are often surprisingly tasteless, perhaps because they travel huge distances from field to market and are bred for their 'travelability'.

Many American gardeners are becoming concerned at the disappearance of their old seed varieties, accelerated by commercial pressures to buy new varieties. On the Students' Farm at the University of California in Davis, primarily a demonstration garden for the students, I saw old varieties being collected, evaluated and saved for seed.

The Students' Garden was full of the sort of food plants which thrive in warm climates but are borderline in England: sesame, quinoa, various kinds of yard-long or cow beans, luffas (young luffas taste like courgettes) and curiosities such as blue popcorn and the 'Moon and Stars' watermelon, so-called after the amazing, bright yellow moon and star markings on its dark green skin. And this was my first encounter with green tomatoes, i.e. tomatoes that are green when mature, and well flavoured with it.

A few days later seedslady Renée Shepherd introduced me to another novelty, a mini-pumpkin, an unlikely thing to emanate from the land of giant pumpkins. Called 'Munchkin', the bright orange, beautifully ridged little pumpkins are only 7.5–10cm/3–4in wide, ideal for baking whole. (There's a similar variety called 'Jack-be-Little'.)

But I still hadn't seen everything in the way of unusual vegetables. My last stop on the west coast was Chino Farms – a Japanese family roadside stall in Del Mar, renowned for the quality and variety of their produce. Take their tomatoes. Yellow tomatoes: a choice of giants, round, pear shaped, plum shaped, cherry size and currant size. Red tomatoes: ditto, green, white and dusky brown tomatoes as well. The dusky browns tasted particularly good.

Aubergines: long and round dark purple; white egg-shaped; round, bright red; round, green with white stripes; and beautiful long, lilac and white ones. Peppers included tiny yellow ones, flat 'bonnet'-shaped ones and long hot 'Jalapeño's. There were pink and green okra, long thin turnips, superbly sweet, gleaming white sweetcorn cobs . . . and so on.

A final thought. Looking back now on a brief visit to that vast American continent, I realize how thankful we should be for our gentle British climate. We don't have to box our roses and yew hedges in for winter, as they do in Milwaukee, or shade our tomatoes from the summer sun, as they do in Arizona, or put electric fences around sweetcorn to fend off the racoons, as I saw in Washington State. We should be thankful too for the wide range of plants we can grow in our more moderate climate – and for our tradition of gardening. I hate to say this, but the typical American front garden is unbelievably boring: a hedgeless grass plot. It may be dotted with trees, if the house is large, with a few evergreen shrubs if it's middle sized, or occasionally brightened with a strip of bedding plants near the house. But it's got nothing on the average English garden.

The Danny Woo P-patch (Community Garden) in Seattle, where only Asians over sixty-two years of age were entitled to have plots. It harboured an astonishing range of Asian plants grown in traditional ways.

Native to Europe, teasels are beautiful, decorative plants, which attract wildlife and have medicinal and practical uses. When introduced to North America, however, they became noxious invasive weeds, aggressively seeding along the interstate highways. A single plant can produce 2,000 seeds.

5 LEARNING FROM THE BOFFINS

Much gardening practice is based on tradition and hearsay, and however curious and experimentally inclined we are, one gardening lifetime isn't long enough, and most gardens not large enough, to try out everything oneself. As a garden writer I spent a lot of time in the 1980s with the boffins, once, believe it or not, attending a carrot conference. (I still have the grinning carrot-shaped biro we were presented with – a very impractical shape for writing.) Don't get alarmed: I've spared you the carrot conference report.

I've selected articles and extracts which I think still chime a practical chord with serious gardeners, though it's interesting how the 'experts' don't always agree. I'm always a little reluctant to write about pests, preferring to turn a blind eye, but they are an inescapable part of gardening life. After all, when two or three vegetable growers get together, you can bet they end up talking about pests. So they get a look in here. 'Vegetables as Medicine and Fodder' on page 203 was a report from an Institute of Biology conference, which opened intriguing global windows on the world of vegetables.

You never quite know what the end result of any article will be. After the piece on deep cultivation appeared I had a letter from a lady saying it had stimulated her to double dig her allotment. She was in her eighties!

LOWDOWN ON WEED SEED
From 'Soil and Soil Pests', *The Garden*, June 1979

The National Vegetable Research Station (NVRS), situated on a 202-hectare/500-acre farm at Wellesbourne near Stratford-upon-Avon, was founded in 1949 as a research station for vegetable crops. Its prime concern is with vegetable crops grown outdoors in this country by commercial growers – crops such as Brussels sprouts, carrots, cabbage, lettuce, onions and beans. There is very often a useful spin-off for amateurs. Sometimes their research findings verify old gardening sayings; sometimes they disprove them; sometimes they indicate new techniques which could be adopted by amateurs.

WEED SEEDS IN THE SOIL

An adage that the NVRS has demonstrated to be true is 'One year's seeds is seven years' weeds'. A team at the NVRS has been trying to answer some basic questions about the weed seed population in the soil: how many weed seeds are there in the soil, at what rate are they lost, what affects this, what is the effect of cultivation on the percentage of weed seeds which germinate, and what other factors affect the number of weed seeds which germinate and the time of year at which they do so?

Some of the answers confirm our worst suspicions. For example, there are likely to be between 5,000 and 10,000 viable, i.e. living, seeds per 1 sq. m/10.7 sq. ft in the top 15cm/6in of soil, which amounts to roughly 20 to 40 million seeds per 0.4 hectares/1 acre. In cultivated ground some of these, such as the familiar groundsel and chickweed, are relatively short lived. But others are long lived – for example, fat hen and fool's parsley, the latter being one of the most persistent. Where fool's parsley seeds were mixed in the surface layers of frequently cultivated soil 20 per cent were still dormant, and viable, five years later. This is apparently due to its exceptionally thick seed coat. Seeds that are left undisturbed can survive far longer, often for many years. The best-known example of this is black nightshade, where there was 80 per cent germination of seeds dug up from soil which had been undisturbed for thirty-nine years.

Two other characteristics of annual weeds contribute to their success as a plant group. They have a very short life cycle, so can often germinate, flower, and go to seed, before a vegetable crop in which they are sitting tenants is lifted from the ground. They also produce immense numbers of seeds: 70,000 from one goodly specimen of fat hen, for example.

When soil is cultivated a certain proportion of seeds germinate on the surface, some germinate under the soil and fail to come up, some are lost due to exposure to birds, etc. Seed counts in the soil show that where soil is cultivated every year, 50 per cent of the weed seed in the soil is lost every year. If this is drawn out on a curve, one can see that it actually takes the proverbial seven years for the seed population to decrease to 1 per cent of its original number.

So the moral of the tale is that, in an ordinary garden, the annual weed population can be kept under control with regular cultivation. The important thing is to prevent seeding, which can cause such an explosion in the weed population. Which, of course, is only scientific corroboration of what every working gardener has learned from experience.

In uncultivated ground less than one-quarter of the weed seeds are lost each year. There is an initial flush of weed growth, but this slowly diminishes, leaving a reserve of weed seed beneath which can remain dormant for a very long time.

When this ground is dug over for use, a huge crop of weed seed will be unleashed. To minimize this, it would be wiser initially to confine cultivation to the surface, just surface hoeing, for example. That is unless there were overriding reasons for doing otherwise.

GREEN MANURING V. WEEDS

Green manuring was the subject of much discussion at the recent Organic Growers Conference, but a novel idea was harnessing the technique to control weeds. The underlying science is that some plants excrete substances which are hostile to certain weeds, so inhibiting their development. The best-known example is the marigold *Tagetes minuta*, a monstrous plant growing 2.3–2.6m/7–8ft high with tiny flowers (hence its somewhat ambiguous name). It is claimed to have an inhibiting effect on certain soil eelworms – as well as on the growth of such weeds as ground elder, convolvulus and twitch. From all accounts it is ineffective until it has reached a height of at least 2m/6ft. It can be grown as a green manure, cutting down and composting the foliage.

Buckwheat is another plant which has some curious, so far unexplained effects on other plants and has, in France, demonstrated its potential for 'cleaning' ground from weeds. Buckwheat seems to be so potent that ground has to be left for a short period after it has been grown, as it is liable to inhibit the germination of whatever is sown next – friend or foe! Worth trying?

....

NVRS is no more as an independent body and has become part of Warwick University.

SOIL COMPACTION AND DEEP DIGGING
From 'Soil and Soil Pests', *The Garden*, June 1979

As so often happens in research, work on one problem yields unexpected information in a completely different field. In this case the objective at NVRS was to investigate the effect of deep placement of fertilizer.

In the experiments some plots were double dug and fertilizer placed at a depth of 46cm/18in, some were simply double dug as control plots, some were cultivated normally. The unexpected result was the increased yields obtained simply by the process of double digging, irrespective of the use of fertilizer.

Pursuing this further, some experimental pits were dug 90cm/3ft deep, the soil being replaced in the order in which it was removed. Broad beans grown on the pit soil gave an increased yield of 95 per cent. This work, of course, was only of academic interest: disturbing soil to a depth of 90cm/3ft is not a practical proposition in everyday cultivation. But what was the explanation?

It is well known that virtually impermeable layers or pans can form in the soil. Sometimes this is a natural hard pan caused by mineral deposits. Sometimes under arable conditions a plough pan can be formed by continued cultivation at the same depth, due to the way one tractor wheel treads in the furrow compressing the soil beneath. Probably the existence of a compacted soil is not always recognized. At Wellesbourne there appeared to be no problem; yet deep cultivation gave remarkable results.

What was actually happening as a result of the soil below being loosened? Subsequent work on the phenomenon has indicated that the effect of breaking up lower levels of soil is directly related to the use of water in the soil. Vegetable plant roots penetrate far deeper than is normally realized; in reasonable conditions the roots of plants such as Brussels sprouts, which are in the ground for a long period, can easily reach depths of 80cm–1m/2½–3ft. The broad bean roots in the double-dug plots grew about 20cm/8in deeper than those in the other plots, and were therefore extracting water from a lower level of soil.

It was also proved that in these plots, when more water was being taken from the lower levels, less was taken from the surface layers, which therefore remained moister for longer.

The significance here is that most of the nutrients available to plants are in the upper layers of the soil, but it is very difficult for plant roots to extract these nutrients from dry soil. In dry spells plants suffer both directly from the shortage of water and, as a secondary effect, from lack of nutrients which become unavailable in dry soil due to lack of water. So the value of double digging, it seemed, lay in keeping the upper layers of the soil moist. (This incidentally seems to be another argument in favour of surface mulching.)

What should amateurs do to benefit from this research? The first thing is to see if there is a compaction problem in one's soil. In good soils where there is continual natural restructuring there would be no problem. Try to examine the soil just below the depth at which it is normally dug, to see if it appears free and open with root penetration to a lower level. If there are signs of compaction, the problem can be cured by manual double digging. It should be quite sufficient to do this once, and from then on to take care to maintain the good structure of the soil by minimizing cultivation. To this end I believe there is a lot to be said for establishing a vegetable garden in narrow beds, each about 90cm/1 yard wide, which can be cultivated entirely from the edges, so eliminating all weight and treading on the soil.

TACKLING BUILDERS' RUBBLE AND RELATED MATTERS
From 'On the Way to Wales and Back', *The Garden*, December 1981

We recently fulfilled a long-cherished wish to visit the National Centre for Alternative Technology (NCAT) at Llwyngwern quarry, Machynlleth, just north of Aberystwyth in Wales. A group of people took over the abandoned quarry tip in 1974 and have converted it into a centre to demonstrate the practical realities of self-sufficiency, in every sense. It is an impressive place, with power generated by harnessing wind, sun and water. They grow most of their own food without using any artificial fertilizers or chemicals.

The centre has one of the few demonstration gardens devoted to organic methods, and is a valuable source of information for gardeners.

One of the most interesting plots contrasts methods of reclaiming quarry waste. The quarry had been abandoned for more than twenty years when it was taken over, so had to be cleared initially of bracken and shrubby growth. While some areas could boast reasonable topsoil, in others the surface consisted of nothing more than mineral slate dust – an inhospitable-looking growing medium. Experimental plots were laid out to compare growth on slate alone, on slate dust mixed with 5–7.5cm/2–3in of compost, and on slate dust covered with 30cm/1ft of soil into which compost had been incorporated. The slate dust is fairly alkaline, which may help to counteract the natural acidity of the Welsh site. The slate dust alone produced, as expected, very poor crops; but crops on slate and compost were quite as good as those on slate, soil and compost. Jeremy Light, who has been responsible for the gardening experiments, feels there is a lesson here for people trying to establish gardens on the equivalent of builders' rubble. Rather than go to the expense of importing costly topsoil, money spent on compost or manure would give as good returns.

This is borne out by my own experience in converting an extremely stony piece of ground, previously part of a farmyard, into cultivated ground. I did no more than cover it in autumn with a layer about 23cm/9in thick of spent mushroom compost, and allowed it to work itself in. The plot was growing tomatoes (of a kind) the following summer.

The concept of 'no digging' appeals to many people for reasons ranging from the ideological to pure laziness. While the general view at NCAT is that digging is necessary in some circumstances – for example, to get rid of a hard pan, or incorporate manure at a deep level – very good crops are being produced on the plot which has not been subjected to conventional digging. The fertility is being maintained by applying compost mulches during the growing season, and mulches of leafmould or bracken in the autumn.

The plot is being compared to one in which there is ordinary digging and compost application, and one in which no compost is added and the only digging is to remove weeds. In the very dry summer three years ago the 'no digging' plot produced the best crops.

In the first year of the experiment soil temperatures were taken at a depth of 23cm/9in to see if mulching prevented the soil from warming up in spring: in fact temperature differences were so slight as to be negligible. In this area of exceptionally high rainfall (between 200 and 230cm/80 and 90in per annum), a great deal of leaching inevitably occurs in winter. For this reason the purpose of the autumn mulches is protective rather than nutritive: hence the use of bracken and leafmould.

KEY FACTS ON COMPOSTING
From 'Organic Growers Conference', *The Garden*, May 1980

Two points about composting were driven home to me during the 1980 Organic Growers Conference. The first was the importance of getting air into the heap, especially in the early phases of decomposition. In farmyards the ideal way of building heaps has proved to be in layers about 30cm/12in thick (allowing at least three to four days to elapse between adding each layer), and using a muck spreader which throws out the material almost in a spray, so that an enormous amount of air is worked into the layers. That is the sort of 'image' one should have in mind when building up a domestic heap – finely cut up, well-mixed material, full of air.

The second point is the need to raise the temperature of the heap to 60°C/140°F to kill off pests, disease and weeds – and make well-rotted compost which is easy to handle. Having, I believe, introduced the soil pest symphilids into my polythene tunnel through using uncomposted farmyard manure, this fact has been brought home to me the hard way.

These temperatures cannot be reached in small heaps, certainly not by the normal domestic practice of adding small quantities of refuse to an open heap. One needs to add at least 0.76 cubic metres/1 cubic yard of waste in one operation to generate the sort of temperatures required – and on a small scale this can only be done by having a 'preliminary' waste bin, mixing all types of rubbish into it, and then when enough is accumulated, turning it into a layer on the compost heap. To conserve heat in the heap it should be well insulated, ideally with timber or breeze-block sides, or sides made with straw bales. And when it has been built up, a thick insulating covering on top, ideally straw, is the best guarantee of the heap maturing well. (We have found seaweed and old carpets work well.)

POTS AND MODULES WIN OVER SEEDBEDS
From 'Soil and Soil Pests', *The Garden*, January 1979

A spin-off from research at NVRS into cabbage root fly demonstrated the value of growing cauliflowers (but it would also apply to other brassicas) in individual pots and planting them out, rather than sowing in rows in a seedbed and pulling seedlings for transplanting. In experiments plants had been potted up in 8cm/3in pots using old peat compost, to which a little sand had been added to make it heavier. Seeds could equally well have been sown in any kind of module.

In the experiments, pot-grown early summer cauliflowers gave good curds two or three weeks earlier than plants raised in a seedbed.

The belief that brassicas need the check of transplanting from a seedbed has been disproved, and for most amateur requirements, a few well-grown individual plants would be of far more value than a larger number of poorer seedlings, the majority of which would be jettisoned. Another tip from them: to get a staggered supply for the household, when it comes to planting out, choose plants of different sizes, rather than just selecting the largest which is what one does instinctively. The largest will mature and produce curds first, but the smaller ones will develop a little later, in their own good time, providing a natural succession.

MAKING THE MOST OF POLYTUNNELS
From 'Growing Vegetables in Plastic Tunnels', *The Garden*, July 1981

Producing out-of-season crops has always been one of the challenges of vegetable growing. Our (wealthier) ancestors enjoyed asparagus at Christmas, kidney beans in April, lettuce all year round, and melons and cucumbers at the most unseasonable times. Originally these feats were accomplished using hotbeds of fermenting horse manure, later with heated greenhouses. The demise of the horse and the rise of the sheikhs – and a few other factors besides – have effectively eliminated these sources of energy as far as the average gardener is concerned. We are left with the skilful utilization of cold greenhouses or unheated tunnels if we are to satisfy our yearnings to cheat the seasons even a little.

This is being written at the end of March. Just to put you in the picture, the rain is beating down almost horizontally, the daffodils are still

prone from storms earlier in the week, and most of this Suffolk vegetable garden is as spongy as a Scottish hillside. (I went out yesterday intending to sow parsnips and carrots and came back musing on the possibilities of cultivating bog myrtle and wondering if it was edible!) The remnants of the overwintered vegetables – Brussels sprouts, chards, kales and leeks – look haggard and unappetizing.

But in the polythene tunnels, which comprise a large and ugly converted Nissen hut and a small LBS Polythene 6m/20ft tunnel, there's a healthy carpet of burgeoning greenery. Endives, lettuces, radishes, chards, sorrel and claytonia in their prime; vigorous patches of mint, chervil and parsley; potatoes under black plastic, hopefully starting into growth, whereas the ground destined for early potatoes outside is literally under water; small patches of cress, rocket and 'Sugar Loaf' chicory seedlings for salads; recently sown 'Karate' cabbage for spring greens; and, courtesy of the mild winter, the last pickings of Chinese cabbage, fennel and a green, leafy continental celery.

A few weeks back a crop of purple-veined Japanese mustard 'Miike Giant' was transplanted outdoors from the tunnel after good pickings all winter; its place has been taken by an experimental patch of green manure, to be dug in, I hope, before planting a summer crop of climbing French beans or tomatoes. What tremendous use can be made of a protected area!

These crops could, of course, be grown just as well in a glasshouse, but polythene-covered structures, whether tunnels or a traditional greenhouse-shaped structure clad with polythene, have two overwhelming advantages for the ordinary vegetable grower. They are a fraction of the cost and are easily erected and dismantled, so can be moved to a fresh site every two or three years, avoiding the build-up of soil diseases which occurs in a permanent greenhouse. They are particularly useful for vegetable growing where the season is short.

The Lee Valley Experimental Horticulture Station at Hoddesdon in Hertfordshire carries out very useful research into polytunnel crops for commercial growers, so I went along to see what had emerged which would be of interest to amateur gardeners. 'Protection', a term which embraces both glass and polythene greenhouses and tunnels, is useful for two main categories of vegetables: those with only a very short period in which they can be grown outdoors (green peppers, aubergines, Chinese cabbage), and those where the season can be extended by growing earlier or later crops (courgettes, sweetcorn, celery).

FRENCH BEANS

Climbing French beans appear to be one of the most rewarding crops under cover. Because they are self-pollinating, they are more suitable than runner beans, which are insect pollinated. This can cause problems indoors, as most pollinating insects prefer to operate outdoors and if, say, bees are introduced into a greenhouse, they cease to work when the temperature becomes too high.

Although dwarf French beans also do well under cover, the climbing beans give higher yields over a season. Of the various types experimented with the shorter, round-podded beans gave only two-thirds of the yield of the flat-podded types. However, they are, quite rightly I think, considered a better-quality bean, commanding higher prices on the market.

For some reason French beans are better raised in small pots 8cm/3½in, or a compartmentalized polystyrene tray such as Propapacks, than in the ordinary soil or peat blocks normally used by growers for plant raising. A trick growers use successfully is to place the seeds on damp newspaper, and two or three hours later to sow seeds which have started to swell in pots loosely filled with peat compost. The purpose of this is not to see if the seed is viable (swelling is a purely mechanical reaction and even dead seeds will swell), but to shorten the period in which they would be in damp peat, which can cause rotting. Three seeds can be sown in each pot. If all three germinate, the weakest is removed before planting.

Lee Valley investigated different spacing distances, and now recommend two plants per station: in other words, planting out as one unit the two plants raised in a pot (quite contrary to anything one had ever thought about root competition) with 30–35cm/12–14in between stations and 1m/40in between rows. Plants did better in single rows than in double rows

Climbing purple French beans making full use of the exceptional height (3.4m/11ft) of our polytunnel, and giving us an early and reliable crop.

(We grew beans this way in the Nissen tunnel last year. They formed an almost impenetrable wall and yields, I'm sure, could have been higher. This year we will try the two-plants-per-station-per-one-string system.) Incidentally there was no stopping of plants, or de-leafing, in the Lee Valley trials.

Lee Valley recommends sowing an unheated crop of climbing French beans in late April or early May, planting out about two weeks later in early to mid-May, and harvesting late July onwards. From my experience I would say it is worth trying earlier sowings (starting in a propagator at the end of March) and hoping for a warm spring to give pickings in June.

They are now investigating the possibility of training the plants inclined at an angle, to see if this will increase the light available to each plant and make picking easier. Another tip: they found the best method of picking, to avoid breaking off the tips of the beans as so easily happens, was to cut them with a short stalk, using spring-loaded Snips.

COURGETTES

Courgettes, like green peppers, can be numbered among those once unknown vegetables which have become widely accepted. (Though it wasn't so long ago that I saw them labelled 'Gorjets' in the Bury St Edmunds market!) It is still not always realized that courgettes are simply marrows picked at a very immature stage, when no more than 10–15cm/4–6in long. As far as I know, any marrow can be grown for use as courgettes, though certain varieties, normally bush rather than trailing varieties, seem to be more productive and make better courgettes.

In a good summer producing an abundance of courgettes outdoors is very easy; in a cold summer the plants are prone to disease and slow to 'get away'. So it can be worth growing even two or three plants under cover.

at the same density. This was attributed to the increased light available to each plant.

French beans can be trained up a vertical string attached to an overhead wire. The two plants at each station happily share the same string, though where three plants were trained up one string experimentally, the yields were lower. Again, light and air circulation seem to be important. Having pairs of plants growing up each string gives more space and ventilation than would be the case with equidistant spacing between single plants, forming a 'wall' of beans.

Our polytunnel was productive all year round. In summer we mulched the paths heavily with straw, which encouraged earthworm activity and created beautiful soil.

For growing under protection without heat Lee Valley recommend sowing in mid- to late April, planting out about two to three weeks later in early to mid-May. This allows harvesting between mid-June and late September. Again, it is probably worth trying earlier sowings, started in a propagator, say at the very end of March or early April, which will pay dividends if the spring is kindly. Last year I made the first plantings in the Nissen tunnel in mid-April, under cloches which were removed a couple of weeks later. The tunnel was so cold and draughty in April 1980 that the double protection at that stage seemed justified. The plants fruited well in advance of any outdoors.

As with French beans, courgettes respond best to being raised in pots rather than soil blocks or modules. Excellent results have been obtained by sowing single seeds in 8cm/3½in pots, only half filled with peat compost, and then planting out at the 'first rough leaf' stage. Suitable spacing is to grow them in two-row beds, with 50cm/20in between plants, and 60cm/24in between rows. Slugs are very attracted to young plants, so precautionary measures should be taken.

Courgettes grow more vigorously under cover than outdoors, and in spite of being bush varieties, a central leader is often produced which is easily damaged underfoot when collecting the fruit. Lee Valley experimented with training this single leader up strings. The idea was to make the bushes more open and keep the head of the plant in the light. In commercial terms the extra work didn't pay, but it would be worth considering for amateur conditions, as a means of improving air circulation, so helping to prevent botrytis, which is a risk to plant and fruit when growth becomes too rampant and bushy.

Once producing, courgettes must be picked regularly when they are young, three times a week if necessary. This is to encourage further fruiting, and in some varieties to catch the fruit before the ends swell into a bulbous shape, which happens if they grow too large.

SWEETCORN

Sweetcorn is another summer crop worth growing under cover. It will crop earlier and more reliably indoors than outdoors, but one of its major assets is that it requires little attention and suffers from few pests and diseases. So it is perhaps worth considering if you plan a long summer holiday. Neighbours might be persuaded to keep an eye on sweetcorn where they would baulk at your tomatoes or cucumbers. As it grows quite tall, it does require a tunnel with a headroom of 2.4m/8ft or more at the ridge.

For protected cropping sweetcorn would be sown in late April, planted in mid-May, and cobs would be ready from late July to mid-August. Because yields are not high, on average only one or two cobs per plant, plants can be packed fairly close together, about 30cm/12in between plants in rows 45cm/18in apart.

Sweetcorn can be sown in individual peat or soil blocks, but if so they must be planted out within five days of germination. This is because the roots grow very rapidly, and if they become blockbound, they never fully recover but remain stunted after planting out. (A leaflet on sweetcorn I received recently from the British seed firm A.L. Tozer stressed the importance of not sowing sweetcorn too early in the open. It needs a soil temperature of at least 10°C/50°F for good germination, and cold weather in the early stages 'can have all sorts of detrimental effects'. The detailed list which followed would have put a 'government health warning' in the shade.)

Lee Valley has had very good results by sowing single seeds in 10cm/3½in pots loosely filled with compost. This produced strong plants which were ready for planting about two weeks later.

It is well known that sweetcorn outdoors should be planted in a block formation to assist pollination, being a wind-pollinated plant. When it is grown under glass, vibrating the plants is recommended to help pollination. Lee Valley suggests 'any means other than water', as the water will dampen the pollen and therefore its transference from male to female flowers is severely reduced.

Shaking the plants two or three times when the pollen is available would be adequate. This ensures that the pollen is transferred from the male flowers on the spike at the top of the plant to the female tassels on the cob. Interestingly the male flowers are normally open, and start to drop pollen, before the tassels are in evidence. Indeed the first flowers to open, which are borne low down on the spike, have often shed their pollen and died before the tassels appear: theirs a pointless and fruitless existence. In most varieties most of the pollination is done by the last flowers to open, those borne at the top of the spike.

Lee Valley also offers a new hint for gauging ripeness in the cob, other than the old method of pressing a thumbnail into the grain. (If it's watery, the cob is unripe; if it's 'milky', it's ripe; if 'doughy', overripe.) As the cob matures the tassels shrivel and die and the cob starts to lean away from the main stem. At maturity it is roughly at a 60-degree angle from the stem, and should snap off easily. If it has to be bent backwards and forwards several times it is not mature, and is not ready for harvesting.

....

The Lee Valley EHS was another victim of what many would consider short-sighted cutbacks.

STORING ROOT VEGETABLES
The Garden, August 1982

As deep freezers have graduated (if that is the right word) from status symbols to basic necessities, so traditional methods of vegetable storage have declined from a major to a minor aspect of vegetable growing. I'm rather sorry. I've always had a soft spot for clamps and 'bran tubs' of beetroot and carrots, and have tended to resist the 'freeze everything' trend — which I gather now embraces root vegetables. What's the point of freezing Brussels sprouts, I ask freezer-fanatic friends as they slave away over their steamers on autumn evenings, when you can pick them fresh from the garden all winter? Winter 1981/2 provided the answer. I was forced to eat my words — there was little else to eat! When the snows drifted against our rabbit-proof fencing the bunnies popped over, and every sprout, savoy and kale plant was eaten to within an inch of ground level.

The loss of brassicas put a premium on roots, and I decided to hedge my bets in future by, on the one hand, freezing more diligently, and on the other, getting up to date on storage of roots.

For the latter I turned to *Know and Grow Vegetables 2*, the recent National Vegetable Research Station (NVRS) publication, which has an excellent chapter on many aspects of vegetable storage. One of the first points it raises is when to sow vegetables for storage. It's a question of timing. They must be sown early enough to mature by winter, but late enough not to become overgrown and tough, as happens with a prolonged growing season. So where root sowings can be spread over several months it suggests, if storage is the objective, sowing at the latest date recommended for any particular variety.

It also suggests that roots for storage should be grown at fairly high densities, to minimize the risk of oversized and coarsened roots. Somewhat contrary to what one might expect, wider spacing should be reserved for the early carrots and beetroot, which benefit most from very rapid growth and minimum competition.

Another fundamental principle is that careful harvesting is the key to successful storage. Root vegetables may look robust, but rough handling easily causes bruising, and this is where the rots will start in store. Any damaged or diseased roots should be used first and never stored. In most cases the leaves should be removed: they act as wicks drawing water out of the roots. Either cut them off, using a sharp knife which is cleaned from time to time, or twist them off. Twisting is always advisable for beetroot, as sap is lost from the cut stems for several days after cutting, heightening the risk of infection.

It is also important not to damage the crown of root crops. If the shoot within the crown is damaged the root becomes moribund, resulting in premature decay.

Should one wash roots before storage? The NVRS view is that where roots are grown in light soils it is unnecessary and could damage them, but in heavy soils, especially if they are lifted in wet condtions, it is advisable to wash off excess soil, which may harbour pests and disease.

All roots start to deteriorate after harvesting, but the rate of deterioration is much slower at low temperatures. For the hardier roots (carrots, parsnips, swedes, turnips), the ideal temperature is 0°C/32°F, with the highest possible humidity.

There are three main options for storing root vegetables: leaving them in the soil, lifting them and storing in clamps, and storing in boxes under cover.

Where it is feasible, there is a lot to be said for leaving them in the soil. This certainly results in the best flavour and texture, for there is the least loss of moisture from the roots. Carrots and parsnips especially benefit, the parsnips becoming sweeter at low temperatures, as some of their starch is converted into sugar. Over long periods beetroot, swedes and turnips keep less well in the soil, as their tissues eventually harden and become woodier. So they are best lifted at some stage during the winter, generally around Christmas.

Most of the common storage roots (potatoes are the outstanding exception) can tolerate light frost, though they are damaged by prolonged heavy frost. So they must be protected if left in the soil. Simply drawing a little soil over the crowns gives some protection: this is all that is required for parsnips. Carrots, swedes, turnips and beetroots need to be covered by 15–20cm/6–8in of insulating material taking precautions against slugs before covering the roots.

The best insulating material is something which can trap air but does not become matted solid when it is wet. NVRS suggests loose straw (particularly wheat straw), leaves, sand, sandy or peaty earth, or polythene sheeting. (The latter sounds rather chilly to me – and I would add bracken to their list.) In some cases it may be necessary to hold the covering in place with say wire hoops or wire netting.

On the whole it is unwise to keep roots in the ground on poorly drained or very heavy soil, though to some extent these conditions can be overcome by growing the roots on raised beds. NVRS also suggest working large quantities of sand into any bed destined for overwintering carrots. And if the crops are badly attacked by pest and disease – aphids, carrot fly or slugs, for example – they should be lifted.

The main disadvantage of storing *in situ* is the unpleasantness of digging up the vegetables when you want them in mid-winter – and the near impossibility of doing so when the ground is frozen solid. However, where the crops are protected with straw the ground is rarely frozen so hard that it is impenetrable with a fork.

It is always worth marking the ends of the rows – before it snows. Every (snowy) year, as I plunge my fork in blind optimism through a secretive blanket of snow to locate buried parsnips, I swear I'll never be caught again.

When it's a question of flavour and condition of the root, clamps, which maintain an even temperature and high humidity, come a close second to keeping vegetables in the soil. They can be made outdoors, or on the floor of an outbuilding or cellar. If outdoors, choose a level well-drained spot, ideally in the lee of a wall.

The base of the clamp is generally a 20cm/8in layer of straw or some other clean material, though the roots can be placed on the bare earth. The roots are then piled carefully on top of the straw, making a heap as large as is required. They are then covered with a second layer of straw of about the same thickness, and at this stage left for a couple of days to sweat. The final covering is a layer of earth up to 15cm/6in thick, taken from around the outside edge of the clamp so as to make a small drainage ditch. Rats and mice occasionally assume a clamp is a winter larder constructed for their benefit. Take precautions against these invaders if necessary.

For swedes, and other very hardy roots such as Witloof chicory or celeriac, the final layer of earth is unnecessary, though in this case the straw may need to be weighted down or anchored in some way. Beetroot stores exceptionally well in a clamp, lasting in good condition until March or April. Unlike most root vegetables, beet can also be stored satisfactorily in polythene sacks.

When storing in boxes, barrels or bins, the idea is to lay down the root vegetables in layers separated by sand, sieved coal or coke ashes, or any material which will allow air and moisture to circulate. The top layer should be covered so that no roots are exposed. It is best to grade the roots, putting the larger ones on the bottom and the smaller ones, which dry out faster, on top.

Boxes can be kept in frost-free sheds or cellars – ideally at a temperature as close to 0°C/32°F as possible. Again, if mice are a likely hazard, take precautions against them. As with any form of root storage, diseased or damaged roots should be stored separately and used first.

Turning to individual root crops, potatoes are mature and ready for harvesting once the leaves have died down naturally. Because they are of South American origin they are susceptible to frost, so must be lifted before the first frost. Wherever possible harvest them in dry conditions, simply rubbing off excess soil. If it is wet at the time, spread them out and dry off the surface moisture before storing.

They are best kept in double-thickness paper sacks, jute or hessian sacks, tied at the neck. Never put them into polythene sacks, which become humid, encouraging sprouting, pests and disease. If the sacks are not of lightproof material, make sure they are stored in the dark or given extra coverage, for light stimulates the formation of poisonous alkaloids in the tubers, turning them green. Potatoes can also be clamped, in this case omitting the straw layers.

NVRS points out that there is no need, immediately on harvest, to put the potatoes somewhere cool. Keeping them for a few weeks at temperatures of 10–15°C/50°–60°F encourages the development of a layer of protective, corky tissue on the skin and the healing of minor wounds. They must eventually be stored in frost-free conditions, in cellars, sheds or a cold room, against an internal wall if possible. If frost is likely, put them on wooden boards to insulate them from below, and give extra protection with newspapers, sacking, old carpets, etc. Prolonged periods at low temperatures (below 4°C/40°F) cause sweetening, and the sugars formed can caramelize on cooking, resulting in blackened, unpleasant-flavoured potatoes.

Once the potatoes start to sprout they lose moisture and become wrinkled. At this stage their storage life can be prolonged for a few weeks by rubbing off the sprouts.

With carrots the root is apparently covered by a thin layer of dead cells, protecting the surface from the abrasive effects of soil particles when it is growing. This protective layer is easily rubbed off during handling or if the carrots are washed, and although it will regenerate, the surface browns and the flavour is impaired in the process. All of which provides an argument for minimum handling, and where the soil is suitable and there are no carrot fly problems, leaving the roots in the ground.

Broken carrots are naturally more susceptible to storage damage, and immature carrots and certain varieties tend to be more brittle than others. For storage 'Chantenay', 'Autumn King' and presumably the Berlicum types have the edge over the Amsterdam and Nantes types, in that they have thicker protective skins, are less brittle, and are less susceptible to freezing. For winter storage or overwintering, NVRS recommend sowing from mid-May to mid-June (in central England), so that they mature in mid-October. These dates should be adjusted for colder and warmer parts of the country.

Where carrots are left in the soil their own leaves form a natural canopy protecting them from the first frosts. About early December, or sooner if there has been a prolonged period of frost with temperatures down to about −5°C/23°F, the leaves blacken and provide no further protection. The carrots should then be protected with insulating material as described earlier. Incidentally, carrot clamps, according to the powers that be, should never be more than 60cm/2ft deep.

Of the more unusual roots kohl rabi is very hardy, and can either be left in the open ground or lifted and stored in boxes. If lifted, a cluster of central leaves should be left on the plant.

The same is true of celeriac, though personally I never lift it, but simply pack straw or bracken in any spaces between the crowns.

Salsify, scorzonera and the Chinese winter radishes can be left in the soil unprotected, though a protective layer will make lifting easier in severe weather. Where winter radishes are concerned I'm now convinced that on heavy, and therefore slug-prone soils, the round types are preferable to the long and are less susceptible to damage. My guess is that the slugs can't get such a good grip on them!

CUTWORM
From 'Soil and Soil Pests', *The Garden*, June 1979

One of the soil pests being studied at NVRS, in Wellesbourne, is the cutworm. Cutworm is a collective name for about ten species of moth which, in the caterpillar stage, do severe damage to a wide range of vegetables – lettuce, potatoes, celery, beet, leek, swede, turnip, etc. The most common and damaging of the group in this country is the turnip moth. Its fleshy, grey/buff caterpillar is fairly commonly encountered in and on the soil.

Attacks of cutworm vary tremendously from year to year, and studies are aiming to find out why. During its life cycle the cutworm could be said to be going down in the world. The adults are on the wing in June and July when they lay their eggs, which hatch in about seven to ten days. The young larvae feed on plant foliage above soil level. The larger caterpillars burrow down into the soil and attack roots and root crops underground. In very hot years some of the large larvae form a soil cocoon and pupate inside in September, hatching out into a second generation in October.

More normally, they overwinter as large larvae in the soil, pupating in the spring to hatch out in summer. An adult moth may lay up to 1,000 or 2,000 eggs in its lifetime.

There seems to be a correlation between dry years and high cutworm population. In a kindly winter large numbers of the caterpillars survive to make a large initial population the following year. With potatoes it has been shown that damage to the crop is minimized by irrigating; it also looks as if some varieties of potatoes may be more susceptible to cutworm damage than others; 'Desirée', for instance, may harbour three times as many cutworms as 'Pentland Dell'.

For amateurs, remedies suggested against cutworm are still reassuringly old fashioned. As one adult cutworm can do a great deal of damage, it is worth catching individuals. They can often be found by scratching in the soil around plants. They can also be attracted to baits, made by mixing bran, honey and water, and putting a blob of the mixture under a block of wood in the vegetable garden.

The baits should be examined in the morning and any caterpillars killed.

WHAT APHIDS GET UP TO
From 'Chelsea: 1980', *The Garden*, September 1980

There were plenty of horrific facts at the Chelsea Flower Show at the University of Reading's exhibit on aphids: one mother aphid can produce 2 tons of aphids in three months; winged aphids fly to 304m/1,000ft; there are 300 to 400 different sorts. Better news, I thought, was that the strains within each aphid species are extremely specific to one type of plant: so at least they are most unlikely to hop from crop to crop in your garden. I also learned that after an aphid has hatched it will make about three forays, over the course of as many days, in search of the food it fancies. If it fails, it then dies of exhaustion. (What beastly odds, I thought on my return home after an overnight stay in London for Chelsea, had drawn an okra-loving brood of aphids to my eight okra seedlings deep in Suffolk, demolishing them completely while my back was turned! Probably the only okra for miles around!)

On practical measures against aphids other than spraying with pesticides, Professor van Emden, who mounted the exhibit, advises keeping plants well watered. When plants get dried out the plant sap becomes concentrated, and hence more attractive, and more nourishing, to aphids.

One line of research showed that plants grown in bark compost tend to be more resistant to aphids. The amino acid spectrum of the plant is evidently altered, rendering them less appetizing. We may hear more of this in the future.

BIOLOGICAL PEST CONTROL IN APPLES
From 'Conference Pickings', *The Garden*, May 1981

At the second Organic Growers Conference, a paper on biological control in apples, given by Dr David Glen of Long Ashton Research Station, brought home forcibly the number of friends one has in an orchard, provided you cultivate rather than crucify them. It is undisputed that the routine, blanket, 'broad spectrum' spraying carried out in many commercial orchards kills off many of the natural predators of common pests. What happens when the spraying stops?

Dr Glen ran through several apple pests discussing their natural enemies. First red spider mite, very rarely a problem in unsprayed orchards, where it is kept under control by predatory mites. But these beneficial mites are killed by many insecticides and fungicides – hence the problem which builds up in sprayed orchards. When amateurs plant fruit trees, red spider may be a problem in the first few years, as trees brought in from nurseries will normally have been sprayed, killing off the predators as well as the pest. However, within a few years the predators will naturally build up a population sufficient to keep the red spider under control.

Earwigs, we were told, should perhaps be considered 'good guys', their record only marred by the holes they sometimes make in fruit. They may be important in keeping apple aphids, including woolly aphid, under control, and they also eat a fair number of codling moth eggs.

The codling moth is an interesting pest from the biological control point of view. Its caterpillars are responsible for that particularly unappetizing debris one finds around the core of apples, and it has always proved a difficult customer to control with the chemicals available to the amateur gardener. The most common amateur remedy has been to tie corrugated cardboard or sacking around the tree trunks, in which it was hoped the caterpillars would spin their cocoons, later being removed or burnt.

But Dr Glen made the point that this is so much unnecessary effort. Research has shown that about 95 per cent of the codling moth larvae are destroyed by great tits and blue tits, who search diligently for them under the bark. The odds are that any caught under the corrugated bands would have been eaten anyway by the tits.

He suggests that the best method of codling moth control is orchard hygiene, removing as many potential bird-proof overwintering sites of codling larvae as possible – for example, wooden stakes which have split or rotted, canes, certain tree ties, hollow weed stems and holes in trees. (I forgot to ask how you remove a hole in a tree!)

The various winter moths which cause corky patches on fruit are another example of pests which are to a limited extent kept under control by their natural predators and parasites.

A common measure against winter moth is to greaseband fruit trees between October and March to catch the wingless females climbing up the trees to lay their eggs. This is rather a chore, as the surface of the bands must be roughened from time to time to remove dead leaves and other debris. And there's a snag: newly hatched larvae spin strands of silk, and can blow considerable distances in the wind, so trees can very easily be reinfected.

Dr Glen made two points here. First, make sure you greaseband all the trees in an orchard. Second, orchards should be isolated from other sources of infection, such as old orchards or broad-leaved woodland, as otherwise much of the value of greasebanding will be lost. He suggests an 'alienation' distance of at least 30m/100ft – ideally 100m/300ft.

Occasionally it is suggested that beneficial insects could be positively encouraged by providing the sort of food and habitat they like – for example, flowering shrubs. So far any research on the subject has been very inconclusive (the fairly extensive trial grounds needed for such work are one stumbling block). It is known, though, that alder windbreaks provide a refuge for the black-kneed capsid, one of the predators of red spider mite.

CURIOUS FACTS ABOUT CLUBROOT
From 'Conference Pickings', *The Garden*, May 1981

At the recent Organic Growers Conference Eliot Coleman reported that at the Coolidge Center in the USA they seemed to get fewer attacks from cabbage root fly when digging in a green manure crop, rather than farmyard manure, before planting brassicas. Secondly, there seems to be a scientific explanation for the view that unbalanced manuring, usually excessive use of nitrogen, increases the likelihood of pest attack. In plant leaves amino acids combine with other nutrients to build up proteins: excessive nitrogen in the leaves results in the presence of free amino acids – and free amino acids are what pests such as aphids and red spider thrive on.

VEGETABLES AS MEDICINE AND FODDER
From 'Vegetables for Feeding People and Livestock', *The Garden*, January 1980

On a worldwide scale vegetables could play an immensely important role – a far greater role than they do at present – in alleviating the problems of disease and malnutrition which afflict huge numbers of the human race.

Nutrition was the starting point at the Institute of Biology conference 'Vegetables for Feeding People and Animals'. Whereas green vegetables have always been considered a source of vitamins and minerals, Professor N.W. Pirie of Rothamsted Experimental Station pointed out that vegetables with dark green leaves are an excellent and overlooked source of very high-quality protein. Leafy vegetables, of course, contain a great deal of water, but on a dry matter basis they contain as much protein as beans, and could yield more human food per hectare per annum than any other crop. In fact an area 15m/50ft square could produce a third of the protein and all the carotene one person needs.

The two limiting factors in the consumption of large quantities of green leaves are that they contain fibre, of which only relatively small amounts can be eaten by human beings, and that, in varying degrees, some species are toxic. This applies mostly to tropical species, which, however, can be rendered harmless by cooking in large quantities of water, or several waters, which are thrown away. The drawback is that vitamins B and C are destroyed by boiling. We are fortunate in that our vegetables can (indeed should) be cooked in small quantities of water or in soups, so making the most of their nutritive value.

It is a tragedy that in some underdeveloped countries where diet is extremely poor there is no tradition of growing vegetables: yet small crops of leafy vegetables grown in the backyard could provide protein, and spell the difference between life and death. A specific example of the potential benefits of using leafy vegetables is in curing the disease xerophthalmia, which causes blindness in an estimated 300,000 children annually. It is now believed that the disease could be prevented simply by the children eating 30–40g/1–1½oz of leafy green vegetables daily.

It is ironical that in some Third World countries large quantities of nutritive indigenous green vegetables were eaten in the past; but as the countries become richer, there is a tendency to adopt the more prestigious Western vegetables – often less well adapted to the climate and giving poorer returns. But these are the crops on which research and marketing resources have been expended. Mankind as a whole would benefit if some of the resources spent on breeding, developing and promoting temperate climate vegetables were diverted to the improvement of leafy and other tropical crops – of which there are many. There is also a need to educate some subsistence communities into the best means of cooking vegetables to maximize their nutritive value.

HARNESSING VEGETABLE WASTE

A pressing problem, all over the world, is the tremendous waste of vegetables once they are produced. In this country it is estimated that the equivalent of 84,000 tons of protein lies wasted on the fields each year, in the form of pea haulm, Brussels sprout tops, carrot tops and so on – all of which could be fed to animals. More waste occurs in trimming for market and processing: 30,000 tons of lettuce, for example, are lost in trimmings. Practical problems arise in using this waste for animals, partly the difficulties inherent in a seasonal supply, partly the difficulties in getting it to the animals. With the modern concentration of markets and processing facilities, there may be more opportunity in future to site animals near these outlets and make use of them. There is also scope for using animals to 'graze' a field from which vegetable crops have been harvested, adding to their fertility in the process.

In tropical countries, where facilities for transport, storage and marketing are poor, losses after harvesting are on an even more immense scale (a programme has been launched to try to cut these losses by half by 1985). Here there is scope for utilizing vegetable waste to feed small animals such as rabbits, guinea pigs or the South American rodent capybara. Professor P.N. Wilson of BOCM Silcock also described systems where vegetable waste is utilized for raising fish. A prime example is the vegetarian Chinese grass carp, which can be fed with vegetable waste. It cannot digest cellulose well, but produces faeces upon which small animals live, which in turn support other species of fish – so a productive biological chain can be built up with vegetable waste as the starting point. The tilapia fish is another suitable candidate, being fed in Africa with the vines from sweet potatoes.

Closer to home is the possibility of using fresh vegetable waste for mushroom growing. It has in fact already been done. For centuries horse manure was considered essential for mushroom growing, but now it is known that what is essential is the lignin and cellulose in the straw: the manure merely accelerated the fermentation. Research workers are experimenting successfully with growing mushrooms on industrial waste, rice straw, shredded paper and other media.

The nutritional image of mushrooms has also changed. Although low in calories, they are rich in minerals, vitamins and protein (containing all the essential amino acids). Today cottage-scale methods of mushroom growing are being encouraged in villages where land and resources are scarce, such as in the Indian Himalayas, as a means of supplementing inadequate diets.

The most unconventional suggestion for using vegetable wastes came from Dr J.M. Walsingham of Reading University. As already mentioned, one of the problems in feeding vegetable waste to warm-blooded animals is the seasonal nature of the supply (in some cases the high moisture content of vegetables also poses a problem). Cold-blooded invertebrates, however, feed irregularly, simply becoming inactive when the food supply dries up. Using this fact snails, slugs, earthworms, as well as the larvae of flies, butterflies, moths and beetles, have been experimented with as converters of vegetable residues.

The ideal creature for the purpose must be easy to handle and useful in some way after consuming the vegetable wastes. Snails have come out well. A snail can eat up to 11 per cent of its body weight in a day; snails can be stored easily(!), they protect themselves by withdrawing into their shell when there is no food and, finally, they can be used to feed humans (in societies where this is acceptable), pigs and hens.

Earthworms also rate high, creating very homogeneous and fertile compost as an end product. Worms are in demand for bait, and as they are very rich in protein, they could, poor things, be dried, ground and added to animal feed.

The larvae of several well-known pests were also considered, amongst them cranefly, leaf miner, carrot fly, large white butterfly, turnip and tomato moth. In most cases it was envisaged that pupae would be fed to livestock. All I can say is that although it may be a wonderfully sound ecological concept, if the practice is developed further, I hope it takes place in controlled premises. The thought of *encouraging* some of those pests . . . Better to compost the vegetable waste, which is a simpler alternative, although leading probably to higher losses of nitrogen and nutrients than when processed through invertebrates.

Dr Walsingham suggested that if the present vegetable wastes in the UK were processed by invertebrates and converted into animal feedstuffs, they could supply 6 per cent of the materials of animal origin currently imported and used in livestock feed.

In rounding off the conference, Professor Kenneth Mellanby pointed out that already world production of wheat is sufficient to provide every person in the world with 1kg/2.2lb of grain each day . . . and eliminate starvation. So what goes wrong? The answer is that a huge proportion of the grain produced is fed to animals. In the USA out of every 750kg/1,650lb of grain available per person per year, only 68kg/149lb are used for human consumption; the rest is fed to animals.

Theoretically, if animals were fed with grain, waste vegetable products, invertebrates such as worms and snails, fodder crops such as turnips, swedes and potatoes in the temperate regions or cassava and sweet potatoes in the tropics, and if legumes such as broad beans and peas were used to supplement or replace the protein in the conventional livestock diet, the grain thus freed could be used to feed the hungry. As someone pointed out, the unsolved problem is how to get the food to the people in need at a price they can afford. The political, economic and sociological answers to that question. I feel, are well beyond the scope of *The Garden*!

This Chinese identification pass probably dates from Manchuria in 1947, when the threatening advance of the Communist armies meant movements were vetted and ID necessary. I was eleven or twelve when the photograph was taken.

6 THE ORIENTAL YEARS

My curiosity about oriental vegetables started, innocently enough, with an intriguing short list of oriental vegetables at the back of the Chiltern Seeds catalogue of unusual seeds. I tried them all, with increasing excitement, soon realizing that the oriental brassicas in particular had huge potential for Western gardens, especially during the autumn-to-spring period. They would make perfect partners to the hardy salad plants we had discovered on our European travels. During the early 1980s my curiosity mushroomed into an obsession.

It has always seemed strange to me that countless ornamental plants from Asia have won a permanent place in Western gardens over the last 200 years, yet Asian vegetables had never gained more than a toehold. We have had tantalizing glimpses of an untapped world through the bamboo curtain; a surprising number reached France in the nineteenth century via interested diplomats and priests, but they never caught on as more than curiosities. Information was sparse. The more I experimented, the more I yearned to see how they were cultivated and used in their homelands of China and Japan, and also, how they were being grown by Asian communities in the West, in Europe, the USA and Canada.

My suspicion that to do so could be a daunting task was reinforced at the Chelsea Flower Show in 1980. I couldn't resist butting in on a conversation between the minders of the National Farmers Union display and their neighbours on the Chinese National Native Produce Corporation's exhibit of *penjing* – Chinese bonsai. 'I would love to see an exhibit of Chinese vegetables at Chelsea,' I said to one of the Chinese. Well, he replied, waving his arms at the vast space around him, it would probably fill the whole marquee, but he would pass on the request to higher quarters!

As I would discover in the next few years, the 'higher quarters' in China's officialdom could be very hard of hearing.

The plan I was hatching was to visit China initially, then Taiwan, then Japan. Japanese seed companies (and to a lesser extent the Taiwanese) were then the main avenue for introducing oriental vegetable seed to the West. Through their business connections with UK seed companies it would be relatively easy to make contacts and arrange visits. Mainland China, with all enterprise under government control, was a different story.

Unlike our Grand Vegetable Tour in Europe in the 1970s, this time I would have to travel alone, leaving Don to look after the children and the market garden. So I plunged again into the world of trip planning, with all the frustrations involved in trying to raise funds or get sponsorship, getting a small group of people together, doing research into what to try to see and where to go, working out potential travel routes and, the biggest hurdle of all, getting permission to travel freely in China and visit research institutions, agricultural centres and communes growing vegetables.

Many leads were pursued – and led nowhere. Regulations were actually tightened in 1982, pithily summarized in a letter from the Chinese Embassy saying, 'It is not convenient to go to China as an ordinary tourist and visit institutions.' One needed to be part of an official exchange programme.

While this was going on I had started lessons in Chinese at the Chinese Language Project in Cambridge. A group of six of us embarked on the O-level Chinese course, but one by one the others dropped out, leaving me alone. The school took pity on me. I suppose even in Cambridge there was a certain novelty value in a middle-aged lady with a hang-up about Chinese vegetables. For a kindly reduced fee I continued with Charles Aylmer, an inspiring teacher, now head of the Chinese Department at the Cambridge University Library.

Our linguistic efforts focused on acquiring enough spoken Chinese to get about and learning some basic horticultural vocabulary. Charles compiled a superb list of the many alternative names for Chinese vegetables, beautifully written in Chinese characters. It was much admired during our eventual travels. We had a great tool in what we called 'The Little Blue Book' – officially the *Beijing Vegetable Production Handbook*, brought back from China by a friend. These little books, the same size and format as Chairman Mao's sayings (huge numbers of printing presses were geared to printing this format), fitted into the pocket of a typical Chinese jacket. We worked through it diligently, along with *600 Practical Chinese Sentences*, which various people recorded on tapes for me. (Chinese language materials were scarce then, compared to today, when learning Chinese is almost a fashion accessory.)

How I enjoyed being a student again, travelling on the train from Bury St Edmunds to Cambridge, biking to my lessons, working hard, and then sometimes reviving my exhausted brain and picking up a little botany in the Cambridge University Botanic Garden!

China has woven itself in and out of our family history. My father had spent time in Hong Kong in the army as a young man, and had returned to China as part of the British Military Mission during the Second World War. He was a fluent speaker of Mandarin, knew some Cantonese, and had a deep knowledge of the country and affection for the Chinese people. These credentials led to his appointment after the war as British Consul General in Dairen (now Dalian), in Manchuria, then later to Harbin, though the intensifying Communist campaign meant he never reached either destination.

7

For over a month we'd had no school, so we started school immediately. It was cold, so we took our stove to school. We had uninterrupted lessons, excepting a short holiday, until Feb. 4th.

On Feb 4th we left Chan Chung and stayed in Mukden for seven weeks, with only a couple of Russian lessons. Finally we flew to Peking. We stayed in the Peking Hotel for a while, and then with the Clubbs. Then to Tientsin, where we stayed at the Court Hotel.

On 3rd April we left on S.S. Hupeh, and arrived in HongKong on the 13th April, 1948. Five days later we came to Kunming by CNAC Skymaster.

For 3 months we'd had had no proper education. so —

The very next day we at the American School.

Manchuria 1947: my sister Erica (front right) and me (front left), forced to wear hats and take part in a sewing bee, at the British Consulate in Mukden (Shenyang). The page is from a 'book' I wrote for my mother called 'My Travels in China'.

As he had been separated from his family for much of the war, he took us along: I was ten, and my sister Erica eight, when we left England in 1946. What an adventurous two and a half years we had, shuttling backwards and forwards between Beijing, Mukden (Shenyang) and Changchun in Manchuria, and eventually, when Changchun was finally cut off by the Communist forces, being evacuated in an American Embassy plane. I was clutching a precious box of caterpillars (the box beautifully made in two compartments by the consulate driver) and a matchbox of Manchurian snails. Somehow, through an aquaintance of my father, I had been made an honorary member of the Malacological Society of London (malacology being the study of molluscs), and had been entrusted with collecting Manchurian snails, a task I took very seriously. My adored Angora rabbit was bequeathed, after a tearful goodbye cuddling it under the sheets in my bed, to the nuns in the convent where we had gone to school. How did those nuns survive that bleak winter? They had nothing.

My father was reappointed to Kunming, in Yunnan, where we led a more settled existence for a year from March 1948. My mother, Dorothy Jacobs-Larkcom, recounted the tale of those two and a half years in her book *As China Fell*.

Our education was patchy indeed. In Beijing we went to a convent for girls, where we were among the few non-Chinese pupils. In the north we learned Russian from a destitute 'White Russian' lady, along with more conventional schooling in a Changchun convent, so cold and so lacking in fuel that we took our own oil stove to school and started each day melting the frozen inkwells. Finally more settled education in a missionary school in Kunming in the south. Along the way, like any children, we picked up some Chinese – with a northern accent.

This, I'm sure, enabled me to make progress when I turned to studying Chinese at the age of forty-nine. The sounds, perhaps even some of the tones, imperfect though they were, were lurking in the recesses of my brain.

It was the Chinese lessons that eventually opened the door to visiting China. The director of the Chinese Language Project was the late Bob Sloss, who was Dean of Darwin College, which had links with the Royal Society. One of the society's duties was arranging scientific exchange visits to China. Bob 'put in a word' in the appropriate ears, and two diligent girls in the Royal Society took up my case, liaising with the Chinese Association for Science and Technology. Even so, it was a long haul. My diary is peppered with 'Ling is waiting to hear from China'. One application lay, unanswered, for eighteen months on a Chinese desk.

By then I had teamed up with garden photographer Pamla Toler. Our original idea was to travel for three months in the autumn, perhaps making a further trip the following spring. But official visits had to have an 'exchange' element (which meant giving lectures), groups ideally had to be of at least fifteen people, and members were expected to be of academic eminence. Neither of us could claim appropriate academic excellence. So a hunt was underway to find suitable eminent scientists to join us, at what was becoming very short notice. It wasn't until May 1985 that the authorities agreed to bend the rules and accept a delegation of four, the other two members being

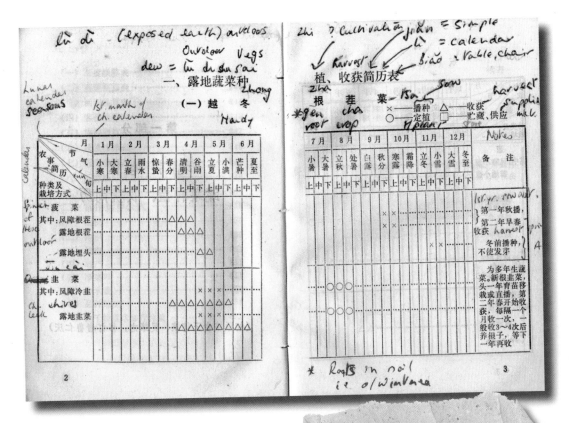

The 'Little Blue Book', officially The Beijing Vegetable Production Handbook, *was a key aid in my attempts to learn Chinese horticultural terms.*

Alan Backhurst, an irrigation expert who had worked in China previously, and his marketing friend Huff Goldsmith. As part of the 'exchange' deal, they both gave lectures on their respective fields, and I gave a slide talk on my work in horticulture to date, and my reasons for visiting China.

I decided to try to give the 'talk' part of my contribution in Chinese, partly to shorten the unbelievably tedious process of every word being translated, and partly to learn more horticultural vocabulary. To this end the Chinese lessons increased in intensity with an army of linguistic helpers. The text of my talk was translated and written in Chinese characters for a Chinese girl to read and tape record; then it was rewritten in pinyin, the romanized script, so that I could read it for the talk. (I never mastered more than a handful of Chinese characters.) Before leaving I played the Chinese tape again and again, and wherever possible in China I listened to it just before each talk to refresh my mind. We probably gave these talks at least half a dozen times to various academic and student audiences. I'll never know if they really understood my Chinese: they would have been much too polite to say if they hadn't. In practice a major problem was the almost continual background noise we had to contend with: we must have hit China in the midst of a construction boom in academe. But I think they appreciated the effort. And once shyness had worn off, the audiences were very responsive, often asking the sort of questions garden club members would have asked back home.

My Chinese was less appreciated by a farmer in what we dubbed the 'biogas' village in Sichuan, where parties of foreign visitors were taken to see exemplary use of methane gas from animal manure for heating, cooking and lighting. Biogas apart, it was an interesting village and a rare visit to the countryside, so Pam and I slipped away from the group to wander around and take photographs of the villagers at work, including a man with his pigs. I tried to say, conversationally, 'What nice pigs you have!' I evidently said, 'What nice chickens you have!' (Wrong word? Wrong tone?) He shook his head in disgust and walked away, presumably thinking foreigners are so stupid they can't tell a pig from a chicken.

The four of us set out in early October 1985 on a three-week exchange trip. We travelled 3,878 kilometres/2,410 miles in China, our visits centred on Beijing, Nanjing, Shanghai, Chengdu and Guangzhou (Canton). I was to spend a further two weeks on my own in Hong Kong, Japan and Taiwan.

As with all organized tours, frustration and elation alternated. The tour's 'official' element manifested itself in long discussions, over elegant cups of tea, on production quotas and the like. For Pam and me, hopeful of producing an illustrated book and/ or magazine articles, getting 'real' pictures was often difficult. We longed to be outside. The workers could well have gone home for lunch before we got to the fields to see them working! It took a while for our guides to understand our (varying) interests, and occasionally to get authority to modify the official programme. But they were unfailingly kind and helpful, we were made welcome everywhere we went, and we saw a wonderful variety of markets, communes, research stations and scenery. With very few exceptions, we enjoyed superb food.

I made a taped diary to send home to the family, and listening to it again many years later, I'm almost ashamed at the continual, mouth-watering references to the dishes we had enjoyed that day. Once or twice Pam and I managed to steal into a kitchen and watch the cooking. What drama: flames leaping around the woks from the gas fires beneath, the gas roaring so loudly you could hardly hear yourself speak, then the sharp sizzle as water was swirled into the hot woks to clean them between operations! The tapes also highlighted the endless urban noise. In Shanghai I simply hung the tape recorder out of the window, in the early hours of the morning, to catch the din of buses, the clatter of the 'four wind' tractors . . .

Shanghai revived childhood memories. We had spent three weeks in the embassy compound on our arrival in China, and to a ten-year-old who had lived only in the countryside, the noise and turmoil of the city, the terrible poverty and the maimed beggars and babies on the streets were overwhelming. I would creep out of the house early in the morning when it was cool, and crouch under one of the shrubs near the road, watching the traffic go by. I still remember vividly men pulling huge cartloads, every muscle straining, their prematurely aged faces etched with pain.

Returning to 1985: our group parted company in Guangzhou, and from then on, I had to become independent. Grey hair, I concluded later, is a great asset when travelling. Whenever the immediate problems of travel seemed bewildering, some kind stranger would take pity on me and help me out. After a couple of pleasant days in Hong Kong, chilling out as they would say today, it was back to work in Japan and Taiwan. How different Japan was to China – and how I missed not knowing a word of the language! But the programmes organized by the different seed companies proved wonderfully complimentary to our Chinese experiences. I learned so much from the trial grounds, the beautifully illustrated seed catalogues and visits to markets, shops and commercial growers. Brief insights into Japanese culture, and regrettably brief glimpses of Japanese gardens and urban planting, whetted my appetite for a future, more leisurely trip, travelling into the interior.

I spent the last few days of my research trip in Taiwan, under the auspices of the Asian Vegetable Research and Development Center in Tainan. They were days packed with vivid encounters. During a visit to a farmer's association my guides and I were invited to join the wedding feast of one of the office workers, for free – the custom was to pay to join in a feast! It was a wonderfully lively affair. Outside the Hsi-lo farmers' market office there was a colourful welcoming sign for the 'English visitor'. So many interesting projects, such warmth and hospitality, and a friendship with research worker Ruey-Hua Lee – a mine of culinary and horticultural information – which has lasted to this day.

I flew home on my fiftieth birthday. What a memorable day that was, spent with the Taiwanese Hu brothers I had met at the airport when I'd arrived! They had offered to meet me on my return to the capital, Taipei, and hearing that my parents had once lived in the consulate in nearby Tamsui, now a national museum, insisted on taking me there, after a merry birthday dimsum lunch. We were almost strangers, I was old enough to be their mother, yet we laughed all day. As it turned out the museum was closed, a national holiday having been declared as elections were being held. Undaunted, one of the brothers took my camera, scaled the walls, and took a couple of snaps of the house. It was just as I remembered it: the thick Portuguese-built walls, the elegant shaded verandah around the upper storey with a view to the beautiful mountains across the river. It was an emotional moment. Thoughts of my parents living there all those years ago, and my sister and me visiting as teenagers, came flooding back. My mother had died in January, and it was money she had left which, in the end, financed my travels. I felt she and my father, who were always supportive of our various ventures, would have been happy to know this. I was always sad that they never saw the outcome, my book *Oriental Vegetables*.

Once home, the immediate task was to make sense of the notebooks, tapes, photos and seed packets I had accumulated. Several Chinese had given me books they had written on vegetables, but sadly, I didn't have the means to get them translated, though I was able to get a popular booklet on Chinese chives translated. What a rich source of unique information it proved to be! Another treasure trove was the 150th anniversary catalogue of the Japanese seed company Takii, a superbly illustrated mine of detailed information on Asiatic vegetables, but of course, all in Japanese. A series of coincidences led me to Ruriko Pilgrim, a Japanese writer and enthusiastic vegetable grower herself, living in Bath. I managed to get a second copy of the prized catalogue, and spent countless hours, often late at night, with Ruriko painstakingly translating key sections. I owe her a tremendous debt. Then the excitement of sowing the seeds I had brought back, seeing how they performed in the UK conditions, and learning to cook them. Our chef friend Ken Toyé delighted in trying out unusual leaves and suggesting ways to use them.

There were still, of course, many gaps in my knowledge: I could have prolonged the research phase for years. Some of the gaps were filled when Jia Wen Wei, a scientist from the Vegetable Research Institute who had met our group in Beijing, came to England with two of her senior colleagues. She was their guide and translator. They accepted our invitation to stay, and I'm afraid I virtually kidnapped the poor girl. I plied her endlessly with questions, went with her to London by train on the next leg of her journey, slept on her hotel floor, and followed her out to the Royal Horticultural Society garden at Wisley on an official trip with her colleagues, one by one ticking off the questions on my list. In her early twenties she had been sent to Inner Mongolia during the Cultural Revolution and, bubbly personality that she was, she had made friends with the villagers and learned from them. I'll always regret that we were never able to arrange a trip back there with her, as she suggested.

There was one more crucial strand to my research: a trip to Canada and the USA to visit growers, seed companies, markets, academics and 'foodies' involved with Asian vegetables. This eventually took place in autumn of 1987.

As I mentioned on page 137, what a productive month that proved to be! The task of finding crucial initiatives fell to a network of old friends such as Jill and the late Bill Lapper in Vancouver, who had known us since my sister and I were children, Bill Hussey in Los Angeles, a family friend since Thailand in the 1950s, my hosts at the various talks I gave in Philadelphia, Seattle and other places, and as always, contacts made through the seed trade. A key contact here, through the late Peter Beemsterboer, Dutch seedsman and a friend since our Grand Vegetable Tour, was Professor Paul Williams at the University of Wisconsin-Madison, plant pathologist by profession and crucifer (brassica) expert and enthusiast, who had visited China as part of an academic delegation in 1977.

Between them they enabled me to see Asian vegetables growing in every setting imaginable, from New Jersey to California to Vancouver, from extensive irrigated ranches to tiny plots. Many of the commercial enterprises were set up by Asians – Chinese, Koreans, Taiwanese – who had relinquished professional careers to return to the soil. And the tiny plots ranged from campus gardens of overseas students, to church projects for refugees, to the P-patches and community gardens of Seattle and Philadelphia. Then there were the seed companies, notably Alf Christianson's in the state of Washington with plot after plot of varieties of Asian greens, side by side, clearly labelled – just what I needed to fill in more gaps on my endless list of queries. I also had the chance to catch up again with the Japanese seed companies Takii and Sakata – more questions answered.

Another exciting source of information was the markets in California. An unforgettable day began at dawn in the Los Angeles wholesale market, where the protective taxi driver refused to let me leave the cab until the man I was meeting had arrived. Someone had been trigger happy lately in a building overlooking the market. The range of imported and USA-grown fruits and vegetables in the market was astonishing. By the end of the day I found myself about 161 kilometres/100 miles north, somewhere in LA's suburbs, I supposed, at a company sprouting beans on a massive scale in old railway carriages. The only affordable way to return to my base in LA by then was to fly in a plane so tiny that the pilot took my luggage – i.e. handbag and camera – up front. The Chinese market in San Francisco was another extraordinary place, so reminiscent of China, with bean curd, ginger, turmeric, pak choi, pickling mustards I had last seen in Taiwan, oriental gourds, and scarcely a sign written in English. I watched in fascination, camera in hand, as a lorryload of waxy-coated Chinese winter melons were carefully unloaded into a basement. Then I was noticed and it was made very clear that photography was unwelcome. I put my camera away smartly.

It had never occurred to me to brush up on my Chinese for this trip, but early on Jane Pepper of the Pennsylvania Horticultural Society and I lost our way in New Jersey, arriving late for a rendezvous at a market garden. The long raised beds of pak choi and amaranthus were deserted, but we found a solitary, elderly Chinese man peering through a mosquito-netted door. He gazed at us blankly. But Mandarin worked, and he reassured us the boss would be back at two. My last days in the USA were a return visit to the Madison campus to attend part of a crucifer workshop, absorbing pearls of wisdom, I hoped, from the erudite of the brasssica world. More gaps filled.

Back home, it was down to work in earnest. It had taken a while to find a publisher for the book I was hoping to write, but eventually John Murray took on the task. After many a hiccup – I learned later the whole project was nearly shelved after I'd handed in the first draft – *Oriental Vegetables* was published in 1991. At the last minute the Japanese publishers Kodansha agreed to publish an American edition, so financing a handful of colour photos. Once again I had worked with the artist Elizabeth Douglass, as I had for almost all my earlier books, posting her bits and pieces of oriental vegetables, photos, pages from catalogues, even seeds for her to grow herself, as reference for her line drawings. It was always a happy working partnership. Fifteen years later an updated version of *Oriental Vegetables* was published by Frances Lincoln – sadly, on grounds of cost, without the colour photos.

The articles reprinted here – some in full, some as extracts – are a selection from those I wrote during what I think of as the Oriental Years. 'Greens from the East' on page 216 won a 'Garden Writer of the Year' award. I was indebted to the gardening magazine *Practical Gardening*, which commissioned articles from my research trip to China and Japan, helped pay my film costs, and continued their support during my American travels. Making ends meet would have been hard without them.

GREENS FROM THE EAST
BBC Gardeners' World, July 1992

From late autumn to early spring, at least half the fresh greens and salads growing in our garden originated in China and Japan. Outdoors, the large, smooth leaves of the hardy komatsunas and the rich green, spicy-flavoured 'Amsoi' mustard rub shoulders with the savoys, Brussels sprouts and kales.

If winter hasn't been too severe, the brilliantly coloured purple mustard, the glossy, deeply serrated mizuna greens, and the symmetrical rosettes of rosette pak choi will be there too. They are a trio of eye-catching plants.

In the unheated polytunnel there is a mass of rich, healthy-looking oriental greenery. This includes several types of pak choi with crunchy white or soft green leaf stalks, the delightful light greens of loose-headed Chinese cabbage, and still more mizuna, accompanied by its narrow-leaved cousin mibuna, both plants forming massive handsome clumps.

Once the days begin to warm up, some of these greens will start bolting, their flowers adding a splash of yellow to the scene. But they won't be wasted. The young flowering shoots, picked in the bud stage, are sweet and tender, with the texture of calabrese or purple-sprouting broccoli.

Different again is a patch of Oriental Saladini seedling mixture, sown very early and ready for cutting within weeks. Being sheltered from the elements, all these indoor plants are wonderfully tender. So, besides being cooked, they will be used in lush, multi-flavoured winter salads, mixed with European salad plants like endive, chicory, corn salad and rocket.

It has taken several years' experimenting, and travels in China, Japan, Taiwan and North America, to track down and learn about these Asian brassicas. The result is I'm absolutely convinced they were tailor made for us.

For a start, they are much faster growing than Western brassicas. Provided they are grown in fertile soil with plenty of moisture, most are ready for harvesting within two months of sowing. Once cut, they continue to produce more edible shoots over a long period.

They are also remarkably vigorous. I came back from holiday last year to find several pak choi plants suffering from cabbage root fly. I dug up the plants, washed off the cabbage root fly grubs, trimmed back the leaves and replanted the pak choi. It never looked back. I don't think you could treat one of our Western cabbages that way.

Many of the oriental greens bolt prematurely if sown early in the year. This is either because they are affected by the day length or by low temperatures during their early growth. On the whole they grow best if sown in July or August, following on neatly after traditional early crops such as broad beans, peas, potatoes, salads or carrots. They can also be sown or planted in greenhouses as late as September following, for example, tomatoes or peppers, utilizing ground which is often bare during winter months.

This is not to say that they can't be grown in spring and early summer. Some modern varieties have good resistance to bolting and can be sown earlier, while others can be grown in spring for harvesting young as seedling crops or small plants, before they get a chance to bolt.

All these oriental greens can be eaten at various stages of growth: as 5–10cm/2–4in high seedlings; as small immature plants; as large mature plants; and as flowering shoots. Some types are grown specifically for their flowering shoots.

In addition, once again reflecting their vigour, they are exemplary cut-and-come-again

Pinning up mustard leaves in our polytunnel, to demonstrate the Chinese practice of drying brassica leaves for use in the winter months.

plants. At almost any stage, individual leaves can be cut for use and the plant will resprout to give further cuttings. And finally, the leaves of some types, generally the pak choi and mustards, can be hung up in the sun and dried for use in winter soups.

Oriental greens range in flavour from mild to spinach-like to spicy. Many have a crunchy texture, especially in the leaf midribs and stalks. They can be cooked as greens or used in soups or salads. While the oriental methods of stir-frying and steaming are ideal, they can be adapted to most Western vegetable recipes, although our traditional method of boiling in water is not recommended.

As a way of getting the feel of the different oriental greens, I worked with the seed company Suffolk Herbs to develop an Oriental Saladini mixture, along the lines of the traditional Italian *misticanza* and French *mesclun* salad mixes. It includes loose-headed Chinese cabbage, green-stemmed pak choi, komatsuna mustard 'Tendergreen', mizuna, mibuna and a purple-leaved mustard.

The mixture can be sown thinly broadcast, or in rows, or in 7.5cm/3in-wide shallow drills, which are best made with an onion hoe. In dry conditions, water the bottom of the drill thoroughly before sowing, sow the seeds, then cover with dry soil, which will act as a mulch, slowing down evaporation and keeping the seeds moist until germination.

For patio or windowsill gardeners, the seeds can be sown in a container or in good potting compost in a seed tray. It will normally be ready for cutting within twenty-five days. For use in salads, cut the seedlings just above the tiny 'seed leaves' when they are about 5cm/2in high. In most cases they will resprout to give at least one further cutting.

Other than mid-summer, it can be sown all year, inside or out, starting under cover in early spring and making the last sowings in early October under cover.

If you want larger stir-fry greens, the seedlings can be thinned to about 2.5cm/1in apart and cut when 15–20cm/6–8in high. Or, leave the seedlings after the first cut, allowing the stronger ones to take over from the weaker and develop into fairly substantial plants.

Another option is to distinguish the different seedlings early on, then transplant some of each kind 30cm/12in apart, allowing them to grow into mature plants. The best time to do this is from late summer sowings.

Oriental brassicas are subject to the same pests and diseases as Western brassicas, slugs and caterpillars being the worst in practice. Growing under very light films or fine nets in the early stages provides protection against flying pests, including cabbage root fly, aphids, butterflies and moths.

HEART OF BEAUTY: CHINA'S SECRET RADISH
Your Garden (Australia), March 1988

As China's bamboo curtain is pulled away, more and more of her secrets are revealed to the outside world. One of these secrets is the Beauty Heart radish, and I don't mind hazarding a guess that in a few years Beauty Heart will be taking the chic restaurants and smart dinner tables of the world by storm. When Pam Toler and I went to China to study vegetable growing, Beauty Heart was one of our most exciting discoveries.

It's a very large radish, 10–12cm/4–5in in diameter and up to 15cm/6in long. But China is a land of huge radishes, and its size alone is not remarkable. What is remarkable is its internal colour. The outer skin is a pale lime green and one would never guess that inside it is white at the outer edges, shading to a beautiful rose and sometimes deep red at the centre. The Chinese name is 'Xin Li Mei', pronounced *shin lee may*, meaning 'heart inside beautiful'.

It tastes as good as it looks: sweet, mild and crisp.

As far as we could see Beauty Heart is grown only in north China in and around Beijing. There it is eaten like a fruit. On autumn evenings, street vendors cut it into cubes and display it with a gas light behind to reveal the colour. 'Radish is better than crisp pears,' they cry out (and the crisp pears of northern China are legendary).

We sampled it shredded and cut into julienne strips – white and pink matchsticks, tipped with the green of the outer skin, served with sugar on top. They looked wonderful on a plate.

It's an autumn or early winter radish, taking about eighty days, nearly three months, to mature in the hot Manchurian summer. It can't be sown until mid-summer. Earlier sowings, reacting to the length of the day, run straight to seed instead of forming a root. Some varieties are grown for lifting in autumn, and are stored for winter in underground pits.

It was while Pam was photographing Beauty Heart and other radishes being lifted in the fields, weighed and carted off to market that she was told about the radishes being carved into flowers for table decorations. It was easy to imagine how lovely the pink and white flesh would look, and we became obsessed with the idea of seeing them being carved.

We took some research station specimens back to the hotel, partly as emergency rations for Pam, who is a vegetarian, and partly in hopes of finding someone to show us how to carve them. We kept them fresh in the bath.

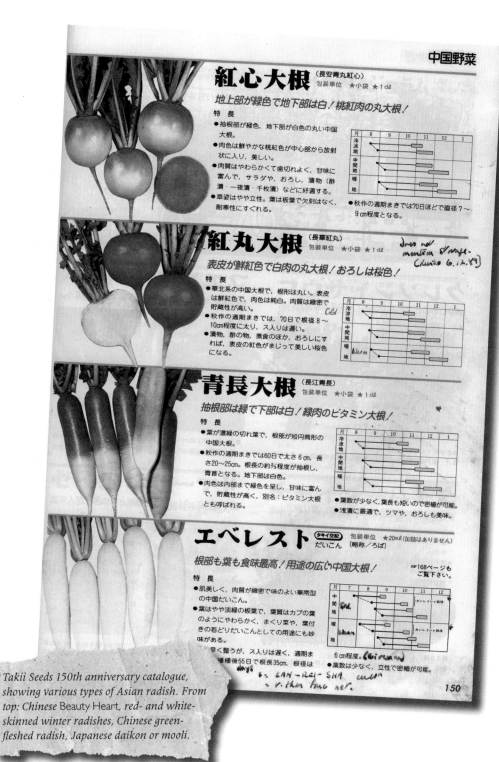

Takii Seeds 150th anniversary catalogue, showing various types of Asian radish. From top: Chinese Beauty Heart, red- and white-skinned winter radishes, Chinese green-fleshed radish, Japanese daikon or mooli.

Chefs skilled in the art of radish carving proved hard to find. The first restaurant we asked told us a special knife was needed – which they didn't have. Later, in our own hotel, they were very sorry, but the only man who could do it was away that day.

With only two hours left in Beijing before our evening train to Nanjing, we braved the famous Peking Hotel. Our guide, still as unused to our ways as we were to hers, was nervous, but, with a little persuasion, asked for a demonstration. The hotel agreed, for a fee, though they wouldn't allow us in the kitchen.

A table was cleared in a lounge for a lady cook. We gave her our radishes. With an enormous, but in fact very ordinary kitchen knife, she sliced off the top – and immediately exclaimed delightedly at the magnificent colour of the breeding station's radish. (Poorer samples can be almost all white with little rose or red in them.) With great speed and dexterity she cut slivers from the sides and centre, and in a few seconds, there was a waterlily.

Continuing to work at top speed she sculpted other flowers – dahlias, chrysanthemums, peonies and lotus – chatting as she worked. She had demonstrated radish carving for President Nixon during his visit . . . they sometimes carve 'green things' like dragonflies and crickets . . . and for banquets they do butterflies.

Now she was really getting into her stride and you felt nothing would stop her, as she cut two thin, rounded slices, just hinged together, for deep red, white-tipped butterfly wings. We could have watched for hours but there was a train to catch. We had to go.

So they put our carved butterfly and flowers into a plastic bag half-filled with water – like goldfish at a fair – and Pam nursed them tenderly for the next sixteen hours on the train. Provided the water is changed frequently, the radishes will keep fresh for several days in a fridge or cool place.

The story ended in our hotel room in Nanjing. Pam was trying to photograph the radishes near the window, using the grey light of a bad-tempered sky. She had floated them in a tray of water to get a reflection. The room maid was watching. Without saying anything, she went off, returning a few minutes later with a few rose leaves and coins – to put in the tray to complete the picture!

Our own Beauty Heart *at last! It took us a few years to grow* Beauty Heart *successfully, but we cracked it by sowing seeds in the polytunnel in July and August, so that they would mature for Christmas.*

BEAN THERE, DONE THAT
Your Garden (Australia), September 1988

For years I've been a compulsive bean sprouter, unable to resist this 5,000-year-old method of producing highly nutritious, tasty food – and the convenience of reaping on Friday what you sowed on Monday. But my bean sprouts were rarely as long, crisp and crunchy as those in Chinese restaurants. There was definitely scope to improve my sprouting technique.

I did once knock on the door of a local Chinese restaurant in Bury St Edmunds to see if I could prise any bean-sprouting secrets out of them. But they proved reluctant to let a foreigner into the kitchen, and all I learned through a barely opened door was that the beans were sprouted somewhere else in large sacks.

So when Pamla Toler and I were in Shanghai on our Chinese 'vegetable tour', we asked if bean sprouting could be added to our itinerary. We would have loved to see how it was done domestically, but that wasn't on. Instead we were taken to the Lu Wan District Non-Staple Food Company bean sprouts factory.

Not only did this give us a fascinating insight into large-scale bean sprouting, but we had a chance to see a bit of Shanghai we suspected wasn't on the normal tourist track. All the 'crowded street' clichés sprang to mind as we wended our way through narrow streets to a brick building in which the basement had been converted into a bean sprouting workshop.

Judging from the battery of dilapidated green pigeonholes for mail inside the entrance, and the cluster of craning necks at every doorway as we went upstairs to the office, a lot of families were living in the rest of the building.

The office was on the bare side – just a large table, cheered by a vase of artificial rosebuds, arum lilies, carnations and shaggy chrysanthemums, and a telephone hanging by a wire to the wall. (I thought at one point they were going to pull it out to put an end to the frequent telephone interruptions.)

With considerable pride the supervisor explained how they had increased productivity tenfold since abandoning the traditional large jars in which sprouts used to be grown, for a semi-automatic 'modern' system.

Now the beans are being grown in concrete tanks, roughly 1m/3ft wide and 1m/3ft deep, and sprinkled automatically every four hours from overhead sprinkler pipes. (As the beans germinate, an enormous amount of heat is generated. In the dark, warm conditions needed for sprouting, they would soon rot if not constantly cooled down by watering. In traditional workshops family members would stay up all night, sloshing water periodically over the beans to keep the temperature down.)

It takes four to seven days, depending on outside temperatures, for the mung beans to reach the optimum 5cm/2in sprout length. They are first soaked in small wooden pails for about eight hours, then put into the tanks in a layer several centimetres deep, covered with thick rice straw matting to keep out the light. By the fifth day they have reached the top of the tank – and increased their bulk and weight sevenfold. So dense are they that it takes considerable strength to pull a handful out of the tank.

Besides mung beans, the factory also sprouted soy beans and horse beans, a kind of broad bean. Mung beans are considered 'cooling' by the Chinese, and are most popular in summer, whereas soy beans are 'warming' and are preferred in winter. The horse beans were sprouted to 2.5cm/1in long.

The basement workshop was dank and gloomy – hardly surprising, with the sprinklers constantly swinging into action over a different batch of tanks. The workers wore huge plastic aprons, tied around their necks with string. It was continuous, three-shift production.

Pam took some beans outside to photograph in natural light. It was a miracle that she succeeded, for immediately a huge crowd gathered, swelled by a group of schoolboys returning home. They all wanted to peep into the camera.

While this was going on I had a chance to marvel at the ingenuity of the occupants of the five-storey building opposite, who had built flimsy bamboo rafts, literally out into space, on which to grow a few plants. The hanging gardens of Shanghai!

Bird cages were perched on rooftops; grannies sat on tiny stools in dark doorways minding the statutory only child. Yarn was being spun down an alley between buildings, and a group of older men and women were playing cards on the pavement.

Piled against the wall across the road were the abandoned pottery sprouting jars. Later I was told how they use the jars at home, covering the beans with a wet cloth and a weight. The beans are rinsed about three times a day, pouring water in, then tipping it out and holding the beans back with a long-handled strainer, so they are disturbed as little as possible. Sometimes large jars with drainage holes in the bottom are used. In very hot weather beans can be ready in as little as three days.

A mistake I used to make at home was to invert the beans into a strainer to wash them. Now at least I know they shouldn't be dislocated.

Later I visited the Asian Vegetable Research and Development Center in Taiwan, where mung and soy beans are two of the crops being investigated. Research there into sprouting had shown that when subjected to pressure, germinating beans produce the gas ethylene, and it is this which promotes the development of fat crispy sprouts, by making the plant cells swell. In fact, both the curved sides of the old-fashioned pottery jars and the rigidity of the concrete tanks create the pressure which is the key to good sprouts. Research had also shown that the smaller the seed, the higher the eventual yield of sprouts. Small bean seeds, however, produce smaller individual sprouts.

When I returned home I decided to try increasing the pressure on beans simply by using a weight. My home-made sprouter was a cheap plastic ice-cream container about 10cm/4in in diameter, with small holes, about 2.5cm/1in apart, made in the bottom with a hot poker. This converted it into a sieve, making it easy to run water through twice daily to rinse the beans without disturbing them.

After removing any cracked beans, they were soaked overnight, drained, and put in the container in a layer about 1cm/½in deep. I covered them with a damp cloth (not having any rice straw matting handy) and a 1kg/over 2lb weight set on a saucer to spread the weight evenly. It did look a little absurd . . . Later I took to using a heavy flintstone, which was much more picturesque. To my astonishment, the germinating beans pushed up this weight as they sprouted. (The weight, of course, has to be removed for the rinsing.)

The end result is far better sprouts than I ever had before, quite up to restaurant standards.

Incidentally if you want to remove any of the little green seed coats which haven't fallen off naturally, plunge the sprouted beans into a bowl of water. The seed coats float to the surface and can be skimmed off. However, no harm comes from eating them.

CHINESE WAYS WITH GARLIC
The Garden, April 1987

Before my recent trip to China I assumed, as I suspect most people do, that garlic is grown for its bulb – that cluster of cloves used almost universally in cooking. It is, of course; but in China that's only part of the story. There it is also widely grown for its young shoots, which are sometimes used green and sometimes blanched, and for its flower stem, which is picked when still fresh, supple and green. Garlic is also conserved in several forms for what euphemistically translates from the Chinese as the 'non-flourishing' periods for vegetables. Besides the mature bulbs we are familiar with, the bulb is pickled, and also made into dried flakes and powder, and frozen. The flower stems are also dried and frozen.

GARLIC SHOOTS

Let's start with garlic grown for its shoots or young leaves, before the original clove has developed and divided into a many-cloved bulb – a common practice in south-east Asia.

Certainly autumn was a good time to be in China to see garlic shoots, for they are a popular winter and spring crop. In early October in Beijing they were already flourishing in the 'improved winter beds' (see page 240) ready for harvesting as a spring treat at Chinese New Year at the end of January. At first sight I mistook them for winter onions, they looked so sturdy and were such a deep green – the leaves looking much lusher than our garlic.

To get shoots, single cloves are planted close, 2.5–3cm/1–1½in apart, for the winter crop in early to mid-September in the Beijing area, at the end of September further south in Nanjing. (This later date would probably be about the right time for any would-be garlic shoot growers in the British Isles.)

It seems the plants are normally harvested whole, and in several markets, both in the north and in Chengdu in west China, I saw shoots being sold with the roots attached. However, I was told the green shoots can be

Green garlic shoots cultivated in north China for the Chinese New Year in specially constructed 'winter beds'. These are protected with plastic film and, as it becomes colder, extra layers of matting.

cut twice, leaving the plant to resprout after the initial cut.

It was several months later that I learned from Professor Jia Wen Wei of the China Academy of Agricultural Sciences in Beijing of the lengths Chinese housewives go to have their own supplies of garlic shoots indoors. Circles of small garlic cloves will be spread on a plate, and threaded together with a peeled piece of bamboo. They will then sprout into a mat-like forest of green shoots for spring. I wonder if I will ever have the patience to try this out for myself.

In some parts of China garlic shoots are preferred blanched, and for this they need to be grown fast so that they are tender, rather than being subjected to the slow, hardening growth of the cold frame. It's an ancient practice, going back to the Han dynasty 2,000 years ago, and again it was Jia Wen Wei who enlightened me.

Garlic was often blanched in rooms indoors, or in so-called 'warm caves'. In Xian in west China they used 'kangs', the traditional Chinese beds raised off the floor so that a charcoal brazier could be popped underneath to heat it. Using the kang heat the garlic was grown under a darkened 'tent'. Garlic forcing and blanching was also done in the traditional clay-walled, lean-to greenhouses, covered with matting to exclude light and heated with a charcoal brazier. Green garlic can also be lifted and blanched in straw shelters, clay pots or by earthing up.

FLOWER STEMS

The flower stems of garlic are harvested in summer when still green. Besides the garlic flavour, they are valued because they retain their bright colour when cooked, giving that visual appeal which is an integral part of Chinese cookery. The stems are surprisingly long: I saw some beautifully packed bunches in Kanda wholesale market in Tokyo, about 45cm/18in long.

Wherever possible the stems are delicately prised off the bulb, leaving the latter intact to mature. This is done in various ways, for example by holding the stem near the base with two bamboo sticks and pulling it away with the other hand. I have an article from a Chinese agricultural journal describing four harvesting methods developed on a commune in Hubei province. The methods include using a sharpened piece of bamboo to slice the stem off, a method where you pinch the stem low down, then pull from above, and another evidently very slow method which produces a very smooth stalk and involves driving a nail into the plant. What ingenuity!

Perhaps in these less thrifty times farmers don't always go to such lengths to save the bulb, for in several markets I saw garlic stems with bulbs attached, sometimes with the inflorescence as well.

Garlic stems can be dried for winter use. Jia Wen Wei described graphically whiling away long winter evenings in Inner Mongolia (where she was sent during the Cultural Revolution) removing the outer skin of the stem with needles. They are hung in the shade to dry in summer, kept in a very dry atmosphere, and reconstituted in water around Chinese New Year. Will this practice survive the advent of television to Chinese homes?

I never discovered if particular strains of garlic were cultivated for the flower stem, but it seems that most Chinese garlic does produce flower stems. Herklots, in Vegetables in South-East Asia, mentions Taiwanese soft- and hard-stem strains, probably equivalent to soft- and hard-necked garlic in the West, the hard necks developing an inflorescence. In Europe, of course, we are conditioned to not wanting our alliums to bolt, though unlike onions, the quality of the garlic bulb seems to be unimpaired by the production of a flower stem.

In my experience only a proportion of garlic bolts each season. A challenge in future summers will be to spot the bolters (one tends to ignore garlic until it is being harvested), to pluck the flower stems carefully from the plant, and to use them to create oriental delicacies – such as the dish of garlic stems and finely sliced pork we were served at the Beijing Vegetable Research Center, or the tasty sliced stems in oil and soya sauce which customers in a Japanese supermarket were being enticed to sample. Garlic stems also mix well, I was told, with the famous lime-preserved, 1,000-year-old Chinese eggs.

MATURE GARLIC

Mature garlic is sold in all shapes and sizes. Typical was a display on a Chengdu street stall, specializing in garlic and ginger. The garlic, laid out in flat, round baskets, was carefully graded. There were large whole bulbs, both white and pinkish, and single cloves, graded into different sizes, as well as 'rounds'. These are the small, round, undivided cloves which result from sowing very small cloves or unfavourable growing conditions: they do, however, develop into mature, large bulbs when planted. We were told that the smallest cloves were bought for planting rather than use in the kitchen. In addition there was peeled garlic – prepared foods for the busy housewife – but it was a man in the background industriously peeling.

The only form of garlic not on that market stall was pickled garlic, but we'd sampled it earlier, in the famous Tian Yuan Zhang Yuan – a hundred-year-old preserved vegetable shop in Beijing (see page 244). It is a sweet pickle. You peel off the skin and eat the clove whole. I thought it quite pleasant, unlike some of the other, extremely dry, acrid pickles we tasted.

A garlic and ginger stall in Chengdu, where every colour and form of garlic was sold, including ready-to-use peeled garlic and undersized cloves planted close for early green shoots.

VEGETABLES IN JAPAN
The Garden, June 1986

For years I've been collecting Japanese seed catalogues because they have been one of the best sources of information on Chinese vegetables available to Westerners. Japan had been my gateway to China. So it seemed to make sense, after a three-and-a-half-week study tour in China, to spend a week in November visiting Japanese seed firms.

The Japanese have very few native vegetables in their essentially mountainous island country, which is probably why they traditionally make such good use of wild plants, fungi and seaweed. Circumstances have forced them to comb less promising habitats, from mountaintop to the sea, for edible plants. It has also, of course, encouraged them to look further afield. In the last hundred years they have introduced vegetables from Europe and China, the latter brought back by soldiers returning from war in China.

With their talent for assimilating, and improving upon, all things foreign, coupled with the range of climatic conditions found in the islands (which stretch over 2,600 kilometres/1,620 miles from north to south), a very wide range of foreign vegetables is both grown and bred in Japan.

Japanese plant breeding has had an enormous impact on our flower and vegetable growing. Many varieties we consider household names have come from Japanese seed firms. So my first visit in Japan was to the largest and best known of these, the Kyoto-based firm of Takii; I happened to arrive during their 150th anniversary celebrations.

Takii have been in the forefront of modern plant breeding since the late 1940s, when they introduced their first hybrid tomato. Their principal plant breeding station and trial grounds are at Kosei, east of Kyoto. The 69 hectare/170 acre site, which includes 48 hectares/118 acres of greenhouses and their own horticultural school for farmers' sons, was created from old pine forest on poor sticky, stony soil. Takii still pays the original owner compensation for his loss of income from the highly rated, extremely expensive matsutake mushroom (*Tricholoba matsutake*) which grew beneath the pines.

Over the years the fertility of the soil has been built up with horse manure, with soil imported from the nearby lake, and by planting sorghum as green manure after the main vegetable crops are lifted. It now produces fine crops; the trials are among the most impressive I have seen anywhere, with a Japanese flavour imparted first by the unnervingly deep bowing of employees as your car arrives, or even passes, subsequently by the excellent tin of hot coffee thrust into your hand on the trial grounds.

Time being short I bypassed the more familar European vegetables and concentrated on the oriental brassicas. For me this was a living museum, the visual aid I'd been needing to piece together the complicated jigsaw of these brassicas, so many at their best in late autumn. There were beautiful, clearly labelled specimens of Chinese cabbage, pak choi, rosette pak choi, flowering brassicas, numerous mustards, komatsuna, that quintissental Japanese vegetable mizuna and, an exciting first for me, its handsome, strap-leaved cousin mibuna.

Brassicas apart, I was fascinated by the trials of *Glebionis coronaria* (syn. *Chrysanthemum coronarium*), alias shungiku, garland chrysan-themum, crown daisy or 'chop suey greens', a fragrant plant much used in oriental cooking. Here were three different types – fine leaved, branching small leaved and large leaved – each

Japanese brassicas, mizuna and mibuna, in the superbly laid out Takii seed trials. These were an invaluable resource for me, in mastering the different varieties of oriental vegetables.

suited to a different season and purpose. And also looking magnificent in November were the Chinese onions, earthed up like our leeks, but in fact forms of the Welsh onion (*Allium fistulosum*). The single-stem onion has a long white shaft; the multi-stemmed is smaller and more branched. Both are extremely popular in the East, where 'our' leeks are comparatively rare. I was puzzled by them in the past, but now, knowing what to expect, I intend to grow them.

The visit ended with a tantalizing drive past huge plots of ornamental kales, those magnificent colourful vegetables used for autumn bedding. (They don't survive severe frost, but try a few under cover for winter. Their bright colours are marvellous for winter salads or simply for garnishing.) As time had run out I had to be content with a couple of snatched photographs from the car window: I'd have loved a longer browse through them.

The following two days were spent in Tokyo, under the wing of Kyowa Seed Company.

First stop, early in the day, was Tokyo's Kanda wholesale market, the largest in Japan. No visitor could fail to be impressed by its cleanliness, the very high standards of packaging and display, and the high quality of the produce itself. Remodelled on the French market system, auctions for different crops – melons, fruit, leafy vegetables – were taking place in different areas. The purple-capped auctioneers stand in a row with samples of produce before them, communicating in a ballet like deaf-and-dumb with the potential buyers, fingers stabbing the air, almost on tip toe in their feverishness.

I don't think I have ever seen such a range of produce in a market. It shattered my assumption that I was beginning to know something about oriental vegetables: there were so many new ones. Most striking perhaps were the long stemmed and root vegetables, such as the 1.2m/4ft long green stems of sweet coltsfoot (*Petasites japonicus*) or the 1.5m/5ft long white stems of *Aralia cordata*, sometimes collected from the wild but here cultivated and blanched by covering with rice husks. Root crops were equally varied. The long thin roots of burdock I recognized, knobbly taro I recognized, but new were the various types of mountain yam or potato (*Dioscorea opposita*) – some long, some heart-shaped.

A great many herbs were being sold, some typically Japanese such as the purple- and green-leaved perilla, often wrapped around other food or vegetables. Others included wasabi, the Japanese ginger, mitsuba, the fine angelica-flavoured stem (a neat matchstick pile might appear artistically on a plate), tiny red seedlings of *Persicaria hydropiper*, also used decoratively, the grass-like salsola, *Oenanthe javanica* (water dropwort), with leaves like watercress, and the elegant flowering stalks of Chinese or garlic chives, *Allium tuberosum*.

Here for the first time I saw boxes of the rarer purple- and common yellow-flowered edible chrysanthemums (shungiku) on sale, and chunky, neatly bunched bundles of rape flowers.

Many familiar vegetables looked different in Kanda market. Cucumbers were tiny – 10–15cm/4–6in long, sweetcorn sold even tinier, baby cobs no more than 6.5cm/3in long. Aubergines were huge, some very long; large pink tomatoes dominated, though cherry tomatoes and yellow tomatoes were also on sale. Carrots were deep red as well as orange, radishes enormous and of many types. A recent idea is the sale of packs of radish seedlings, an appetizing mustard and cress substitute and something we could copy here.

It could be said that the rest of the day was spent underground – in the basement of Tokyo department stores, to be precise. For these are crammed with food counters and stalls, and provide an excellent opportunity to see what the Japanese customer expects – and gets. As in the market, the care that goes into presentation and display is astonishing. Immaculately arranged fish, garnished with chrysanthemum flowers; counters where at least ten types of fungi were displayed in wicker baskets, nestling between sprigs of conifer and fir cones; extensive counters of beautifully presented pickled vegetables – for example jars of black pickled aubergines, green stem and leaf mustards, reddened turnips, deep red cucumbers and kimchi, the famous Korean pickle of Chinese cabbage, cucumber and radish spiced with garlic and ginger. Prepared foods were there for customers to sample. I had a taste of calabrese salad, mixed with egg white and shrimps, and garlic stalks in oil and soya sauce. All in all, living proof of a society where vegetables are highly valued, appreciated for their decorative and nutritional quality, and used widely, both raw and cooked.

The following day was spent in the intensively farmed, fertile countryside of the Bōsō peninsula, south-east of Tokyo.

We visited two holdings. They had the feel of market gardens anywhere. It could have been the fens, though I wondered if fenmen would take to the *jikatabi*, the traditional growers' footwear – light rubber soles, calf-gripping cotton leggings with a comical mitten-like foot, the big toe separated from the others. Everyone wore them – far lighter than wellies! A homely touch by the grower's house was a group of large-flowered chrysanthemums, protected from the rain by a brolly; and opposite a typical Japanese copse of conifers (*Podocarpus*?), the branches being rigidly trained to form horizontal layers.

Crops we saw here included a polytunnel of turnips, so tender we just crunched them raw, and immaculate fields of single-stem onion.

These take a year from sowing to harvest and are earthed up several times to create the very long blanched shafts.

The second holding was a long narrow strip, and here I saw many traditional crops – for example lotus, now dying back in the pond (root and seed are eaten), a field of Japanese daikon sticking out of the ground like sugar beet, corners of coltsfoot and perilla, and mizuna and other mustards alongside mulched strawberries. The highlight for me was an energetic demonstration of how to lift burdock and taro. A narrow-bladed mattock was used to cleave the soil and extricate the deep roots. Sufficient to convince me that these two vegetables will never become popular in England.

My last day was spent with world-famous Sakata Seed. Their founder, Takeo Sakata, died only in 1984 at the age of ninety-five, active almost to the end.

The whole day was spent at their vegetable breeding station in Kimitsu, where the station director and an agricultural professor contrived patiently to answer all the questions I had been accumulating, by working through their catalogue, pulling ancient tomes off the shelves, and drawing on their knowledge. They enabled me to unravel many mysteries – the different types of daikon (sweet and sharp, storage and fresh); the different mizunas; which Chinese chives to grow for leaf, which for stem and flower buds; and the many different types of Chinese cabbage.

I'll keep my feet dry this year with the *jitakabi* I bought in a small local shop and think fond farewell thoughts of the Narita Hotel, where, on a high bank opposite the main entrance, the hotel emblem is picked out in ornamental kales.

PEACE WORKERS
Practical Gardening, December 1986

My interest in Japanese gardens was probably kindled in an enforced wait at Trafalgar Square many moons ago. To kill time I popped into Charing Cross Library and more or less at random took a book on Japanese gardening from the shelves. I left utterly spellbound by a vision of exquisite simple gardens of raked sand or gravel and 'pictures' made from stones and a few very carefully chosen plants. So during my brief visit to Japan last year to study vegetables I determined, if time allowed, to see something of Japanese gardens.

An opportunity arose in Kyoto, with half a day free. My seedsmen contacts couldn't think of any famous gardens in Kyoto (never ask seedsmen about gardens), but as I flicked through the commercial 'bumf' in my hotel bedroom a sheet fell out: 'The 10 Best Gardens in Kyoto'. The answer to my prayers? Most required special permits to visit them, impossible to get at short notice, I soon discovered. But I selected two on the outskirts of the city near the zoo that were open to the public – the modern 'stream garden' of Murin-an, and the dry landscaped Zen garden of Nanzen-ji temple.

I could write a book on getting there by public transport – the mysteries of finding the bus station, then the bus, then the right stop and finally the garden of Murin-an itself, for there was nothing to indicate that the closed door in the street was an entrance to a garden rather than a house.

One of the smartly dressed and well-equipped gardeners, wearing the light jikatabi footwear, in the peaceful Murin-an stream garden in Kyoto.

It was a narrow, rectangular garden, 12–15m/40–50ft wide, probably between 0.2–0.3 hectares/½–¾ acre) in size and typical, I think, of the Japanese 'tea garden' style. Near the entrance was the tea house, a simple building raised on low stilts, the doors rolled back so that visitors could sit on the matted floor and contemplate the garden. At the far end, hidden from view, was a small waterfall feeding into two pools from which came two streams, one bubbling down the left-hand side of the garden, the other smaller stream on the right-hand side soon disappearing underground then re-emerging to join its sister stream

near the tea house. Narrow gravelled paths meandered through the garden, up one side to the waterfall, down the other, following the contours of the streams.

The garden was shielded from the outer world by a frame of trees – conifers, maples starting to turn orange and large ginkgos already a beautiful autumnal yellow. Within the garden were smaller trees, many of them pines (popular because they symbolize longevity), several planted in typical Japanese style at the edge of the pool. There were bamboos too, and near the entrance a little grove of conifers and evergreen shrubs, and a group of acers, the ground between them a smooth carpet of green moss. Moss in Japan is treated with the respect we reserve for grass.

What was strange to English eyes was the lack of colourful flowers, but that again is typically Japanese. To quote from *Gardens of Japan*, written by Harada in 1928, 'Japanese gardens aim for simplicity rather than gaiety.'

Murin-an certainly had a quality of stillness and serenity and I was surprised at the number of businessmen who seemed to have come there to enjoy it in their lunch hour. Apart from the raucous shrieks of the zoo monkeys across the road there was little sound other than that of moving water. The still effect, I think, was created by the grey stones and low, rounded hillocks of neatly trimmed dwarf azaleas and box – trimmed to represent rocks – which edged the stream and were placed in key spots on the central grassed slope. Stones sometimes protruded into the paths, or formed stepping stones across the stream. The art of using stepping stones, down to the shape and surfaces of the stone themselves, is part of the complex tradition of Japanese gardening.

There seemed to be five gardeners working in the garden, all smartly dressed, several wearing the comic *jikatabi*.

Watching the gardeners work made one appreciate the extraordinary attention to detail which characterizes Japanese gardening. One man was carefully re-edging a sunken path, making a tiny earth margin by the bank, smoothing the surface gravel with a board, picking up dead leaves. Two others were up splayed bamboo ladders in the pine trees, painstakingly removing dead pine needles and probably, according to what I've read subsequently, picking off the tips of young shoots to preserve the shape and energy of the trees. Another was clipping bamboo, his tools in a neat holster around his waist. Pruning and trimming: these skills lie at the heart of Japanese gardening, seen as a means not of curbing plants but of allowing the 'ideal beauty' within the plant to emerge.

A TASTE OF TAIWAN
The Garden, August 1986

My destination last November was the Asian Vegetable Research and Development Center (AVRDC) in Taiwan, situated near Tainan in the tropical part of the island, about 257 kilometres/160 miles south of the capital Taipei. The slow train journey between the two, along the eastern coastal plain, proved a wonderful introduction to the island's geography and agriculture, even providing peeps into its history, culture and modern prosperity.

It was November in the 'hot dry' season, following the 'hot wet' months of June to August, to be followed in turn by the 'cool dry' season from December to February and the 'cool wet' season from March to May.

There were glimpses of rice grain drying, inches deep, in village courtyards, spreading right to the doors of the verandahed houses with their curving grey and red tiled roofs. On the return journey, in the (unseasonal) rain, the rice had been pulled up into heaps and covered with bright red and bright green tarpaulins for protection.

The passing scene was often more 'Chinese' than in modern China, with pagodas and temples, quite frequently under construction, as well as ground-consuming ancestral graves and the tiny countryside shrines with their offerings – both now disappeared from mainland China. But typical of Chinese culture everywhere were the intensively cultivated plots of vegetables and seedlings alongside the railway tracks.

I spent two action-packed days at AVRDC, under their helpful and hospitable guidance, travelling south one day, north the next, so seeing a lot of the countryside. The starting point each day was a market, the first in Lujhu, run by the Taoyuan County Farmers' Association Agricultural Products Company in the heart of a cauliflower and calabrese growing area. Produce was coming in by every imaginable form of transport – lorry, tractor, oxen, motorbike, cart, bicycle, shoulder poles. Taiwan is a major exporter of fresh fruit and vegetables, exported from the port of Kaohsiung to Singapore, Malaysia, Hong Kong, Japan, Indonesia.

Calabrese was one of the main vegetables being handled that day. The largest heads were for local consumption (no one-child families here); the smaller ones, neatly decapitated, were for export to Japan, catering to the small Japanese family. So what to do with the long, unwanted stalks? Gangs of brightly dressed women, clad in the traditional sun-protecting garb of straw hats over headscarves and long-sleeved blouses, were peeling the stalks (the peel went for pig food) and slicing them for pickles.

The other market, at Hsi-lo, was more varied and far more chaotic, market stalls spilling out on to a nearby street where the mêlée of manoeuvring vans, motorbike carts and hand-pulled carts made movement almost impossible. Here were familiar vegetables like radishes, asparagus, peppers, green beans, leaf beet, sweetcorn, green onions, Chinese celery and Chinese cabbage, and, less familiar, the popular local variety of tomatoes, green with big red blobs at the blossom end, amaranthus, bamboo shoots, bottle gourds and the bitter melon or karela, with its striking crocodile-like skin.

What caught my eye were the pickling mustards so loved by the Chinese. Here at last I saw cartloads of the grotesque, knobbly-stemmed pickling mustard (it's the stem that is used), and the almost savoy-like headed pickling mustard, a brilliant green. On the edge of the market we came across a family making pickles, sitting on tiny stools under a tarpaulin propped up by bamboo poles. They were pickling the 'pickling melon' (stem mustards were waiting their turn on the pavement). The melons look rather like overweight greenhouse cucumbers some being about 30cm/12in long, are first quartered, then deseeded, then packed into large wooden tubs and sprinkled liberally with salt before being weighted down by a pyramid of enormous smooth stones. They are left for twenty-four hours before water is drained off and they are ready for sale.

A little further down the road were several traditional pickling houses, no longer used — rounded, tubby little structures with thatched roofs, raised slightly off the ground and entered via a ladder.

Not far from Hsi-lo we passed a village famous for its onions. Bunches of the long white-shafted, leek-like Chinese onions were hanging up all through the village.

One of the most serious brassica pests in Asia is the caterpillar of the diamond back moth. Near Lujhu AVRDC was experimenting with a biological control by introducing a parasitic Indonesian bee (*Diadegma eucerophaga*), which lays eggs in the moth larvae, so destroying them. The cauliflower fields were dotted with neat little white houses on stilts for the bees, with a row of tagetes planted down the garden path, so to speak, providing them with the nectar they apparently required.

Taiwan, unlike mainland China, has its own independent seed companies, one of the best known being the Known-You Seed Company, based in Kaohsiung.

Their research director, Mr Chung-Hsiung Yu, was a mine of practical information on Chinese vegetables. His horticultural bible, incidentally, was the late Dr Herklots' *Vegetables in South-East Asia*. He took me on an interesting detour to some allotments on the edge of the city. Sadly, like so many plots on the outskirts of cities all over Asia, these were already overshadowed by the construction of ugly modern buildings which would engulf them the following year. But like allotments anywhere, they would be intensively used to the eleventh hour. In 2m/6ft-wide sunken beds all sorts of things were being grown – several types of mustard and Chinese cabbage, flowering kales, both the round- and pointed-leaved types, the water spinach *Ipomoea aquatica*, but here grown on land, young and maturing pak choi and, now that temperatures were cool enough, lettuce.

The raised paths between the plots were crammed with plants, making it hard to walk along without slipping into a muddy, irrigated bed. Some were planted with young papayas

In the wide sunken beds of a Taiwanese allotment pak choi is being cut at the seedling or 'chicken feather' stage. Shortly afterwards these productive allotments succumbed to urban development.

and mangoes, probably destined to be moved to a new site; others with flowers – cockscomb, canna lilies, daylilies (the flowers are eaten); also medicinal herbs and culinary herbs such as basil and the perennial *Gynura bicolor*, the '*bicolor*' presumably referring to the purple underside to the green leaf. Allotment tenants ranged from elderly peasants to a trendy young gent in tracksuit, listening to his transistor radio.

Back at AVRDC I was especially interested in the Home Gardens programme, developed by a nutritionist, the late Dr Jack Gershon. Its object is to alleviate the serious diet deficiencies of poorer people in underdeveloped countries, particularly in Asia. Vegetables contain calcium, iron, vitamins A and C, and in the case of dark green leaves, some valuable protein. Lack of vitamin A causes the blinding disease xerophthalmia in children, but it can be prevented, and reversed in the early stages, with a regular intake of vitamin A. But vegetables are too expensive for many poor people to buy. Is it possible for families of five people, with very small garden plots, to grow enough vegetables to meet their daily basic nutritional requirements?

Following this line of thought small trial plots 4m × 4.5m/13ft × 14ft 9in were established at AVRDC for three countries – Thailand, Indonesia and the Philippines, growing both 'culturally acceptable' and nutritious vegetables. There was also a 'Vitamin A' garden, concentrating on fruits and vegetables rich in vitamin A.

A related project is the school garden. Many Asian children take a rice lunch box to school, which, for the poorer children, is of low nutritional value. The idea was to demonstrate how schools could grow fresh vegetables, to be stir-fried on the spot, to add to the lunch boxes and supplement their diet.

The school garden concentrated on easily grown vegetables, so that even if a professional did the initial cultivation and planting, the children could weed, pick off pests and harvest. In the '85 to '86 season the 10 × 18m/33 × 59ft plot produced over 16kg/35lb of vegetables a day, enough to give 142 children half a cup of freshly cooked vegetables every day of the school year, so contributing to their nutritional needs. Already school gardens based on this model have been established successfully in Thailand.

Another interesting project, with increasing relevance in an ever-drier world, was a permanent, dry-land, sheet composting garden, designed to retain moisture and so extend the vegetable growing season in dry climates. Utilizing permaculture concepts developed by Bill Mollison in Tasmania, beds are made up with different layers of organic material. The lowest, a high-nitrogen layer, is covered with cardboard, newspaper, underfelt or similar material to prevent weed penetration. This in turn is covered with a nutrient-rich layer of manure or compost, and topped with 15cm/6in of organic material such as rice hulls, nut shells or leafmould to prevent evaporation. Holes are made in the cardboard layer for planting. In work to date the garden required 20 per cent less water than adjacent control plots, and produced excellent crops.

VANCOUVER: A GROWING CITY
Practical Gardening, July 1988

Vancouver in British Columbia was a major port of call on my travels to the American continent last autumn, not least because it has one of the largest Chinese populations outside mainland China.

I found the epicentre of Chinese cultivation in the leafy suburbs of Burnaby along the banks of the Fraser River. Here, in the area known as the Big Bend, is a string of between thirty and forty small Chinese-owned farms – Kwong Lee, Hop On Farms, Wing Wong. These are the last of a once huge Chinese market-garden industry, originating in the nineteenth century, now all but squeezed out by industrial and urban development.

Looking down on these farms from Marine Drive, where many have farm shops which are more like mini supermarkets, is like looking at a photograph of China. Immaculate, parallel, raised beds stretch down towards the river, densely planted with European and Chinese vegetables, a sea of greens of infinite shades. The landscape is pocked with giant white parasols under which old and young Chinese sit bunching radishes, green onions or pak choi. From dawn to dusk straw-hatted figures work in the fields, sowing, transplanting, hand weeding.

The peaty alluvial soil here is wonderfully fertile – 90cm/3ft deep and over 30 per cent organic matter (ordinary mineral soils have about 3 per cent). In true Chinese style the farms are very intensively worked, most of the land producing three crops a year. Takings are said to be ten times higher than on conventional market gardens in British Columbia. Small though the area is, it produces a huge percentage of the province's fresh vegetables, exporting to the eastern United States in spring.

No one knows if the farms will survive the next twenty years. Not only are there enormous pressures on the land, but the young generation of Chinese is not prepared to work the lengthy hours. It's not surprising. One retired farmer reminisced over the days when he helped his father deliver vegetables to Vancouver in narrow carts (they had to be narrow to cope with the streets of China town). That was at three in the morning – often after no more than two hours sleep.

The intensely cultivated Chinese market gardens in the Big Bend of the Fraser River in Vancouver. Left: me talking to a man working in the fields. Right: a lady bunching green onions.

The gardens have indeed survived. Photos on the Internet, taken only a few months ago, are almost identical to those I took over twenty years ago.

CHINESE METHODS OF PEST AND DISEASE CONTROL
The Garden, November 1984

Since time immemorial (the records go back to BC), China has suffered from plagues of migratory insects. Locusts are among the best known – in the 1930s trains used to be stopped in their tracks by locusts on the line – but equally devastating are grain pests like the caterpillar of the oriental armyworm moth, the brown plant hopper and the rice leaf roller.

For a long time it wasn't appreciated that these pests were migratory: it was thought they just appeared. But back in the 1950s the Chinese started perfecting techniques for trapping insects,

spraying them with a dye, releasing them, and seeing where they turned up. The first marked releases were of armyworm moths, some of which were recaptured nearly 1,500 kilometres/932 miles away. Slowly a picture of their origins and movements, and those of various other pestilential insects, was pieced together, looked at in relation to wind and weather records, and techniques evolved for forecasting when and where attacks were likely to occur.

The knowledge was put to work in devising long-term measures for combating pests, such as draining swamps to eliminate winter breeding places, and in establishing forecasting stations.

FORECASTING STATIONS

Feeding the people is such a high priority in China, the margins between success and failure so fine, and the potential damage caused by pests of such serious consequence that a lot of money has been invested in setting up a remarkable network of forecasting stations. These are used for short-, medium- and long-term warnings of outbreaks of all sorts of pests and diseases all over the country.

The system is headed by a central state forecasting station, supported by a vast network of subsidiary stations. In addition each of the 52,000 agricultural communes could have about four forecasters. So thousands of 'spotters' pass information to the authorities, who notify the communes of likely outbreaks and appropriate measures. These are relayed to workers in the field by telephone, radio, even loud speakers.

Successful forecasting depends on widespread monitoring of insects and the build-up of their populations – and an impressive battery of techniques is used in gathering this information. At an experimental level insects are trapped by aircraft or with unmanned radio-controlled target aircraft, or even caught at sea with insect traps on ocean-going vessels.

At a more humdrum level insects are caught in traps, which for the armyworm, to take one example, include light traps, molasses traps, traps made from straw bundles tied to windbreaks, and traps made of three millet straws in the ground, in which the moths lay their eggs. There could be about 100 light traps and 100 molasses traps in each province and 1,000 straw bundles – each examined daily, with numbers of insects caught, their sexual maturity and other relevant factors recorded.

All these facts would be passed to the nearest forecasting centre every few days. Very large catches, say over 1,000 insects, would merit the use of telegrams. Lucky China – still 'backward' enough to have a telegram service!

To monitor the likely outbreak of diseases, spore collection devices are used, while vegetable crops are examined regularly to see what problems may be developing.

Educating people about pests and diseases receives a lot of attention. It is estimated that about 15 million people in China can recognize common pests and diseases. Dozens of pest posters are seen in the countryside, and manuals and handbooks on pests and diseases are sold in ordinary bookshops.

One result of this widespread recognition of pests and diseases is that agricultural workers are likely to spot, say, a diseased caterpillar, which could be the starting point for the manufacture of a biological control agent. In one case caterpillars with virus diseases were brought into a research station by peasants, were being stored until required, then crushed, mixed with water, and sprayed on crops to infect caterpillars with the disease and so control them.

PREVENTION MEASURES

Many Chinese cultural practices help to prevent the spread of pests and diseases. An American delegation (co-authors of *Vegetable Farming Systems in China*, 1981), which visited China in 1977, suggested the relative lack of soil-borne diseases such as clubroot was due to a combination of high levels of organic matter in the soil, rigorous crop rotation, and in some cases flooding as part of the rotation, where rice or water crops such as lotus are grown.

The care lavished on crops also plays its part. A great deal of hand weeding is done to keep crops clean, but perhaps more important, as soon as a crop is harvested, all leafy remains are removed from the fields, so preventing any build-up of pests and diseases on crop residues. Cabbage leaves would be used fresh or dried to feed cattle, pigs or fish; the leaves of legumes, cucurbits and solanaceous crops would be fed to livestock or composted. In the south bacterial rot of Chinese cabbage is combated by ploughing in all crop residues. The soil is then left to bake in the sun for several days before the ground is replanted.

Another element of 'preventive medicine' is the use of natural genetic resistance. In complete contrast to the West, where identical varieties and strains of seed are distributed internationally by large seed companies, seed in China is still almost entirely selected and produced at local level. Almost every commune has members who concentrate on seed production, and they are continually selecting varieties and strains adapted to local conditions, with tolerance or resistance to pests, diseases and climatic conditions encountered locally.

To minimize the use of chemical sprays, the traps used for monitoring pests are also used to catch and control pests. For example, very simple traps for aphids consist of 50cm/1½ft squares of polythene sheeting, yellow and covered with grease. These are staked upright throughout a crop, at the rate of between 15 and 30 per hectare/2.4 acres. Various coloured sheets were tried out, but yellow proved the most attractive to aphids. (I've often noticed how insects accumulate on yellow clothes on the washing line.) Shallow yellow bowls containing water are also used to trap aphids. In one instance it was claimed that the use of these traps halved the amount of chemicals needed for aphid control. Although yellow water traps are used in Europe to monitor aphids and other insects, they don't seem to be used by gardeners to control pests. Worth a try, perhaps.

In greenhouses greased yellow sheets are used to attract whitefly, in conjunction with the use of the parasite *Encarsia formosa*.

Black light traps are another kind of trap used for flying insects. These consist of 20–30-watt fluorescent black lights, to which the insects are attracted, then deflected into vessels beneath which are sometimes filled with water. (Water used for cooking rice might be used in the traps.) The traps are placed permanently in the fields, in some with the extra refinement of a wire grid which electrocutes the insects. In others a film of kerosene or insecticide might be added to the water to trap and kill the insects more effectively. In a typically Chinese touch, the insects falling into the water or traps are collected and fed to fish or pigs (they're a good source of protein), or put back on the fields as a source of organic nitrogen.

In Shandong province the American delegation came across a curious practice, reputedly going back 1,400 years, of applying sulphur to the roots of poorly growing aubergines. They speculated on whether the sulphur acted as a fungicide, or in correcting minor element deficiencies by increasing the soil acidity. Even today in Jekiang sulphur and lime are incorporated into the soil after removing aubergines infected with verticillium wilt.

Biological control is widely practised in China, in forestry, in farming, and on fruit and vegetable crops. A 1977 survey indicated that it was used on 6.6 million hectares/16 million acres of crops, the agents ranging from the whitefly parasite *Encarsia formosa* (the technique was introduced from the UK) to bacteria, viruses, lacewings and even ants, spiders and ducks. Biological control is favoured by the Chinese partly because of the rapidity with which insect resistance to chemicals would build up in their intensive cropping, and partly from a concern for the environment. In an area north of Beijing an extensive biological control programme has been introduced to avoid pollution of a huge irrigation reservoir, which also produces large quantities of fish.

One of the most commonly used biological control agents is the bacterium *Bacillus thuringiensis* and related species, to control caterpillars. Although the bacillus is sometimes made in factories in the cities, it is also made on a large scale at local level – even in pots at home.

Among the more recently developed forms of biological control are antibiotics, effective against diseases on rice, fruit and other crops. One of the first to be made was *Streptomyces* *qingfengmyceticus* (*qingfeng* meaning 'bumper harvest'). Within two years of its discovery a handbook was available telling people how it could be made by production teams on the communes.

Beneficial insects such as ladybirds and hoverflies are encouraged. In some areas the wheat fields are swept with nets to collect ladybird beetles, which are then let loose in vegetable crops. Spraying with chemicals is stopped while this is being done. Work is also under way to improve the fertility of beneficial insects by feeding them with special diets – homogenized pig's liver, honey and hormones

Biological control in Taiwan. Above: experimental 'houses' for a parasitic bee introduced to control diamond back moth caterpillars. Below: herding ducks through rice paddy fields to gobble up pests.

from juveniles in the case of ladybirds in a Beijing research programme.

Lacewing flies, which also feed on aphids, are raised on the famous Evergreen Commune in Beijing. The adults lay their eggs on coils of paper, which are cut into small pieces each with four or five eggs, and distributed among the vegetable crops.

I learned of one of the most intriguing, and perhaps earliest examples of biological control from Dr H.T. Huang, a scientist working on biological control in the United States. In Guangdong, near Guangzhou (Canton), ants are used to control pests in the citrus orchards, records indicating that their use dates back to fourth century AD. The ants, *Oecophylla smaragdina*, are slightly larger than common garden ants and normally build nests of about 45cm/18in diameter in the Chinese olive. This grows in a slightly warmer area than citrus. During the winter the ant nests would be collected by local farmers, put into rush bags, and sold to the citrus growers – at a price. A grower would buy a few nests and place them in strategic trees in his grove. He would then make little overhead bamboo bridges, from one tree to the next, so that the ants could cross over and build nests in neighbouring trees. Eventually there would be a nest in every tree. To prevent the ants wandering further afield mineral oil was sometimes spread on the bark of the trees, or circular troughs filled with water were built around each trunk.

These carnivorous ants did a wonderful job in controlling beetles, stink bugs and other citrus pests, while leaving the beneficial insects intact. Their main disadvantage was that they had an association with mealy bugs, who were also a pest, and spread them around the trees. However, by and large they were an effective means of control, though the bridge building and other tasks were laborious. However, when DDT was introduced most of the growers abandoned their traditional methods in favour of DDT. Twenty years later they have the problem of resistance to DDT – and the authorities are currently encouraging them to return to the ants.

Records of a very similar use of ants were recently discovered in the Yemen. Here the nests were brought down from the mountains in early spring and put in date trees to control their pests. Again, with the advent of DDT the method went completely out of use: only a few old men can now remember the ants being used.

Ducks too have a long pedigree in China as a means of biological control. In ancient times when crops were being devastated by pests, the day would sometimes be saved by the arrival of flocks of birds. So the idea arose of raising ducks for the purpose – not leaving it to chance. Today flocks of young ducks, sometimes as many as 1,200 ducklings, are herded through paddy fields during the day to feed on insect pests – then rounded up at night.

The Chinese approach can be summed up in the slogan painted on the forecasting station walls: 'Try to control infestations, but if necessary, use an integrated approach.' We're catching up in the West!

Since I wrote this the use of yellow sticky traps has become widespread in gardeners' greenhouses, monitoring and controlling whitefly, greenfly, thrips and other pests.

MADE IN CHINA
Practical Gardening, November 1986

Like any gardener travelling abroad, on my recent trip to China I was curious to see how ordinary gardening operations are done – sowing, planting, cultivating – and what tools were used.

To start with seed and sowing. In China they still tend to broadcast seed – just throwing it out in easy sweeping gestures, the traditional method of sowing since time immemorial, raking the ground afterwards to cover the seed. Brightly painted enamel bowls of seed were a common sight in the field, as communes save most of their own seed. You often find little patches of plants left in a corner for a seed crop.

In the Flower Commune in Beijing we watched them drying and winnowing seed, in a sunny, concreted yard. Chinese chives and beans were laid out to dry, and when the seed didn't fall out naturally, the stalks were beaten with gnarled sticks to extract it. There were even chives drying on a roof top, a long ladder leaning against the house to reach them. Seed was being tossed in shallow half-moon baskets to separate it from the chaff, then, when cleaned, collected in picturesque wide baskets.

The few seed shops we found were fun, with a lovely old-fashioned look about them. One Shanghai one had samples germinating on the counter – living proof of their quality. Another had big pictures on the wall, giving customers hints on how to grow vegetables. A seedsman in a Nanjing market wrapped all his seed in paper cones. Don't ask me why, but the paper happened to be old English song sheets. So I got local radish seed wrapped in 'London Bridge is Falling Down'!

A seed merchant in a Nanjing street market. Among the unusual seeds he was selling was the 'weed' shepherd's purse, which is cultivated in China.

Typical Chinese intercropping in 'island beds' in the Guangzhou suburbs; here lettuce was planted between peas. The site was surrounded by municipal rubbish, which was sifted for use as fertilizer.

I was very surprised to find that knives seemed to be the favourite tool for planting. One evening we found a gang of girls from the Long March Commune planting celery by the roadside in Shanghai. They were all using a knife like a rather stocky butcher's cleaver. With the blade they cut a slit in the soil, then put in the seedling and stubbed it firm with the end of the handle. I was so intrigued I asked where we could buy the knives, and they directed us to a shop a few minutes away.

It was very sparsely stocked. There were a couple of buckets for sale, some of the planting knives, half wrapped in paper on a shelf at the back, a few wrapped brooms in the corner, some jars of chemicals, a few postcards and some lovely, simple Chinese cups. Just an abacus and a spike for receipts on the counter. Seeing we wanted to take photos, the owner immediately got out the feather duster and had everyone scurrying removing empty bottles from the visible shelves and replacing them with full ones. I got a couple of knives for 75p each. In other places I saw straight-bladed, diamond and triangular-shaped knives being used both for planting and weeding. Most of the weeds,

incidentally, were very familiar: our common foes know no boundaries.

As to where they plant, the cliché that the Chinese don't waste an inch of space is certainly true (it's equally true of the Japanese). A few gaps in a row of cabbages, pest damage maybe, and spinach seedlings are soon growing in the gap. In the Long March Commune they were planting celery around the cauliflowers that were nearly ready to harvest, carefully tying up the cauliflower leaves so they could plant the celery as close as possible. Fruit trees and ordinary trees are often undercropped with vegetables in the early stages, and we were told of hundreds of intercropping systems, often with tall bamboo canes supporting beans, cucumbers and gourds overhead in combination with low growing, shade-loving crops. Time and again we saw onions and garlic growing in broken pots and bowls, perched on low walls, on tin drums, on any space available.

Trying to buy gardening tools led me to some interesting shops off the tourist trail. One evening in Taiwan a Chinese friend, Ruey-Hua Li, took me on her moped into the nearest town in search of tools. The main tool shop had closed (it was, after all, eight in the evening), but another was still open and we sorted through piles of hand-made workmanlike tools. I bought a combined hoe and rake – a hand tool cleverly made from an old saw, with the serrated saw edge for raking, and the flat edge on the other side for hoeing. I also bought a beautiful trowel and a serrated 'banana knife' for cutting crops, so named after its sickle shape.

Much of the heavy cultivation and digging in the East is done with a kind of mattock that looks like a cross between a spade and a shovel, with a slightly concave, pointed blade. After the soil is dug or ploughed it is sometimes broken down further with a rake with a 2m/7ft-long bamboo handle and four large, flattish prongs. It looked a very cumbersome tool, but I asked if I could try one out and was surprised at how light it was, and how easily it broke down what looked like heavy, lumpy soil. That made me realize, too, the superb structure of this intensively worked soil near the cities, the result of centuries of working in organic matter.

China is an enormous country, but the amount of land suitable for cultivation is pitifully small, not much larger than the size of England. The fact that they now feed a population of a billion from this acreage is largely due to the traditional recycling of all wastes, particularly human manure or night soil, as it is politely called. Even today, though there's a move towards the use of artificial fertilizers, signs of the old sytems are everywhere, such as the barrel-like night-soil carts, which, in the absence of any mains sewer systems, collect waste from receptacles in the city every night and take them out to the countryside. In the suburbs and countryside there are many pits, some open, some covered, where the night soil is left to ferment for a month or so to destroy disease organisms; and at the edges of the fields are large stone jars where it is stored before being diluted and used on the crops.

An interesting feature of vegetable growing in the Far East is the way land is divided into beds. Frequently they are rectangular and

There are sophisticated ways of watering and simple ways. Here a simpler method was being used. The individual attention given to every plant was a salutary lesson from China.

slightly sunken, so that they can be flooded easily for irrigation. Far more picturesque is the flooded furrow system, where the land is built up into raised beds, 60cm/2ft high, 1.2–1.5m/4–5ft wide, several running in parallel and each completely surrounded by furrows of water.

We found a lovely example of these island beds in the suburbs of Guangzhou (Canton) one Sunday morning. It was buzzing with activity, everybody shielded from the sun by straw hats (or white cotton hats for the trendy young), and trousers rolled above the knee as much of the work was done standing in the water-filled furrows. You could see every stage of cultivation: ploughing with buffaloes, hoeing, planting, harvesting (a man was cutting the 'Chinese tea plant' with a blade attached to his finger), applying fertilizer and watering, in one case simply by splashing water by hand from the furrows on to the crops. Everything was being carried on shoulder poles. Because this was the cooler weather of early autumn the crops being grown were all ones that could be grown in

Europe in summer – ordinary and stem lettuce, pak choi, flowering Chinese cabbages and kales, ordinary cabbage, radish and peas.

A vegetable that is popular all over China is Chinese or garlic chives (*Allium tuberosum*). For years it has been one of my favourite oriental plants. The pale green, narrow, flattish leaves have a lovely mild flavour, somewhere between garlic and chives, and the white flower heads are very decorative in the garden or, when dried, for flower arranging. In China the flowers are used to make pickles and as a spice. I'd heard that these chives were blanched in the Far East, but it wasn't until we reached Guangzhou that we actually saw it being done. Several methods are used but here, after cutting back the green leaves, the stumps were covered with miniature clay 'chimney pots' about 30cm/1ft high. The little armies of pots, marching down the length of an island bed, were very eye-catching. Most of the pots had a lid on top and on top of the lid, a blob of mud. This was partly to slow down evaporation and partly to make sure the lid

After harvesting the leaves of Chinese chives, the plants are covered with clay pots to produce sweetly flavoured blanched shoots. The blobs of clay increase humidity in the pots and make them more stable.

stayed on in a high wind. Inside the pots the chives would grow long, thin and pale yellow, giving them a special, sought-after flavour. The night before being cut for market, we were told, the lid would be taken off, so they'd grow just that little bit longer in the dark hours.

In Beijing we were lucky to arrive at the right time to see another fascinating Chinese technique: making the 'winter beds'. Winters in the north are very severe and a lot of vegetables are protected in shallow pits, rather like a sunken version of the traditional cold frame, sloping to the south. They are made in the ground after the summer crops are cleared, and cleverly constructed to make the most of the winter sunlight. Nowadays they are generally covered first with polythene, laid over a bamboo framework and later, when temperatures are too low for anything to grow, with heavy matting.

The cold beds are used to store some vegetables and to overwinter others. Vegetables that are lifted and transplanted into the frames are called 'false plants'. When we saw them some had already been planted with garlic cloves, planted very close together, to get green garlic shoots in time for the New Year festivities.

UBIQUITOUS PICKLING
From 'A Taste of Shanghai', *Practical Gardening*, October 1986

In China, a country with climatic extremes which make vegetable growing impossible for much of the year in many regions, the art of preserving vegetables, in all sorts of ways, has been perfected.

Time and again on my travels, when I asked how a vegetable was used, the answer was 'for pickles'. Nothing, it seems, can't be pickled. In Beijing we squirmed our way into an unbelievably crowded 100-year-old pickles shop where pickled garlic, radish, cucumber, peppers, cabbage, mustards – you name it – were selling like hot cakes. The walls of the shop were lined with angled mirrors, so even from the back of the crowd you could pick out the reflection of your favourite pickle or pickle mixture, piled high in blue and white enamel bowls and what looked like biscuit tins. Most of those I sampled seemed unbearably dry and salty. They go beautifully with porridge or noodles at breakfast, I was assured.

I never did acquire the taste, although I think the pickling mustards have fantastic flavour – unpickled.

Making 'quick pickles' from the Taiwanese pickling melon. Sliced melons are sprinkled liberally with salt, covered with huge stones and pressed for twenty-four hours before being drained and sold as fresh pickles.

Vegetables have probably been grown for 2,000 years on the unique reclaimed island beds or hortillonages of Amiens. Many today have second-home owners, as in this typical family garden.

7 A WORLD OF VEGETABLES

Vegetable growing seemed to shed its Cinderella image in the 1990s, bringing an insatiable demand for books about vegetables. The year 1991 saw me working on another new edition of the Royal Horticultural Society's classic *Vegetable Garden Displayed*. Then came the chance to revise *Vegetables for Small Gardens* (a revised version of *Vegetables from Small Gardens*, published in 1986) and *Salads the Year Round*, and these came out as a paperback pair, *Vegetables for Small Gardens* and *Salads for Small Gardens*, in 1995.

My 'big project' was a book on potagers, *Creative Vegetable Gardening*, eventually published by Mitchell Beazley in 1997. Photography was a key element, with garden photographer Steve Robson commissioned for the book. Researching photogenic potagers, in the UK and overseas, and growing illustrative material myself took a lot of time and energy. The first summer was disastrously dry: few gardens looked as they should. Our spirits sank. The following year Steve went to the USA, following up leads from my research trip in 1995. The book was saved, I always felt, by what he captured in his two short weeks there. I had a wonderfully supportive editor in Selina Higgins – decisive, efficient, helpful, the best of naggers. She even tried to waylay a furious, fiery fax I sent to the art editor when I learned no one was going to photograph the patterns I had been growing for months, which had reached perfection. She failed. I lost. And still regret they were never captured on film.

I contributed the vegetable sections to two substantial garden manuals, *The Complete Manual of Organic Gardening* and the RHS *Encyclopedia of Gardening*. And I earned the chance to buy the RHS *Dictionary of Gardening* at a greatly reduced price by pointing out, in the nick of time, that they had forgotten to include parsnips! Then *BBC Gardeners' World* magazine was launched, and from 1991 to 1995 I had the rewarding job of writing its monthly kitchen garden column. I continued writing for the RHS journal *The Garden*, as well as for *Organic Garden* and other amateur and trade journals.

In 1992 I became the vegetable consultant for the six-part Channel Four TV series *Grow Your Greens, Eat Your Greens*, presented by Sophie Grigson. What fun that was! Nothing like working with a bunch of youngsters to shed the years. To conform with the

Neighbours enjoying the peaceful community garden created at the Bromley by Bow Centre in east London, on the site of a derelict park.

dress code I nearly cut off my jeans above the knees, with suitably jagged edges! I loved the insight into film-making – after all, I had tried for a job with the Canadian film board thirty years previously. We filmed the 'oriental greens' programme at Montrose Farm, and I wrote the *Grow Your Greens* booklet that accompanied the 'growing' part of the series. What gems were there to be extracted from the recordings made with the growers and gardeners who had taken part!

I got involved with other projects: the abortive Earth Centre millennium project in Doncaster, reclaiming an open-cast coal mine. I felt my age there, striding over the bulldozed bare-field site in a hard hat, and cynicism reared its head at the sheer impracticality of some of the ideas being floated. Strange to read now that the site has been locked for years and 'community activists' are struggling to reclaim it. I gather Mother Nature has been doing her share of reclamation. A far more satisfying involvement was with the Bromley by Bow project in East London, one of the most deprived urban areas in the UK. The centre got in touch after reading my article on US community gardens (see page 257), and in due course we helped convert concrete into vegetable gardens, wove willow fences, participated in their vibrant, multi-racial summer fair, and arranged an outing for a group of youngsters to Montrose Farm. 'Is this still England?' one of them asked us on arrival. We will never forget their excitement at picking flowers for a salad, hunting down quiz clues in the garden, climbing a tree, moving the henhouse . . . Each child went home clutching an egg – the hens laid just enough that day. We learnt later that when they returned even the 'toughies' who hung around the centre were moved to docile curiosity by the sight of those carefully clutched eggs. The colourful drawings and pencilled letters the kids sent us afterwards were the richest of rewards.

Rewarding too was the weekend we opened the garden for the Organic Garden scheme. Nearly seven hundred people edged their way along the narrow beds in the one-way system we had devised, and pored over the detailed notes I had – inevitably – written, and some, no doubt, enjoyed the view over the neighbouring fields from the newly built compost loo. Sharing, and learning from each other, is a big part of gardening.

The demand for talks gave the chance to travel, not just in the UK but to Ireland, Sweden, Holland, Belgium, France and the USA. Wherever possible Don went with me. In those pre-email days planning consumed hours, and of course lecture tours are exhausting. But what golden opportunities to see new places, to appreciate the problems posed by less benign climates than ours, and above all, to meet lively people from all walks of life, bound together by a love of gardening! I always returned refreshed and aglow with new ideas.

The 1990s had their highs and lows – accolades and rejections. To explain the need for accolades. Writing books, in my experience, is an absurd way to earn a living. Great excitement with the advance royalty cheque when a deal is signed, followed by a smaller one, usually, when the manuscript is handed in a year or so later, and another when the book is published. Then the penny drops. These are not earnings, these are loans. Slowly, book sale by book sale, the author repays the loan with royalty earnings: only when the advance is fully repaid do you start to earn. Maybe. It took over ten years with both *Oriental Vegetables* and *Creative Vegetable Gardening* – and shortly afterwards both went out of print. Hence another gripe (it must be therapeutic to get these off my chest): nobody tells the author his or her book is going out of print. I've several times discovered only by ordering my books myself. What is stock control for, I wondered, when I informed one publisher my book was out of print? They hadn't realized. They checked the computer. It wasn't there. Why? Because when stock was exhausted it simply 'fell off' the computer!

Which may help explain why accolades, in the form of people appreciating your work, letting you know it has helped, influenced, amused them, are music to the writer's ears. They make it all worthwhile. The little accolades that came along – several articles winning Garden Writers' Guild awards, *Salad Garden* being nominated a 'book of the century' in a 1999 BBC *Food Programme* – meant a lot. As did the unexpected, and deeply appreciated, RHS Gold Veitch Memorial Medal in 1993.

But I can't avoid the dark cloud, and rejection, which marked the end of the decade. Once again *The Vegetable Garden Displayed* was being updated, and I was asked to do it for what would have been the third time. This time the RHS were co-publishing with Dorling Kindersley, supreme marketers, and dare I say it, hard taskmasters, and it was 'going global'. It would be sold all over the world; semi-tropical, even tropical vegetables were to be included. I couldn't bear it. How could I write about growing peanuts for the allotment holder in Lincoln? How could this most authoritative of books, the acknowledged 'bible' of vegetable growing in the UK for over half a century, be reduced to one size fits all?

There was the usual tight deadline, and while arguments raged, I spent nights up in London on friends' floors, so that I could spend full days in the DK office selecting photos before the writing started. There were other problems: my agent and the chief negotiator couldn't agree terms, and two cataract operations were imminent. So I had a cataract operation, and in the recovery period, off we went to Sicily in the camper van for December and January. I assumed, on our return and after the second operation, all would be sorted. But little had changed. Optimistically, I started work on the 'background' chapters, soil, shelter and so on, rather proud of the soil chapter, which I felt, after picking the brains of experts on the subject, one of the best I had written. But still no contract, still no decision, but hints of a 'black copy', i.e. relevant local text, for the overseas editions. Then, out of the blue, a letter saying that no agreement had been reached and I was sacked. I couldn't believe it. Every day I expected a word from the RHS, the publishers, my agent, saying it had all been sorted and we could get back to work. It never happened. I felt a kind of desperate isolation I have never felt before, or since. Several weeks later a senior editor phoned me to apologize. The first kind word – and the floodgates burst. All I could do was sob into the phone. I appreciated her courage in phoning me. But it was a long time before the sense of betrayal faded, and never since have I started work on a project without a firm contract.

It was hard selecting a handful of articles and extracts to represent the 1990s. In the end I left out 'how to grow' articles, opting for a handful which stemmed from overseas trips, highlighting unusual aspects of horticulture (the Amiens *hortillonnages* and Sooke Harbour hotel still flourish), a few light-hearted personal ones, the story of the original *Vegetable Garden Displayed*, and the first in the *Gardeners' World* series, which, I was surprised to discover, was about global warming. Twenty years ago. And here am I thinking it is a new problem.

OUR CHANGING WEATHER PATTERNS
BBC Gardeners' World, April 1991

Digging the fruit cage in January last year, I was astonished to find that this normally waterlogged corner of our heavy clay garden in Suffolk was bone dry.

Shortly afterwards I learned that in some parts of southern England, soil water reserves were so low it would take several months of high rainfall to return them to their normal levels.

Experts agree on one thing. Over the next few decades the world is likely to warm up and rainfall will probably increase on a world scale. In Europe, the wet areas (such as northern England) will probably get wetter and the dry areas (southern England) drier. Much of Europe will have longer, hotter and drier summers.

We may be able to grow more tender crops further north because of the increase in the number of growing days in the north of the British Isles. Warmer winters may mean an increase in pests and diseases, where higher temperatures and higher rainfall coincide. It looks as if we are going to have to be very adaptable.

Last year some surprising plants proved drought resistant in my kitchen garden, for example rhubarb, parsnips and scorzonera. I think they get their roots down deep while there is still moisture in the soil. Other successes were courgettes, Swiss chard, the new red-flowered strawberries and Chinese chives.

To give my vegetables a better chance, I'll be planting them further apart, as they do in the desert, so that each plant can draw moisture from as wide an area as possible. I'll raise more plants in modules or small pots.

The better the root system developed before planting out, the better the plant's chances of survival.

By growing more overwintering green manures, such as tares and grazing rye, I will allow rain to seep in rather than run off. Green manures also help condition the soil when dug in, so helping conserve moisture. I vow to collect more rainfall in tubs and make fewer bonfires, which add to the greenhouse gases.

If I lived in an area of increasing rainfall I'd be thinking in terms of raised beds to increase drainage, and constructing walk-in and low polytunnels to give plants more protection.

WARTIME BABY
The Garden, March 1992

I started working on the 1991 revision of *The Vegetable Garden Displayed* while on a train. Not far short of Edinburgh a fellow passenger leant across and declared, 'I've got the first edition of that.' Our subsequent conversation brought home to me that 'VGD' was heading for its fiftieth anniversary, and spanning as it did the era from the Second World War in the 1940s to the threat of global warming in the 1990s, it was something of a social document. I thought it would be fun to delve into its early history, via the RHS archives, to see how the many editions reflected the changes which have taken place in half a century's kitchen gardening.

The Vegetable Garden Displayed was a wartime baby. Within a month of the outbreak of war the Royal Horticultural Society Council was doing its bit by publishing an inexpensive pamphlet on *Simple Vegetable Cooking*. It sold like hot cakes. Quick on its heels was a broadside chart for allotment holders, varnished on one side so it could be pinned on outdoor noticeboards. By late 1940 plans were afoot to support the 'Dig for Victory' campaign with an 'illustrated vegetable gardening book'.

The eminent scientist Sir Daniel Hall, then in his early seventies, was responsible for all these publications. His obituary in the *RHS Journal*, in 1942, described his role: 'In 1939, as a bit of

The cover of the first edition of the 'illustrated vegetable gardening book' conceived as part of the Second World War 'Dig for Victory' campaign. It eventually sold in millions.

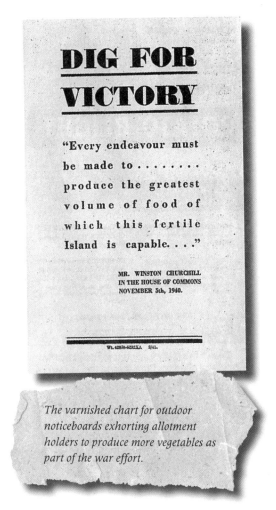

DIG FOR VICTORY

"Every endeavour must
be made to . . . .
produce the greatest
volume of food of
which this fertile
Island is capable. . . ."

MR. WINSTON CHURCHILL
IN THE HOUSE OF COMMONS
NOVEMBER 5th, 1940.

WL 42976-6232XA. 2/41.

The varnished chart for outdoor noticeboards exhorting allotment holders to produce more vegetables as part of the war effort.

'considered this too dear for the probable purchasing public', and asked him to produce a simplified form which could be sold for 1s., or, if the Ministry of Agriculture could be persuaded to assist, up to 1s. 6d. They later agreed that for illustration purposes 'the photogravure process should be adopted' and that 'advertisements should be incorporated'.

By January progress was reported on 'the photographic enlargements of vegetable growing for the vegetable book'. By February, Mr R. Hudson, Minister of Agriculture and Fisheries, and Lord Woolton, Minister of Food, had agreed to write a foreword. Council had also agreed that 'a copy of the ministerial plan from the Growmore leaflet No. 1: vegetable growing in private gardens and allotments should be included in the Society's book', as they felt 'it was very essential there should be one voice in giving advice'. (They might have sympathized with my struggle, when revising the text forty years later, to harmonize contradictory advice from research station experts.)

Nothing captures the mood of the times better than the advertisements and exhortations in the first edition. 'Your Garden is part of the National Defences. Don't arm it with poor weapons' (Suttons Seeds, illustrated with a bunch of carrots bearing a remarkable resemblance to a cluster of falling bombs). 'When buying sprayers insist on buying British. Don't grow your fruit with foreign-made machines' (Four Oaks Sprayers). 'Speed up the Nation's Food Supply . . . by sowing Fogwills' Best Result Seed.' Chase Continuous Cloches advertised a booklet impertinently called *Cloches versus Hitler* by Mr Charles Wyse-Gardner (a pseudonym adopted by Major Jocelyn Chase).

A surprising number of the companies advertising in 1941 still exist, or their names are associated with products or varieties that are still well known: Suttons, Fisons, Garotta,

war work, he undertook the task of Editor of the Society's publications, and discharged this new and last task with great distinction.' By the time of his death the year-old *Vegetable Garden Displayed* was already well launched on its long and successful career. Three impressions, totalling 75,000 copies, were printed and sold in 1941.

The 'illustrated vegetable growing book' was first mentioned in RHS Council minutes on 1 October 1940. Sir Daniel presented the Council with a proof of a proposed page, and estimated the cost at 2s. 6d. per copy. Council

Plant Protection, Pan Brittanica Industries, Stonor tomatoes, Rivers fruit, Corry's Slug Death, Growmore fertilizer, Chase Cloches. Casualties include Ryders Seeds and, to the best of my knowledge, the Ichthemic Guano Company of Ipswich, who in 1940 claim to have sold Tomorite to 200,000 amateur gardeners.

The exhortations were most evident in the ministerial forewords. Lord Woolton was strongest on the military implications. 'This is a Food War. Every extra row of vegetables in allotments saves shipping. If we grow more potatoes we need not import so much Wheat.' Stored carrots and swedes could replace imported fruit in winter. We should grow our own onions instead of importing 90 per cent. He saw the vegetable garden as 'our National Vegetable Chest yielding a large proportion of the vitamins which protect us against infection' and concluded with the stirring words, 'The battle on the Kitchen Front cannot be won without help from the Kitchen Garden.'

The Minister of Agriculture and Fisheries, after commending the hundreds of practical men (no women?) from the society who enlisted as volunteers advising 'Dig for Victory' projects, stressed the need for 'orderly planning'. The challenge, he said, was to provide vegetables all year round, not just in summer but 'in the dark days of winter when the food problem reaches its most acute phase'. This was indeed a preoccupation: articles on continuity planning, late sowings in autumn, the use of cloches, frames and greenhouse, were all directed to this end. I can't help feeling it is just as relevant today.

The book was a success from the start. By February 1942, a quarter of a million had been printed and it was making a profit of over £1,000, 'entirely due to the advertisement revenue'. To keep in profit and to keep the price low (it had doubled to 2s. by the eighth impression in 1944), the society was continually negotiating

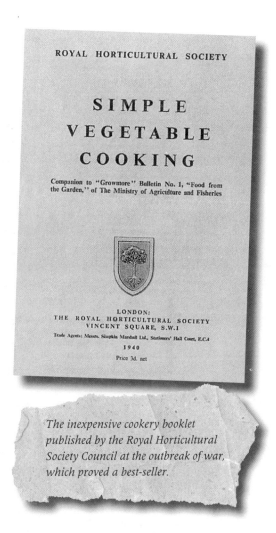

The inexpensive cookery booklet published by the Royal Horticultural Society Council at the outbreak of war, which proved a best-seller.

improved terms from the distributors, Messrs Simpkin & Marshall, who evidently struck a hard bargain. But the limiting factor on production was the paper shortage, both during the war years and as late as 1947, when the severe weather of that year precipitated the fuel crisis and a 10 per cent cut in paper quotas.

The paper question first surfaced in October 1941 at a meeting to discuss the Secretary's 'Schedule of Paper Consumption'. Council agreed to apply to Paper Control to reprint a further 50,000 copies – which would consume 175cwt of paper out of the society's allocation of 785cwt for the year. (Annual consumption pre-war had been over twice this amount.) A few months later they were in touch with Paper Control again, seeing the need for a 50,000 or 70,000 run for the fifth impression. They wanted advertisements in it, a view endorsed by the Ministry of Agriculture who were supporting the application for paper. Authorization was a long time coming and then was only for 50,000 and a weight that would exclude advertisements. So negotiations were put in hand for a smaller edition with advertisements. (An irony today, when the number of ads so often determines the size of an issue.) Council having learned from experience, application for paper for the sixth impression was put in hand in advance in 1943, but the situation was so serious by then the society was only allowed to print half the required number of copies.

Shortly after the war *The Vegetable Garden Displayed* was translated into German. Lt. Col. M. Wilson, commanding 617 Detachment, Military government, BAOR, requested permisson to translate it 'for the sake of encouraging and helping food production in Germany'. In 1953 Council declared their intention to keep *Vegetable Garden Displayed* in print as long as possible. In 1959 they rejected an offer from Penguin to take it over. In 1978 it was published in Dutch.

In its early days *The Vegetable Garden Displayed* was directed primarily at the novice. The text was compiled anonymously by staff at Wisley, and was notable for its clarity and brevity: this was a time for instructions, not explanations. The story was told through the sepia photos, taken by Norman Gould and James Wilson. Norman Gould was the society's taxonomist, and, apart from war service, spent his working life at Wisley. *The Story of the RHS* relates that he 'had no desire to work anywhere else though he had tempting offers'. The waistcoated models in

the early editions were Wisley staff Ollie Sink, George Hacker and Freddie Millard, the latter sometimes sporting a cap, sometimes a trilby. The photos were taken on the society's trial grounds in the village of Wisley: the slate-roofed house which featured in the background was used by staff, but demolished in the late 1950s.

For the 1961 edition a number of new photos were taken by photographer Ernest Crowson. The new model, in this and all the editions up to 1981, was the late Bertie Doe, who retired as Vegetable Trials Supervisor in 1987. He recalls Ernest Crowson's 'massive camera', and his disappearance under a black cloth to take the picture. New photography was undertaken for the 1981 revision, this time by Mr L. Hammett, of the Harry Smith Horticultural Photographic Collection, who made regular trips to Wisley to capture a year's operations. The 1981 edition broke into colour for the pest and disease section, but it wasn't until 1991 that a decision was taken to re-photograph entirely in colour. This task fell to freelance photographer Jacqui Hurst, who over nine months made frequent raids on Wisley (at dawn, to avoid the attentions of the visitors), armed with home-made cakes and biscuits to soften the intrusions of a photographer. The key model, this time, was Colin Martin.

The range of vegetables covered has increased dramatically. In 1941, only the most basic vegetables were included. In 1961, sweetcorn and the new 'self-blanching' celery were added. The inclusion of more luxurious vegetables, such as asparagus and globe artichoke, came in 1970. By 1981 horizons were expanding rapidly; the long list of new entries included aubergine, peppers, pumpkins, salsify and scorzonera, fennel, kohl rabi, chicories, Chinese cabbage, and minor salad plants like corn salad, the purslanes and salad rocket. In the 1991 edition a place was found for several new oriental vegetables, along with sorrel, seakale, iceplant and dandelion. (How did dandelion escape inclusion in the wartime edition?)

Tools and techniques have changed too. In 1941 bell-glass cloches were still in use. In 1961, the revision now the responsibility of Trials Recorder Pat Walker, comprehensive sections were added on irrigation and mechanical cultivators. A vast collection of hand tools, including ridgers, a crumbler-weeder and a pronged-weeder, were photographed in 1971. In 1981 we went to town on cloches; in 1991 there are new sections on walk-in polytunnels and 'floating' films.

The use of chemicals has gone through several cycles. The first edition shows soda and copper being mixed in buckets to make Burgundy mixture to spray potatoes against blight. From the '60s to the '80s a wide range of chemicals was advocated, but several, aldrin and DDT to name two, have now been withdrawn. In acknowledging the growing number of 'organic' gardeners the new edition lays greater emphasis on preventive measures and a return to some of the safer chemicals, such as derris, which was one of the most popular remedies in 1941. Green manuring, in response to the shortage of farmyard manure and the organic mood of today, also features more strongly.

The impact of scientific research, filtering down to the amateur from the commercial grower, has become more marked with each edition. The first mention of F_1 hybrids and pelleted seed came in 1975; by 1981 'varieties' were becoming cultivars, and the seed raising section covered seed treatments, disease resistance, seed storage, fluid sowing and the use of soil blocks. But scarcely a word on saving your own seed, which in wartime was recommended for a number of vegetables.

Space-saving ideas, such as 'mini-cauliflowers' and 'leaf lettuce', were developed by the National Vegetable Research Station, and their research into spacing led to recommendations for closer, often equidistant spacing. A natural development has been the adoption of the 'bed system' by amateur gardeners. In early editions intercropping and successive sowing plans were the main means suggested for increasing productivity.

Research has also knocked a few traditional practices on the head, such as the need to bend onion leaves over to make the bulbs ripen, and spraying the flowers of runner beans so they will set. The rather rigid cropping guide, based on a three-year-rotation (now known to be ineffective against most soil pests), was for many years the basis of the model garden at Wisley. I imagine that most of us are relieved to know that this has been replaced by a more flexible approach.

I was surprised to learn that onion sets only 'came in' in the 1961 revision. Wisley apparently played a role in their development. Also surprising to find that autumn sowing of broad beans was not advocated until 1975. But probably the most noticeable change is in cultivars: in a few cases the 'Trustworthy Varieties' recommended in 1941 are still with us: 'French Breakfast' and 'Sparkler' radish, 'Epicure' and 'Arran Pilot' potatoes. Otherwise they have been superseded. With the brassicas the F_1 hybrids have taken over. How many of us can remember the Brussels sprouts 'Harrison's XXX' or 'Wroxton'? Yet looking at the sepia photo of a surprisingly well-buttoned sprout plant, the now demolished house a vague outline through the winter mist, I couldn't help wondering if we have made quite as much progress as we sometimes think.

Garden Answers, June 1993

It wasn't until I started writing this article that my first little garden flashed into my mind – its main occupant a straggly and lopsided lavender bush given to me by our aged neighbour, Mr Grist. As a kid, I loved talking to him over the fence, though I was never sure if he was pulling my leg when he said they invited the pig into the sitting room on Christmas day. I think it was probably true!

That urge to chatter to people about what they do has never left me and may explain why I eventually became a journalist. The interest in gardening, I suspect, came via an interest in the sacrificial wireworms I took to the hens on my father's behalf when he 'dug for victory' on wartime leave; then came a passion for caterpillars and snails, then frogs, then birds. I built a hide one summer and spent several enjoyable weeks literally eyeball to eyeball with a thrush.

I always loved the garden and from an early age 'helped'. For a while, a rather proper professional gardener, Mr Rosier, did a day a week in our garden. I remember being enormously proud when I overheard him saying to my mother, 'Miss Joy has made a good job of those rose beds.'

The war ended, my father joined the diplomatic service, and we exchanged the security of Berkshire for a nomadic life in north China – already seriously disrupted by the Communist army's progress south. Back to England and boarding school, where a sympathetic headmistress said I could keep my caterpillars provided they weren't a nuisance to anyone. But they discouraged me from my dream of becoming a vet, so the vague desire for an 'outdoor career' led me to horticulture and Wye College.

First there was a year's practical work in a traditional walled garden. What a lot I learned from gentle Alf Gower, the head gardener – everything from diligent pot washing to tying peach trees to the walls with 'bass' (what we now know more commonly as raffia).

As soon as I graduated I went to join my parents in north Thailand, where I found work teaching American children. Here I earned my first money from horticulture. The World Bank asked me to write a paper on the future of the horticultural industry in Northern Thailand – a wonderful excuse to travel around the countryside asking questions. I made my first forays into Chinese market gardens, never guessing that I would be doing the same thing in China – and Canada and the USA – a quarter of a century later.

Marriage, moving to the countryside and the arrival of children brought me back again to horticulture. I was able to spend hours in our Suffolk garden, growing vegetables.

There's nothing like a ten-year break to make you question everything you were taught. Why plant vegetables in rows with all that wasted space between? Equal spacing makes much more sense. I got the experimenting bug, trying out growing methods, new materials and every vegetable I could find in the catalogues. I kept notes compulsively.

Children gave me my first push in the organic direction. Perhaps the turning point, etched indelibly in my memory, was the day I sprayed the apples with a tar oil wash, turned round to check baby Brendan in his pram, and was horrified to find him covered in oily black spots. I decided then and there that babies and chemicals didn't mix, and have been a committed organic gardener ever since.

from COMMUNITY SERVICE
The Garden, March 1996

Edible landscaping, or the idea of prettifying your kitchen plot, is big news in North America. So off I went, when researching my book on the decorative vegetable garden, to see how community gardeners grow vegetables and fruit in their often tiny plots. My travels started in New York, and I spent three days visiting a handful of the thousands of community gardens in this city.

Superficially, the community garden network in the USA is the counterpart of the UK's allotments, but the gardens are very different, because they really are community based – sometimes linked to just a few blocks of buildings in a street. They display enormous variation, not just in size, location and the ethnic mix of the occupants but in legal status, ethos and origins.

Many owe their existence to the tenacity of a single person or a few neighbours who have got together and decided to make use of a vacant building lot. The fact that there may well have been legal battles along the way with the authorities, the owners or potential developers probably accounts for the exceptionally strong sense of commitment and identity. Some groups have battled with bulldozers, and the threat of being scheduled for development hangs over many sites. A plethora of supportive groups has evolved to help would-be community gardens legally, financially, or with gardening expertise and resources.

The legal status of a community garden ranges from the security of site ownership to blatant squatting, but the majority are on long- or short-term leases from city authorities, intermediary bodies or private owners.

One of the best-known and longest-established gardens in New York is the Liz Christy Bowery-Houston Community Garden in Lower East Side Manhattan, founded in 1973 by the original Green Guerilla group, of which Liz Christy was a member. It is a narrow, green oasis squeezed between a tall, ivy-clad building and the pavement railings on a busy, noisy, accident-ridden intersection. The City fathers agreed to lease the land for $1 month, and soon there were sixty raised beds in it, mainly growing vegetables.

Its character has evolved in the intervening years, and what strikes you today is its air of permanence. The site boasts a grove of birch trees, a dawn redwood and established fruit trees, while a vine clambers 9m/30ft up one wall. From the entrance a winding path leads past a beautiful shaded border of variegated and white-flowered plants, opening out into a general-purpose area with a small lawn, paving stones and a tiny pond overhung by an elegant dierama. There is a weeping peach, clumps of ornamental grasses – even space for a little summer house and a working beehive.

Today the garden accommodates thirty-five different plots, each exhibiting its own character. In such limited space combining vegetables and flowers is commonplace –here, typically, towering amaranthus, sunflowers and tithonia at the back, tomatoes, okra, aubergines and peppers in front.

This garden is known for its strict rules. A points system is operated: gardeners have to submit their plans every six months, and if they are deemed to be letting the side down, out they go. It has its quirky features – a three-legged black cat that helps control the vermin, a scarecrow in an 'Aids Awareness' T-shirt and a bucket on the tree for donations for the subsoil irrigation system they are hoping to install.

Community garden landmark in New York: Eddie's pop art construction, made from the city's abandoned toys and debris. The Fire Department turned a blind eye to its flouting of local laws.

Like all the gardens I visited, it was open to the public at certain times.

It is a shock to realize how small a community plot can be in the States. At the Campus Road Gardens in Brooklyn, thirty gardeners are squeezed into a 15 × 61m/50 × 200ft area, with plots of 2.5 × 3 or 3 × 3m/8 × 10 or 10 × 10ft. This site was designed by a member who had previously farmed in Guyana, and was typical in having a colourful communal area with benches, paving, a hosta border, and flower beds filled with bulbs in spring and annuals in summer. Also characteristic is its ethnic mix – nine nationalities (Caribbean predominating) looked after the thirty plots. I loved the homely touches: the hand-painted signs, the little statues popped in among the plants, bitter melon trained on a dead tree trunk 'St Vincent' style. Vegetables, flowers and herbs are bedfellows – curly kales, broccoli, tomatillos and okra rub shoulders with cosmos, French marigolds, coleus, black-eyed Susan, zinnias and Mediterranean and eastern herbs. Also typical were the rough-and-ready paths of bricks, boards, rocks and stones hauled from derelict sites.

It was the twenty-nine-member garden on, I think, 9th Street and Avenue C – a beautifully designed site adjoining a derelict air-conditioner factory – where rubble was rebuilt on rubble to create a tiny sunken garden, and a mock well was constructed from old bricks in the communal area. In its limited space was a small table, a seat, raised beds, a shrine, statues, several brightly coloured vases and a runner bean in a pot climbing up into the overhanging ailanthus, all linked with a meandering path painstakingly pieced together with fragments of mosaic. One plot had simply been converted into a 3 × 3m/10 × 10ft pond; there were plenty of vegetables, too. In a highly productive Spanish plot, I chatted to an Iranian girl growing tomatoes, basil, cabbages, sage, dill and the striking, red-stemmed 'Red Stalker' ornamental sweetcorn.

I also took in one of New York's community garden landmarks – Eddie's three-storey pop art edifice built in the East 6th and Avenue B gardens. Its plastic dolls, rocking horses and urban bric-a-brac peering down saucily from every corner are a source of amusement for passers-by. (The New York Fire Department had turned a blind eye to its law infringements.) This is a 117-plot site – average plot size 1.2 × 2.5m/4 × 8ft – where planting started in 1982. Much of the early planting was fruit trees, so today's occupants share damsons, pears, nectarines, peaches and grapes. The communal area has been redesigned with seats for elderly people and a stage where the harvest festival and corn roast, poetry readings, events for handicapped people and flower shows are held. It is true community gardening, and seems a far cry from our British allotments.

I have a feeling that in the years since this was written, community gardens and allotments in the UK have moved far closer to the American concept.

THE FLOATING GARDENS OF AMIENS
The Garden, September 1996

The *hortillonnages* is a small area of reclaimed marshland in the Somme on the outskirts of Amiens, capital of Picardy. Vegetables have been grown here for probably 2,000 years. At the turn of the century there were nearly 1,000 *aires* (island plots) and as many *hortillons* (owner/growers) cultivating 350 hectares/870 acres. Today there are fewer than a dozen genuine *hortillons* on a total of 25 hectares/62 acres.

Far more of the plots are now second homes, or more accurately second gardens, owned in the main by city weekenders. So as you drift quietly through on the flat-bottomed boats there can be leeks and cabbages on one side, and on the other coarse grass lawns, shrubberies, exuberantly planted flower borders, discordant cypresses, a little polytunnel, even a replica of your boat planted with flowers. There is a backdrop of willow and alder, glimpses of the Gothic spire of Amiens cathedral in the distance and families of mallards scuttling away into the darkness of the overhung *fossés* (narrow, privately owned canals).

There is documentary evidence to suggest that the *hortillonnages* were already being cultivated at the time of the Roman occupation:

In spite of the problems posed by transporting everything by water, the remarkably fertile soil of the island beds of Amiens is still used for the production of commercial vegetable crops.

maybe it was Caesar's soldiers who named them *hortolani* after the Latin *hortus* for a garden. Peat was already being extracted for fuel from the vast deposits in the Somme's alluvial plain; the excavated sites were filled with water and later made into canals. Peat extraction continued into the nineteenth century, when mechanical diggers created characteristically straight-edged sites. In the Middle Ages the neighbouring communes drained the area and created the modern network of irrigation canals and *aires* that have produced vegetables ever since.

The *hortillonnages* were once so extensive that they surrounded Amiens, extending to within a stone's throw of the cathedral, the foundations of which were laid in 1220, reputedly on the 'artichoke field' donated by the *hortillons*. Today Amiens engulfs the *hortillonnages*. They have been eroded steadily by the demands of progress, starting with the sixteenth-century citadel fortifications which nibbled into the western extremities. Then in 1825 the Somme was canalized at Amiens, effectively confining the *hortillonnages*' waterways between the upper and lower locks.

Far more serious was the construction of railways in the 1830s, followed by almost continual urban development. The fatal blow was nearly dealt in 1975, with a proposal for a major bypass and associated construction through the area. It would no doubt have happened, had it not been for Nisso Pelossof, Greek by birth but Amiénois by adoption, and imbued with a love of the *hortillonnages*. He spearheaded a campaign to stop the bypass and preserve the area, in the process founding the remarkable Association which now effectively manages the *hortillonnages*.

The *hortillonnages* had been in serious decline from the late 1920s, mainly because of competition from earlier, cheaper produce freighted in from the south. Production on the *hortillonnages* is difficult and labour intensive. Not only is everything – from manure to the vegetables themselves – transported by boat or carried over the small, humpback bridges, but there is a constant, unremitting struggle against soil erosion and loss of fertility.

The highly fertile soil in the *aires* looks like wet clay, but is an extraordinarily porous mixture of alluvial silt, peat, chalk and gravel, which ran through my fingers like coarse salt. It drains rapidly, needs constant watering, and is continually being washed out into the *rieux* (wide public waterways). This both erodes the banks and silts up the gentle flow of the shallow waterways – rarely more than 1–1½m/3–4ft in depth – on which the entire irrigation and drainage system depends.

By using an inverted shovel (*drague*) the *hortillons* traditionally hauled the mud back out of the *rieux* and the *fossés*, spreading it on the land as a fertilizer and to replace the lost soil. It was also tamped down to reinforce the sloping banks. If this job is neglected, or an *aire* is abandoned, the banks collapse, and the land virtually sinks beneath the encroaching waters. Problems occurred where the 'weekenders' did not appreciate the communal need to keep banks in repair, or blocked off their *fossés* to guard their privacy.

Under Nisso Pelossof's presidency, the Association, which now employs about thirty people, undertook the immense task of restoration. Registry records were consulted to establish the boundaries of the *aires*, but modern solutions were sought for the problems of maintenance and the battle against twentieth-century pollution such as rubbish dumping and sewage. Any remedy had to be practical, aesthetic and ecologically sensitive because the *hortillonnages* are rich in natural history: plant, bird, insect and fish life are abundant. Wild swans are a feature of the area, and in the past were rounded up on the first Tuesday of August to mark the beaks and establish ownership of the cygnets.

The *rieux* are now dredged mechanically with the aid of a pump which works in shallow water. This separates out debris, and extracts 80 per cent of the moisture from the mud before discharging it on the *aires* in a semi-compact state via flexible piping.

The Association is experimenting with methods for reinforcing the banks, which in many cases were shored up with unsightly concrete slabs and sheets of metal, alien to plant life, weighty, and prone to collapsing into the waterways, causing blockages.

One success has been the use of water-resistant 2½m/8ft acacia poles, driven deep into the canal at the angle of the slope. They, in turn, support treated oak planks, behind which excavated mud is deposited. Plants, which have a stabilizing effect, establish just above the water line. Some of the original renovated wood embankments have now lasted twenty years.

The work is largely financed by tourism, with 60,000 visitors a year being taken on a 3-kilometre/2-mile circuit into the *hortillonnages* in the traditional *bateaux à cornet*. These unique flat-bottomed boats have been used by the *hortillons* since the eighteenth century. Made of oak, tarred or painted black, they are up to 10m/33ft long, wide in the centre to allow the easy stacking of vegetables, and with an extended prow stretching upwards at a 30-degree angle. This enables them to rise over the sloped banks of the *aire* for loading and unloading.

Once the current was subdued by the canalization, the rudder was abandoned and the boats were steered by a pole, though most *hortillons* today have outboard motors. Tourist boats, however, have been fitted with electric motors, which are almost pollution-free, create no wash, and are silent but for the gentlest purr.

The *aires*, which are retained in the same families for generations, vary in size from less than one to several hectares/2–7 acres. They are workable almost all year enabling the *hortillons* to produce up to five salad crops a year. I saw endive, a wide variety of lettuce and chicory when I was there in July.

The combination of fertility and good drainage is excellent for root crops and brassicas such as Brussels sprouts, cauliflowers and cabbages. Celery, onions, leeks, garlic, parsley, French beans, pumpkins, globe artichokes and rhubarb are among other vegetables grown commercially, as well as strawberries, currants, gooseberries and flower crops.

Some plots look immaculate but others distinctly weedy. This is probably on purpose, in the long-held belief that weeds have a humidifying influence on the vegetables and attract insects. In most cases the approach is 'fairly organic', relying for fertility on the dredged mud and horse manure – which farmers unload at various 'manure ports' for collection by boat. Pests – rarely a problem until mid-summer aphids arrive – are controlled with minimal spraying.

The vegetable markets have always been one of the most picturesque aspects of the *hortillonnages*. In the past, hundreds of boats would stream into Amiens for the thrice-weekly 'market on the water'.

The beautifully displayed produce was sold directly from the boats, the *hortillonnes* (owners' wives), wearing traditional sleeveless bodices, aprons and the weatherproof *grimpe* headdress, being in charge. At the end of the day the lines of boats would be towed back upstream, the *hortillons* walking along the tow paths, towing ropes straining over their shoulders.

Visitors can still get a taste of the past at the twice-weekly quayside markets, or at the colourful *hortillonnages* festivals in June and September.

GOURMET GARDENERS
The Garden, August 1997

Back in the 1970s, *The Edible Ornamental Garden* by John E. Bryan and Coralie Castle opened my eyes to the hundreds of ornamental plants which had a culinary use. For years I dreamed of creating a beautiful garden where every plant was edible. I never quite realized that dream myself, but I know a couple who have – Sinclair and Frédérique Philip, the owners of Sooke Harbour House on Vancouver Island, off the western coast of Canada.

It is hard to write about Sooke without recourse to superlatives. In a perfect setting, the hotel, a friendly clapboard farmhouse perched on a promontory, overlooks the Juan de Fuca Strait, with glorious views to the Olympic Peninsula mountains in Washington State. The guest rooms all have their own nautical or botanical character – I stayed in the Edible Blossoms Room, where every flower in the room could be eaten.

Above all, it is the food which is renowned and has deservedly won many accolades; Sooke was recently voted one of the best twenty-five hotels in the world by a gourmet magazine. Which brings us to the garden. The philosophy behind the food served at Sooke Harbour House is that it should all be 'in season' and grown or gathered locally. So while you won't find a lemon in the kitchen, a prolonged foray in the garden will reveal several substitutes: the flowers of tuberous begonias (which are cut finely into vinaigrettes), lemon verbena (carefully dried in a desiccator for winter), lemon grass and rhubarb (the juiced stems have a citrus flavour).

With very few exceptions, everything in the garden, from the conifers and broadleaf trees to the weeds, is utilized in the kitchen. More than six hundred edible plants are cultivated.

As the immediate garden is no more than 0.8 hectares/2 acres, the basic, bulkier vegetables are bought from nearby holdings (organically grown wherever possible). The hotel garden provides the less common vegetables (such as oriental greens and the tuberous nasturtium mashua), an extraordinary range of unusual salad ingredients, flavouring herbs and a wonderful assortment of berried fruit. The sea and seashore are the outlying larder, providing all sorts of edible seaweeds together with an astonishing range of fish and seafood.

At first sight it is not obvious that the garden is what Americans call an 'edible landscape'. Its edibility is unobtrusive. A kiwi fruit vine (*Actinidia deliciosa*) clambers over the entrance porch. Most visitors would be surprised to learn that the colourful flower beds near by, where daylilies, fuchsias, roses, tuberous begonias and *Salvia patens* are threaded through with borage, calendula, lemon balm and bergamot, will be raided for the evening meal.

Only the imposing silhouette of walking stick kale a few yards from the front door might raise an eyebrow. The peeled stems are cooked, the leaves are used as wrappers for the food, and the plants are left to seed because the large yellow flowers are sweet and tasty, and serve to attract humming birds.

More obviously purposeful are the workmanlike sets of vegetable beds on the gentle, seaward slope. Flanked by flower beds and lawn, the rectangular beds are edged in Douglas fir boards about 23cm/9in high, painted a calming blue green. The beds are of varying lengths, all 1m/3ft wide, so easily accessible to the chefs, whatever the weather. The paths between them are mulched with Douglas fir bark or sawdust, and kept relatively weed free by burning off young weeds with a blowtorch soon after the last spring frosts.

Even familiar vegetables are not grown in entirely conventional ways or for the normal purpose. The dwarf runner bean 'Dwarf Bees' is grown for its flowers, while the white form of carrot (basically a fodder carrot but none the less edible for that) is used for juicing. Peas are grown for the whole pea shoots and flowers, which are put into salads, as well as for the pods. And they grow a Quebec broad bean, known colloquially as 'Gourgane', notable for its thin, very palatable skin.

Vegetables are planted to look decorative. Curly endive, always a pretty plant, is planted in swathes alternating with colourful red and red-tinged lettuces such as 'Speckles', 'Ruby' and the deeply curled 'Valeria'. Various types of kale are dotted about, adding colour, texture and form. These include the gaudy ornamental kales, along with ordinary curly kale and the purple-tinged 'Ragged Jack' (looking lovely next to 'Lollo Rossa' lettuce) and Russian kale. Oriental vegetables such as the jagged-leaved mizuna, Chinese artichoke, garlic chives, pak choi, the red and green forms of the Japanese herb perilla or shiso and shungiku (chrysanthemum greens) all add vitality to the beds.

Self-seeding is encouraged, as proved by the abundance of dill, fennel, coriander, calendula, chickweed and the North American native winter purslane (*Claytonia perfoliata*, formerly *Montia perfoliata*). This bounty of self-sown seedlings is scooped up by eager chefs for seasoning, salads, soups or some niche in the day's menu.

There were many plants I didn't recognize, but my ignorance was rectified by the knowledgeable head gardener, Byron Cook. One delicate curiosity turned out to be *Nigella sativa* (black

Edged with Douglas fir boards, the vegetable beds at Sooke Harbour House in Canada grow an astonishing range of edible plants for the internationally acclaimed hotel and restaurant.

cumin), its pale blue flowers similar to those of love-in-a-mist. It is traditionally grown for its black seed, but at Sooke the flowers are also used in stuffing rock fish and halibut. Another unrecognized plant was *Lomatium nudicaule* (Indian celery), a local wild plant with celery-flavoured seeds. The use of this, and many other plants in the garden, is derived from the native Indian plant lore. Curiosity and experiment diffuse the gardening and cooking at Sooke, giving both an exciting edge.

The garden at Sooke is, unsurprisingly, run organically. If plants prove susceptible to pests or diseases they are abandoned: Byron considers there are enough naturally robust plants to supply the hotel's needs. Building up soil fertility is a key to this robustness. The acidic soil is naturally poor, but a great deal of effort has gone into improving it over the seventeen years that Sinclair and Frédérique have lived there. In the early days 'we traded dinners for farmyard manure'.

No potential source of organic matter is overlooked: their own compost, mushroom compost and huge quantities of seaweed. Seaweed is collected in winter and spread thickly on any beds that are not being used. It is also shredded for use as a mulch or for adding to the compost heaps.

The maritime climate is a huge asset in maintaining kitchen supplies all year, and frosts are not often experienced before November. To protect winter crops from the elements, extensive sections of the vegetable beds are covered, in autumn, with closely fitting, hinged, clear plastic-covered wooden frames. In this snug environment a wonderful variety of herbs, salads, and edible flowers supply pickings, albeit scantier, in the colder months.

To me the most endearing aspect of Sooke is the way every element and feature in the garden utilizes dual-purpose plants. I made a pre-breakfast tour around the garden on my last visit. It was a radiant October day – doubly welcome in the wake of an exceptionally severe storm.

Out from my ground floor room on to the lawn, with a bed of scented *Pelargonium tomentosum* and herbs on one side, and on the other, discreetly screening the jacuzzi and sitting area, what can only be called a hedge of herbs. Giant rosemary and bay bushes, seeding fennel, sages, the shrubby pineapple guava or feijoa (barely hardy at Sooke) combined with spiky yucca plants. These last two are grown for the edible flowers; yucca flowers have a pea-like flavour.

Down to the sea, on the right-hand side, a high bank is planted with ground-covering edible berries, including the brightly coloured bearberry, *Arctostaphylos uva-ursi* 'Vancouver Jade', known locally as kinnikinick, the aggressive creeping raspberry *Rubus calcyinoides* and *Rubus* species salmonberry and thimbleberry, grown for both berries and shoots.

Back up to the inn, with the smell of baking bread wafting from the house, I marvel at the window boxes outside the dining room, crammed with ornamental edibles – miniature fuchsias, alpine strawberries, pinks, shiso, purple sage, nasturtiums, pelargonium 'Attar of Roses', ornamental kale. On the wall, figs and passion flowers flourish, though edible passion fruits are only produced in hot summers.

Handy to the nearby kitchen door, mashua (*Tropaeolum tuberosum*) scrambles over a dwarf Scot's pine. The Sooke chefs bake, fry and pickle these nasturtium tubers, and also make them into a sorbet. Leaves and the almond-flavoured flowers are also used. Although a long season is needed for it to form tubers, mashua does well at Sooke, sometimes growing as a vine up fences, sometimes as sprawling ground cover, and usefully tolerating relatively shaded situations.

Above the house there are examples of edible ground cover. Corsican mint (*Mentha requienii*) lurks in crevices on a flight of wooden steps. It is used to flavour ice cream and is encouraged in shaded positions like this one, where it grows a little taller. Further up a mound is carpeted with thymes: lemon, common (constantly picked for the kitchen) and woolly thyme, which breaks the rules by being grown simply because Sinclair likes it.

In the background throughout the garden are grand fir (*Abies grandis*) trees. For the Indians, the needles were an important source of vitamin C, but at Sooke it is used, both fresh and dried, for everything from flavouring sorbets to a base for roasting fish, or in fish 'smokes'. It has a long-lasting limey, citrus flavour.

The last word should go to a tree that, sadly, is no longer there. A magnificent, 250-year-old big leaf maple (*Acer macrophyllum*) until recently stood guardian over the main entrance, with chervil, sweet woodruff and even daylilies and tuberous-rooted begonias tolerating the shade beneath. The native Indians ate the seeds, but at Sooke they cook the flowers dipped in batter. Even the young leaves of this maple can be 50cm/20in in diameter; I had seen them in their autumn glory as understorey trees in the local temperate rainforests, so could appreciate what was lost when it had to be felled. Happily, lots of maple seedlings are now starting to appear – true to the spirit of the garden. For this really is a place where Mother Nature is given reign, only being curbed lightly to ensure that the twin goals of producing glorious food, in a beautiful setting, are met.

VIEWPOINT: ARTISTRY IN THE VEGETABLE PLOT
The Garden, February 1998

Ugly rumours have been reaching my ears: people are knocking potagers. They are, it seems, a fashion on its way out. Passé.

In a wonderfully humorous article several years ago, columnist and allotment holder Michael Leapman decried 'the disconcerting trend towards growing vegetables for their appearance'. More recently, Stephen Anderton, discussing 'What is a garden?', loftily proclaimed: 'Vegetable gardening is a happy mechanical process, free of the possibilities and responsibilities of ornamental gardening.' He then dismissed ornamental potagers as a 'relatively naïve art'.

Since I have spent twenty years encouraging the making of beautiful vegetable gardens, this to me is like stepping on nails in threadbare wellies. How dare they imply that because a kitchen garden is functional, it is unnecessary, or worse, pretentious, to make it lovely? Don't people have ornate tiles in their bathrooms, and decorate their kitchens?

The term potager, as a concept, has strayed far from its original French roots as a down-to-earth kitchen garden producing the vegetables for soup or *potage*. The world's best-known potager, Villandry in the Loire, gave the word a far grander meaning. It now conjures up formal patterns of symmetrical beds edged with precision-clipped box enclosing swathes of coloured vegetables, framed with espaliered fences and linked to neighbouring beds with elegant walkways, fountains and arbours.

Fragments of these ideas have percolated through to ordinary gardeners, imperceptibly breaking down the rigid division between ornamental and productive gardens. Vegetables now appear among the flowers, and flowers among the vegetables, but there are bolder and more intricate manifestations, from magnificent alleyways of trained fruit to elaborate tapestries of intercropped vegetables. My favourite definition of a potager, if I can be pompous enough to quote myself, is 'any vegetable garden touched with the paintbrush of imagination'. This embraces a wide spectrum, with what you might call 'posh potagers' at one end and 'people's potagers' at the other.

It is undeniable that creating and maintaining a 'posh potager' requires an enormous commitment on the part of the owner, in terms of technical and creative skill, time, diligence and sheer energy. England's best-known potager, Rosemary Verey's at Barnsley House, Gloucestershire, testifies to all these qualities. Gardeners from all over the world have been inspired to imitate the intricate design, the skilfully trained topiaries and box edges, the espalier apples grafted to make a screen, the apple and pear 'goblets'.

Barnsley is a beacon but is no longer alone. The quickest flick through the National Gardens Scheme's 'Yellow Book' will show that new potagers are popping up everywhere – 'recently established ornamental vegetable garden', 'potager in progress'. No sign of a passing fad there. I hope all these new potagers are feeding both the belly and the soul, unlike one (undoubtedly 'posh') potager I heard about, where the owners were so often absent the untouched vegetables were ploughed in at the end of the season. If that is not a crime, it's a crying shame.

I am intrigued by the creativity that seems to be unleashed, or finds expression, in potager gardening. Is it a coincidence that the most exciting potagers I have found – large and small – have been made by artists: potters, painters, interior designers, sculptors. It seems natural

to them to harness the palette of edible plants to paint pictures. By chance last summer I came across two examples of what I have to call 'rainbow gardens'. At Bosmelet in Normandy, each square in a classic chateau potager is devoted to a different band of colours, echoed in the plantings against the adjacent walls. Interspliced vegetables and cut flowers create a magical display. Then in a Munach Community in Denmark, I found a remarkable garden of medicinal and culinary herbs, vegetables, fruit and flowers, fanning boldly across a sloping field in colourful rays of the rainbow's spectrum. Two other potagers which have inspired me are Annie Huntington's the Old Rectory in Northamptonshire and Eugenie van Weede's Bingerden in Holland.

The marriage between art and plot is as evident at the 'people's' end of the potager spectrum. I'm thinking of the Belltown P-Patch (community garden) in Seattle, a small green oasis in what was an industrial area, with a sizeable artist population. So perhaps it is not surprising that someone had made a striking wrought-iron gateway of garden tools, while ironwork onions and mosaic butterflies adorned the fence. Typical of American community gardens, the tiny individual plots are miniature landscapes, where vegetables and herbs mingle with flowers, climbers, shrubs, minuscule ponds, arbours and statues. Nothing is taboo: they are full of humour and fun.

The same exuberant, mould-breaking enthusiasm is appearing in Britain. The Cameron Community Garden in East London, for one, is a hotbed of creativity, with the centrepiece a thatched, rose-covered old barge used as a tool shed. Scarecrows, maize mazes, beans climbing up sunflowers or sweetcorn – all are fun, and potagers are the place for them.

A common charge levelled at potagers is that the 'picture' has to be sacrificed to supply

Above: the Munach rainbow herb garden in Denmark, which inspired our fan potager in Ireland. Below: Don and me on our first visit.

the kitchen. Is this so different from ordinary gardens? Are these always perfect? Are there no sickly, mildewed Michaelmas daisies smudging the landscape? Pull the other one. As I write this in November, my own herbaceous border is desolate – straggly stalks amid shapeless, soggy mounds of decaying perennials – but just round the corner is my winter potager, glowing with the rusty red of 'Redbor' curly kale and the fine blue-green plumes of black kale. Speckled chicories give ground cover and, until a heavy frost, I'll enjoy the orange, red and pink stems of 'Bright Lights' (syn. 'Rainbow') Swiss chard.

I recently heard of a British housing estate where the owners were forbidden to grow vegetables. Please someone, tell the authorities responsible for this decree about potagers. Explain that fennels, artichokes and asparagus have fantastic foliage and that parsley, mizuna greens and 'Lollo' lettuce will outshine lobelia for edging a bed. A few leeks or red lettuces look spectacular if left to run to seed. Suggest they plant a circular bed with cabbage – yes cabbage: savoys, red cabbage and 'January King', with perhaps a purple oriental mustard thrown in. Passers-by will stop to admire the glowing colours and metallic sheens and may even ask what the vegetables are. Emphasize it can be done in a matter of months. Potagers passé? Not at all: they're the gardens of the future.

A DAY IN JOY LARKCOM'S LIFE, 13 FEBRUARY 1998
Garden Writers' Guild Newsletter, March 1998

My day's divided into chunks.

GETTING GOING CHUNK
Won't reveal what time I get up. Would love to see dawn rising, but my biological clock disagrees. Aim to be at my desk by nine, but first

- Five minutes' back exercises (becoming essential, but the most boring five minutes of the day).
- About quarter of an hour at the piano – pure 'treat'.
- Rain gauge readings, complicated by the cloche frame to prevent our epileptic, plastic-and-metal-fetished goose attacking it. Now the sap's rising he's at his most belligerent. Another day without a trace of moisture.
- Check propagator house – watering and 'stroking' overwintered brassica and biennial seedlings to harden them off. First peep of strawberry 'Temptation' seedlings. You never lose the thrill of seeds germinating.

TO THE DESK
Essential paperwork takes an hour. Dying to get back to 'seed stock' records and sorting (seventeen) seed boxes – really the basis of all my work. Must: dry the silica gel, chuck old seed and enter new, go through 1997 records, seed trial notes and catalogues, decide this year's experiments, rotation and potager plans, order seeds and finally print month-by-month sowing lists. Mid-Feb already and scarcely begun. Shall I do the legume boxes today? No, must go through notes from yesterday's excellent HDRA course on green manures and municipal composting while fresh in my mind. Great that real organic research is being done at last. Here comes the post – half hour sorting books to review, flower seeds, bills . . . (At least phone calls fewer on Fridays! Crunch time for editorial offices and everyone else knocks off early?)

LUNCH CHUNK
Completely knackered by lunchtime. Usually escape to old caravan for twenty-minute nap with hot-water bottle and alarm clock. No phones; just fresh air and bird song. So warm today 'napped' outside. Heaven. Completely refreshed for afternoon indoor chunk.

AFTERNOON INDOOR CHUNK
Back to green manures; taking ages. By 4.00 p.m. dying to get to garden. A thousand tasks to choose from. Prune vines (*very* overdue)? Plant lettuce? Opted to weed, tie, mulch polytunnel sweet peas. Sown in August, they're romping. Noticed dense sowing of 'Frisby' lettuce in mid-October for salad seedlings very successful. Climate warming has its advantages.

EVENING CHUNK
Came in when virtually dark. Prepared 'Roseval' and 'Golden Wonder' spuds to chit upstairs, on thick bed of paper and cloth so can Maxicrop them. Slumped in kitchen reading the papers. Much easier to read than write. 7 p.m. phone. *Very* apologetic garden magazine. They've a Q&A 'your ideal garden' feature. Monday deadline, eminent gent has let them down . . . Could you ?????? Decided I couldn't . . . not as well as 'A day in the life of . . .' Friday night we swim and 'Mac' gets switched off before midnight! And soppy weekend ahead? (We met thirty years ago on Valentine's Day . . . can't let that go unmarked.) Why don't the genetic engineers work on a longer day instead of weedkiller-resistant maize?

A decade later, starting work on this book at my desk in Ireland. Keeping records and making notes still take up much of the working day – and night!

GARDENER UNDER THE SPOTLIGHT
Garden Answers, July 1998

WHAT'S YOUR FAVOURITE PLANT
AND WHY?

It has to be sweet pea – not just any sweet pea, but the dainty, beautifully fragrant old variety *Lathyrus odoratus* 'Cupani'. I sow it every year in August and grow it alongside my polytunnel veggies in winter. Life looks up the moment I pick the first bloom for my desk in early May. Sweet peas have sentimental connections, too. I did my year's pre-college practical work with Alfred Gower, a wise gardener and champion sweet pea grower, and the first present my future husband ever bought me was a bag of pig muck for my London sweet pea trench.

WHAT'S YOUR WORST GARDEN
NIGHTMARE?

Incapacity – above all the thought of not being able to see. I couldn't bear to miss all those amazing plant combinations that just 'happen' without ever being planned, and the continual play of light on plants which is one of the greatest joys of gardening.

WHAT'S YOUR FAVOURITE GARDEN
AND WHY?

I would love to return to Balata, in Martinique in the Caribbean. I can't remember ever feeling so excited at discovering a garden. It was full of extraordinary plants like the rasta palm, which really does have long dangling black dreadlocks that later turn into necklaces of the most life-like beads. When I made a dash for shelter (it's in the rainforest, and there's a downpour every few minutes) I came face to face with my first heliconia with its banana-like leaves. It was startling – the most brilliant colour I've ever seen. The garden was like a painting, with amazing contrasts of leaf sizes, textures and colour, layer upon layer of intertwining vegetation, rubbery stems and bright bromeliads or urn plants pinned to tree trunks like Christmas decorations. It was fairyland.

WHERE WOULD YOU LIKE YOUR GARDEN
TO BE?

Having gardened for thirty years on completely flat land in dry East Anglia next to a mushroom factory, I'd like to be somewhere with gentle undulations, twice the rainfall, and a beautiful view.*

My favourite sweet pea, the superbly scented and beautifully coloured 'Cupani', entangled in an apple arch in our Irish garden. Never a year goes by without my growing it.

WHAT'S THE BEST BIT OF GARDENING ADVICE YOU'VE BEEN GIVEN?

'Co-operate with the weather', from a farmer neighbour. This particularly applies to sowing and planting. It's madness to do either when conditions are too cold, too wet or too dry.

WHICH PIECE OF GARDENING ADVICE HAVE YOU IGNORED?

I've ignored a great deal of what I was taught at college, and traditional 'wisdom'. The 'rules' on spacing, once I started to think about them, struck me as absurd. There's no good reason for growing vegetables lined up close in widely spaced rows. It's far more productive to space plants evenly and forget about rows. That way they all receive equal amounts of light, moisture and nutrients, and keep down weeds by forming a leafy canopy over the ground.

WHAT'S YOUR FAVOURITE GARDENING BOOK?

The Vegetable Garden by brothers Vilmorin-Andrieux – from the famous French seedsmen family. My edition, revised by the English garden writer W. Robinson, dates from 1885. It covers more vegetables, more accurately and lucidly, than any other book I have ever found. It also tells you how long seed remains viable, which no modern gardening book does. My copy, bought second-hand many years ago, is full of neat little notes and cuttings from newspapers pasted in by some previous owner. I felt destiny meant me to have it. It needs re-binding but I can't bear to be parted from it.

Balata Garden in Martinique at the edge of the tropical rainforest. Its exuberant and imaginative planting captivated me utterly, and is imprinted on my memory.

*A dream I realized in Ireland.

The potager at Bingerden, in Holland – surely one of my favourites, bursting with colour and creativity. A quiet feature is this scalloped bench, framed with carefully trained whitebeam (Sorbus aria 'Lutescens'), and silhouetted against the boundary hornbeam hedge and crisply trained finial.

8 JUST VEGETATING

It was great news when *The Kitchen Garden*, a magazine devoted entirely to vegetable and fruit growing, burst on the scene in 1997, beautifully produced and illustrated, and intelligently edited by enthusiasts for enthusiasts. I wrote for it for seven years, starting my bimonthly 'Just Vegetating' column in 1998. What a chance to air my views and recount my doings on any topic I wanted! During this time we moved to Ireland and 'semi-retirement' (about which more in the next chapter). I'm glad to say the magazine, although now under new ownership, is still going strong. 'At the Seed Trials' (page 289) won the Garden Writers' Guild Journalist of the Year award in 2001.

ON COLOUR
'Just Vegetating', *The Kitchen Garden*, November 1998

I've only got to be out working in my kitchen garden for a few minutes before thoughts swirl into my mind. As I sow or plant or hoe, the thoughts take wing – whisking me back to distant times and places and fragments of past conversations, or bringing into focus the relevance of something I have just seen or read. Or they may project me into the future, perhaps with a mundane mental note to plant, say, leeks deeper, earlier or closer next year.

Occasionally they spark an 'idea' and I get that frisson of excitement which makes gardeners instantly forgive and forget the trials of the current season and long for the next, so that they can grow this, or try that, or put so and so in that awful corner. Most of my thoughts float off like soap bubbles, disintegrating, forgotten, but a few are captured – grubby notes in a muddied notebook – eventually wending their way into garden plans, books, articles. And now I have the luxury of following where they lead and sharing them with the readers of *The Kitchen Garden* in this bimonthly column, 'Just Vegetating'. I hope we all enjoy the result.

This last summer, colour has dominated my garden thoughts. 'Joy appreciates pretty colour' an art teacher once wrote in my school report. I appreciated her valiant search to say something kind about a pupil with a total inability to draw, paint or express herself artistically. But I think it was true. Few aspects of my kitchen garden give me as much pure pleasure as its colour.

I'm lifted every morning when I look over the half-moon blue gate to the weaving lines and patches of blue grey leeks in my so-called 'waves' to the clumps of gentian-blue chicory on the far side. (Ridiculous to call a chicory 'gentian' blue, but the flowers have that sky-blue clarity that makes me think of gentians.) What a fleeting moment of glory! By a sunny midday the flowers are closed, the clumps (which come from a handful of winter chicories left to flower) a dingy brown. A few more flowers may deign to appear in the cool of evening, but that's when the evening primroses take the baton and illuminate the garden. I planted them originally because they are reputed to have edible roots, though in our heavy soil the roots proved so spindly I've never put it to the test. But once established, of course, they seed themselves in paths and beds and borders and it takes a heart of steel to uproot them. I'll pass them late afternoon without noticing them – but half an hour later and the beautiful, clear yellow flowers are wide open, innocently demanding attention. When did it happen? If I stood by a plant, would I catch them opening? The daylilies are the same: suddenly ablaze in the evening light as if a switch had been turned on.

Every year I try different ways of weaving colour into the vegetable garden. This year I encased the new runner bean 'Hestia', a dwarf form of the much loved orange/pink and white-flowered 'Painted Lady', in a diamond-shaped frame of alternating leeks and 'Bull's Blood' beetroot. For anyone who doesn't know this old variety of beet, it has deep burgundy, glossy leaves which remain brilliantly coloured all winter – and no mean beetroots either.

The adjacent diamond-shaped patch was a hand-sown mixture of early carrots and annuals, in this case ornamental grasses, pheasant's eye (*Adonis aestivalis*) and Midget Series cornflower. The idea here is that the patch looks 'flowery' all summer, but in its heart the carrots are slowly developing, largely undiscovered by carrot fly. As it happened, one of the cornflowers was a near-black crimson and it chanced to flower right next to the beetroot. To a closet lover of clashing colours, it was a thrilling juxtaposition. In its turn the carrot patch was edged with *Tagetes* 'Orange Gem' – an edible flower with an uncanny flavour of oranges. But what a colour! In dull evening light in particular it visibly glowed – the colour emanating from those tiny flowers seemed to penetrate the onlooker. I really felt it did me good.

Well, perhaps it did! To digress a moment. A kitchen garden which has enthralled me, on account of its colourfulness, is Hadspen in Somerset, run by Nori and Sandra Pope. No space here to detail their exciting use and exploitation of colour, but a few weeks ago I was given a copy of their new book *Colour by Design* and it told me things about colour, and made me think about colour as I never have before. I was intrigued to learn that men and women literally see colours differently. It's mostly to do with the numbers of rods and cones in the eye, but men only store colour on one side of the brain – poor dears – so they can't recall colours so well. (They compensate with better depth perception.) I learned that deep reds get 'lost' as blacks in the background so are best placed in the foreground, but to get back to the point, orange really does appear to be therapeutic. One study indicated that children's IQs were raised appreciably in an orange setting.

I've never quite pulled off a long-held ambition to create a 'red square' in my winter potager, using plants like red mustard, Treviso chicory, purple sage, purple sprouts, red cabbage. So I turned for inspiration to the Popes' chapter on 'plum' colours – which seemed to embrace my intended spectrum. Forget winter: within a few moments I'd decided on the colour schemes for next year's carrots-and-annuals patch. I'll be mixing the carrot seed with dark plum cornflower and scabious – *Centaurea cyanus* 'Black Ball' and *Scabiosa atropurpurea* 'Ace of Spades' to be precise. Both have light foliage, so they won't swamp the carrots. They're already on my 1999 seed shopping list. And perhaps I'll throw in a few really dark poppies to complete the effect.

One of our happiest memories of this past summer will be the day a minibusload of children from the Bromley-by-Bow East London Community Project visited our garden. They ranged from about eight to twelve in age, and few, I think, had ever been in the country before, let alone in a vegetable garden like ours. After they went home we received a wonderful batch of letters and brilliantly coloured drawings. That was proof to me that they had seen, and responded to, the colour in our veggy patch.

....

Hadspen is no longer managed by Nori and Sandra Pope, and is 'currently closed while being redesigned'.

ON FLAVOUR
'Just Vegetating', *The Kitchen Garden*, January 1999

It's so easy, at this time of year, to pop into the shed, dip your hand into a paper sack, and pull out a few spuds for supper. Baked tonight? OK, let's have a few 'Picasso'. Or shall we try the 'Golden Wonder'? They should have matured by now. All that rushing in and out between heavy showers in late September was worth it. What a chore it seemed then, lifting a few at a time, sorting the damaged from the prime, and drying them off outdoors or in the polytunnel before bagging them! I was quite pleased with my refined potato harvesting techniques in 1998. Normally I put them on the ground to dry but this time I found a nice slatted shelf from a dismantled greenhouse, propped it up on a couple of bricks, and laid the best tubers one end and 'seconds' the other. They got 'ventilated' from below and above and dried relatively fast. I had heavy plastic sheeting at the ready to cover them if short showers threatened, and the whole shelf could be carried under cover quickly if necessary. Why had I never thought of this before?

As usual tiddly ones went straight into a bucket for the hens, rotting blighted ones into a bucket for the bonfire. Luckily both were few. But you never really know till you start lifting. You hold your breath as you move from variety to variety, and what a sense of exhilaration, when the first plunge of the fork reveals lovely big, healthy tubers! What must it have been like, in the Irish famine, to find nothing on plant after plant? And it still happens. My thoughts flew to the peasants in those parts of Russia where heavy rainfall last summer devastated the potato crop. For us it's a nuisance and irritation to lose our home-grown potatoes; for them it is a catastrophe.

Another irritation, of course, is slug damage. Now I don't intend to dwell on slugs (it's a beautiful day and I don't want to depress my spirits), but watching out for their damage is an integral part of potato lifting. I can never quite believe those neat little rounded holes are made by slugs; they look much too small. But watching a jet-black Houdini of a slug easing its way out of a drying spud quelled any doubts. He'd have been better advised to stay put. But it's curious how they are attracted to some varieties more than others. You wouldn't really credit a slug with such subtleties of palate. Is there a Delia Smith of the 'Slug Culinary News' down there saying 'Picasso' and 'Maris Bard' are delicious, 'Kestrel' should be left alone and 'Charlotte' and 'Ratte' are not worth the trouble? (I'm basing this on the results of the Gardeners' World TV slug trial findings, which were announced while I was lifting.) Is it texture or taste they go for? We're certainly not on the same taste wavelength. 'Charlotte' and 'Ratte' happen to be two I rate very highly for flavour, especially in salads. But then they loved 'Roseval', another superb salad variety.

Taste buds are supposed to get less discerning as you get older. Well, that's one part of the ageing process – about the only one – which hasn't got to me yet. Where vegetables are concerned I think I'm getting more and more discerning. I just can't be bothered with vegetables that don't taste really good. But what a tricky business flavour is! Not only is it very personal and subjective, but it is so variable. With tomatoes, for example, flavour seems to change from truss to truss, from plant to plant, and from week to week.

Last season I found myself reversing all my long-held opinions on tomato flavour. For years I'd advised anyone who asked about good flavour to go for the continental 'Marmande' type, or the cherry tomatoes, like 'Gardener's Delight', 'Cherry Belle' and 'Sungold'. I know last summer was sunless, but I was very disappointed by the 'Marmande' types in particular. Lovely fleshiness, it's true, but where was the flavour? I've a nasty suspicion that it is being sacrificed in the modern strains as smoothness and regularity become the main criteria for selection. The cherry tomatoes were fine in mid-summer, but, with the exception of 'Sungold', which really is a winner, they'd all lost that 'special' quality by the end of summer.

It's extraordinarily difficult to carry out unbiased flavour tests. You can only taste so many tomatoes in a row. But I have one infallible test – infallible because of my innate greed. It's the where-do-my-footsteps-take-me-when-I'm-picking-tomatoes-for-lunch? test. And last summer there was no doubt. They didn't take me to the little polytunnel where the 'Marmande's and cherry tomatoes were growing. They took me unerringly to the old Nissen tunnel, where I'd planted 'Typhoon', 'Cristal', 'Brigade' and 'Santa'. Those were my favourites.

Mind you 'Santa', which has little tear-dropped fruits, had a strange aftertaste early in the season but got better and better, and 'Cristal' and 'Typhoon' have quite tough skins (but I'm all in favour of roughage). 'Brigade' is so firm that I was trying to save them (along with 'Britain's Breakfast') for freezing, but treated myself and friends to a few early and late in the season. How I enjoyed them all then, and how I miss them now! And to think of all those poor people without gardens who have to make do with supermarket tomatoes and never really know what a tomato can taste like! Yes, I know the supermarkets are trying. But they need to try harder.

I was at a seed firm's pumpkin and squash open day last autumn, chatting to one of its staff about the increased interest supermarkets are taking in the various squashes. And what are they focusing on? Spaghetti marrow. Now if there's one member of the squash family which is utterly tasteless it's spaghetti marrow. OK, its innards tumble out in spaghetti-like strands when it's cooked, but you need every herb and spice in the cupboard to give it a modicum of flavour. Fearful of my own prejudice, I've grown them again and again, in spite of vowing not to give them space. (They do have the merit of covering trellises and supports very rapidly.) But I've yet to detect a hint of natural flavour. Supermarkets would be much better to go for the pretty little 'Patty Pan' squashes if they want something eye-catching and edible.

One last thought. George Beaven, a retired friend from the seed trade, came round the garden a few weeks back, and saw the remnants of my giant maize plants with the climbing beans scrambling up them. 'That's how the Serbians used to grow them,' he said. In the past he inspected seed crops in predominantly Serb villages on the Hungarian/Yugoslavian border. The villagers grew the maize for their livestock,

the beans for themselves. At the time of writing Kosovo dominates the news: it's nice to think of Serbs in a different light.

I thought I'd better check availability of my top tomatoes listed above, and finding no trace of 'Cristal' in any current catalogues, I phoned D.T. Brown, my original supplier, to have a little whinge. What I got was a rational, but curious, explanation. It seems that 'Cristal', which is a commercial growers' variety, has indeed been widely acclaimed in various tests for its flavour, but has an unfortunate habit of 'breaking down', i.e. producing all sorts of strange fruits, when grown in certain circumstances. The 'circumstances' seem to occur mainly in northern parts of the country. One customer was so irate he drove his family from the Lake District to the Brown office in Poulton-le-Fylde, and threatened the manager, Dr David Booth, with his misshapen fruits. For once EU legislation is not to blame!

ON ODDITIES
'Just Vegetating', *The Kitchen Garden*, March 1999

I've been thinking about oddities – in other words unusual vegetables – and two remarks from the past sprang to mind. Many years ago I was planning to write a book on unusual vegetables, and my dear, ever-helpful mother insisted I went to see 'a very clever man in the village who knows all about unusual vegetables'. Goodness knows what my opening remark was, but he cut me down to size with his. 'If a vegetable's unusual there's a very good reason. It's worthless!' The other remark was at the end of a garden talk. In a rather querulous, challenging tone a male voice piped up: 'I don't suppose you grow anything as ordinary as a lettuce.' Both men! Sorry about that, but

strangely the male sex does seem to be the more conservative where trying something different, especially vegetables, is concerned.

There are two points to make. First, what is 'exotic' one day may become mainstream the next. Obvious examples are potatoes and tomatoes – both considered suspect novelties when introduced to European shores in the sixteenth century. What garden or household is without them today? Admittedly there are unlikely to be many, if any, undiscovered 'mainstay' vegetables out there now, given modern communications, but here we come to the flip side of exoticism: there are countless curiosities, new flavours, enticing-looking plants which can enrich our cuisines. Two of my favourite herbs, basil and coriander, were virtually unknown here not so long ago, but what marvellous, and to me indispensable, flavours they are. And neither is particularly hard to grow.

In my experience, unusual vegetables fall into two categories. They either won't grow; or they grow amazingly well, but you don't know what to do with them when you've got them. In the first category I put okra (I don't care what anybody says, I've never yet had a flourishing plant), my much-loved lablab beans (which seem to need a longer, warmer season of shortening days) and those huge Chinese wax or fuzzy gourds, though I did get a couple of passable, endearingly fuzzy, ones last year, so maybe I'm getting a (well-deserved?) breakthrough there.

There have been several candidates for the second category. An early one was garden huckleberry. I rather assumed it needed coddling so planted it in a small greenhouse. The plant took it over completely, long lank stems producing an enormous crop of large, jet-black berries. Make them into pies everyone said, and we did. The taste was, well, unusual, but the appearance startlingly dramatic. Imagine coils of thick white double cream sinking into the glossily purplish surface of the cooked berries. But even so, there really is a limit to the number of huckleberry pies you can consume.

Last season I was sent a trial sample of a purple variety of tomatillo and soon discovered I had another profligate novelty on my hands. The plant is closely related to cape gooseberry, but the fruits, which lurk within a papery husk, look like unripe green tomatoes. In spite of the cold start to a rather miserable summer they grew brilliantly in the unheated polytunnel. But I was uncertain when to pick them. Should I wait for them to turn purple? Then they began falling on the ground in such profusion (were

they underwatered?) that we decided they must be ready for use. But what next? It's common knowledge that they're a standard ingredient in Mexican cookery, but we're not well stocked with Mexican recipe books.

American seedswoman Renée Shepherd to the rescue: my husband Don made some superb salsa verde, a cold sauce, from one of her recipes. I loved its compelling, mysterious taste, and ate it with anything and everything – fish, vegetable dishes, baked potatoes. But it wasn't until I read what Michael Michaud and Christine McFadden had to say in their new book, *Cool Green Leaves and Red Hot Peppers*, that I really cracked the problems of harvesting (when green and immature), and learned with delight that fresh tomatillos can be kept in the fridge for several weeks, and deep frozen for several months. That knowledge came a little too late. A second batch of picked tomatillos spent several weeks in our 'back door' greenhouse, overlooked until I spotted a rather sinister black slime oozing over the wooden bench. Suspecting at least a cat-related crime, I investigated further, only to discover that our lovely tomatillos were turning into compost, not salsa. I guiltily rescued the few that were still firm. This year I'll grow them again, and I promise to pick, use and store them properly.

It's not often that vegetables, ordinary or extraordinary, get into the national press. But last year there was a lot of publicity for some colourful carrots – purple, white, yellow, and purple with an orange core amongst other combinations – bred by the Dutch seed company Bejo and being trialled and marketed in the UK by Elsoms Seeds. Within a couple of years we'll be tempting our vegophobic children with colourful carrot snacks, and restaurants will be tempting you with rainbow whirls of grated or delicately steamed carrots.

I must admit I was excited by the news, and Don and I had an enjoyable morning on the trial ground, tasting them and marvelling at how the purple colour rubs off like a dye on your fingers. We enjoyed their flavour and found them sweet. But we had another personal reason for being interested.

One of the people who had encouraged us to embark on our Grand Vegetable Tour about twenty years ago was Allan Jackson ('Jacko' to his friends and students), who had been my lecturer in market gardening at Wye College. So before leaving we visited him, then happily retired in west Wales, for some final advice on what to look for. Top of his list were red Italian chicories and purple carrots. These, he said, were being studied before the last war because of their high vitamin A content, which helps to prevent night blindness, but somehow they had disappeared. We did eventually find purple carrots, in a funny little shop in Portugal where we were buying a Christmas chicken, but we failed, in spite of constant enquiries, to get any seed.

So the re-emergence of purple carrots was a wheel turning full circle, and I'd planned to phone Jacko the following week to tell him all about them. Sadly, that very week, I heard he had died at the age of eighty-six. So I would like to dedicate this column to his memory. Thanks, Jacko, for your unstinting help and encouragement to us and generations of horticultural students. We'll miss you.

IN SICILY
'Just Vegetating', *The Kitchen Garden*, May 1999

I'll come clean. My husband Don and I escaped the worst of last winter touring Sicily in a camper van: six weeks of bright blue skies (well, most of the time), beautiful landscapes and seascapes, gloriously fresh food and wine at moderate prices, and something ancient or interesting around every corner. It was a long-held dream come true.

Before leaving I unearthed some notes I'd made nearly twenty years ago, intrigued then by both Sicily's modern vegetable production and its rich horticultural and culinary history. This stems from a balmy climate and fertile valleys, coupled with its pivotal geographic position, since prehistoric times a stepping stone between the European and African continents.

This was intended to be a 'non-work-related' holiday. But I can't help it: vegetables beckon. Before I know it the notebook and camera are out and precious van space is filled with odd little bunches of greens. On this trip two factors limited accurate observations and fact finding. First, I'd had a cataract operation three weeks before leaving, with the second due on my return. So while one eye was now mildly short-sighted, the other was extremely so and never the twain would meet. Binoculars helped for middle and long distance, but most things, including the wild flowers at my feet and trees overhead, were softly blurred. Second, my Italian is rudimentary. I'm a past master at making a little language go a long way where vegetables are concerned, but I'd have gleaned a lot more information if I'd been more fluent.

The first vegetables to beckon were cauliflowers. They reign in winter in Sicily. Within five minutes of stepping ashore in the twilight at Palermo, we were easing our way through a thronging street lined with fruit and vegetable stalls. While oranges, lemons, glossy black aubergines and stark white fennel bulbs gleamed from orderly ranks, the caulis were piled high – a few ordinary white ones, but mostly eye-catching purple and lime-green ones. In due course we tried both (excellent flavours), the purple one bought from a travelling fruit and veg van in Enna, advertising his presence with a loud hailer. We ended our trip in the fishing village of Sferracavallo outside Palermo, where every morning we were woken romantically by loud street cries. Bread? Oranges? On the last morning I downed my toothbrush to find out: it proved to be green-curded cauliflowers sold from a three-wheeler van. I watched three being carefully placed on a doorstep opposite. I expect they'd been cut that morning. *Cavolo celi*, I think they called them in Palermo, and *cavolino* in Trapani.

The New Year period is also the peak season for globe artichokes. Wherever we went, their long greyish leaves and thistle heads were draped untidily over little handcarts and trestles. Tureens of freshly boiled heads and stems, almost equally delicious, were on sale as street food in Palermo. We saw vast fields of artichokes growing on the coastal plains, and on a farm near Gela were shown an experimental variety from Naples, with heads so large they commanded three times the normal price.

This was where we solved another mystery. Alongside the globe artichokes we'd often seen small bunches of artichoke-like leaves, apparently called *cardone* – which I'd always interpreted as cardoons. But they weren't the large blanched cardoon stems I knew. We'd bought some and followed the greengrocer's simple advice: boil until soft, and eat dipped in salt – though next day our visiting friend created a lemon-based salad dressing which went beautifully with them. But what were these *cardone*? I asked the Gela

Market stall in Trapani, Sicily, selling the beautiful green cauliflowers that were ubiquitous on our winter trip.

farmers, and in reply one of them plunged into the artichoke field, sliced off a leafy offshoot at ground level, stripped off a couple of outer leaves, and offered me a taste of the inner stem on the tip of his penknife. It had that subtle, edgy, cardoon flavour. Eat them raw was their advice.

We were able to try all sorts of local vegetables and dishes. In Agrigento I bought some shaggy, dandelion-like leaves with little pieces of root attached, which I assumed were wild chicory. They were excellent boiled: the best flavour really is in that slither of root. In a pizzeria I had a superb plate of roasted red chicory – salted, lightly brushed with olive oil, then cooked like the pizzas in a wood-fired oven.

A brief encounter in the small town of Scicli led to a tiny sprig of steamed borage one night. The cobbled road we'd followed up through the town became a rocky footpath leading into the countryside, and passing us, on their way down, were a group holding bundles of leaves. The old lady volunteered they were 'borrago' and they'd collected them to eat. They looked smoother and darker than our borage. Could they be comfrey? On retracing our steps later what should I find but a bunch they had dropped. Unashamedly I took it home. It was borage and was quite palatable steamed. So the Italian peasant tradition of gathering edible wild plants lives on.

Typically Italian, too, are the *cima di rapa*, bunches of turnip tops on the verge of flowering, and similarly various young cabbage and mustard rape greens – rough-and-ready poor-man's fare. I asked to photograph an elderly man selling them, but when I tried to buy a couple of bunches as a thank-you, he insisted on giving them to me. I'd bought some previously from another elderly man selling from a roadside cart in Mazara del Vallo. He told me to boil them and dress them with oil and lemon juice. They were surprisingly good.

I love the way you pick up cooking tips when travelling. In the attractive port of Trapani we bought a long, pale green courgette, which I thought might be the variety 'Cocozelle'. The lady at the till took it upon herself to tell me how to cook it. Cut in slices and sprinkle with salt – and with a large knife she delicately marked the thickness of the slices on its skin. Then put olive oil in a 'padella'. I guessed a frying pan, but sensing my momentary doubt, she dived under the counter and brought out an illustrated kitchen catalogue to confirm it. Not too much oil, not too little, but it must be really hot. A quick fry on each side. And to indicate how exceptionally good the outcome would be, she plunged her forefinger in her cheek and twisted it round in that wonderfully expressive Italian gesture. I got a pat on the cheek when I thanked her for the cookery lesson. By then all the customers were discussing the merits of the courgette: how they were much cheaper in summer, and how these winter ones were grown in polytunnels.

Along the south coast from Portopalo on the eastern tip of Sicily to Agrigento, polythene often stretched as far as the eye could see: large timber-framed structures with plastic pushed up along the sides for ventilation and steel hoop tunnels, roughly 1.5m/5ft high and sometimes over 30m/100ft long, with pairs of neat round, dinner-plate ventilation holes along their entire length. By the way, the plastic is collected and recycled into useful products.

Mario Mennella, our Italian plant breeder friend, gave us an introduction to a commercial tomato *azienda* (nursery) south-west of Vittoria, and we spent a night there – locked with the night watchman behind electronically operated gates guarding 40 hectares/over 100 acres of tomatoes! Mostly destined for export to northern Europe, the two main varieties were a cherry tomato, 'Chico Rosso', and a large round Dutch variety, 'Durinta' – used fresh and for salsa. They gave us a huge box when we left, picked 'on the vine', some ripe, some still green to ripen over the next few weeks. They smelt and tasted wonderful. We tried to give a few away to a garage owner who'd helped us. He declined politely: 'We don't eat tomatoes in winter. We eat lettuce and oranges at this time of year!'

Inevitably, I got that old urge to talk to some market gardeners. Back in Palermo at the end of our trip we had a cheery hour in the Capo vegetable market, asking about the neat little bundles of young spinach (spiga) and scarole (giri), and being introduced to the Sicilian and Palermo dialect names for different vegetables. What chance does a foreigner have? As for market gardens, just follow the Corso del Mille from the Central station until about 4 kilometres/2½ miles out of the city . . .

It wasn't quite that simple, but we did find them, like 'suburban' market gardens the world over threatened by the encroachment of the cities they traditionally supplied.

Winter crops of spinach, calabrese, cauliflowers, fennel and brassica greens were densely planted in wide beds separated with irrigation channels, with a few immaculately ridged bare plots prepared for the summer crops of tomatoes, beans, melons, peppers and aubergines. We talked to a couple harvesting their young 'spinach'. Later, when I looked carefully at the leaves they gave us (apologizing profusely for their being unwashed), I realized they were in fact young chard, with the lovely pink blush on the stem found in some Italian chard varieties. This crop was sown directly in the ground from October to July, and harvested forty days later. I found myself thinking of China: the same intense cultivation, harvesting crops young and the ingrained belief that vegetables should be eaten the day they are harvested.

I must mention two (yellow) things: citron and Bermuda buttercup. Citron are fruits that look like enormous lemons. Their tiny core and outer peel have a strong lemon flavour, but it's the mild, sweet-flavoured pith that is used. It was great in a fennel salad. The Bermuda buttercup (Oxalis pes-caprae) is a brilliant yellow-flowered weed originally introduced from South Africa. It colours the Sicilian winter landscape – cultivated fields, vineyards, olive and orange orchards. It must be the most pernicious and persistent of Sicily's many invaders.

ON LABOUR SAVING
'Just Vegetating', The Kitchen Garden, July 1999

In honest moments recently I've acknowledged that an instinct for labour saving (my labour) is beginning to dominate my gardening. I've always, perforce, been an evening gardener, and in the past often found myself sowing and planting by moonlight. Not because I'm a believer in moon planting theories. (I've always argued that whatever the influence of the moon's phase, in practice immediate factors, like the state of the soil, have more bearing on a plant's growth.) It's just that obsessive gardeners don't stop when darkness falls . . . there's always one more weed to pull up. But now a little voice murmurs: it can wait till tomorrow. And another little voice says: just enjoy the evening. Lean on the fork a moment or two and listen to the nightingales. This happens to be excellent advice, as at the time of writing our nightingales have just returned, and have been singing their gorgeous hearts out, night and day.

So with a busy summer ahead, and less regular help than last year, I had a serious think in spring about how to make the vegetable garden less demanding, while keeping us supplied with veggies, producing some surplus bits and pieces to sell to local restaurants and shops and, above all, being a lovely place to work in – at a gentle pace in the evening.

First thought: simplify. The most complex areas in our kitchen garden are the little summer and winter potagers. Both have about eight beds or sections, with edges planted with edible crops. Normally each section is planted differently, which is fiddly, and takes a lot of planning and executing. This year I'm settling, in both potagers, for four bold circular bands embracing all the beds. It will drive a coach and horses through the underlying rotation scheme, but I'll risk it. On the whole the diversity of crops in the potagers seems to prevent pests and diseases building up seriously. Whether the circles will look breathtaking or a mess remains to be seen. Early indications are that the reservoir of dill, calendula and red orach seed in the soil is producing a vigorous crop of self-sown seedlings, which will disturb current sowings. Will I have a psychological block over pulling them out – knowing they'll be usable and possibly sellable? Will this 'simplified' idea prove labour intensive?

I always make trouble for myself by trying too many varieties of everything. Tomatoes are the worst. So many tempting new and heirloom varieties to try, yet I'm loath to sacrifice favourites to make space for the untried. We never manage to grow fewer than twenty-four varieties, which is quite enough to raise, keep labelled, and record properly. This year I vowed to restrict it to a dozen. So much for resolve: the final list was eighteen, a modest improvement on last year. But just after they'd all been sown along comes a sample packet of 'Pendulina Orange' with an irresistible description: 'bright orange, squarish little fruits, superb flavour, heavy yielder, suitable for containers'. It sounded so like my beloved little American variety 'Whippersnapper', now difficult to obtain. I caved in. Nineteen varieties it will be.

The most obvious way of cutting down on work is to grow perennials and self-seeding vegetables. Robert Hart, of 'forest garden' fame (see page 288), is one of the main exponents of perennial vegetables. I remember being a little sceptical when I first visited his garden back in the 1970s, but now I appreciate the value of those unflagging clumps of good King Henry, sorrel and brassicas such as perennial kale – which only need occasional renewal. Until recently I'd never considered perpetual spinach a perennial, but now I realize it's the queen of self-perpetuating vegetables. If cut regularly the rootstock seems to keep going for years – we're eating from plants originally sown three years ago. On top of that, let an occasional plant run to seed, and it self-seeds. Well, that's the only way I can account for its welcome presence in various corners of the garden, shiny leaves ready in the 'hungry gap' in April and May.

Winter salad plants are amongst the best self-seeders. Being small-leaved and tasty as small young leaves (baby leaves in modern parlance) it doesn't matter if they are crowded. I have wonderful self-perpetuating patches of lamb's lettuce, land cress, rocket and winter purslane. Not to mention edible weeds like chickweed, hairy bitter cress and one of my favourites, the spicily flavoured field penny cress. All there for the taking in spring. Dandelions too: but here the trick is to cover the leafy plant with a lightproof bucket or even a plate to blanch them. This transforms the flavour of the leaves from a stringency few palates can tolerate raw into a refreshingly lively taste. The creamy, jagged, blanched leaves look theatrical in salads. Blanching also stops them flowering and spreading.

The most surprising self-seeding perennial is asparagus. I've lost track of the number of times we've tried to establish asparagus beds: bindweed was the death of several in their vulnerable early years. Yet occupying one end of a border in my winter potager is a huge, self-sown asparagus plant. In late April we picked the biggest crop of the lushest spears we have ever had from this plant. Makes you think. All that money spent buying expensive all-female, modern hybrid varieties, preparing the ground carefully, laying the thongs over a neatly rounded ridge . . . and this orphan of unknown provenance outshines them all. Jerusalem artichokes – there's another that keeps itself going. Any unlifted tuber will sprout cheerily the following season, and so on *ad infinitum*. I've never noticed any deterioration in vigour, even when they've inhabited the same spot for years. A true DIY veg.

Let's leave low-maintenance plants and turn to labour-saving techniques. Mulching heads my list. I can't stand bare soil in the kitchen garden. It's just inviting moisture to evaporate and weeds to germinate. Last winter a farming neighbour bequeathed us a trailerload of 'spoilt' old, wet straw. I couldn't have asked for a better present. Nothing does more good to our heavy soil than mulching with old straw. And the luxury of being extravagant with it! I'll start by covering the paths in the polytunnel. In due course the summer paths become winter beds, and while the straw looks good and feels nice underfoot, it is amazing what it does to the texture of the soil beneath. It also encourages masses of earthworms to carry on the good work. All in all, straw mulching saves us loads of time and effort in weeding, watering and working in compost.

We also cover potatoes with straw after they're planted. Here I have a tussle with my husband. He says the shoots struggle to come up through it and it encourages slugs. He may have a point – especially after the drenching rains we had this spring – but I value the initial protection against frost, its role in keeping moisture in the soil (the key to heavy potato crops here) and, again, its dramatic effect on the soil. Potatoes + straw is one of the main planks in fertility building in our rotation scheme.

A couple of months ago *The Kitchen Garden* reported work at the Henry Doubleday Research Association which showed that mulching with straw offered potatoes some protection against blight. You still need to cut back the haulm when the blight first becomes apparent, but the blight spores are trapped on the straw and tuber damage is limited. Wonderful to find a justification for what you want to do anyway.

Having the right tools makes all the difference to getting work done easily and tirelessly. My favourite is a Chinese hand tool, onion hoe size, made from an old saw. The jagged saw blade serves as a rake, and the smooth edge as a hoe. I use it constantly for all my wide drill sowings. At Chelsea one year I tried to persuade the tool makers Burgon & Ball to manufacture it, but sadly, the economics of launching new tools these days was prohibitive.

Earlier this year a group of us had a fascinating visit to the company's factory in Sheffield, seeing the traditional skills that go into making its shears and scythes. We finished up at the Abbeydale industrial hamlet, once the hub of water-powered scythe production, now individual workshops. I took along my Chinese tool and asked scythe grinder Ron Staley, who still sharpens all the Burgon & Ball scythes, to sharpen the Chinese hoe blade. I never expected such a spectacle. He does the grinding suspended in a leather harness overhanging the rotating grinding stone. I'll treat my tool with even greater respect from now on!

ON BREAKING WITH CONVENTION
'Just Vegetating', *The Kitchen Garden*, September 1999

Last week I was in the restaurant at the Chaumont Garden Festival in France eating an entrée described as '*mesclun*'. The festival's theme this year is potagers or kitchen gardens; hence a strong potager influence in the restaurant menu. My '*mesclun*' proved to be an elegant little tower of filo pastry, with a deeply curled lettuce leaf embedded in the tower, a pink rose petal, a white rose petal and a borage flower peeping from the top. Around the base was an array of lightly battered vegetables and flowers – a nasturtium crisped into a butterfly, a beet so baby it was less than an index finger in diameter, battered mini-courgettes and carrots and so on. A little precious perhaps, but a picture of culinary delight.

I first encountered *mesclun* in its Italian form, *misticanza*, over twenty years ago. Both words are used for traditional seed mixtures sown to provide an instant blend of a dozen or so different salad plants, cut as seedlings. Over time we've grown and marketed our own bags of mixed salad, christening them Saladini. But we've always served them with a classic French dressing, albeit tossing a handful of edible flower petals over them at the last moment. In all those years, it never occurred to me to house them in a turret of filo pastry, bedecked with delicately battered miniature vegetables.

Which set me musing on how conventional we vegetable growers are. Our predominant instinct is to stick to the tried and tested. Well, most of the time. But shadowing that conventional strand in our psyche is a parallel, subversive strand: curiosity. That's the one that urges you to try new varieties and new methods, to sow at a different time from normal, and to compare varieties and methods so you'll know another time which horse to back. Provided, of course, you remember, or record, the results.

I've a German friend, Ulrike Paradine, who has almost none of the conventional strand, and I'm tempted to say has the 'gift' of curiosity. Into her small garden are packed edible plants and herbs from all corners of the globe, and she scours the globe, via catalogues, colleagues and the Internet, to obtain seeds and plants and information on growing and using them. I'm full of admiration, but sometimes I find myself wondering if curiosity is a blessing or a curse.

Why can't I just sow two identical rows, instead of carrying out a mini-experiment with every sowing? Earlier this year I sowed two rows of mixed lettuce in fairly dry weather, one normally, the other using that old trick of drenching the drill before sowing and covering the seed with a dry mulch. I've been advocating the latter for so long to overcome germination problems in dry weather that I thought it was time to compare the methods side by side. What happened? Neither germinated well. Duff lot of seed, I fear!

Sometimes you have to take a mental leap over the conventional strand to indulge the curiosity strand. Several years ago I first heard of the work done by Stan Finch and his colleagues at Horticulture Research International, into undersowing brassicas with clover to deter flying pests – notably butterflies, cabbage root fly and aphids. It seems the pests are attracted to the odour of brassicas growing in bare soil, but prefer to land on something green.

If nothing but cabbages are growing there they land on them. But if there's another nice patch of green, it's a 50:50 chance they'll land on it instead. Then, sensing something's amiss, off they fly instead of settling down, noticeably reducing pest attacks.

While clover works well as a green decoy, weeds can be pretty effective too. This may be one reason why the slightly weedy plots of organic growers and gardeners appear to have lower pest levels than conventional pristine, weed-free plots.

To date, I've never tried this out. Curiosity over-ridden by laziness? You have to get the clover well established first, leaving spaces to plant the brassicas later. The clover should be about halfway up the brassicas when they are planted – say 8cm/3in high for brassicas that are about 15cm/6in high.

I've now firmly resolved to try it two ways. Late this summer I will sow some crimson clover as a winter green manure, leaving gaps or tramlines for planting out overwintered cauliflowers and red cabbage next spring. I'll cut back the crimson flowers to keep it nice and dense. Then I'm going to sow trefoil, another clover, in late April or May, giving it two months to grow before planting the winter brassicas in June and July. Now I really should establish a control bed, without clover, in another part of the garden. Will I get around to it?

One new technique I have tried out this year is planting potatoes in late July to get new potatoes at Christmas. Taking a leaf from commercial practice, Marshalls Seeds have held back tubers in cold store, so they are raring to go when planted in July and August. Years ago I dug up early potatoes and buried them in a tin for new potatoes at Christmas, an old practice I had read about somewhere. What did I get? Some very rusty, waterlogged potatoes. This sounds a much better idea – provided I can keep potato blight at bay. Apparently Maxicrop sprays help improve blight resistance – so there's another experiment to carry out. It's going to be a busy autumn.

MUSINGS FROM MICHIGAN
'Just Vegetating', *The Kitchen Garden*, June 2000

You never know where vegetables are going to take you. In March this year I was invited to give a couple of talks at the Michigan Herb Associates (MHA) annual conference in East Lansing – so off I went to the American Midwest. It never occurred to me I'd return with my head buzzing with analemmatic sundials and geodesic domes, and resolving to mow a maze in the lawn and wash my hair in rosemary to stimulate my memory. Nor did I expect to witness Harry Potter dowsing (successfully) for water in the conference lecture hall. His dowsing rod was two sawn-off wire coat hangers.

America is full of surprises, and although gardening is still far from being the national pastime it is here, in the last decade, to quote my 'Master Gardener' guide in Toledo, it is 'fast becoming a passion'. In the gardening circles I was in the air was thick with ideas and energy. Perhaps you need that passion to overcome the problems they face in some parts of the country. In the two days I was in East Lansing there was a 60-degree temperature drop. And the four-legged pests are horrendous. Next time you bemoan the ravages of mice, moles and rabbits, just be thankful you don't have racoons, possums, porcupines, gophers, bears, deer, ground hogs . . . and that was just the big ones. (I didn't like the sound of the squash borer either.)

The MHA conference was held on Michigan State University campus. In the spring mid-term break its doors are thrown open to the public in Agriculture and Resources Week, which offers an extraordinary range of courses and gatherings with rural leanings. As far as I know, we have nothing quite like it.

This year the MHA's chosen herbs were rosemary and thyme. I was captivated by a slide of a lawn into which thyme (ordinary broad-leaved thyme was the suspect), had 'escaped' and was flowering with abandon. So I may be planting a few patches of rooted thyme cuttings in our rough-and-ready lawn this summer. Other interesting snippets? Llamas produce excellent dung and deposit it neatly in one spot; and rose water was the most popular flavour in the world before the discovery of vanilla. I've added pineapple sage and coriander to my list of edible flowers, after briefly visiting an MHA-supported research project into growing edible flowers in winter, with artificial light and heat. The sage flowers were exquisitely sweet.

So to labyrinths and mazes, and the differences between them. A labyrinth, I learned, is a simple path, classically eleven concentric circles leading to the centre and back out. 'Walking the labyrinth' has a calming effect and in the US small therapeutic labyrinths are being made in churches, hospitals, prisons, even in people's back yards. The materials used range from grass and herb-edged paths to canvas (indoors). Mazes, on the other hand, are puzzles for fun and entertainment, full of dead ends and deceptions. They're becoming very popular, too, with farmers planting vast 'maize mazes' in the fields.

Next topic was analemmatic sundials, i.e. sundials where a human figure acts as the gnomon, or shadow-casting marker. To give an accurate reading this has to be moved daily according to the calendar: a human gnomon 'moves' by simply standing in the appropriate spot for the day.

The inclusion of mazes, labyrinths and sundials in the conference programme reflected the interests of conference organizer Jane Taylor. Jane was also the prime mover and first curator of the famous 4-H Children's Garden on the MSU campus, where, you've guessed it, there's an analemmatic sundial and an Alice in Wonderland maze.

I'm always interested in ways of getting kids gardening, so once the conference was over, Jane and I went to the Children's Garden – inevitably bleak in mid-March Michigan. In the early planning stages Jane 'consulted' children on what they wanted, and to my delight, vegetables were high on their list. So vegetables figure largely in many of the sixty-odd 'theme' gardens. The Rainbow Garden, for example, is planted to illustrate the edible plants associated with the many ethnic groups in the US: Hispanic, African and Asian Americans, the Pioneers, North American Indians, plus an ever changing International segment.

There are more vegetables in the raised bed kitchen garden near outdoor cooking facilities, and in a raised bed designed for handicapped children. Here mini vegs are grown at eye level and young wheelchair visitors can peer into a low glass panel to see root crops growing. A realistic sheep grazes in the Forage Garden, a simple frame can be woven with vines or flax in the Flax and Fibre Garden, climbing beans, sunflowers and giant grasses romp in the Jack and Giant Garden. The whole garden is rich in imaginative details, justifying its description as 'the most creative half acre in the USA'.

ROBERT HART
From 'Just Vegetating', *The Kitchen Garden*, June 2000

Robert Hart, standing in front of a Swiss nut pine in his forest garden at Wenlock Edge in Shropshire, where he put his creative and philosophical ideals into practice.

On my return from the US I was very sad to learn of the death of Robert Hart, philosopher, idealist, pioneer gardener and creator of a tiny 'forest garden' on Wenlock Edge in Shropshire. Driven by the desire to alleviate world hunger, Robert was an early advocate of self-sustaining systems, such as agroforestry/permaculture. In his forest garden, imitating the ecosystem of the natural forest, half-standard fruit and nut trees provided shelter for shade-tolerant berries such as gooseberries. As ground cover beneath them and in mini clearings among them were vegetables and herbs, mainly perennials or natural self-seeders, while climbers were trained up trees and over fences and buildings.

I visited Robert's garden many times over the years, always returning inspired and with pages of copious notes. I remember once following behind him as he pulled an endless supply of onion sets and garlic cloves from his pockets, planting them at random to deter slugs and snails. Maybe it worked: there were surprisingly few in his damp garden.

Robert devoted his life to nursing his mentally handicapped brother and rarely travelled far from Wenlock Edge. But his work reached the corners of the globe, and he drew enormous pleasure from his many visitors, particularly young people. He was passionate both about the healing qualities of wild and salad plants, and the joy of making gardens beautiful, tranquil places. I'll miss him, and treasure the good King Henry plants he gave me over twenty-five years ago. It was one of his favourite perennials. His work lives on in several books, including *Forest Gardening* and *Beyond the Forest Garden*, and the booklet *The Forest Garden*.

AT THE SEED TRIALS
'Just Vegetating', *The Kitchen Garden*, December 2000

'Going round the seed trials' is a long-established and enjoyable summer ritual for garden writers. These are the trials run by the retail seed companies, who supply seed to amateur gardeners, and the 'trade' seed companies such as Tozer and Elsoms, who supply commercial growers and also act as wholesalers to the retail seed companies.

A seed trial is essentially a large-scale exercise in quality control. The cool, unpredictable UK climate is generally unsuitable for seed production, so most of our seed comes from overseas, nowadays from all corners of the globe. As with any crop, quality varies from year to year for all sorts of reasons – and the main way seed companies check what they are getting is to try them out in the field. So batches from different sources are grown, side by side, in endless short rows. This quickly shows up any that germinate badly, or are not what they purport to be, and in the case of 'mixtures', whether they are genuinely balanced, attractive mixtures or not.

Trials also provide an opportunity to compare the old with the new. Are the varieties which companies are breeding themselves, and those in the pipeline from other sources, really better than what has gone before? Are they higher yielding, faster maturing, more disease or weather resistant? Sometimes it's hard to tell; sometimes an outstanding variety really does stand out dramatically. An example of this is cucumbers with mildew resistance. In greenhouse trials you may see plant after plant with sickly grey, mildewed leaves, but among them will be a few completely healthy plants, perhaps 'Brunex', 'Tyria', or 'Passandra' – varieties clearly resistant to mildew.

I was once on a trial ground after an unexpectedly heavy frost in early November. Every row of curly parsley had crumpled with one exception, the variety 'Favorit', an 'industrial' variety. It was far and away the hardiest. Trials also afford a chance to make close observations of varieties as they grow – valuable information for company and customer alike.

Organizing trials is a complex and expensive business. George Beaven, once responsible for the vegetable seed trials at Hurst Seeds, told me that at any one time they could be trialling over seven thousand different lines – and that was in the days before computers. Simply assembling the seed from the multitudinous sources, in time for either the spring or summer sowings, was a mammoth task.

Then sowings have to be carefully planned and grouped, rotation systems worked out, and soil conditions, as far as possible, made even across the ground. Occasionally something goes wrong. I remember seeing a swathe of gaps and miserable plants in one trial ground. They traced it to the residue of a weedkiller applied a couple of seasons previously.

Yes, trials have their tribulations. This year at the Suttons trial ground, part of the plot, near a newly tarmacked car park, was flooded. The previous year vandals broke in and chucked some of the records into a rain barrel – including the courgette yield trials. They repeated the trials this year. Let's hope the books are under lock and key this time.

Elsoms trial grounds in Lincolnshire had floods a few days before their summer open day for growers; and on top of that, the heavy, silty soil had capped into a crispy crust which had to be broken up with a push hoe. Capping soils are the kiss of death for many germinating seedlings, but it was interesting to see how beet

Left: carefully breaking the capped soil on Elsoms Seeds' trial ground in Lincolnshire. Right: neat lettuce trial at Tozer Seeds in Surrey.

and spinach were among the few strong enough to break through. Opt for them if you have a capping soil.

Trial sites are often woefully bleak. I've seen double rows of sunflowers grown as windbreaks for squashes, and climbing runner and French beans in a corral of 1.8–2.1m/6–7ft-high windbreak netting. Thompson & Morgan's site is on poor soil in a very exposed position without irrigation facilities. It really does sort the sheep from the goats: only the fittest survive.

Many trials this year suffered from harsh winds in spring, followed by low light levels and cold nights extending into early summer. Even in July Unwins Seeds recorded 8°C/46.6°F at night on their Cambridgeshire trial ground. Gardeners, of course, suffer the same conditions, so trial results are a microcosm of what happens in the outside world. It's a truism that every season is different; for this reason no variety should be judged on one season alone.

Try anything new for two or three years before passing final judgment.

The trials for commercial growers often provide a peep into the future. What the professionals are growing today filters down to amateurs in due course. It was on Elsoms' trial grounds that I first saw the red curly kale 'Redbor', pink-tinged savoys like 'Colorsa', the improved modern varieties of red chicories and the stunning range of coloured lettuces which are now commonplace in supermarkets and restaurants.

One year I visited their carrot trials and was bowled over by the experimental purple, red, yellow and white carrots. Some tasted gorgeous, but there have been a few hiccups in getting them on the market.

Another glimpse into the fast-approaching future was gained at Tozer's trials, where they try out all manner of greens for use as 'baby leaves', in salads and stir-fries. The closely sown, superbly grown rows, harvested only a few inches high, are a picture: lush, bright and colourful. On the home front this is what I call cut-and-come-again (CCA) but in the commercial world they cut once then re-sow. Either way, it's a highly productive concept I've been enthusing over for years. Yet here were all sorts of things I'd never considered for CCA, from different types of spinach to kales, sorrel, mixed orach and a fascinating range of oriental greens.

I'm always picking up hints on growing techniques and pest control on trial grounds. I was intrigued at how extensively Suttons were using fleece over young crops of kohl rabi, turnips, cabbage and oriental vegetables as protection against flying brassica pests. Carrots and parsley were sometimes grown to maturity under fleece, in this case warding off carrot fly. The edges of the fleece are simply anchored with soil – fiddly perhaps, but it causes less damage than pegs.

Interestingly, sweetcorn 'Indian Summer' that had been sown outside then covered with fleece was ahead of pot-raised plants. Both lots were well earthed up.

Trials give you new ideas and shake up or confirm old ones. I'm always surprised at how well aubergines and basil do outdoors on Unwins' exposed Cambridgeshire site (I'd never risk either outside myself). I reinforced my belief that the semi-leafless pea 'Markana' is the most 'self-supporting', and that dwarf runner beans, especially the bi-coloured 'Hestia', make colourful and decorative ground cover.

Finally a bit of seed trade gossip. Would you believe it, EU regulations allow seed companies to mix lettuce and endive in the same packet, but not lettuce and chicory. Since they call endive *chicorée* on the Continent, and what we call chicory *endive*, there must be some very confused bureaucrats in Brussels!

. . . .

Coloured carrots are now widely available but, sadly, the savoy 'Colorsa' has disappeared. That's the way it goes.

THE TRADITIONAL KITCHEN GARDEN AT HEX
'Just Vegetating', *The Kitchen Garden*, March 2001

I've never been as enthusiastic about garden restorations as I should be – and that goes for historic kitchen gardens. I can't quite suppress the sentiment (allegedly voiced by President Nixon about trees) 'seen one, and you've seen 'em all'. I get far more excited about imaginative, contemporary approaches to vegetable growing. But when it comes to traditions being maintained – that's a different story. So let me share the delights of a recent autumnal visit to

the kitchen garden at Hex castle, in Belgium which has been in continual use since 1770.

Set in the gently rolling Hesbaye countryside south-east of Brussels, Hex castle was built in the late eighteenth century by Charles-François de Velbrück, the arts-loving Prince Bishop of Liège. Elaborate formal gardens were made close to the castle, the surrounding parkland was landscaped à la 'Capability' Brown (a lake was later excavated by hand) while ground south-west of the chateau was terraced to make the potager and orchards. Walls were built to enclose the kitchen garden, and giving it its unique, theatrical quality, the immense wall on its north-east side. Rising probably 4m/13ft from the potager to the terrace above, crowned with an elegant eighteenth-century cast-iron balustrade where old climbing roses mingle with the ivies, a pleached lime walk runs along much of its length. From the formal garden on this upper terrace the garden is reached through fine eighteenth-century wrought-iron gates. A beautiful double stone stairway leads from the gardens down to the potager.

Leaning over the balustrade the visitor gets an unforgettable vista of a serene, colourful, highly ordered garden. The main working area is a vast, box-edged, dahlia-fringed rectangle, where long rows of vegetables stretch from side to side, interspersed with parallel rows of fruit, herbs or flowers. Pears, figs, vines and roses are trained against the walls, and on the far side, filling niches between old pears and recently planted quinces, soft fruit bushes edge the outer path. At either end the main bed is flanked with borders of shrubs, herbs and flowers.

Separated from the main ground by a wide path, and running parallel to the high outer wall, is a gently sloping bed about 3.5m/12ft wide. Box-edged again, and backed by the gnarled, lichened branches of old, drawf espalier apples, this well-drained, south-west-facing slope is the warmest ground in the garden. Its whole length is packed with annual and perennial herbs, salads and sun-loving vegetables like peppers and aubergines, and cutting flowers for the house. Looking towards the castle, still within the confines of this 0.8 hectare/2 acre garden, are grassed orchards of apples and pears, and at the far end, the vegetable cellars. At the nearer end are two greenhouses and a small walled nursery area. Overlooking the garden is the church and

the benign white façade of the parish priest's house, demolished in the eighteenth century and rebuilt on the other side of the road, to make way for the garden walls.

This is a potager in the original sense of the word – a working kitchen garden. And it's a potager which is cherished and used to the full by its current owners, Count Ghislain d'Ursel and his wife Stéphanie, who took over in 1997. The family spend their weekends at Hex, but his wife and children return to Brussels and schooling during the week. Frequent business engagements take the count into Brussels during the week, his car always packed with fresh vegetables, herbs and fruits, maybe even a couple of dishes prepared by the Hex cook. Having spent much of his childhood at Hex, his conversation is coloured with childhood memories of the garden and the ethos of 'living by the seasons'. It's a concept his wife, with her urban background, still sometimes finds alien when planning the weekly menus. But they live off the fresh produce from the garden. Every morning the gardener reports to the cook on what fruit and vegetables are in their prime.

Ghislain d'Ursel is determined that the kitchen garden, though rooted in the past, embraces the new. His object is to bring the best-quality produce to the table all year round. Seakale, for example, has been introduced to help fill the spring gap, notoriously long in this part of Belgium where winter temperatures can drop to below −15°C/5°F. A modern cold store prolongs the fresh fruit season.

The potager and formal gardens are managed with three permanent gardeners (two have been there for twenty-eight years, one for thirty-three), with two extra workers during the summer. The box edges – there is well over half a mile of box edging in the potager – are now cut under contract. A key element in the potager, most of the box (*Buxus sempervirens* 'Suffruticosa') was planted forty years ago, but some was replaced seven years ago from their own cuttings. It is a remarkably slow-growing strain. When trouble strikes, as in a recent case of die-back attributed to weedkiller drift, it responded well to being cut back severely.

The original potager was laid out in hundreds of small squares, each devoted to a single kind of vegetable and each edged with box. Imagine the maintenance! When the count's late parents, Nanda and Michel d'Ursel, returned from the Congo to settle in Hex in the 1960s they converted the potager into its present, more practical form. Sadly, there are no photos of the original gardens.

In those days the gardener would get up at midnight and again at 4.00 a.m. to stoke the greenhouse boiler. Like many traditional gardeners, he took as his garden guide *The Calendar of Saints*: asparagus cutting finished on St John's Day and so on. Nanda d'Ursel, from all accounts a remarkable gardener herself, learnt much from this old gardener (who worked, incidentally, in old-fashioned clogs).

The rich, heavy soil in the garden has been enriched with soil from the woodlands, and is kept fertile with manure from the farm, rotovated in as soon as weather allows in spring. As far as possible, organic methods are used, an exception being weedkillers on the paths.

I can't think of any kitchen garden where a wider range of crops is grown. Besides all the traditional standbys, from asparagus and leeks to cauliflower and sweetcorn and an astonishing range of herbs, there are copious supplies of those vegetables I associate with Belgium. These include exceptionally tall climbing beans (some are grown to dry for winter), corn salad, endives, Witloof chicory and cardoons. I was taken by the double sowings in the corn salad strip. Fearing poor germination, a second sowing was made right alongside the first, a couple of weeks later. As it happened both came through. But what a neat way to double your money: corn salad is such a slow-growing, low-yielding plant.

Hex Castle is renowned for its 200-year-old *caves* (cellars), where vegetables are still stored in the methods widely used before the advent of domestic freezers. Entered through a small door in the high potager wall, the cellars extend underground beneath the formal prince's garden on the upper terrace. (Worryingly, they are starting to get leakage from above.) Five vaulted chambers are supported by pillars made from the local river Meuse blue stone, the same stone that frames the castle windows.

The outer cellar walls are 1m/3ft thick, maintaining an ambient winter temperature of about 5–6°C/42°F. The vegetables are planted in narrow timber-edged beds of soil which line the walls. Here red and white cabbages are plunged up to their heads in orderly rows, along with celeriac, celery and dandelion, the latter loosing its bitterness as the leaves blanch in the darkness. Carrots, turnips and scorzonera are laid flat in layers and overed with soil. Pumpkins are stored here too. Some of the white cabbage is used to make their own sauerkraut, using a recipe Nanda d'Ursel was given by nuns.

The winter vegetables are dug out of the potager and transferred to the cellars between 1 and 15 October. We arrived mid-afternoon on 3 October, just in time to see the last of the cardoons being dug up, carefully lifted on to a hand cart, tied in place and pushed through the garden and up the slope into the cellars. We watched them being gently replanted. Within a month the stems would have become white and tender and ready for the kitchen.

The next day we watched the Witloof chicories being dug up. Most of these are cut back and replanted close together outside, covered with leaves and soil. This traditional method is said to produce the best-flavoured chicons. But head gardener Dirk Ysebaert

Looking down on the kitchen garden at Hex Castle, in Belgium, which has been in continuous cultivation for over 200 years growing vegetables, herbs, flowers and fruit for the household.

explained how a third of them are now held back in the cold store, at 0°C/32°F, then planted later in the cellar for a successive crop. Endives, too, are blanched by covering with leaves *in situ*.

Fruit abounds at Hex, in and around the potager. Many of the cherries are old local varieties. This year red, white and yellow varieties all fruited well – presented at table in the form of the Belgian flag, a family tradition. There are medlars, quinces, wonderful old mulberries and the gorgeously flavoured white-fruited raspberry 'Surprise d'Automne' – a variety 'that has always been here'.

'Brown Turkey' and 'Brunswick' figs flourish in the old vinery, though it wasn't until the vines were removed that they started to fruit well. As for apples and pears, the count has embarked on a major replanting programme. The Gembloux research station (which we had visited on our Grand Vegetable Tour in 1976) has helped to identify the old varieties at Hex, and an enthusiastic amateur has given scions of old pear varieties, which are being propagated in the potager, and will eventually fill gaps on the wall.

Only well-flavoured varieties will be planted. Current favourites include 'Doyenné du Comice', 'Triomphe de Vienne' and 'Marguérite Marillat'. Old and modern varieties of apple rub shoulders; apart from being used fresh, copious quantities of apple juice are made at a local press. They also make juice from a Caucasian pear – once it has rotted.

Hex is about three hours' drive from Calais, and holds two garden festivals each year, in June and September. For further information, see their website, www.hex.be.

REMEMBERING ROSEMARY
'Just Vegetating', *The Kitchen Garden*, October 2001

It is now several months since Rosemary Verey, the garden designer and writer, died, and I would like to make this 'Just Vegetating' hers by 'Remembering Rosemary'. Over the years we spent a lot of time 'just vegetating', in person and by post, swapping seeds and useful addresses, discussing successes and failures and the practicalities of growing vegetables – the typical hobnobbing of vegetable fanatics. I am lucky to be one of the many people, scattered over the gardening world, on whom she had an enormous influence.

We started corresponding in 1978 after Rosemary had seen an article I had written in the *RHS Journal* about red Italian chicories. They sounded just the sort of thing she needed for her recently designed potager at Barnsley in Gloucestershire, and typically, she was dying to know more. We met a few months later at a side door of the V&A Museum. 'You must be Joy' . . . 'You must be Rosemary!' She was wearing one of the pretty waistcoats which were her hallmark.

We were attending a meeting about the forthcoming Victoria and Albert exhibition *The Garden: A Celebration of One Thousand Years of British Gardening* (see page 126). The eminent taxonomist William Stearn, who by a sad coincidence died in his nineties only a few days before Rosemary, had withdrawn from working on the history of vegetables section and somebody – I'm not sure if it was Rosemary or not – had suggested me to take his place. Of course, in the unchanging way of these things, time was running out. The exhibition opening was only a few months away.

Rosemary Verey, who taught me so much about garden history and potagers, trimming the herbs in the intricate little herb garden at Barnsley House.

Rosemary soon ascertained that I knew very little about the history of vegetables, indeed about history of any sort, and took it upon herself to put this right. She issued a warm invitation to Barnsley House and let me loose in her superb library of historical gardening books. But first the little problem of my English history, a peripatetic education having left a yawning gulf between the Roman invasion of Britain and the repeal of the Corn Laws.

Rosemary got hold of a huge sheet of paper, and filled it with dates, dynasties, kings, queens, Cromwell and key historic events. Then she let me, thus equipped, embark on unravelling the history of vegetables, what vegetable was introduced when, and so on, extracting information from her rare, beautiful, often fragile-looking historical books.

As a short cut she wrote out a set of index cards – I have them on my desk now. Although I didn't realize it at first, they would prove to be windows on a new world which was opening up for me:

ABERCROMBIE, J, eighteenth C
　　1776 *Every Man His Own Gardener*
BRADLEY, RICHARD, eighteenth C
　　1726 *New Improvements of Planting and Gardening*
EVELYN, J., seventeenth C
　　1699 *A Discourse of Sallets*
HIBBERD, SHIRLEY, nineteenth C
　　?1877 *The Amateur's Kitchen Garden*
LANGLEY, BATTY, eighteenth C
　　1728 *New Principles of Gardening*
LAWSON, WILLIAM, seventeenth C
　　1618 *Country Housewife's Garden*

– and many more. The last was her favourite. She steeped herself in this parson's down-to-earth writing, 300 years later embodying the principles he expounded in the design and management of what was to become her world-famous kitchen garden potager.

The seeds of my own obsession with potagers and the concept of making the kitchen garden a beautiful place had been sown a couple of years earlier, in 1976, with a visit to the recently restored potager at Villandry in the Loire Valley (see page 39). Here at Barnsley, Rosemary was pouring her talent for design into her young potager, which, unlike Villandry, was a size and scale that ordinary mortals could identify with. As it was for the thousands of visitors who have visited it in the intervening years, it was a source of inspiration to me.

In the 1980s I collaborated with Christopher Lloyd on a series for the *Observer* on 'Dream Gardens', the idea being to analyse gardens of a particular style, so that gardeners could extract and utilize ideas from them. One of our chosen gardens was the Barnsley potager. What an opportunity to spend several days studying it and learning from it.

Rosemary had a mathematical mind and often said that she was obsessed with patterns. Nothing gave her more pleasure than 'sitting down and drawing up patterns'. A key element in the potager was its patterns. Not just the varying bed patterns in the different sections of the potager, but the patterns in the way the bricks in the paths were laid, in the symmetrically trained goblet apples and pears, in the interplanting within the beds, even in the supports erected for runner beans and peas. Studying the garden, I learned the value of a bold structure, here created with box edges, pockmarked with round box balls, with taller golden privet and variegated box at the corners, stark in winter, but as strikingly beautiful then as they would be in summer.

I absorbed her lessons on dimensions – 'horizontal, vertical and distant'. Paths led to arbours, key paths were accented with verticals, for example standard gooseberries in the early days, later largely replaced with fastigiate upright box. I learned the value of transplanting to keep the potager 'busy', with plants always at the ready, the usefulness of alpine strawberries, carrots, even mitsuba for natural edges, and the beauty of beds devoted solely to one vegetable.

Rosemary was the most practical of gardeners – forever on the lookout for sensible solutions to the problems plants pose. My notebooks were crammed with sketches of her fruit training systems, arches put up for the fragrant, old-fashioned sweet peas, names of suppliers. Typical of her practical approach was the way she transplanted an elderly box hedge someone was uprooting – far too old to replant, in most people's eyes. She simply dug it up and replanted its scruffy bare stems at a 45-degree angle in a trench. As upright shoots sprouted from the old stems they were earthed up, becoming her new box edges.

Rosemary was driven by a desire to share knowledge. She was unfailingly generous in sharing her invaluable books, her time and her knowledge, and had a sponge-like desire to learn herself. I remember being grilled on how to set up a propagator and the use of artificial lighting (I've never mastered it – but she did). And she hated obstructions being put in the way of sharing knowledge. When we were working on the V&A exhibition a visiting TV researcher left some notes on the kitchen sideboard with the address of a Dr S – coupled with a summary of the history of vegetables: what a contact Dr S would be! Would the researcher pass on the address? No way would he breach this confidence – but he would pass on my address, then Dr S could contact me if he so desired. With time running out, this seemed too long-winded to contemplate. I mentioned it to Rosemary.

During lunch she popped into the kitchen, and later furtively handed me a piece of paper. 'Here, I've jotted down the address. Not a word!'

I should add that Dr S and I have been good friends for the last twenty years.

My last visit to Barnsley was almost exactly a year before Rosemary died, to take a small part in the video that was being made about her life and garden. By then her health was troubling her and she had relinquished the management of the garden to her son, Charles. I crept out into the potager early in the morning, and once again, was completely captivated by its abundance, the interplanting, the simple beauty of the Welsh poppies and blue polemoniums which had self-seeded everywhere, the deep reds of the 'Bijou' lettuce . . .

It is a wonderful creation. But like the innovator she always was, Rosemary was equally excited by what she was doing in her now infinitely smaller garden on her patio. She had acquired a host of barrels of different shapes and sizes, installed a drip irrigation system, and transferred all her potager ideas on interplanting and intermingling flowers, vegetables, herbs and fruits into those barrels. She was so proud of having picked our supper salad the previous night from her patio garden.

'Joy,' she said emphatically the next morning, 'we must make sure the television people do something on my barrels.' And we did. If, in a few years' time, I find myself limited to a patio garden, I know I'll be turning, once again, to Rosemary's notes.

Thank you, Rosemary, for affectionately sharing so much and for the books you wrote. A long line of tradition is being carried on. You were inspired by the gardeners of the past, and I suspect that generations still unborn will be encouraged by your writings to create beautiful gardens.

THE ORGANIC SALAD GARDEN
'Just Vegetating', *The Kitchen Garden*, December 2001

Last month the new edition of my book *The Salad Garden* was published, and I'm unashamedly taking the opportunity to look back with nostalgia at its origins in 1984 and to marvel at how much the salad scene has changed in the ensuing decade and a half. The new edition is called *The Organic Salad Garden*. Not just because 'organics are in', but because now I simply can't conceive of growing tasty nutritious salad plants, most of which are eaten raw, and blighting their wholesomeness with toxic chemicals. If pests, diseases or weeds sometimes get the upper hand, so be it. I dare say I was occasionally provoked into using the odd slug pellet in the early 1980s, but the slug hunting by torchlight habit is now deeply engrained. And I suspect that goes for many enthusiastic salad growers.

The seeds of the idea for *The Salad Garden* were sown in 1976 to 1977, the year our family spent travelling around Europe in a caravan. Our main discovery was the unusual, wonderfully diverse, colourful and often remarkably hardy salad plants which were so widely grown on the Continent and were then scarcely known in the British Isles.

Once we had shaken off the dust of travel and become accustomed to the luxury of getting hot water, any water, simply by turning on a tap, I collected all our newfound information on salad plants into *Salads the Year Round*, which was published in 1980. As its author I had ambivalent feelings towards it. Casting false modesty aside, I felt it was packed with detail which would enable newcomers and seasoned gardeners to discover and grow this vast new range of salad plants – but how dedicated you had to be to wade through the solid pages of print! And there wasn't a drop of colour. How could you convey the beautiful reds and textures of Italian chicories and 'Lollo' lettuce without colour? My pleas even for a cover that would illustrate the unfamiliar salads fell on deaf ears.

Then along came the publisher Frances Lincoln, proposing an illustrated salad book, *The Salad Garden*, with photos taken especially for it by botanical photographer Roger Phillips. So we set to growing all the plants, and every two weeks or so Roger, his assistant Jacqui Hurst and members of the Frances Lincoln art department would turn up at Montrose Farm, pick the fresh samples, and photograph them in the makeshift studio set up in our barn. Often the day would end with Ethel Minogue and Paul Laurenson, who ran a Cambridge restaurant, making a beautiful salad photograph, which we would scoff with relish when our work was done.

Gradually 1984 began to seem a long time ago; as I worked on other aspects of vegetable growing, notably Asian vegetables and the concept of the ornamental kitchen garden or potager, I longed to update *The Salad Garden*. Again, my pleas fell on deaf ears, or so it seemed to me. (Publisher/author relationships are not unlike marriage, with their own forms of marital deafness. Perhaps understandably, new projects are the focus of attention: updating old ones is less exciting.) But God bless the millennium. In a BBC radio food programme late in 1999 guest speakers were invited to pick their 'book of the century' and organic grower, food buff and writer Michael Michaud chose *The Salad Garden*, enthusing about it in his unique way. (Some people suggested I bribed him; I swear I did no such thing.) The happy result, for me, was a rekindling of enthusiasm for the book, and the longed-for chance to update it and bring it into the twenty-first century.

ORIENTAL SALADINI
FAST GROWING • NUTRITIOUS
TASTY • PRODUCTIVE

SUFFOLK HERBS
HERBS • WILD FLOWERS • VEGETABLES

Left: a bowl of September Saladini. We grew and sold these mixed salads to Wholefood in London and locally. Right: the original seed packet of Oriental Saladini, which we developed with Suffolk Herbs.

So what is new? Or perhaps it is more appropriate to ask 'What is old and has been rediscovered?' One answer, to my great delight, is the concept of the mixed salad, a European tradition. Not only are these mixtures such as our own Saladini visually appealing, and an exciting medley of complementary flavours, but I've always felt they were extraordinarily economic. Time and again I'm convinced there is not enough in the garden for a decent salad, especially in winter, yet by picking a leaf here and another there, suddenly a salad of sufficiency had been gathered. The oriental vegetables I studied after the original *Salad Garden* was written proved the ideal candidates for salad mixtures. It gives me great satisfaction now to see, in many supermarkets, packs of salad which I suspect have evolved from the old *mesclun* and the Oriental Saladini I launched with Suffolk Herbs. Only a few weeks ago I was talking to some of the Waitrose supermarket buyers, persuading them of the merits of oriental vegetables. So if you chance upon crunchy radish seed pods, spicy radish seedlings or delicious pea shoots in a supermarket in the near or distant future, I might have had a hand in it. (All, of course, are easily grown at home.)

Closely linked with the mixed salads is the idea of cut-and-come-again crops – all those leafy things that can be cut carefully when a few inches high, at their most tasty and nutritious, and will often resprout to give lots more cuttings. Wonderfully productive and a boon to people who are short of space. The idea of growing seedlings for salads is very old – even lemon and orange pips were sprouted in the seventeenth century – and this can be done on a windowsill. It has endless potential: only this autumn Unwins Seeds launched their Kitchen Crop kits of edible seedlings. My favourites were red cabbage and carrot seedlings – neither of which I had grown before to eat at this stage.

So there's always more to be discovered about what can be grown for salads. In the last few years I've done several trials with members of the kale family, often sowing them in my polytunnel in September for winter and spring crops of cut-and-come-again seedlings. Tuscan

kale, 'Redbor' kale (beautiful but perhaps just a little tough), and the thin-leaved 'Hungry Gap' and 'Pentland Brig' kales have all found favour – and hence a spot in *The Organic Salad Garden*.

Lastly, my chef friend Ken Toyé helped me update the recipes for this new edition, adapting them to a more weight-conscious public and adding a few for the new salad crops. I hope the book will encourage a whole new generation of kitchen gardeners to grow their own salads.

ON TOMATOES
'Just Vegetating', *The Kitchen Garden*, June 2005

Never before have I picked the last tomatoes from the previous season on the day I started sowing the new crop. It was 6 March – and the last two tomatoes, clinging to a bedraggled, leafless stem, still had flavour. It's an unexpected bonus from our mild West Cork climate that greenhouse tomato plants, provided they remain healthy, keep on growing and fruiting till very late in the season.

It wasn't until our second Irish season that we started growing tomatoes. We grew them in the greenhouse and outside, though from what I'd heard from other gardeners, I didn't have high hopes of success outdoors. Summers can be grey and windy with high humidity. But we were lucky. That summer was a scorcher, and they did well.

Number one enemy here – as in the rest of the British Isles – is tomato/potato blight. It thrives in maritime conditions, and with neighbouring farmers growing potatoes, there's a high risk of infection.

I'm a great believer in putting up a barrier against the airborne blight spores, so that first crop of outdoor tomatoes was surrounded with a 1m/over-3ft-high barrier of Monarflex UV

Sheeting, a heavy-duty, fairly rigid, transparent plastic which is easily battened to wooden posts. There's no pretending it keeps off blight permanently: it is a delaying tactic. But the delay enables you to get a better crop than would otherwise be possible. Blight eventually struck in the greenhouse, but by regularly removing infected leaves plants continued cropping into the New Year.

A brief digression. In our northern Europe climate I've never gone along with the popular conception that outdoor tomatoes always taste better than the same varieties grown indoors. Quite the reverse in some years.

The real hope for conquering blight for us organic gardeners lies in using blight-resistant tomatoes, and 2003 was the first year I'd grown the much-vaunted French-bred variety 'Ferline' F_1, a solid-fruited 'Marmande' type with reputedly high resistance to blight. I was very impressed. Repeated trials in 2004, a much 'blightier' year, bore this out. Here's a note I wrote to Kitchen Garden editor Andrew on 6 October: 'Full marks to 'Ferline' in its second year. Still OK outdoors when everything else is blackened and browned with blight. Still picking wonderfully tasty toms from the greenhouse.' It made me realize what a debt we gardeners owe to the enterprise of plant breeders, who bring us these improved varieties.

Which takes me to Torre del Greco, south of Naples, and passionate Italian tomato breeder Mario Mennella of mfm International. We first met Mario in 1977 on our Grand Vegetable Tour, and last September he and his wife invited us back to see his tomatoes, an irresistible invitation.

For many years a flower breeder, Mario turned to tomatoes in 1989 when he realized that the local tomatoes were being taken over by American varieties. He likens plant breeding to a musician combining notes to create new music. He starts by imagining a certain type of tomato, visualizes the qualities it needs, takes the germplasm from his 400 lines of tomatoes, thinks 'this will go with that', combines it accordingly . . . and with luck, eventually breeds the perfect tomato for the purpose in mind.

He specializes in cherry tomatoes, industrial tomatoes (the long solid type used for canning, typified by 'San Marzano', which originated 30 kilometres/18 miles inland) and fresh tomatoes. These include green ones – highly valued in Sicily – and pink varieties, which Mario feels can be the best flavoured of all. Then there are the yellows.

Mario's breeding work starts in his 'pyjama trials', the trial ground right behind the house so often visited in pyjamas! Here, surrounded by palms, edible cactus and bougainvillea, in the shadow of Mount Vesuvius and benefiting from the rich lava soil, are rows and rows of parent lines and trial crosses. On our end-of-season visit the picturesque scene was completed by two nuns picking the surplus fruit for their orphanage.

Meanwhile the seed was being harvested. The ripe tomatoes are put in buckets, pulverized with an electric beater, then left in their juice to ferment for forty-eight hours before being washed through a sieve. Finally they are dried in a heavily shaded glasshouse in neat little piles, each eventually bundled in windbreak net. Each carefully coded and labelled bundle is a 'treasure' in Mario's eyes. One plant can produce about 20 gm/¾oz of seed, but it takes about 1kg/2.2lb to do trials of a new variety all over the world.

As is well known, the original tomatoes to emerge from the American tropics in the sixteenth century were yellow: hence their early name, *pomodoro* (golden apples). Long overshadowed by reds, yellows are fighting back and are now all the rage in California, especially with organic farmers. European breeders are hugely excited by them. Yellow tomatoes have very little lycopene, which gives red tomatoes their colour and reputedly the acidity which exacerbates arthritis.

One day a yellow 'San Marzano' turned up in Mario's breeding programme, and with the resulting varieties he has pioneered the canning of yellow tomatoes with a local organic processor, is experimenting with bottling and juicing yellows, and has persuaded a well-known Sorrento restaurant to make its classical fish soup with yellow, instead of red tomatoes. His variety 'Yellow Punch' is a bush variety with firm plum-type fruits turning slightly orange when ripe; it keeps well on the bush for many weeks. Another yellow curiosity in the pyjama trials was an apple-like variety, with exceptional firmness and durability. It may one day become a naturally 'long-life' variety.

The last word goes to another type of long-life tomato. Hanging in the Mennella kitchen, and under cover beside the outdoor barbecue, were tight clusters of gleaming, plum-shaped tomatoes for winter use. *Spongillo*, I think they are called locally. In an old Vesuvius tradition, the bunches

Left: the late Mario Mennella, tomato breeder, in his beloved 'pyjama trials' in the shadow of Mount Vesuvius. Right: nuns picking the surplus tomatoes at the end of the season.

are twisted around in a U-shape and with some varieties, can be up to 1m/over 3ft long. When the fruits mature and turn red water is withheld: the resulting stress makes them hang on the stem rather than dropping off. Mario's variety 'Pendolino' can keep for about eight months, until May with luck, 'bringing the sun of summer into winter'. The tomatoes wouldn't, of course, have the flavour of fresh tomatoes, but are used in cooking. Mario made us a lovely bruschetta from them on our last evening.

In the Puglia region local yellow varieties are used for this purpose, and Colin Simpson, of Simpson's Seeds, tells me that they had success with the variety 'Yellow Butterfly': 'We hung trusses in the office and picked right through winter.'

Stop press: one of Mario's varieties, 'Maxantia', is currently in trials for reputed anti-carcinogenic properties.

ON THE DILEMMAS AND VAGARIES OF SEED SOWING
'Just Vegetating', *The Kitchen Garden*, August 2005

I've always envied decisive people, the sort who say, 'Right, I'll sow parsnips outside today.' Instead here's the sort of dialogue I'm likely to have with myself:

'It's such a nice day. Should I sow parsnips outside?'

'Better not, the weather could still turn nasty.'

'But it's April.'

'Yes, but there's been a lot of rain and wind and the soil's still cold. Didn't you make three sowings last year before you had any success outdoors?'

'Well, that could have been the seed.'

'But you did that germination test and germination was virtually 100 per cent indoors.'

So I close the argument with, 'Then I'd better sow indoors and prick them out into modules to be on the safe side, though it does seem a lot of work for parsnips.'

And after all that dithering I'm quite likely to sow one lot in the garden and another indoors, to be on the safe side. Just for the record, my first outdoor sowing this year was on 2 April, with seed that I had tested indoors because it was a year old and there was virtually 100 per cent germination.

So I confidently sowed outside. But they didn't come through. I blame the cold spring winds, which desiccated the soil and made it 'cap', which can be fatal for emerging seedlings. So I resowed in modules in early May. With hindsight, I should have painstakingly pricked out the germinated seeds after the earlier test (see below) either into a seed tray or, better still, into small modules, for planting out as young seedlings. Still, we're lucky here in West Cork. With our fertile, well-drained soil and high light intensity, parsnips grow fast once the winds abate. We've had fine crops from May sowings.

One of the commonest dilemmas facing gardeners is whether to risk sowing old seed. Wastage goes against the grain, but has to be balanced against the waste of time, space, and resources such as propagator, greenhouse space and prepared garden soil, if the seed proves duff.

There are so many factors affecting seed viability – that almost mystical ability to remain fresh and to germinate. Quite apart from significant inherent differences, how the seed is stored has a noticeable effect, and even the conditions under which it was harvested. We can't do anything about that, but keeping seed cool and dry is very important. The ideal is an airtight tin with silica gel crystals in it to absorb moisture. Keeping seed in damp sheds and hot kitchens is never advisable, and I'm always wary of buying seed from garden centres, shops or street stalls if I see the sun has been beating down on the seed rack.

But there are mysteries. Take peas. A seedsman with many years' experience of peas told me that they can remain viable for up to eight years, but viability starts to fall off after three years, especially for the wrinkle-seeded types. Last year, 2004, I had abysmal results with sowing two lots of 2002 seed, but good germination from much older seed dating from 1998. And a while back I germinated the purple-seeded dun pea after keeping it for twelve years. So you can never presume anything.

Another thing I have learned is not to blame the seed if it fails to show. Give it a second chance. This year I was on the verge of chucking out lettuce and pea seed, neither of which had germinated (indoors) first time round, but got good germination when I tried again. What went wrong the first time? Who knows? Something in the compost? Drying out at a critical stage? Temperature too high or too low?

If in doubt, do a germination test. I put samples on moist paper in little foil dishes, into a propagator at about 20°C/68°F. I usually cover them with kitchen foil, to keep them dark and conserve moisture – unless they are types which require light to germinate, such as celery.

I try to sow a round number, so it is easy to work out the percentage which germinate. In most cases, if they haven't germinated within a couple of weeks, or less than 35–40 per cent have germinated, you're better off buying fresh seed. After all, germination is going to be far lower in garden soil outdoors.

Of course, if they do germinate you then have the task of transferring these fragile-looking germinated seeds, desperately clinging to their base of paper towelling, into seed trays or modules. They usually germinate in twos and threes, and I dither again over whether to transfer them when they have virtually just sprouted, so less damage is likely but there's almost nothing to get hold of, or to wait until the gossamer roots are a little more substantial but probably more vulnerable.

I tend to opt for the latter and gently 'flood' the paper towelling so that the roots 'float' free, and pick them up with a sharp point, sometimes even on the tip of a broken shard of glass, to transfer them into a tiny hole made with a miniature dibber in sowing or potting compost. It is rewarding when the seedlings peep through a few days later. Seed and time have both been saved.

In my early days as a garden writer I remember talking to the late Jim Unwin, of Unwins Seeds, about customers' complaints. He said they got more complaints about French bean germination than anything else.

Yet when they sowed them themselves, the seeds were fine. They'd just been sown in the wrong conditions.

French beans cannot tolerate cold damp soil and poor weather: they just rot. Far better to delay until the soil is warm. But we gardeners are impatient creatures with itchy fingers. My itchy fingers have led to so many French bean failures that nowadays I almost always sow them indoors in 5–7cm/2–3in modules, currently in Fertile Fibre multipurpose compost, for planting out when the time is ripe – after hardening off well.

Now that's a link in the chain that can go wrong and where it's tempting to cut corners. Plants raised indoors are exceptionally soft and really do need to be gradually acclimatized to tougher conditions before being planted out in the open. Ideally this should be done over two or three weeks, but in the bedlam of spring sowings I rarely remember to note when I first put a tray outside.

I'm lucky in our new place. There's a low stone wall with a flat slate top right outside the greenhouse which is ideal for hardening off; plus a bit of ground between greenhouse and wall where plants can be put for a little more protection in the early stages. It's a quick operation to put them out in the morning and back at night – provided you remember.

Earlier this year I forgot to bring in my cabbages one night. They were January-sown summer and red cabbage, beautiful little plants. As luck would have it, it was a nasty night. The next morning they looked dreadful – limp, bent over, some of the stems cracked. They looked at me reproachfully; my sense of guilt was overwhelming. They eventually recovered, but it took a while.

My hardening off area is deceptively idyllic. I've several times failed to notice, especially during the later leave-them-out-all-the-time stage, that seedlings were disappearing. Lifting up the trays I would find a fat slug or snail beneath, replete and sleeping soundly during the day. I add to the problem by standing small pots in seed trays lined with plastic to prevent them drying out, and damp plastic is a magnet to slugs and snails. Now I compulsively lift seed and module trays any time I'm passing and peer beneath.

I don't know why I don't follow my own advice and adopt the Japanese 'stroking' technique instead of moving plants in and out. With a piece of paper or cardboard, and sometimes a special brush, they brush seedlings back and forth, twice a day, for about a minute a time. It 'bashes' the plants as much as exposure to the elements and saves all the moving. Perhaps I have that old-fashioned feeling that 'fresh air does them good'. Or if I'm honest I just enjoy the activity – handling all those seedlings first thing on a beautiful morning and last thing at night – like putting children to bed.

I'll end with a long-nurtured, probably out-of-character, plea for standardization. Why do plant pots come in so many shapes, making it impossible to stack them in satisfying little pyramids? I recently washed twenty small, square, black pots. There were thirteen different patterns! That's worse than the orphanage of unmatching navy and black socks I'm harbouring upstairs. We need a national sock day in which lost socks can be reunited with their like and a pot swap day for gardeners.

P.S Just after finishing this article I discovered why I gave up brushing seedlings. Global warming went into remission here, and we had three days of exceptionally damaging vicious east winds. There was no way the seedlings, being hardened off, could have been put back outside. So I started stroking them. It takes forever, because you can only do one 'arm's stretch' at a time. Great for small numbers, I'd say.

Tessa Traeger's portrait of me with a garlic flower stem, taken in our polytunnel for the National Portrait Galley's exhibition of gardeners, The Gardener's Labyrinth. *Photographers love the diffuse light created by the cloudy polythene film.*

9 NEW CENTURY, NEW GARDEN

How fast the first decade of the twenty-first century has flown! Had I really been writing about vegetables for over thirty-five years when it began – forty-five years now? As the various economic crises deepened, so the interest in vegetables increased, giving me a chance to update all the books I had written. After *The Salad Garden* became *The Organic Salad Garden* in 2001, a much enlarged *Vegetables for Small Gardens* became *Grow Your Own Vegetables* in 2002, followed by new editions of *Oriental Vegetables* and *Creative Vegetable Gardening* in 2007 and 2008.

A consequence of being around a long time, and your erstwhile scorned subject acquiring fashion status, is the 'Can I come and interview you?' syndrome. As a life-long journalist, I hate being interviewed. I hate the almost invariably obvious questions, which elicit parrot-like replies. I don't really like telling other people about my garden so that they can write about it; I'd rather write about it myself. But worst of all are the unending requests for 'sound bites': 'your ten top tips', 'five favourite plants', 'why old people enjoy gardening?', 'what plants have you killed?' features . . . Cheap copy for editors, totally undemanding material for readers, I mutter, as I grumpily perform yet again, on the assumption that some publicity is better than no publicity. And the nightmare of being photographed, dreaded from 'straight hair and National Health glasses teenager' onwards. That paralysing woodenness when a lens hoves into view. How do other people know what to do with their hands and look natural? And who wants to be photographed as they stumble into old age? Where can you hide all those chins?

There have been exceptions. I was thrilled to be one of the gardeners photographed by Tessa Traeger for the 2002 National Portrait Gallery exhibition *A Gardener's Labyrinth*. The gallery even used the Joan of Arc-like silhouette of me holding a flowering garlic stem for the exhibition invitations. My only pin-up moment. (The chin problem was solved by looking skyward, but there were fewer chins then.) In 2005, I was one of the 'heroes' in the BBC *British Gardening Heroes* TV series, programmes that took time to capture the personality and life's work of the seven participants. We really enjoyed the filming at Donaghmore, with a sensitive crew and interviewer perched for hours on our stairs, even if Don and I had to collect seaweed on the beach again, and again, and again – until in playful frustration Don thrust a forkful of smelly seaweed almost into my face, and of course that was the take they used. A good experience, too, was being interviewed for the British Library Oral Archive on gardeners, which took several days and delved back to wartime childhood. Some day I'll go and listen to what I said. Another high spot in the decade was the Lifetime Achievement Award from the Garden Writers' Guild: nothing is as heart-warming as being honoured by your peers. A bonus was the prize money of £200, almost exactly the sum needed to pay for the evergreen holm oak hedge I had surreptitiously ordered to plant behind my new herbaceous borders. We'd spent so much on windbreaks and trees that this was a guilty extravagance. Now I felt I had earned it, and what a fabulous backdrop it has become!

So to 'the last chapter' – Donaghmore. All our married lives we had talked of moving to Ireland. Years ago, attracted by those drifts of fertile seaweed on the western beaches, we mulled over the possibilities of growing vegetables for hotels and restaurants. Life swept us along on a different course. So it wasn't until our mid-sixties, retirement beckoning, that we uprooted ourselves and moved to West Cork. We found a farmhouse in a beautiful spot near the sea, and in the years since have been totally engrossed in creating a new garden on the windswept, almost bare site. It's been a wonderfully rewarding experience, the satisfaction multiplied a hundredfold by the appreciative interest in what we have done by neighbours and the people of West Cork, many embracing gardening for the first time.

Congratulations from Alan Titchmarsh after I was awarded the Garden Writers' Guild Lifetime Achievement Award in 2003.

Making Donaghmore's garden has played such a huge part in our lives in this last decade that I feel compelled to share the story, so here it is, albeit in shortened form. Our early experiences, and tackling the crucial windbreak fence, are based on 'A Clean Slate' and 'Batten Down the Hatches', articles written for *Kitchen Garden* and *Weekend Telegraph* respectively. Subsequent progress is telescoped into 'What Happened Next'. Other writing in the 2000s is represented by a miscellany of articles and even a couple of the dreaded sound bites. 'A Nomadic Good Life' is a slightly shortened version of my opening contribution to a debate on 'The Good Life' at the Garden History Museum exhibition in 2009, while 'The Writer in the Garden' was my entry to a joint British Library/RHS competition, associated with the 2004 'The Year of the Garden' exhibition. It didn't get anywhere, but I felt it distilled the essence of being a garden writer.

A CLEAN SLATE
The Kitchen Garden, February 2003

15.8.02 FIRST PEAS. Yes, that diary entry was in capitals, reflecting our excitement and undiluted joy at the first fruits (botanically speaking) from our new garden. We'd had lots of cut-and-come-again salad and spinach leaves by then, but those first peas, sown in early May, marked a milestone.

In early April we had said goodbye to Montrose Farm in Suffolk, where we had gardened for well over thirty years, and moved to West Cork in southern Ireland. With retirement (of sorts) ahead, we had downsized from 0.75 hectares/2 acres to 0.2 hectares/½ acre, exchanging a pancake-flat garden for a gentle slope, and one crammed with established fruit and vegetables, with a huge polytunnel and handy propagation house, for what was essentially a bare field. We were starting again with a clean slate.

Donaghmore Farmhouse, our new home, is a traditional, south-facing Irish farmhouse set comfortably halfway down a hill only 700 metres/½ mile from the sea. The sea lies to the south and west, hidden from sight by the hill and the lie of the land, but on stormy nights and in the aftermath of storms we hear its thundering – strangely like the roar of a motorway. Most of the garden can be seen from the house – a lawn and a couple of stone-edged flower beds near by, and beyond, the small field where I plan to make a fan-shaped potager. In addition there's a 10m/33ft-wide strip of land alongside the house and outbuildings on the west side, the buildings framing a courtyard. For years I've hankered for a courtyard. A dream fulfilled? We're planning to build a greenhouse linking the house and stables.

The soil, climate and situation are very different from our East Anglian garden. There we had a heavy, cold, poorly drained clay soil, though years of working in manure and compost had made it rich and fertile. The soil here is light, alkaline, remarkably well drained and fertile – there is valuable farmland all around – but in places it is only a thin layer above the slatey subsoil. As we have only dug a few beds so far, we have much to learn about it. This is the first time I've gardened on light soil, and I still marvel at how easy it is to hand weed. Just a light touch and up they come – couch grass and docks excepted.

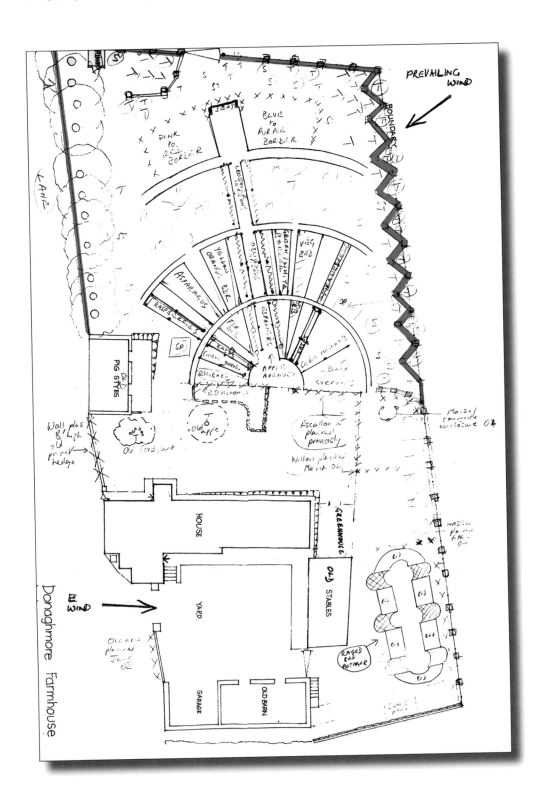

The maritime climate is benign. Frosts – certainly prolonged or severe frosts – are rare, they say. Yet the minimum temperature fell to 2°C/37°F on 23 October, so I hope they're right. As for the annual rainfall, it could easily be double the 50cm/20in or so we were used to in East Anglia. Our first May here was the coldest and wettest for something like twenty years and October was the wettest on record. Friends and neighbours continually apologize for our rude introduction to the area. But, as so often near the coast, rainy squalls seem to hop over us and fall inland. My hunch is that in the long term we are going to complain more about drought than wet. We shall see. But I'm avoiding the real issue – the wind. Now that should be in capitals.

It's the Atlantic out there, and there's nothing between us and Boston, 3,218 kilometres/2,000 miles or so away. The whole of our garden is exposed to the south-west wind. And as if that wasn't enough, it funnels through farm gates into the courtyard of my dreams, becoming a whirlwind of unimaginable maliciousness. This wind is a vandal, knocking off twigs and flowers, decapitating trees. Back in October it uprooted a maturing 'Romanesco' cauliflower, dumping it unceremoniously on the grass.

The few trees in the immediate vicinity tell the story. The ageing sycamores along our top boundary form a 45-degree silhouette: the lowest on the windward side offers some protection to its neighbour, which therefore grows slightly taller, giving a little protection to its neighbour and so on. These sycamores, and their ageing brethren on our eastern boundary, were almost completely defoliated by a storm in late May. To my amazement they had produced a second crop of leaves a month later. The branches on an elder in the hedge were burnt black, to a depth of almost 60cm/2ft, by that May storm, illustrating clearly that the winds are laden with salt. While the prevailing wind is from the south-west, at times a vicious, albeit less salt-laden wind attacks us from the east, and there's the north wind as well. The garden, however, is less exposed on the east and north, sheltered to some extent by the house itself, aided by a mighty privet hedge near the house. Privet deserves more recognition for its ability to withstand salt-laden wind.

So our gardening lives are dominated by the necessity to erect and grow windbreaks. And how we appreciate the calm days: THEY get capital letter entries in the diary!

While wind is enemy number one, slugs are a close second. I'm very conscious that embarking on slug stories is like asking visitors what their journey was like and ten minutes later regretting the enquiry. But sorry, I can't resist. The year 2002 was a horrendous slug year for us all: they were literally front-page news. But in my traumatized state after our move (I couldn't bear to think about gardening for at least six weeks), I was slow to appreciate what a force slugs were going to be at Donaghmore. The following, not in any logical order, are some of the thoughts, notes and observations accumulated during the first six months' campaign against Donaghmore's slugs.

- Realized there was a problem in May. Seedlings sown in modules were disappearing after germination. Lifted module tray and found numerous slugs and snails beneath. Decided night patrols necessary.
- Reverted to old technique of collecting by torchlight. Using beer cans with water in the bottom so that the can remains upright if put into the ground, leaving hands free to collect. Slugs popped into hole at top. In spring/early summer here still light at 11.00 p.m. Had to explain to (teetotal) farming neighbours, meeting us beer cans in hand, we're not alcoholics.

- Soon realized extent of slug population. In early days beer can often crammed solid with slugs. Literally no room for more. Started counting while collecting – out of curiosity and to relieve boredom. Rarely turned in before reaching 100; not infrequently 200.
- Extraordinary diversity of slugs – from 'little grey jobs' to sinister sturdy humpback blacks and greys, to large blacks, to long lean greenish-brown mottled ones. Different types predominant in different parts of garden: i.e. lots of large blacks in longish grass at foot of stone-edged bed; green/brown mottled numerous on old stone steps to ruined barn and close to house; humpy ones nearest neighbouring field; small greys ubiquitous.
- Largest obviously easiest to find: noticeably fewer by autumn.
- Where are they coming from? Answer 1. Stone walls. Up earlier than normal one morning, went to spot where I'm nurturing a slug-prone fem, and saw numerous slugs beating for cover in adjacent wall. Just in time to prise a few backwards out of cracks. Any loose stone serves as slug sanctuary. Long-term plan is to build raised veg. beds of stone. Must be well and truly mortared so no hiding places. Answer 2: Grass. Our bare field a vast reservoir of slugs. Visualize it as the maquis where guerillas hide until darkness gives cover to emerge and attack. Must keep grass mown much more closely near beds. (Heard of gardener here who mows at dusk to catch the emerging hordes. Sympathize.) Lot to be said for surrounding veg. beds with gravel.
- Is temperature critical? Early on realized warm nights meant more large slugs, fewer 'standard' ones. First found thousands on grass on morning when ambient temperature about 13°C/55°F. Was staggered at numbers

out and about in broad daylight. Following day about a degree warmer, and not a daytime slug in sight.
- Snails like it pitch black. One very dark night found far more snails than normal and noticed same again when similarly dark about a month later.
- Are slugs carnivorous? Several times found snail bodies (? originally crushed by me or birds), with crowds of slugs converging on them to feed. Suspect the very large slugs are carnivorous – though that doesn't stop them eating vegetation too.
- Are slugs territorial? Most nights find say about twelve on pak choi rows or circle of 'Little Gem' lettuce, three on globe artichoke and so on. Over a week collect seven times that number on those plants. Why aren't they all there at once? Do first arrivals send out vibes saying 'my patch for the night'? If first arrivals 'despatched', have a new crowd moved in by 2.00 a.m.?
- Reflections on mulching. Alerted to downside of mulching when realized small pile of hay was hotbed of sluggery. Equally numerous under any plastic mulches. In early dry spell mulched all new plantings; mulching lifetime habit and organic gardening mantra. But undoubtedly encourages slugs here. Need to rethink?
- The numbers game. October calculations. Have collected for at least 5 months, i.e. approximately 150 days, at least 100 a day (conservative estimate as husband Don doesn't count his catch), i.e. total of 15,000 – and still more there! Just before starting to write this (writers grasp at any means of procrastination), decided on a morning swoop as no slug hunting during two previous nights of high winds and torrential rain. Quickly collected well over 200, including masses under recently cleared

mulching mats. Two hours later popped out to check something, decided on a second peep under mulching mats and collected another 50! No-win situation? Don't think so. There are encouraging signs. It's taking longer to collect 100, there are far fewer monsters and middle-sized slugs, and more tiny, recently hatched ones, so we're making inroads on the next generation. The main lesson I've learned is to delay planting until seedlings or plants are a reasonable size and can withstand some slug damage, coupled with extra vigilance in the early stages, especially with susceptible plants like lettuces, globe artichokes, pak choi and other brassicas.

Enough of slugs. Optimism prevails. We fell in love with the house and its situation and took pot luck on the garden. We have been lucky: it could have been pure rock or worse, bog. That would take us far more years, and much more energy, to tame. Moreover, we inherited a huge heap of muck and there is wonderful seaweed neatly deposited on a beach less than ten minutes away. In fact, it's a gorgeous day, it's low tide, I must sign off and go and get some!

Don at work collecting fresh seaweed from nearby Ballinglanna beach, where it piles up after a south-west wind. We put it straight on the beds as a mulch.

BATTEN DOWN THE HATCHES
Saturday Telegraph, 21 February 2004

It was obvious from the outset that unless we put up or grew windbreaks to tame the wind, we would never make the garden of our dreams. In those early months we became windbreak bores. We talked about windbreaks, read about windbreaks, visited windswept gardens and sought advice on posts (concrete or wood?), nets and fabrics, trees and hedges which tolerate salt and wind and alkaline soil, planting distances, planting patterns and so on. Friends drew me diagrams of wind flows. I bought a hand-held anemometer.

Meanwhile the outline of our dream garden was taking shape in our minds. The relatively narrow piece of ground alongside the house, averaging 6m/20ft wide, was the easiest to shelter so would be the main vegetable garden and the immediate priority. In the larger, far more exposed ground in front of the house (very roughly 30m/100ft square) the long-

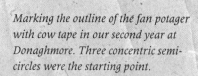

Marking the outline of the fan potager with cow tape in our second year at Donaghmore. Three concentric semi-circles were the starting point.

term plan was to make a fan-shaped 'potager' of fruit, flowers and perennial vegetables. The ribs of the fan would be rows of soft fruit and hopefully apples, trained as cordons and espaliers, so that they could be protected with short parallel windbreaks. The potager would be surrounded with a shelter belt of trees and shrubs, underplanted with naturalized bulbs. Everything depended on establishing shelter.

We started by planting Rugosa roses on the bank along the lane, hopefully filling gaps between the sycamores. Our farming neighbour appeared with several gigantic used tyres to slip over the young plants: two or three tiers give good protection. Later he reappeared with wooden pallets, and we discovered how upended pallets make excellent temporary, even semi-permanent, windbreaks, easily anchored by driving poles down the centre.

Our early attempts at erecting windbreaks on the west flank of the vegetable garden were amateurish, banging in 4.5 × 4.5cm/3 × 3in posts and battening on old netting windbreak. Underlying stones impeded progress (we eventually learned to make an initial hole with a heavy metal bar), inquisitive neighbouring cows took a fancy to the net, and when winds struck the posts keeled and the net sagged. To save the day we grew our first vegetables under low hoop tunnels, covered with Enviromesh netting.

The first permanent shelter was a drystone wall along the northern boundary of the vegetable garden, beautifully built by stonemason Henry FitzGerald, using stone from our ruined barn. The heat radiating from that wall was blissful.

In winter, bearing in mind local advice to 'make it as strong as humanly possible', we started on the perimeter windbreak fence. Its purpose was to protect the trees and shrubs we would plant for the shelter belt and hedges.

We opted for a 1.9m/6ft-high fence of square, treated, softwood 15 × 7.5cm/6 × 3in posts, 2.4m/8ft long, concreted into the ground to a depth of 60cm/2ft. These hefty posts were 2.4m/8ft apart, each with three cross pieces to which windbreak net was battened. Alongside the vegetable garden the fence was straight, but it zigzagged unconventionally down the western side, clad with immensely strong black Nicofence, an almost wire-like net. Whispers reached our ears that the zigzag was the subject of discussion in the local pub.

Where did I get this idea of a zigzag fence? An escape from straight lines? Possibly. (It has an intriguing concertina profile from above.) A super-strong construction? Yes. Probably above all I was convinced it offered an increase

Early planting in the zigzag windbreak, which offered exceptional strength and increased shelter against the prevailing wind, as well as making an interesting pattern.

in shelter, not just from shifting winds, but because of the calm spot you seem to get, right up against a windbreak on the windward side. Surely, given help, trees could grow there?

In recent strong winds, armed with anemometer, I found that winds gusting to 20mph in open ground were reduced to 10mph within the zigzag. What I hadn't foreseen was how those outside trees would be protected from the east wind, which set in, with unexpected viciousness, the moment we had the south-west windbreak completed. The inner row of zigzag posts, incidentally, is 1.9m/6ft away from the outer.

Countless telephone hours went into sourcing the posts and net. I was still struggling with the local lingo, as doubtless they were with mine. A hot tip led us to what seemed to be a chemist's shop for the Nicofence net, word of mouth into finding Cronin Danjoe Highland Fencing to do the job . . . 'but probably not until after Christmas'. They would hire a local mini digger to make the holes. We lined up 4 tons of gravel for the concrete mix, bags of cement, pounds of galvanized nails – and dismantled our rough-and-ready windbreak. On the foggiest of December days, before Christmas, they appeared. The promised digger was unavailable, so they brought an extra man – a club bouncer by night – instead. A happy accident: the smaller

holes dug by hand required less concrete, and we would have run out of gravel.

What a magnificent job they did, breaking up rock with a metal bar, digging the holes with the long tapering blade of the Irish spade, manoeuvring posts around the trees we'd already planted, carefully setting the 'zigzag' posts at an angle. They got in half the posts the first day. The next day brought torrential rain, but there they were, in ocean-going rain gear, to finish the job and attach the windbreak. Don helped sawing battens to size, and at the end of the day, holding the torch. We appreciated their skills even more when we tackled the outstanding bits of netting ourselves, and, months later, concreted in a few posts for the final windbreak strip separating the potager and vegetable garden.

One problem remained: two 3.6m/12ft-wide, five-bar farm gates to the garden created wicked wind funnels. There is no simple way of battening windbreak net to metal bars. So we got hold of the rigid polythene windbreak we had used as ventilation panels in our old polytunnel, and using mason's line threaded through a bodkin, tied it through the ventilation holes to the gate bars.

We're keeping our fingers crossed. As all our neighbours keep telling us, we haven't seen a real storm yet!

DONAGHMORE: WHAT HAPPENED NEXT

The hefty posts and severe black net of the windbreak looked stark that first winter, softened only by two clumps of young Italian alders we had planted in spring. Fast growing, pretty, highly recommended, what an excellent choice they were! 'Our wood' we called them as we looked down on their youthful tops. Now they tower over us.

Deciding what else to plant in the shelter belt was daunting. I nearly wore out my new *Hillier Manual* searching for trees and shrubs that were wind and salt resistant, and would tolerate our surprisingly alkaline soil, look nice and require little upkeep. 'You want a thicket', we were told by people who had established gardens in exposed sites. So we aimed for three to four staggered rows, with the toughest trees on the outside, and the more tender, shrubbier species closest to the garden. We mixed evergreens, deciduous trees and conifers, including plenty with decorative berries, bark, blossom or fruits. As hedges would mean upkeep, the only hedge initially was olearia, planted on two sides of the vegetable strip. (We had to remind ourselves this was a retirement garden, and hedges could reach monstrous proportions in this fertile soil and mild climate.) The holm oak behind the herbaceous borders came later.

During that first dormant season we planted over seventy trees and shrubs, usually two or three of each. Nine years on the original windbreak is still rock solid, but almost invisible. The diversity of the shelter belt is a continual joy, and from late January onwards there is a gorgeous sequence of daffodils, mostly shorter, wind-resistant varieties, given to our young garden by Taylor Bulbs that first spring.

Meanwhile another dream was being realized. We sorely missed the polytunnels and greenhouse we had left behind. What could be done? The only practical spot for a tunnel would obscure the recently built stone wall. How about linking the house and old stables, and closing the wind funnelling gap between them, with a purpose-built greenhouse? We consulted builders and friends. They shook their heads gravely at the awkward discrepancies in height and pitch of the neighbouring roofs. Not so Malcolm Rowley. He surveyed the scene and pronounced it 'do-able', and several wintry months later we had a beautiful 6 × 4.6m/20 × 15ft galvanized steel greenhouse, nearly 3.5m/11½ft high at the ridge. Built from imported steel and glass from dismantled Dutch greenhouses, it was wonderfully strong, as it had to be, facing into the south-west gales. Drawing on Malcolm's skills and creativity, we incorporated all sorts of practical features. As Malcolm lived a fair distance away he often stayed the night, and I got a free ventilator for every night's 'B&B'. What a bargain for a ventilation-hungry organic gardener! In due course Malcolm built two brick-edged raised beds. The central bed had a wide end to double as a seat, while the bed against the house gable had rounded corners, making it easier to manoeuvre barrows, and 'Joy's bites', indents enabling me to reach the wall for picking and tying. We diverted water from the central gutter into an internal tank, made a propagator to fit my standard seed trays, a potting bench with a gap for sweeping out debris, and handy shelves for pots and trays, and laid slate tiles on the floor and staging. Best of all, the house was threaded with sturdy straining wires in every direction – the stuff of gardener's dreams.

With the artificial windbreak in place and shelter belt planted, the scene was set for our biggest project: making a potager on the slope in front of our house. The moment I set eyes on our future garden a vision of the Munach Community's herb garden in Denmark, which we had visited a few years previously, sprang into my mind. In that magical garden bands of herbs, each a colour of the rainbow spectrum, radiated across a sloping field in three sweeping arcs, the bands outlined by low hedges of blue willow stretching up the field. Munach was our inspiration, but on our much smaller site, the rainbow became a simpler fan, its 'spokes' windbreaks alongside cordoned soft fruit. And up the centre we created 'apple alley', fourteen varieties of apples, trained as cordons and espaliers, with windbreak net on either side. The rainbow colours morphed into four flower borders. At the top the fan opens out into a pair of herbaceous borders — essentially blue and silver on one side, pinks, reds and purples on the other. In the semi-circle arc below a pie-shaped yellow and bronze bed on the east is matched by a green, white and variegated bed on the west. 'Naff', an eminent garden designer recently remarked to me about these apparently now outdated colour concepts; but after years of concentrating on vegetables, how I've enjoyed planning and planting these beds. Naffness be damned!

Fitting between the 'spokes' of the fan are pie-shaped beds of varying sizes where we rotate vegetables, strawberries and annual flowers for cutting. One has become a prolific asparagus bed, another a rhubarb patch. Apple alley is now graced with several arches over which hops, several sorts of berries (fairly unsuccessfully) and more recently apples (much more successfully) are trained, mingling with sweet peas in summer.

As we harvest the apples, protect the gooseberries and redcurrants from birds, feast on blackcurrants, and enjoy the late 'Joan J' raspberries, we think back warmly to the gang of Rossinver Organic Centre students who,

in a couple of days, dug out those early beds. With less fondness we remember the hours spent driving in galvanized steel pipes for the windbreak supports, drilling holes for supporting wires or to bolt on timber to which we battened the windbreak net. How many drill bits did we wear out? A miracle our marriage survived.

'Don, I've had an idea.' How Don dreads those words, harbingers of hard work ahead! Raised beds were the last idea. The ground was beginning to recede (older people will know what I mean), a dodgy knee and ailing back the culprits. I had long pondered over making truly raised beds, but how to overcome the severity of bunker-like beds edged with sleepers? The clue lay in a seat overlooking Clonakilty Bay, with a little plaque stating 'made from recycled plastic' and a Cork city phone number.

And so we built a raised bed potager of tongue-and-grooved recycled plastic boards. Inexperienced handymen that we are, it took nearly five months. Perhaps it was a mistake to start on April Fool's Day. Its heart is four rectangular beds, in pairs, 3m/10ft long, 1.3m/4ft wide and 0.6m/2ft high. The boards are bolted to sturdy posts with handsome, neatly aligned, coach bolts. The quartet are 'rounded off' with a semicircular bed at each end, the outer curve of stone (elegantly built by Hendrik Lepel), the inner edges recycled plastic, with a small slate seat set in each, looking along the central grass path. Giving the potager picturesque unity (in my biased eyes), each bed is linked to its neighbour with a simple 'rebar' arch covered with chicken wire. Over this frame honeysuckles, blackberries and grey-stemmed raspberries clamber, joined in summer by 'Crown Prince' pumpkins, peering down saucily from the top of the arch, climbing French and runner beans and masses and masses of sweet peas. Top dressings of compost and seaweed keep the beds fertile, and we harvest an abundance of vegetables all year round.

It's proved a very good idea. But I've promised not to have any more – well, unless I have a brilliant idea for converting Donaghmore into a low-maintenance garden suitable for old age, my original intention. Heart ruled over head.

An 'apple alley' – of apples trained as espaliers, single and double cordons and arches – forms the backbone of the fan potager. Lines of soft fruit radiate out on either side.

The newly built raised beds made from recycled plastic, linked with simple rebor and wire arches. The arches were soon clad with fruit, climbing beans, sweet peas, gourds and honeysuckle.

BACK TO THE CHOPPING BOARD
The Garden, July 2000

There is plenty of evidence that the British are becoming more adventurous about food, cooking and the vegetables that we grow to eat, but ancient prejudices about what part of any vegetable is eaten are still firmly entrenched, I suspect. So much so that I notice a streak of one-upmanship in those who dare to be different: 'We eat beetroot leaves'; 'Have you tried broad bean tops?'; 'What about pumpkin flowers?'

And they are right, of course. All these parts are palatable. It is also true that many ordinary vegetables have potentially tasty parts that are never allowed to develop, or end up on the compost heap. I have found quite a few over the years, and here are some favourites.

Take, for example, the core in a cabbage head. It has stacks of flavour, but needs to be grated or finely sliced if it is cooked with the cabbage leaves. Ironically, modern plant breeders are making this core even smaller.

Among my favourite 'alternative bits' are radish seed pods. After being told many years ago they are widely eaten in India, I now leave some large winter radishes to run to seed in spring. One large radish root produces an enormous number of seed pods over many weeks. The pods are crisp – they must be picked while fresh and green – and vary in their heat, but many people prefer their flavour to that of normal radishes. I toss them raw into salads and stir-fries. While any cultivar can be used, in my experience the larger ones such as the Japanese *daikon* and giant overwintering types tend to produce more succulent pods. Our ancestors appear to have used them too: there is a recipe for pickled radish pods in John Evelyn's *Acetaria*, which was written in 1699. The German cultivar 'München Bier' and the heritage variety 'Rat's Tail' are summer-sown radishes that are good for pod production.

In my heavy soil the roots of salsify and scorzonera never thrive, but I now leave them for a second season to flower, and cut the buds, just before they open, with a few inches of stem attached. Steam or boil them lightly, let them cool and dress with vinaigrette. They go particularly well with smoked fish.

Blanching the young spring leaves of salsify and scorzonera is a practice deserving a revival. The easiest method is to wait until the roots sprout in spring, then cover with at least 10cm/4in of straw or dried leaves. The young shoots push through as pale 'chards' – a delicacy in salads, much like the chicons of Witloof chicory. Witloof was originally grown for its root: according to one tale, a Belgian farmer threw some into a shed one winter, only to discover them in spring, bursting into life. The naturally blanched shoots tasted good, and the Witloof chicory industry was born.

The young shoots of swedes can be forced too. I have done it under the glasshouse staging by covering the roots with black plastic film laid over wire hoops. They have a crisp texture and interesting flavour.

One of my 'discoveries' was how good the stalks of globe artichokes are. I now cut young artichokes with 8–10cm/3–4in of stem, and cook them whole. Stems have the true artichoke flavour, without all the painstaking effort required to eat the heads. I see that the *River Café Cookbook Green* uses the stems, peeled, chopped and lightly cooked with parsley and garlic, but young stems would not need peeling.

The leaves of semi-leafless peas grow as a mass of curled tendrils, which are a superb substitute for Chinese 'pea shoots'. Picked young, they have exquisite flavour, and can be used raw in salads or steamed. 'Markana' is a good cultivar for the purpose. Development of its pods is unhampered by judiciously picking the tendrils.

You can use all parts of Chinese or garlic chives (*Allium tuberosum*). In China it is grown for its garlic-flavoured leaves, used green or creamy yellow after blanching under clay pots. Other parts used are the highly flavoured flowers (to make a spicy jam) and the flowering stem, picked in bud. This is considered a great delicacy. The stems are carefully harvested. The same is true of the flower stem of garlic. In the West, we have selected garlic that does not flower, but this is not so in China. Dual-purpose garlics are favoured. Therefore, if you find your garlic bolting prematurely, cut off and savour the flowering stem. You will still get a perfectly usable garlic bulb later.

The squash family is another where we overlook edible parts – although stuffing courgette, marrow and pumpkin flowers no longer raises eyebrows. (They also make a pleasant, light soup.) In Asia the tendrils and tender shoot tips are harvested. The top 15cm/6in or so make good greens, steamed or boiled.

I had never thought of eating calabrese stems – until I went to a Taiwanese market. A group of women were industriously chopping off the calabrese heads, peeling the stems and trimming the core so that it could be pickled.

Next time I harvest it I shall see what the stems taste like.

In the huge households of the seventeenth century, ranks of frames in the walled gardens burgeoned with forced salad seedlings in spring. We should do more of this: seedlings grow fast, give high returns, and are tasty and nutritious. Turnips, mustards, broad and curled cresses, spinach, scurvy grass and radish seedlings were all used. Seedling radish is popular today in Japan, sold in punnets much like our mustard and cress. To this list of salads I would add curly endive, lettuce (especially 'Salad Bowl' types) and the oriental greens such as pak choi, mizuna and mibuna. They are superb in salads.

The last word should go to edible flowers, widely used in the past and currently in vogue again, though still considered a little daring. Besides those flowers that have a reputation for being edible – daylilies, nasturtiums, pot marigolds – there are a number of ordinary vegetables and herbs which produce flowers worth eating. Among my favourites are salad rocket, winter purslane, chives, coriander and chicory. They all add decisive flavours to mixed salads and, in the case of coriander and chives, cooked dishes. Not only do they enrich the palate, they add texture and colour to the garden. A single plant of chicory – Witloof, 'Sugar Loaf' or a red radicchio – when allowed to seed becomes a gorgeous 1.5–1.8m/5–6ft clump, the stems sparkling with clear-blue flowers over many weeks. Can you ask more of a humble vegetable?

DEAR FATHER CHRISTMAS
Garden Inspirations, December 2000

Dear Father Christmas

Please could I have an organic control for bindweed? I had a two-week holiday in June (I know that's an indictable offence for gardeners), and when I returned fruit trees, herbaceous plants and climbing vegetables were all smothered in bindweed. I had to liberate them by cutting it away with scissors. Don't tell me to use heavy mulches like carpets to control it. OK, it works to some extent, but the roots coil up beneath like a cobra ready to strike when the mulch is removed or breaks down.

If you've nothing to offer, as compensation please tell me one good use for the plants. Most weeds have medicinal value. (The Romans introduced ground elder to cure gout, and one day I may be grateful for that.) But I've never heard of a single useful thing about bindweed. No, it's not beautiful either. Beauty's in the eye of the beholder, and to this beholder those flowers are leering at me audaciously, trumpeting the fact that they've got away!

This is from a magazine issue that focused on ageing. 'High-profile' enthusiasts were asked, 'Why do people develop a passion for gardening in their later years?' I was impressed by the company I was in!

....

WHY 'OLDIES' TURN TO GARDENING
Guardian Weekend magazine, 28 October 2006

Gardening has always been part of my life, so it's never been a question of gardening more. But I'm preoccupied with how you adapt your gardening to your ageing self . . . as you become aware of it. I remember clearly the first time I had to bend down to get closer to a plant I couldn't see standing up, and that was twenty years ago. In my new garden, started in my late sixties, all the fruit trees are cordons or espaliers – easy to manage from the ground, and very productive.

I'm sure the element of escapism gets stronger. Older people have more time to think. Global warming, wars, man's inhumanity to man – the scale of the problems that face future generations can be utterly overwhelming. But gardening is a politics-free zone. Gardening and music are wonderful escapes.

I think the sense of wonder increases. I recently had a disease where, for a while, I might have lost my sight. I looked at plants then as I never have before. The intensity of colours, the patterns, the amazing changes from day to day. It's mind-blowing, as youngsters say.

You can get very set in your ways as you age, but gardening keeps you alert. I don't think I ever walk round the garden without noticing something, learning something. Perhaps, above all, that's why it remains such a joy as you get older.

A NOMADIC GOOD LIFE
Garden Museum debate on 'The Good Life', 5 October 2009,
reprinted in *The Garden Museum Journal*, spring 2010

I can remember very clearly the first time I heard the expression 'the good life' back in the 1960s. A visitor came into our Suffolk farmhouse, walked into the kitchen, looked around, and said, 'This is the good life.'

We didn't have TV and had no idea what he meant. We just thought it was a polite way of saying, 'What an untidy kitchen!' In which case we've been living the good life ever since.

Looking back, we probably were trying to lead the good life: our first real home, 0.8 hectares/2 acres of land, new baby . . .

I have to say at the outset that if 'the good life' is shorthand for trying to be self-sufficient, as I assume it is, it's a terrible misnomer.

- The good life is extremely hard.
- It leaves no time to do anything else.
- It means you go to bed exhausted every night, dreaming of bananas.

Two examples of our failed good lifery spring to mind: chickens and rose hip syrup. First, chickens. We seem to attract chickens – other people's cast-offs, typically 'divorce' chickens when households split up.

The man we bought the house from (not a question of divorce, I should make clear), left us about forty, all ages and sexes, with the parting words 'You'll have to cull the young cockerels.' This we tried to do.

At the scraggy pullet stage you can't tell the difference by looking. So, armed with the NFU (National Farmers' Union) handbook on chicken rearing, we set out to cull cockerels. You go out at dusk when they're roosting, pick them off the perch one by one, do a bit of judicious groping in the nether region and if it seems spacious down there assume it's a female. (The space is where the eggs come out later.)

We did this diligently by torchlight and found our first cockerel. Exhausted by then, Don couldn't face doing the deed, so we put the cockerel into a cage for the night. When we went out next morning . . . IT HAD LAID AN EGG!

Now rose hip syrup. As a wartime baby, I was brought up to believe the survival of the nation was due to cod liver oil, which was vile, malt, which was gorgeous, and rose hip syrup, which was deliciously sweet.

We had masses of rose hips down our Suffolk farm track. I had to make rose hip syrup. Have any of you tried to make rose hip syrup?

Well, I collected the hips, getting stung by nettles and scratched in the process, boiled them for hours, mixed them with something else, strained them and what did I get? A tiny jar of something with a very strange appearance and texture that nobody would touch.

Now perhaps it is time to be a little more serious. Over the years, we ('we' includes my husband, Don, who has always done the hard work while I get the credit) have encouraged people to grow more, to be more adventurous with what they grew and to grow organically.

The starting point, as many of you already know, was our year-long Grand Vegetable Tour in 1976 and '77, travelling round Europe with a caravan. Our kids were aged five and seven when we set out.

Why did we go? First, we wanted an excuse for an adventure and to travel together. We had both been wanderers before we got married, and various 'escape schemes', like teaching in Ethiopia or teaching Eskimos, as they were then known, had fallen through.

Second, we wanted to collect endangered

vegetable varieties. Largely due to Lawrence Hills, founder of the Henry Doubleday Research Association, there was a growing awareness of their importance, and, perhaps as a result, the national Vegetable Gene Bank was being established at Wellesbourne in Warwickshire.

Third, while writing my first book, *Vegetables from Small Gardens*, I kept hearing about intensive vegetable growing systems on the Continent, and I was curious to track them down.

I could talk all night about that year, but, apart from all we learned, about salad plants in particular, the immediate outcome was collecting seed of over 150 endangered cultivars for the gene bank, some of which have since been used in breeding.

To earn a living on our return we started growing organically and marketing mixed salads for Wholefood in Baker Street, the first wholefood shop in London. We also collaborated with the nearby seed company Suffolk Herbs to import Italian seed, which eventually led to supermarkets taking up the idea of mixed salad bags, so widespread now.

Another significant event on our return was the Victoria and Albert Museum exhibition *The Garden: A Celebration of One Thousand Years of British Gardening*. Through this I met the late Rosemary Verey, was let loose in her amazing library of old books, and realized the plants we were introducing had all been grown here centuries ago. Why had they disappeared? I've always suggested, perhaps flippantly, that Queen Victoria and Brussels sprouts came in, and everything else went out.

To keep within my ten minutes I'll have to telescope several years . . . but must mention some personal obsessions which I think have a bearing on 'the good life' today.

Oriental vegetables is one. I experimented with them in our garden for many years, and eventually went to China, Japan, the USA and Canada to learn more before writing *Oriental Vegetables*. What is significant for us today, I am convinced, is that so many of the Chinese and Japanese greens lend themselves to being grown as low-energy winter crops.

Then there's the organic movement. We were involved from the start in the Organic Growers' Association, and I was one of the few who reported the early conferences, on which much scorn was poured by the mainstream press. The mood changed after one of the most hostile journalists drove into a spray drift on a return journey. He became a more balanced commentator after that! Today 'organic' is mainstream. There's been a huge change in attitude.

Potagers have been another passion. The whole idea of making the vegetable garden a beautiful place has caught on, and has encouraged all sorts of people of grow fruit and vegetables.

I have to mention the USA. I have researched most books in the US and always returned invigorated. I first encountered 'guerilla gardeners' (currently hitting the headlines here) in New York back in the 1980s, and have been so inspired by the energy and imagination in the community gardens I visited all over the USA, as well as by wonderful examples of the cultivation of Asian vegetables and stunning potagers.

I was asked to reflect on my experiences past and present (in ten minutes?), and say what I think we should do in the future.

The future is global warming, and I have to say I'm profoundly depressed about it. Every day there is more serious evidence about what is happening. Every time a baby is born the joy is mixed with fear about what the world will be like when they're my age.

Governments seem unable to take the necessary bold steps to avert catastrophe; individuals make no more than token changes in their lifestyle. We're all guilty. After all, I flew here today.

But – and it is a very big 'but' – all sorts of good things are happening. My experience of the present, since we retired to Ireland a few years ago, is almost entirely Irish. I had intended to spend the rest of my days gardening gently, reading, listening to music, perhaps learning Irish, but my cover was blown early, and the enthusiasm with which the younger generation are embracing gardening and all aspects of 'the good life' is amazing – and I've become part of it.

In the Celtic Tiger years people shed their cabbages, kales and spuds, which were the hallmark of poverty. They forgot how to garden. I can't tell you how many people have told me they remember their grannies growing things, and now want to do the same. And it's happening. Our home town, Clonakilty, has its Sustainable Clonakilty plan, and is setting up allotments and gardening projects in schools. The same is true of several small towns near by.

Several weeks ago I took part in the first 'Grow It Yourself Ireland' conference in Waterford, initiated by ex-IT journalist Mike Kelly. He left it all to become more self-sufficient, and after a while felt he'd like to swap ideas and get advice from others doing the same. So he organized a meeting in the local library, expecting about ten people to turn up. In fact 100 turned up, and the first 'Grow It Yourself Ireland' group was formed.

I've never been to a conference where there was such a buzz, so much enthusiasm, and so much shared expertise. They had a full house of 200 delegates, and 48 of them volunteered to set up local groups – and there have been many more since. That's going to touch an enormous number of people.

I'm well aware there are wonderful initiatives like this everywhere. They have so many obvious benefits – the huge satisfaction of growing your own (hopefully chemical free), the community spirit engendered, the erosion of food miles and, I dare I add, increased sales of gardening books!

So what should we do? Keep encouraging and participating in small local enterprises. After all, the world is the sum of its parts: each part is someone's locality.

THE WRITER IN THE GARDEN
British Library/RHS competition entry, 2004, unpublished

Step out into the garden, grab a hoe, start sowing seeds, or weeding, or carting manure, or pruning – anything – and a curious chemistry comes into play in a garden writer's mind. Words that indoors lurked just beyond reach, agonizingly elusive, now fly through the open window into the outdoor mind, begging to be captured and written down, to be woven into sentences. Sometimes they land boldly in complete sentences or even paragraphs. They spring to mind, whirling and pushing, jostling like baby cuckoos, struggling to occupy the mind's space and oust all other thoughts. For there are other thoughts: observations, ideas, solutions, connections, and above all memories, drifting in more gently, but with sparkling clarity, almost as soon as hand and soil or hand and tool make contact.

Is garden writing bondage? Is it impossible for a writer to relinquish that compulsion to tell, to describe, to teach, to entertain, and instead to simply enjoy the pure delights of gardening.

Millions of words have been poured into describing these pure, simple joys. Is the garden writer alone unable to thrill at the first shoots appearing, to marvel at a rare combination of colour and form, or let the spirits soar in response to the warm sun, a gentle breeze, the light on a plant, a robin perched near by – without the curse of rendering it into prose for someone else?

Yes, and no. For simply being in a garden liberates the writer's spirit. Within moments the magic starts to work, worries melt, tiredness drops away. And the memories steal in, triggered by trivialities but soaring away to distant friends, far away places, times long gone. Six decades of precious memories. That not-so-innocent wireworm triggers the earliest of them all. It's wartime, I'm six years old or so, my Daddy's home on leave, 'digging for victory', turning over rough grass. He passes me the gleaming wireworms to feed the wartime hens. A bottle of Bulmer's cider propped near by. Fast forward to peacetime a few years later and he's planting shrubs and teaching me their names. *Ceratostigma willmottianum*, *Caryopteris* x *clandonensis*. What amazing names they seemed! How proud I was to learn them! So many names forgotten since. Why do these two remain? Only now can I imagine the joy it must have been, after the frenzy of war, to be discovering shrubs and planting them. How little we know our parents!

Another misplaced label. Scratching birds I suppose. But there we go – whirring back again. Now I'm the parent. Our first garden. The first chance to experiment. Masses of seedlings are hardening off outside, each neatly labelled. And then I spot my baby crawling down the garden path, a clutch of labels in his teeth. His revenge for the tar oil wash that drifted on to his pram a few months before? My darling baby hauntingly covered with black splodges. I've never sprayed fruit since.

Pests, mice . . . and my apprenticeship year in the nearly lost world of private gardens. And it's not the smell of roses but toasted cheese. Yes, with a lit match we toasted the cheese for the mousetraps, then set them carefully among the cyclamen on the greenhouse staging. And I can see us out there for the afternoon break: adored head gardener Mr Gower, gaunt, slow-working Mr F, the cheeky Welshman, lovely Jess the maid who'd break for the garden whenever free . . . and Mrs F, bringing us a pot of tea. That undrinkable tea, steeped on the hob all day. In turn we'd shield each other and silently pour our cups away. In a flash it's a tropical Indian evening, in the Cultural Attaché's garden. Gin and tonics. But the gin so weak, tepid and vile I quietly turn to pour it on the grass. And am face to face with another guest doing the same. The suppressed giggles are with me still.

A moment's sadness by the lemon balm. I'd always meant to tell John Peel its tale: my dear friend Mandy in his mother's Irish garden, collecting salad by torchlight and taking a cutting home . . . Too late now – all those loved people gone.

Just look at that. The cat's above me, pacing the windbreak fence. As she moves, her shadow glides along the wall at right angles. Will shadow and substance meet at the corner? It's beautiful. It's eerie. How to describe it? Oh no, they've invaded again, the baby cuckoos, the writer writing. Can I never just be a gardener, in a garden, gardening?

From the top: me in the kitchen garden at Montrose Farm; a corner of the blue border at Donaghmore, backed by a holm oak hedge; Don shaping the fast-growing escallonia hedge at Donaghmore into a scalloped outline.

From the top: Donaghmore, looking north over the borders to the hills behind; the purpose-built greenhouse, which adjoins the house; the view south over the red and green borders, showing the original sycamores shorn by the south westerlies.

INDEX

Page numbers in *italics* refer to illustrations.

ACKNOWLEDGMENTS

In *Just Vegetating* I've been looking back over four decades as a freelance garden writer and journalist with an unquenchable desire to experiment and then pass on what I have learnt. Like all journalists, that means I've been a spider at the centre of a giant web, reaching out to countless individuals whose help, knowledge, experience, time, generosity and contacts I have tapped mercilessly. Some have become lifelong friends, some I have never met. Many have been acknowledged and thanked when I completed the books and articles to which they contributed or were involved in, but there are others who have never been thanked, who probably never realized they were part of the spider's web. So thank you now: all those people who wrote and shared titbits of interesting information and their gardens and enterprises; the man in the warehouse who put the clamping order on copies of *Salads for Small Gardens* to prevent them from being sent to Holland for pulping; the kindly constructive criticism from the late Franz Lammer, who translated *The Salad Garden* into Dutch; the travelling salesman who gave me the tip about picking up tiny seeds with a piece of broken glass; the many seedsmen who supplied me with samples and facts; the researchers; the collaborators in projects where the spirit of helpfulness prevailed and made them such a joy to work with; those overworked people in publishing companies where the same, far more often than not, has been the case, to those involved at Frances Lincoln and especially to the book's wonderfully constructive editor, Anne Askwith, to Becky Clarke, whose design has so captured the feel I wanted, and to Jo Christian and John Nicoll for their unflagging support over many years; to the friends and acquaintances who were cajoled into driving this reluctant driver to gardens, meetings, research stations, plots of every imaginable kind all over the world; and above all, to my family, who have put up with a mother, wife and grandmother obsessed with vegetables.

My thanks to the following publications for the use of their articles:
BBC Gardeners 'World, Daily Telegraph, Farmers Weekly, The Garden, Garden Answers, Garden Media Group Newsletter, Garden News, Garden Museum Journal, Gardeners' Chronicle, Guardian Weekend, Kitchen Garden, Observer, Saturday Telegraph, Practical Gardening, World Gastronomy, *Your Garden*

PICTURE CREDITS

6 *Daily Telegraph*; 19 *Farmers Weekly*; 41 Tom Wright; 90 below left Don Pollard; 134 John Walker; 139 right Stephen Robson; 142 garden plan Yvonne Green; 143 above left Jerry Harpur, below right Stephen Robson; 154 Alain Garsmeur; 155 Jacqui Hurst; 170 Charles Hall; 217 *Gardeners' World*; 235 left Bill Lapper; 246 and 259 Sophie Lloyd; 267 below Anemette Olesen; 269 Brendan Pollard; 270 Jane Sebire; 299 right seed packet design Elizabeth Douglass; 306 Tessa Traeger; 308 Garden Media Guild; 310 Richard Grierson; 318 below Jane Powers; 326 above Anemette Olesen, below Richard Johnston; 326 centre and 327 above and below Jane Sebire. Portrait on back flap of jacket Tadg Spillane.